THE
UNHEAVENLY
CITY
REVISITED

Books by Edward C. Banfield

GOVERNMENT PROJECT

THE MORAL BASIS OF A BACKWARD SOCIETY

URBAN GOVERNMENT: A READER

POLITICAL INFLUENCE

BIG CITY POLITICS

POLITICS, PLANNING, AND THE PUBLIC INTEREST
(*with Martin Meyerson*)

GOVERNMENT AND HOUSING IN METROPOLITAN AREAS
(*with Morton Grodzins*)

CITY POLITICS
(*with James Q. Wilson*)

BOSTON: THE JOB AHEAD
(*with Martin Meyerson*)

THE UNHEAVENLY CITY: THE NATURE AND
FUTURE OF OUR URBAN CRISIS

THE UNHEAVENLY CITY REVISITED

THE UNHEAVENLY CITY REVISITED

by EDWARD C. BANFIELD

A Revision of *The Unheavenly City*

LITTLE, BROWN AND COMPANY • BOSTON • TORONTO

PUBLISHER'S NOTE

Ever since its publication in 1970, Edward C. Banfield's *The Unheavenly City* has provoked intense discussion among students, scholars, and general readers alike. And today, some twenty-two printings later, it remains one of the most widely read and widely debated of all books on contemporary American urban problems.

The Unheavenly City Revisited constitutes a thorough revision and substantial expansion of the original text of *The Unheavenly City*. Although the author's main theses and the order and structure of the chapters in both volumes remain the same, *The Unheavenly City Revisited* unquestionably supplants the earlier volume and will, we trust, bring Mr. Banfield's work to the attention of many new readers, as well as provide significant new information for those already familiar with the book in its original version.

The title *The Unheavenly City Revisited* is intended to distinguish the present book from its original version and to prevent any possibility of confusion between the two.

Chapter 9, "Rioting Mainly for Fun and Profit," appeared originally in somewhat different form in *The Metropolitan Enigma*, published by Harvard University Press, 1968.

Part of Chapter 11, "Why Government Cannot Solve the Urban Problem," appeared originally in different form in *Daedalus*, Fall, 1968, and is reprinted by permission of the American Academy of Arts and Sciences. Copyright © 1968 by the American Academy of Arts and Sciences.

Published simultaneously in Canada
by Little, Brown & Company (Canada) Limited

PRINTED IN THE UNITED STATES OF AMERICA

Come hither, and I will show you, an admirable Spectacle! 'Tis an Heavenly CITY. . . . A CITY to be inhabited by an Innumerable Company of Angels, and by the Spirits of Just Men . . .
Put on thy beautiful Garments,
O America, the Holy City!
— Cotton Mather, *Theopolis Americana: An Essay on the Golden Street of the Holy City* (1710)

Preface to *The Unheavenly City Revisited*

THIS book has given rise to a great deal of controversy in the four years since it appeared. Moreover, the problems of the cities have changed. These are the two principal reasons for this "revisit."

I have taken very seriously the many criticisms, not all of them unsympathetic to my point of view, by reviewers and by colleagues and many readers who were kind enough to write me (review articles are listed in the appendix). On some points of importance I have modified, or completely changed, my views. In a great many places I have recognized, and I hope eliminated, ambiguities of language or confusions of thought that created confusion (and often outrage), and diverted readers from the ideas that I was trying to convey.

Some of the changes I have made so that my meaning will be clear on matters of very great importance. The best example is my discussion of the lower-class (radically present-oriented) style of life. By treating the lower-class culture in Chapter Three and waiting until Chapter Ten to acknowledge that the same pattern of behavior may result from situational causes (hopeless poverty, for example), I made it unnecessarily difficult for many readers to either understand or accept what I was saying. The present version will I hope much reduce this difficulty.

I had hoped that by this time I would be able to present data supporting my view that the cultural differences among the several social classes can be explained by differences of time horizon. This view was advanced as an heuristic hypothesis, but it was taken by many readers as an assertion of fact. I had hoped too that I could give some reasonably reliable estimates of the sizes of the classes as I define them. Unfortunately neither is yet possible; so far as I have been able to discover, appropriate data do not exist.

Although I have worked hardest on clarifying my argument, I have also taken account of some recent developments that seem to be significant — for example, changes in the growth and distribution of population, in the unemployment problem, and in our knowledge about the effects of compensatory education, public health, and other policy areas. On the whole, however, I have found that the wealth of data that have become available since the book was written (the 200,000 pages of the 1970 Census are the most important source) has confirmed, or at any rate supported, the main elements of my earlier analysis.

Because the book has proved to be so controversial and because it is being used in a wide variety of college courses, I have cited many more authorities, and a much wider range of them, than I did before. I make no pretense of "covering" the literature, however, because this is not intended to be that kind of book and because I take up so many matters in it. This is an essay — as I said in the preface to the original version, "an attempt by a social scientist to think about the problems of the city in the light of scholarly findings."

It was never my purpose to write a "how-to-do-it" book for the solution of urban problems. One of my main contentions is that we do not know and never can know what the real nature of the problem is, let alone what might "work" to alleviate or solve it. Therefore I was — and am — precluded from making short-run forecasts or from prescribing cures. The "recommendations" in the next-to-the-last chapter were intended, as some discerning readers recognized, merely as a take-off point for a discussion of the political circumstances that make such recommendations pointless. To bring my account of the city's development "up to date" by introducing data on the "trends" of the last two or three years — such as the apparent decline in heroin use and the apparent drop in some kinds of crime — would be a very dubious enterprise. It takes more than a few years to make a "trend." Witness the "crisis of youth unrest" that superseded the "urban crisis" three or four months after this book was first published and, within a year or two, disappeared, to be followed by other "crises" in rapid succession. If my essential argument about the economic, cultural, and political processes of American city growth is to be either confirmed or disconfirmed, it will have to be not three or four but twenty or thirty years hence.

For much the same reasons, I cannot find a way to make the book much less controversial. Clarifying myself will, I trust, reduce the amount of outcry over views erroneously attributed to me, although experience tells me that I should not expect too much in this respect. It would have been impossible to be more explicit in saying that the lower class, as I defined it, was not to be equated either with the poor or the black, but this did not deter many people from insisting that I meant the opposite of what I wrote.

The principal — and I am afraid ineradicable — source of controversy, however, is that my main points are deeply subversive of opinions and beliefs to which many highly intelligent and well-informed people are wedded, and without which the world would perhaps be unendurable for them. What most distresses my critics is not that I have (as they suppose) made conjectures that are not in accord with the facts. Rather it is, first, that I have asserted (and anyone who reflects knows it to be true) that conjectures unsupported, or slightly supported, by facts are the stuff of which social policies must always mainly be made. And, second, *my* conjecture is that owing to the nature of man and society (more particularly, American culture and institutions) we cannot "solve" our serious problems by rational management. Indeed, by trying we are almost certain to make matters worse.

My "revisit" has therefore not changed the book in any essentials, and I am afraid that, although it should be less irritating, those who did not like it before will not like it now.

I wish to express my thanks and appreciation to Professors Frank F. Furstenburg of the University of Pennsylvania and Shigeo Nohara of the University of Delaware for their advice and criticism. I am particularly indebted to my old friend Julius Margolis for his painstaking before-and-after review of the manuscript and to the Fels Center of Government of which he is director for affording me ideal conditions in which to work. Mrs. Rachel Munafo and Mrs. Lenore Stiber gave indispensable assistance as research assistant and secretary-typist respectively. I should like also to acknowledge the help given by Miss Nancy Smith, librarian at the Fels Center, and Dr. David I. Lazar.

Preface to *The Unheavenly City*

THIS book will probably strike many readers as the work of an ill-tempered and mean-spirited fellow. I would not mind that especially if I did not think that it might prevent them from taking its argument as seriously as they should. I should like therefore to assure the reader that I am as well-meaning — probably even as soft-hearted — as he. But facts are facts, however unpleasant, and they have to be faced unblinkingly by anyone who really wants to improve matters in the cities.

It is, of course, impossible to be an expert on urban affairs — the range of subject matter is far too great. One can, however, learn enough of several disciplines to make useful applications of some of their major ideas and findings. This is what I have tried to do. Although I draw on work in economics, sociology, political science, psychology, history, planning, and other fields, this book is not really a work of social science. Rather, it is an attempt by a social scientist to think about the problems of the cities in the light of scholarly findings. If the attempt is thought presumptuous, I offer two defenses. First, the alternative — to discuss the problems of the city in the light of a single discipline — is clearly worse; better to be presumptuous than wrong. Second, one need not have a profound knowledge of any discipline in order to make the use of it that I am making, provided that one receives criticism from those who are specialists.

Fortunately, I have had a great deal of such criticism. Much came from Harvard students, undergraduates as well as graduates, some of whom had detailed and often firsthand knowledge of matters about which I knew little. In addition, I have to thank the following for reading particular chapters: Gary Becker, James S. Coleman, M. Kimbrough Marshall, Christopher De Muth, John F. Kain, Bruce

Kovner, Garth Mangum, Gary T. Marx, Thomas A. Reppetto, David Riesman, Martin Shefter, and Lester C. Thurow. The entire, or almost entire, manuscript was read by Martin Meyerson, Margy Ellin Meyerson, Milton Friedman, Frances Fox Piven, and James Q. Wilson. Margaret Locke and Mark Petri provided research assistance in the early stages of the work. Lawrence D. Brown, who prepared the manuscript for the press, called attention to and helped eliminate numerous confusions of thought; if it were not for him the book would be in many respects poorer. Mrs. Carla Kirmani was a painstaking typist. I am very grateful to them all. I am grateful also to the Joint Center for Urban Studies of the Massachusetts Institute of Technology and Harvard University, which supported the undertaking generously over a considerable period.

Although written for this book, Chapter Nine appeared first in James Q. Wilson, ed., *The Metropolitan Enigma* (Cambridge, Mass.: Harvard University Press, 1968). Chapter Eleven is a much-revised version of an article that appeared in the Fall, 1968, issue of *Daedalus*.

1970   E.C.B.

Contents

THE
UNHEAVENLY
CITY
REVISITED

CHAPTER ONE

Introduction

... the clock is ticking, time is moving ... , we must ask ourselves every night when we go home, are we doing all that we should do in our nation's capital, in all the other big cities of the country.
— President Johnson, after the Watts Riot,
August 1965

A few years ago we constantly heard that urban America was on the brink of collapse. It was one minute to midnight, we were told. ... Today, America is no longer coming apart. ... The hour of crisis is passed.
— President Nixon, March 1973

THE reason for juxtaposing the quotations above is not to suggest that whereas a few years ago the cities were in great peril now all is well with them. Rather it is to call attention both to the simplistic nature of all such sweeping judgments and to the fact that one's perception of urban America is a function of time and place and also, if one is a politician, of whatever winds are blowing. A few blocks' walk through the heart of any large city was enough in 1965 — and is enough in 1973 — to show much that was (and is) in crying need of improvement. That a society so technologically advanced and prosperous has many hundreds of blocks ranging from dreary to dismal is disturbing at least and when one takes into account that by the end of the century the urban population will be at least 20 percent larger than in 1970, with six out of every ten persons living in a metropolitan area of more than a million, the prospect may appear alarming.

There is, however, another side to the matter. The plain fact is that the overwhelming majority of city dwellers live more comfortably and conveniently than ever before. They have more and better housing, more and better schools, more and better transportation, and so on. By any conceivable measure of material welfare the present generation of urban Americans is, on the whole, better off than any other large group of people has ever been anywhere. What is more, there is every reason to expect that the general level of comfort and convenience will continue to rise at an even more rapid rate through the foreseeable future.

It is true that many people do not share, or do not share fully, this general prosperity, some because they are the victims of racial prejudice and others for other reasons that are equally beyond their control. If the chorus of complaint about the city arose mainly from these disadvantaged people or on behalf of them, it would be entirely understandable, especially if their numbers were increasing and their plight were getting worse. But the fact is that until very recently most of the talk about the urban crisis has had to do with the comfort, convenience, and business advantage of the well-off white majority and not with the more serious problems of the poor, the Negro, and others who stand outside the charmed circle. And the fact also is that the number of those standing outside the circle is decreasing, as is the relative disadvantage that they suffer. There is still much poverty and much racial discrimination. But there is less of both than ever before.

The question arises, therefore, not of whether we are faced with an urban crisis, but rather, *in what sense* we are faced with one. Whose interest and what interests are involved? How deeply? What should be done? Given the political and other realities of the situation, what *can* be done?

The first need is to clear away some semantic confusions. Consider the statement, so frequently used to alarm luncheon groups, that more than 70 percent of the population now lives in urban places and that this number may increase to nearly 90 percent in the next two decades if present trends continue. Such figures give the impression of standing room only in the city, but what exactly do they mean?

When we are told that the population of the United States is rapidly becoming overwhelmingly urban, we probably suppose this to mean that most people are coming to live in the big cities. This is true in one sense but false in another. It is true that most people live closer physically and psychologically to a big city than ever before; rural occupations and a rural style of life are no longer widespread. On the other hand, the percentage of the population living in cities of 250,000 or more (there are only fifty-six of them) is about the same now as it was in 1920. In Census terminology an "urban place" is any settlement having a population of 2,500 or more; obviously places of 2,500 are not what we have in mind when we use words like "urban" and "city."[1] It is somewhat misleading to say that the country is becoming more urban, when what is meant is that more people are living in places like White River Junction, Vermont (pop. 6,311), and fewer in places like Boston, Massachusetts (pop. 641,000). But it is not *altogether* misleading, for most of the small urban places are now close enough (in terms of time and other costs of travel) to large cities to be part of a metropolitan complex. White River Junction, for example, is now very much influenced by Boston. The average population density in all "urban areas," however, has been decreasing: from 5,408 per square mile in 1950 to 3,752 in 1960, to 3,376 in 1970.

A great many so-called urban problems are really conditions that we either cannot eliminate or do not want to incur the disadvantages of eliminating. Consider the "problem of congestion." The presence of a great many people in one place is a cause of inconvenience, to say the least. But the advantages of having so many people in one place far outweigh these inconveniences, and we cannot possibly have the advantages without the disadvantages. To "eliminate congestion" in the city must mean eliminating the city's reason for being. Congestion in the city is a "problem" only in the sense that congestion in Times Square on New Year's Eve is one; in fact, of course, people come to the city, just as they do to Times Square, precisely *because* it is congested. If it were not congested, it would not be worth coming to.

Strictly speaking, a problem exists only as we should want something different from what we do want or as by better management we could get a larger total of what we want. If we think it a good thing that many people have the satisfaction of driving their cars in and out of the city, and if we see no way of arranging the situation to get them in and out more conveniently that does not entail more than offsetting disadvantages for them or others, then we ought not to speak of a "traffic congestion problem." By the same token, urban sprawl is a "problem," as opposed to a "condition," only if (1) fewer people should have the satisfaction of living in the low-density fringe of the city, or (2) we might, by better planning, build homes in the fringe without destroying so much landscape and without incurring costs (for example, higher per-unit construction costs) or forgoing benefits (for example, a larger number of low-income families who can have the satisfaction of living in the low-density area) of greater value than the saving in landscape.

Few problems, in this strict sense, are anywhere near as big as they seem. The amount of urban sprawl that could be eliminated simply by better planning — that is, without the sacrifice of other ends that are also wanted, such as giving the satisfaction of owning a house and yard to many low-income people — is probably trivial as compared to the total urban sprawl (that is, to the "problem" defined simple-mindedly as "a condition that is unpleasant").

Many so-called urban problems (crime is a conspicuous exception) are more characteristic of rural and small-town places than of cities. Housing is generally worse in rural areas, for example, and so are schools. "Low verbal ability," Sloan R. Wayland of Columbia Teachers College has written, "is described as though it could only happen in an urban slum." Actually, he points out, all but a very small fraction of mankind has always been "culturally deprived," and the task of formal education has always been to attack such conditions.[2]

Most of the "problems" that are generally supposed to constitute "the urban crisis" could not conceivably lead to disaster. They are — some of them — important in the sense that a bad cold is important, but they are not critical in the sense that a cancer is critical. They have to do with comfort, convenience, amenity, and business advantage, all of which are important, but they do not affect either the essential welfare of individuals or what may be called the good health of the society.

Consider, for example, an item that often appears near the top of the list of complaints about the city — the journey to work. It takes the average commuter between 21 and 34 minutes to get to work (the difference in the average time depending upon the population of the metropolitan area).[3] It would, of course, be very nice if the journey to work were much shorter. No one can suppose, however, that the essential welfare of many people would be much affected even if it were fifteen minutes longer. Certainly its being longer or shorter would not make the difference between a good society and a bad.

Another matter causing widespread alarm is the decline of the central business district, by which is meant the loss of patronage to downtown department stores, theaters, restaurants, museums, and so on, which has resulted from the movement of many well-off people to suburbs. Clearly, the movement of good customers from one place to another involves inconvenience and business loss to many people, especially to the owners of real estate that is no longer in so great demand. These losses, however, are essentially no different from those that occur from other causes — say, a shift of consumers' tastes that suddenly renders a once-valuable patent valueless. Moreover, though some lose by the change, others gain by it: the overall gain of wealth by building in the suburbs may more than offset the loss of it caused by letting the downtown deteriorate.

There are those who claim that cultural and intellectual activity flourishes only in big cities and that therefore the decline of the downtown business districts and the replacement of cities by suburbs threatens the very survival of civilization. This claim is farfetched, to say the very least, if it means that we cannot have good music and good theater (not to mention philosophy, literature, and science) unless customers do their shopping in the downtown districts of Oakland, St. Louis, Nashville, Boston, and so on, rather than in the suburbs around them. Public efforts to preserve the downtown districts of these and other cities may perhaps be worth what they cost — although, so far as cultural and intellectual activities are concerned, there is no reason to assume that public efforts would not bring at least as much return if directed to metropolitan areas as wholes. The return, however, will be in the comfort, convenience, and business advantage of the relatively well-off and not in anyone's essential welfare.

The same can be said about efforts to "beautify" the cities. That for the most part the cities are dreary and depressing if not offensively ugly may be granted: the desirability of improving their appearance, even if only a little, cannot be questioned. It is very doubtful, however, that people are dehumanized (to use a favorite word of those who complain about the cities) by the ugliness of the city or that they would be in any sense humanized by its being made beautiful. (If they were humanized, they would doubtless build beautiful cities, but that is an entirely different matter. One has only to read Machiavelli's Florentine Histories to see that living in a beautiful city is not in itself enough to bring out the best in one. So far as their humanity is concerned, the people of, say, Jersey City compare very favorably to the Florentines of the era of that city's greatest glory.) At worst, the American city's ugliness — or, more, its lack of splendor or charm — occasions loss of visual pleasure. This loss is an important one (it is surely much larger than most people realize), but it cannot lead to any kind of disaster either for the individual or for the society.

Air pollution comes closer than any of these problems to threatening essential welfare, as opposed to comfort, convenience, amenity, and business advantage. Some people die early because of it and many more suffer various degrees of bad health; there is also some possibility (no one knows how much) that a meteorological coincidence (an "air inversion") over a large city might suddenly kill thousands or even tens of thousands. Important as it is, however, the air pollution problem is rather minor as compared to other threats to health and welfare not generally regarded as "crises."[4] Moreover, steps are being taken to clear the air. The Clean Air Act Amendment of 1970 is expected to reduce pollution from auto emissions (by far the most serious source) to half of what they were in 1967 (the base year) by 1980 and to a quarter by 1985.[5]

Many of the "problems" that are supposed to constitute the "crisis" could be quickly and easily solved, or much alleviated, by the application of well-known measures that lie right at hand. In some instances, the money cost of these measures would be very small. For example, the rush-hour traffic problem in the central cities (which, incidentally, is almost the whole of the traffic problem in these cities) could be much reduced and in some cases eliminated entirely just by staggering working hours in the largest offices and factories. Manhattan presents the hardest case of all, but even there, an elaborate study showed, rush-hour crowding could be reduced by 25 percent, enough to make the strap-hanger reasonably comfortable.[6] Another quick and easy way of improving urban transportation in most cities would be to eliminate a mass of archaic regulations on the granting of public transit and taxi franchises. At present, the cities are in effect going out of their way to place obstacles in the paths of those who might offer the public better transportation.[7] Metropolitan transportation could also easily be improved in those areas — there are a number of them — where extensive expressway networks link the downtown with outlying cities and towns. In these areas, according to the Harvard economist John F. Kain, "all that is currently needed to create extensive metropolitan rapid transit systems . . . is a limited outlay for instrumentation, some modification of ramp arrangement and design, and most importantly *a policy decision to keep congestion at very low levels during peak hours and to provide priority access for public transit vehicles.*"[8]

The "price" of solving, or alleviating, some much-talked-about city problems, it would appear from this, may be largely political. Keeping congestion at low levels at peak hours would necessitate placing high toll charges on roads at the very times when most people want to use them; some would regard this as grossly unfair (as indeed in a way it would be) and so the probabilities are that if any official had the authority to make the decision (none does, which is part of the problem) he would not raise tolls at rush hours for fear of being voted out of office.

If the transportation problem is basically political, so is the revenue problem. A great part of the wealth of our country is in the cities. When a mayor says that his city is on the verge of bankruptcy, he means that when the time comes to run for reelection he wants to be able to claim credit for straightening out a mess that was left him by his predecessor. What he means when he says that his city *must* have state or federal aid to finance some improvements is (1) the taxpayers of the city (or some important group of them) would rather go without the improvement than pay for it themselves; or (2) although they would pay for it themselves if they had to, they would much prefer to have some other taxpayers pay for it. Rarely if ever does a mayor who makes such a statement mean (1) that for the city to pay for the improvement would necessarily force some taxpayers into poverty; or (2) that the city could not raise the money even if it were willing to force some of its taxpayers into poverty. In short, the "revenue crisis" mainly reflects the fact that people hate to pay taxes and that they think that by crying poverty they can shift some of the bill to someone else.[9]

To some extent, also, the revenue problem of the cities arises from the way jurisdictional boundaries are drawn or, more precisely, from what are considered to be inequities resulting from the movement of taxable wealth from one side of a boundary line to another. When many large taxpayers move to the suburbs, the central city must tax those who remain at a higher rate if it is to maintain the same level of services. The "problem" in this case is not that the taxpayers who remain are absolutely unable to pay the increased taxes; rather, it is that they do not want to pay them and that they consider it unfair that they should have to pay more simply because other people have moved away. The simple and costless solution (in all but a political sense) would be to charge nonresidents for services that they receive from the city or, failing that, to redraw the boundary lines so that everyone in the metropolitan area would be taxed on the same basis. As the historian Kenneth T. Jackson points out, those central cities that are declining in numbers of residents and in wealth are doing so because their state legislatures will not permit them to enlarge their boundaries by annexations; even before the Civil War many large cities would have been surrounded by suburbs — and therefore suffering from the same revenue problem — if they had not been permitted to annex freely.[10]

That we have not yet been willing to pay the price of solving, or alleviating, such "problems" even when the price is a very small one suggests that they are not really critical. Indeed, one might say that, by definition, a critical problem is one that people *are* willing to pay a considerable price to have solved.

With regard to these problems for which solutions are at hand, we will know that a real crisis impends when we see the solutions actually being applied. The solution, that is, will be applied when — and only when — the inconvenience or other disadvantage of allowing the problem to continue unabated is judged to have become greater than that of taking the necessary measures to abate it. In other words, a bad-but-not-quite-critical problem is one that it would almost-but-not-quite pay us to do something about.

If some real disaster impends in the city, it is not because parking spaces are hard to find, because architecture is bad, because department store sales are declining, or even because taxes are rising. If there is a genuine crisis, it has to do with the essential welfare of individuals or with the good health of the society, not merely with comfort, convenience, amenity, and business advantage, important as these are. It is not necessary here to try to define "essential welfare" rigorously: it is enough to say that whatever may cause people to die before their time, to suffer serious impairment of their health or of their powers, to waste their lives, to be deeply unhappy or happy in a way that is less than human affects their essential welfare. It is harder to indicate in a sentence or two what is meant by the "good health" of the society. The ability of the society to maintain itself as a going concern is certainly a primary consideration; so is its free and democratic character. In the last analysis, however, the quality of a society must be judged by its tendency to produce desirable human types; the healthy society, then, is one that not only stays alive but also moves in the direction of giving greater scope and expression to what is distinctively human. In general, of course, what serves the essential welfare of individuals also promotes the good health of the society; there are occasions, however, when the two goals conflict. In such cases, the essential welfare of individuals must be sacrificed for the good health of the society. This happens on a very large scale when there is a war, but it may happen at other times as well. The conditions about which we should be most concerned, therefore, are those that affect, or may affect, the good health of the society. If there is an urban crisis in any ultimate sense, it must be constituted of these conditions.

It is a good deal easier to say what matters are not serious (that is, do not affect either the essential welfare of individuals or the good health of the society) than it is to say what ones are. It is clear, however, that crime, poverty, ignorance, and racial (and other) injustices are among the most important of the general conditions affecting the essential welfare of individuals. It is plausible, too, to suppose that these conditions have a very direct bearing upon the good health of the society, although in this connection other factors that are much harder to guess about — for example, the nature and strength of the consensual bonds that hold the society together — may be much more important. To begin with, anyway, it seems reasonable to look in these general directions for what may be called the serious problems of the cities.

It is clear at the outset that serious problems directly affect only a rather small minority of the whole urban population. In the relatively new residential suburbs and in the better residential neighborhoods in the outlying parts of the central cities and in the older, larger, suburbs, the overwhelming majority of people are safely above the poverty line, have at least a high school education, and do not suffer from racial discrimination. For something like two-thirds of all city dwellers, the urban problems that touch them directly have to do with comfort, convenience, amenity, and business advantage. In the terminology used here, such problems are "important" but not "serious." In many cases, they cannot even fairly be called important; a considerable part of the urban population — those who reside in the "nicer" suburbs — lives under material conditions that will be hard to improve upon.

The serious problems are to be found in all large cities and in most small ones. But they affect only parts of these cities — mainly the inner parts of the larger ones — and only a small proportion of the whole urban population. Crime is a partial exception, but in Chicago (so the Violence Commission was told) a person who lives in the inner city faces a yearly risk of 1 in 77 of being assaulted whereas for those who live in the better areas of the city the risk is only 1 in 2,000 and for those who live in the rich suburbs only 1 in 10,000.[11] Apart from those in the inner districts, which comprise about 10 to 20 percent of the city's total area, there are few serious urban problems. If what really matters is the essential welfare of individuals and the good health of the society, as opposed to comfort, convenience, amenity, and business advantage, then the problem is less an "urban" one than an "inner-(big)-city" one.

Although the poor and the black (and in some cities other minority groups also) are concentrated in the inner city and although the districts in which they live include many blocks of unrelieved squalor, it should not be supposed that the "poverty areas" of the inner cities are uniformly black, poor, or squalid. This can be seen from the findings of a special survey made in 1970 and 1971 by the Census of what it defined as the "low-income areas" of fifty-one of the largest cities.[12] A brief listing of some of these findings should dispel any notion that an inner-city "poverty area" is occupied only by the "disinherited."

Of the almost nine million persons aged sixteen or over who were counted, half were black and 35 percent non-Spanish white.

More than three-fourths reported incomes *above* the poverty level.

The median income of a male-headed family was $7,782 (the comparable figure for the United States population as a whole was $10,480).

Among such families, 25 percent of the white and 20 percent of the Negro reported incomes above $12,000.

Of the nearly two million persons below the poverty level, whites and blacks were distributed in about the same proportion as in the whole "poverty area" population. (Spanish families were considerably overrepresented among the poor in the nineteen cities where they were numerous enough to be surveyed separately.)

The median income of male-headed white families was $425 more than that of black and the median income of black $849 more than Spanish.

In twenty-one of the fifty-one cities, however, the blacks in poverty areas had higher median family incomes than whites and in twelve more cities the difference (in favor of the whites) was trivial — less than 5 percent.

The median years of schooling for persons twenty-five years of age or older was almost identical — 10 and a small fraction — for whites and blacks, males and females; for persons twenty-five to thirty-four it was also almost identical and surprisingly high: twelve and a small fraction.

Although a large share of the income of many families went for housing, the reverse was also true: 40 percent of white and 25 percent of Negro (male-headed) families paid less than 10 percent of their income for housing. Ninety percent of the white and 80 percent of the black (male-headed) families had housing that was not over-crowded — that is, there was at least one room per person.

Of the nearly nine million persons aged sixteen or over, 478,000 (9.6 percent of those in the labor force) were unemployed. Less than half of these had been laid off; most had either quit or were just entering the labor force. Only 82,000 had been unemployed for as long as six months. Most were teenagers or unattached men and women in their early twenties, and many of these were students who wanted part-time or summer jobs.

The unemployment rate among male Negro family heads was 5.3 percent; among male white (non-Spanish) family heads it was 4.5 percent.

About 10 percent of those *not* in the labor force said that they intended looking for a job (most non-participants were housewives, of course). Asked why they did not look, "inability to find work" was given as a reason by 8,000 males and 24,000 females. Of these, 25 percent were aged 16-21. Asked what would be their minimum acceptable wage, the median figure given by black males in this age group was $83 weekly; whites expected one dollar more. Both black and white men who were heads of families expected $108.

Within or overlapping, some "poverty areas" are huge enclaves — a few have populations of several hundred thousand — that are almost entirely Negro or, in some cities, Puerto Rican or Mexican-American.[13] These enclaves — they are often called ghettoes, but as will be explained in Chapter Four this usage is extremely ambiguous — constitute a problem that is both serious and unique to the large cities. The problem arises because the enclaves are psychologically — and in some degree physically — cut off from the rest of the city. Whatever may be the effect of this on the welfare of the individual — and it may possibly be trivial — it is clear that the existence of a large enclave of persons who perceive themselves, and are perceived by others, as having a separate identity, not sharing, or not sharing fully, the attachment that others feel to the "city," constitutes a potential hazard not only to present peace and order but — what is more important — to the well-being of the society over the long run. Problems of individual welfare may be no greater by virtue of the fact that people live together in huge enclaves rather than in relative isolation on farms and in small towns, although about this one cannot be sure (such problems *appear* greater when people live in enclaves, of course, but this is because they are too conspicuous to be ignored). The problem that they may present to the good health of the society, however, is very different in kind and vastly greater in importance solely by virtue of their living in huge enclaves. Unlike those who live on farms and in small towns, disaffected people who are massed together may develop a collective consciousness and sense of identity. From some standpoints it may be highly desirable that they do so: feeling the strength of their numbers may give them confidence and encourage them to act politically and in other ways that will help them. On the other hand, the effect of numbers may be to support attitudes and institutions that will hamper progress. There is no doubt, however, that such enclaves represent a threat to peace and order, one made greater by the high proportion of young people in them. As the Commission on Population Growth and the American Future recently remarked,

The decade 1960 to 1970 saw a doubling of the number of young black men and women aged 15 to 24 in the metropolitan areas of every part of the nation except the south. This increase, twice that for comparable white youth, was the result of higher black fertility to begin with, participation in the post-World War II baby boom, and continued migration away from southern rural poverty. The result has been more and more young black people ill-equipped to cope with the demands of urban life, more likely to wind up unemployed or in dead-end, low-paying jobs, and caught in the vicious wheel of poverty, welfare, degradation, and crime.

The facts we have cited describe a crisis for our society. They add up to a demographic recipe for more turmoil in our cities, more bitterness among our "have-nots," and greater divisiveness among all of our peoples.[14]

The political danger in the presence of great concentrations of people who feel little attachment to the society has long been regarded by some as *the* serious problem of the cities — the one problem that might eventuate in disaster for the society. "The dark ghettoes," Dr. Clark has written, "now represent a nuclear stockpile which can annihilate the very foundations of America."[15] These words bring to mind the apprehensions that were expressed by some of the

Founding Fathers and that Tocqueville set forth in a famous passage of *Democracy in America:*

The United States has no metropolis, but it already contains several very large cities. Philadelphia reckoned 161,000 inhabitants, and New York 202,000, in the year 1830. The lower ranks which inhabit these cities constitute a rabble even more formidable than the populace of European towns. They consist of freed blacks, in the first place, who are condemned by the laws and by public opinion to a hereditary state of misery and degradation. They also contain a multitude of Europeans who have been driven to the shores of the New World by their misfortunes or their misconduct; and they bring to the United States all our greatest vices, without any of those interests which counteract their baneful influence. As inhabitants of a country where they have no civil rights, they are ready to turn all the passions which agitate the community to their own advantage; thus, within the last few months, serious riots have broken out in Philadelphia and New York. Disturbances of this kind are unknown in the rest of the country, which is not alarmed by them, because the population of the cities has hitherto exercised neither power nor influence over the rural districts.

Nevertheless, I look upon the size of certain American cities, and especially on the nature of their population, as a real danger which threatens the future security of the democratic republics of the New World; and I venture to predict that they will perish from this circumstance, unless the government succeeds in creating an armed force which, while it remains under the control of the majority of the nation, will be independent of the town population and able to repress its excesses.[16]

Strange as it may seem, the mammoth government programs to aid the cities are directed mainly toward the problems of comfort, convenience, amenity, and business advantage. Insofar as they have an effect on the serious problems, it is, on the whole, to aggravate them.

Two programs account for a very large part of federal government expenditure for the improvement of the cities (as opposed to the maintenance of more or less routine functions). Neither is intended to deal with the serious problems. Both make them worse.

The improvement of urban transportation is one program. The federal contribution for urban highway construction and improvement, which as long ago as 1960 was more than $1 billion a year, has since doubled. The main effect of urban expressways, for which most of the money is spent, is to enable suburbanites to move about the metropolitan area more conveniently, to open up some areas for business and residential expansion, and to bring a few more customers from the suburbs downtown to shop. These are worthy objects when considered by themselves; in context, however, their justification is doubtful, for their principal effect is to encourage — in effect to subsidize — further movement of industry, commerce, and relatively well-off residents (mostly white) from the inner city. This, of course, makes matters worse for the poor by reducing the number of jobs for them and by making neighborhoods, schools, and other community facilities still more segregated. These injuries are only partially offset by enabling a certain number of the inner-city poor to commute to jobs in the suburbs.

The huge expenditure being made for improvement of mass transit — $1 billion in fiscal 1974 — may be justifiable for the contribution that it will make to comfort, convenience, and business advantage. It will not, however, make any contribution to the solution of the serious problems of the city. Even if every city had a subway as fancy as Moscow's, all these problems would remain.

The second great federal urban program concerns housing and renewal. Since the creation in 1934 of the Federal Housing Authority (FHA), the government has subsidized home building on a vast scale by insuring mortgages that are written on easy terms and, in the case of the Veterans Administration (VA), by guaranteeing mortgages. Most of the mortgages have been for the purchase of *new* homes. (This was partly because FHA wanted gilt-edged collateral behind the mortgages that it insured, but it was also because it shared the American predilection for newness.) It was cheaper to build on vacant land, but there was little such land left in the central cities and in their larger, older suburbs; therefore, most of the new homes were built in new suburbs. These were almost always zoned so as to exclude the relatively few Negroes and other "undesirables" who could afford to build new houses and until late 1962 (when a presidential order barred discrimination in federally aided housing) FHA acted on its own to encourage all-white developments by instructing its appraisers to make low ratings of properties in neighborhoods occupied by what its Underwriting Manual termed "inharmonious racial or nationality groups" and by recommending a model racial restrictive covenant.[17]

In effect, then, the FHA and VA programs have subsidized the movement of the white middle class out of the central cities and older suburbs while at the same time penalizing investment in the rehabilitation of the run-down neighborhoods of these older cities. The poor — especially the Negro poor — have not received any direct benefit from these programs. (They have, however, received a very substantial unintended and indirect benefit, as will be explained later, because the departure of the white middle class has made more housing available to them.) After the appointment of Robert C. Weaver as head of the Housing and Home Finance Agency, FHA changed its regulations to encourage the rehabilitation of existing houses and neighborhoods. Very few such loans have been made, however.

Urban renewal has also turned out to be mainly for the advantage of the well-off — indeed, of the rich — and to do the poor more harm than good. The purpose of the federal housing program was declared by Congress to be "the realization as soon as feasible of the goal of a decent home and a suitable living environment for every American family." In practice, however, the principal objectives of the renewal program have been to attract the middle class back into the central city (as well as to slow its exodus out of the city) and to stabilize and restore the central business districts.[18] Unfortunately, these objectives can be served only at the expense of the poor. Hundreds of thousands of low-income people, most of them Negroes or Puerto Ricans, have been forced out of low-cost housing, by no means all of it substandard, in order to make way for luxury apartments, office buildings, hotels, civic centers, industrial parks, and the like. Insofar as renewal has involved the "conservation" or "rehabilitation" of residential areas, its effect has been to keep the poorest of the poor out of these neighborhoods — that is, to keep them in the highest-density slums. "At a cost of more than three billion dollars," sociologist Scott Greer wrote in 1965, "the Urban Renewal Agency (URA) has succeeded in materially reducing the supply of low-cost housing in American cities."[19]

The injury to the poor inflicted by renewal has not been offset by benefits to them in the form of public housing (that is, housing owned by public bodies and rented by them to families deemed eligible on income and other grounds). With the important exception of New York and the less important ones of some Southern cities, such housing is not a significant part of the total supply. Moreover, the poorest of the poor are usually, for one reason or another, ineligible for public housing.

Another housing program that has subsidized the relatively well-off and hastened their movement out of the central city is seldom thought of as a housing program at all. It consists of benefits to homeowners under the federal income tax laws. *The President's Fourth Annual Report on National Housing Goals*, issued in 1972, estimated that by allowing homeowners to deduct mortgage interest and property taxes from their gross incomes federal revenues had been reduced by $4.7 billion the previous year.[20] The subsidies, the report said, "are worth relatively more to higher income homeowners." Renters were not benefited at all except as owners might pass some of their tax savings on to them. To dramatize the inequity of these arrangements, a tax authority testifying before a Senate subcommittee imagined what it would sound like if a housing program having the same effects were to be proposed to Congress:

> We have a program to assist people who own homes. . . . If there is a married couple with more than $200,000 of income, why for each $100 of mortgage that they have, HUD will pay that couple $70. On the other hand, if there is a married couple with an income of $10,000, then under this HUD program we will pay that married couple only $19 on their $100 mortgage interest bill. And, of course, if they are too poor to pay an income tax then we are not going to pay them anything.[21]

Obviously these various government programs work at cross-purposes, one undoing (or *trying* to undo) what another does (or *tries* to do). The expressway and (with minor exceptions) the housing programs in effect pay the middle-class person to leave the central city for the suburbs. At the same time, the urban renewal and mass transit programs pay him to stay in the central city or to move back to it. ". . . [F]ederal housing programs over the years," the presidential report cited above acknowledges, "have contributed to rapid suburbanization and unplanned urban sprawl, to growing residential separation of the races, and to the concentration of the poor and minorities in decaying central cities."[22] In the opinion of the economist

Richard Muth, expressways ("the major contributor to urban decentralization in the postwar period") and federal aids to home ownership may have caused the land area of cities to be as much as 17 percent larger than it would otherwise be and the central city's share of the urbanized area population to be 3 to 7 percent smaller.[23]

In at least one respect, however, these government programs are consistent: they aim at problems of comfort, convenience, amenity, and business advantage, not at ones involving the essential welfare of individuals or the good health of the society. Indeed, on the contrary, they all sacrifice these latter, more important interests for the sake of the former, less important ones. In this the urban programs are no different from a great many other government programs. Price production programs in agriculture, Theodore Schultz has remarked, take up almost all the time of the Department of Agriculture, the agricultural committees of Congress, and the farm organizations, and exhaust the influence of farm people. But these programs, he says, "do not improve the schooling of farm children, they do not reduce the inequalities in personal distribution of wealth and income, they do not remove the causes of poverty in agriculture, nor do they alleviate it. On the contrary, they worsen the personal distribution of income within agriculture."[24]

It is widely supposed that the serious problems of the cities are unprecedented both in kind and in magnitude. Between 1950 and 1960 there occurred the greatest population increase in the nation's history. At the same time, a considerable part of the white middle class moved to the newer suburbs, and its place in the central cities and older suburbs was taken by Negroes (and in New York by Puerto Ricans as well). These and other events — especially the civil rights revolution — are widely supposed to have changed completely the character of "the urban problem."

If the present situation is indeed radically different from previous ones, then we have nothing to go on in judging what is likely to happen next. At the very least, we face a crisis of uncertainty.

In a real sense, of course, *every* situation is unique. Even in making statistical probability judgments, one must decide on more or less subjective grounds whether it is reasonable to treat certain events as if they were the "same." The National Safety Council, for example, must decide whether cars, highways, and drivers this year are enough like those of past years to justify predicting future experience from past. From a logical standpoint, it is no more possible to decide this question in a purely objective way than it is to decide, for example, whether the composition of the urban population is now so different from what it was that nothing can be inferred from the past about the future. Karl and Alma Taeuber are both right and wrong when they write that we do not know enough about immigrant and Negro assimilation patterns to be able to compare the two and that "such evidence as we could compile indicates that it is more likely to be misleading than instructive to make such comparisons."[25] They are certainly right in saying that one can only guess whether the pattern of Negro assimilation will resemble that of the immigrant. But they are wrong to imply that we can avoid making guesses and still compare things that are not known to be alike in all respects except one. (What, after all, would be the point of comparing immigrant and Negro assimilation patterns if we knew that the only difference between the two was, say, skin color?) They are also wrong in suggesting that the evidence indicates anything about what is likely to be instructive. If there were enough evidence to indicate that, there would be enough to indicate what is likely to happen; indeed, a judgment as to what is likely to be instructive is inseparable from one as to what is likely to happen. Strictly speaking, the Taeubers' statement expresses *their* guess as to what the evidence indicates.

The facts by no means compel one to take the view that the serious problems of the cities are unprecedented either in kind or in magnitude. That the population of metropolitan areas increased during the 1960's by nearly 17 percent to a record high of 139,374,000 persons need not hold much significance from the present standpoint: American cities have frequently grown at fantastic rates (consider the growth of Chicago from a prairie village of 4,470 in 1840 to a metropolis of more than a million in fifty years). In any case, the present population increase is leaving most cities less rather than more crowded. In the 1960's, 130 of the 292 central cities lost population, and the aggregate of their loss was 2.25 million persons; this was a greater decline than in the previous decade. Density of population in the central cities fell from 7,786 per square mile in 1950 to 4,463 in 1970; the comparable figures for suburban areas are 3,167 and 2,627.[26] Looking to the future, there is every reason to expect the trend toward "decongestion" to continue. But even if it were to reverse itself, there would be no obvious cause for concern. As Irving Hoch, a researcher for Resources for the Future has remarked, there has been much sound and fury about the presumed ill effects of city size and density on health and welfare but there is little hard evidence on the subject; moreover, such evidence as points in one direction can be countered by other evidence pointing in the opposite direction.[27]

The movement of farm and rural people (mostly Negroes and Puerto Ricans) to the large Northern cities was much smaller in the 1960's than in the previous decade and the outlook is for a continued decline both because natural increase was less during the 1960's and because rural areas appear to be retaining a higher proportion of their growth.[28] But even at its height the migration of Negroes and Puerto Ricans to the big cities was no more than about equal to immigration from Italy in its peak decade. (In New York, Chicago, and many other cities in 1910, two out of every three schoolchildren were the sons and daughters of immigrants.) When one takes into account the vastly greater size and wealth of the cities now as compared to half a century or more ago, it is obvious that by the only relevant measure — namely, the number of immigrants relative to the capacity of the cities to provide for them and to absorb them — the movement from the South and from Puerto Rico has been not large but small.

In many important respects the material conditions of life in the cities have long been improving. Incomes have increased steadily. In the 1960's, for example, white income rose by 69 percent and black income by 100 percent. Despite this relative gain, the income of black families was still somewhat less than two-thirds that of whites. Housing is also better and consumption of it more than doubled in real per capita terms between 1950 and 1970. As Dean Dick Netzer has written,

Not only has the housing improved, but also there have been huge investments in supporting public and institutional facilities — schools, twenty-year period, about $200 billion has been invested by state and local governments in new public facilities in metropolitan areas, almost as much as the total investment in new housing in these areas during the period. This hardly supports the charge that ours is a society of "public squalor amidst private opulence."[29]

At the turn of the century only one child in fifteen went beyond elementary school; now well over half finish high school. In this period blacks have increased the amount of their schooling faster than whites; in 1900 they averaged three years less than whites, but the present generation of pupils is expected to get almost as much, or — if comparison is made among pupils with about the same test scores — slightly more.[30] (In 1972, for the first time, the percentage of black and other minority-race high school graduates enrolling in college was the same as for whites). As these figures imply, racial discrimination has declined dramatically since the Second World War. Studies made over a period of almost thirty years by the National Opinion Research Center reveal a trend "distinctly toward increasing approval of integration" with the highest pro-integration scores among the young and among residents of the largest metropolitan areas.[31]

The very movements that in some cities or parts of cities signalize, or constitute, an improvement in the situation tend, of course, to make matters worse in other places. For example, in Philadelphia the population of the districts designated "low income" by the Census dropped from more than 900,000 to nearly 800,000 in the 1960's. This happened partly because many families, black as well as white, became able to afford to move to better neighborhoods. The consequence of their moving out of the "low-income" areas, however, was to widen the income gap between those areas and the rest of the city. In other words, the poverty of the "low-income" areas has been intensified relative to other areas even though — conceivably — it may be that no one in any of them is poorer than before. (As a practical matter, there can be little doubt that the departure of the better-off families *does* entail disadvantages for those who remain.)

Surprising as it may seem, most Americans are reasonably well satisfied with their neighborhoods. A recent poll found that those who live in rural areas and in small towns are more likely to say that they are satisfied than those who live in cities, and, as one would expect, the well-off are more likely to be satisfied than the poor. But even among blacks (seven out of ten of whom are city dwellers) only 17 percent say that they are dissatisfied with their neighborhoods.[32]

If the situation is improving, why, it may be asked, is there so much talk of an urban crisis? The answer is that the improvements in performance, great as they have been, have not kept pace with rising expectations. In other words, although things have been getting better absolutely, they have been getting worse *relative to what we think they should be.* And this is because, as a people, we seem to act on the advice of the old jingle:

> *Good, better, best,*
> *Never let it rest*
> *Until your good is better*
> *And your better best.*

Consider the poverty problem, for example. Irving Kristol has pointed out that for nearly a century all studies, in all countries, have concluded that a third, a fourth, or a fifth of the nation in question is below the poverty line.[33] "Obviously," he remarks, "if one defines the poverty line as that which places one-fifth of the nation below it, then one-fifth of the nation will always be below the poverty line." The point is that even if everyone is better off there will be as much poverty as ever, provided that the line is redefined upward. Kristol notes that whereas in the depths of the Depression, F.D.R. found only one-third of the nation "ill-housed, ill-clad, ill-nourished," Leon Keyserling, a former head of the Council of Economic Advisers, in 1962 published a book called *Poverty and Deprivation in the U.S. — the Plight of Two-Fifths of a Nation.*

Much the same thing has happened with respect to most urban problems. Police brutality, for example, would be a rather minor problem if we judged it by a fixed standard; it is a growing problem because we judge it by an ever more exacting standard. A generation ago the term meant hitting someone on the head with a nightstick. Now it often means something quite different:

What the Negro community is presently complaining about when it cries "police brutality" is the more subtle attack on personal dignity that mani-

fests itself in unexplainable questionings and searches, in hostile and inso-
lent attitudes toward groups of young Negroes on the street, or in cars, and
in the use of disrespectful and sometimes racist language. . . .[34]

Following Kristol, one can say that if the "police brutality line" is
defined as that which places one-fifth of all police behavior below it,
then one-fifth of all police behavior will always be brutal.

The school dropout problem is an even more striking example. At
the turn of the century, when almost everyone was a dropout, the
term and the "problem" did not exist. It was not until the 1960's,
when for the first time a majority of boys and girls were graduating
from high school and practically all had at least some high school
training, that the "dropout problem" became acute. Then, although
the dropout rate was still declining, various cities developed at least
fifty-five separate programs to deal with the problem. Hundreds of
articles on it were published in professional journals, the National
Education Association established a special action project to deal
with it, and the Commissioner of Education, the Secretary of Labor,
and the President all made public statements on it.[35] Obviously, if one
defines the "inadequate amount of schooling line" as that which
places one-fifth of all boys and girls below it, then one-fifth of all boys
and girls will always be receiving an inadequate amount of schooling.

Whatever our educational standards are today, Wayland writes,
they will be higher tomorrow. He summarizes the received doctrine in
these words:

Start the child in school earlier; keep him in school more and more
months of the year; retain all who start to school for twelve to fourteen
years; expect him to learn more and more during this period, in wider and
wider areas of human experience, under the guidance of a teacher, who has
had more and more training, and who is assisted by more and more specialists, who provide an ever-expanding range of services, with access to
more and more detailed personal records, based on more and more carefully validated tests.[36]

To a large extent, then, our urban problems are like the mechanical
rabbit at the racetrack, which is set to keep just ahead of the dogs no
matter how fast they may run. Our performance is better and better,
but because we set our standards and expectations to keep ahead of
performance, the problems are never any nearer to solution. Indeed,

if standards and expectations rise *faster* than performance, the problems may get (relatively) worse as they get (absolutely) better.

Some may say that since almost everything about the city can stand improvement (to put it mildly), this mechanical rabbit effect is a good thing in that it spurs us on to make constant progress. No doubt this is true to some extent. On the other hand, there is danger that we may mistake failure to progress as fast as we would like for failure to progress at all and, in panic, rush into ill-considered measures that will only make matters worse. After all, an "urban crisis" that results largely from rising standards and expectations is not the sort of crisis that, unless something drastic is done, is bound to lead to disaster. To treat it as if it were might be a very serious mistake.

This danger is greatest in matters where our standards are unreasonably high. The effect of too-high standards cannot be to spur us on to reach the prescribed level of performance sooner than we otherwise would, when that level is impossible of attainment. At the same time, these standards may cause us to adopt measures that are wasteful and injurious and, in the long run, to conclude from the inevitable failure of these measures that there is something fundamentally wrong with our society.

To extend the range of present Department of Health, Education and Welfare services equitably — to all those similarly situated in need — would require an *additional* cost roughly equivalent to the *entire federal budget*, Elliot L. Richardson reported as he left the secretaryship of that department.[37] His point was that expectations, indeed claims authorized by Congress, far exceeded the capacity of the government to provide. "One can imagine," he said somberly, "a point of reckoning at which the magnitude of the ill-treated problems is fully perceived — along with a profound sense of failure. And one can only hope that the troubled reaction toward the institutions held accountable would be reasoned and responsible."

CHAPTER TWO

The Logic of Metropolitan Growth

... within a very recent period three new factors have been suddenly developed which promise to exert a powerful influence on the problems of city and country life. These are the trolley, the bicycle, and the telephone. It is impossible to foresee at present just what their influence is to be on the question of the distribution of population; but this much is certain, that it adds from five to fifteen miles to the radius of every large town.

It is by such apparently unimportant, trifling, and inconspicuous forces that civilization is swayed and moulded in its evolutions and no man can foresee them or say whither they lead. . . .

— F. J. Kingsbury, 1895

MUCH of what has happened — as well as of what is happening — in the typical city or metropolitan area can be understood in terms of three imperatives.[1] The first is demographic: if the population of a city increases, the city must expand in one direction or another — up, down, or from the center outward. The second is technological: if it is feasible to transport large numbers of people outward (by train, bus, and automobile) but not upward or downward (by elevator), the city must expand outward. The third is economic: if the distribution of wealth and income is such that some can afford new housing and the time and money to commute considerable distances to work while others cannot, the expanding periphery of the city must be occupied by the first group (the "well-off") while the older, inner parts of the city, where most of the jobs for the unskilled are, must be occupied by the second group (the "not well-off").

The word "imperatives" is used to emphasize the inexorable, constraining character of the three factors that together comprise the logic of metropolitan growth. Indeed, the principal purpose of this chapter is to show that, given a rate of population growth, a transportation technology, and a distribution of income, certain consequences must inevitably follow; that the city and its hinterland must develop according to a predictable pattern and that even an all-wise and all-powerful government could not change this pattern except by first changing the conditions that give rise to it. The argument is not that nothing can be done to improve matters. Rather, it is that only those things can be done which lie within the boundaries — rather narrow ones, to be sure — fixed by the logic of the growth process. Nor is it argued that the only factors influencing metropolitan development are those that relate to population, technology, and income. Countless others also influence it. Two of these other factors are of key importance, even though they are not part of the logic of the process. They will be discussed in the following two chapters (on class culture and race).

This chapter, highly schematic, describes in a generalized way how most American cities, small as well as large, have developed and are still developing, but it does not describe completely (or perhaps even accurately) how any *particular* city has developed. The city under discussion here is a highly simplified model. Its residents have no class, ethnic, or racial attributes (they will acquire them in the next two chapters). They are neither rich nor poor; instead, they are "well-off" or "not well-off," depending upon whether or not they can afford to buy new homes and to commute a considerable distance — requiring, say, half an hour or more — to work.

If the reader finds himself perplexed and irked at an account of metropolitan growth that deals only with demographic, technological, and economic factors, ignoring such others of obvious importance as racial discrimination, he is asked to be patient. This simplification is for analytical purposes, and the necessary complications — but *only* the necessary ones — will be introduced later on. The method is to start with the simplest possible model of urban growth and then (in the next two chapters) to elaborate on it.

The logic of metropolitan growth began unfolding the moment the cities were founded and it has not changed since. More than a century ago, in 1857, a select committee of the state legislature described the forces that were shaping New York. These were, as the committee made clear, the same forces that had always been shaping it. And they were the same ones that are shaping it and other cities still:

As our wharves became crowded with warehouses, and encompassed with bustle and noise, the wealthier citizens, who peopled old "Knicker-bocker" mansions, near the bay, transferred their residence to streets beyond the din; compensating for remoteness from their counting houses, by the advantages of increased quiet and luxury. Their habitations then passed into the hands, on the one side, of boarding house keepers, on the other, of real estate agents; and here, in its beginning, the tenant house became a real blessing to that class of industrious poor whose small earn-ings limited their expenses and whose employment in workshops, stores, and about the wharves and thoroughfares, rendered a near residence of much importance. At this period, rents were moderate, and a mechanic with family could hire two or more comfortable and even commodious apartments, in a house once occupied by wealthy people, for less than half what he is now obliged to pay for narrow and unhealthy quarters. This state of tenantry comfort did not, however, continue long; for the rapid march of improvement speedily enhanced the value of property in the lower wards of the city, and as this took place, rents rose, and accommodations decreased in the same proportion. At first the better class of tenants submitted to retain their single floors, or two and three rooms, at the onerous rates, but this rendered them poorer, and those who were able to do so, followed the example of former proprietors, and emigrated to the upper wards. The spacious dwelling houses then fell before improvements, or languished for a season, as tenant houses of the type which is now the prevailing evil of our city; that is to say, their large rooms were partitioned into several smaller ones (without regard to proper light or ventilation), the rates of rent being lower in proportion to space or height from the street; and they soon became filled, from cellar to garret, with a class of tenantry living from hand to mouth, loose in morals, improvident in habits, degraded or squalid as beggary itself.[2]

What was happening in New York (and elsewhere as well) was the expansion of the city outward under the pressure of growth at its center. Typically, land closest to the point of original settlement (always the point most accessible to waterborne transportation) became the site of the central business district. Great accessibility to wharves, markets, shops, and offices, and later to railheads, meant that commercial and industrial activities had to be located there; the closer a site was to the most accessible center, the more it tended to be worth. Accordingly, most people lived on the outskirts of the central business district, where land prices were not prohibitively high. Only the very rich, to whom the price of land did not matter, and the very poor, who occupied undesirable sites near factories and wharves and endured great overcrowding, lived in the very center of the city.

As the central business district grew, it absorbed the residential neighborhoods adjacent to it. The people who lived in them were pushed outward into unsettled or sparsely settled districts where land prices were still low. To say that they were "pushed" makes it sound as if they went against their wills. Probably most were glad to go. Those who owned their homes profited from the rise in prices; they could sell an old house close to the business district for enough with which to build a new and bigger one at the periphery of the city.

Much of the housing taken over in this way was torn down to make room for factories, stores, and offices. Some, however, was converted to more intensive residential use. When the only transportation was by horse, almost everyone lived within walking distance of his job in the central business district. Even afterward, when one could take a trolley to work, factory workers and office and store clerks generally preferred to pay relatively high rents for crowded quarters from which they could walk to work rather than spend the time and money to commute from neighborhoods where rents were lower. The central business district was therefore ringed with rooming houses and tenements. These establishments could afford the expensive land because they used it intensively. At the end of the last century, for example, some lodging houses in Chicago accommodated (if that is the word) as many as a thousand lodgers a night.

As the populations and income of the city grew, so did the number and proportion of those (the "well-off") who could afford new homes. In the nature of the case, most new homes had to be built at the periphery of the expanding city, where there was vacant land. In the 1830's the large cities — New York, Boston, and Philadelphia — saw the introduction of omnibuses which were usually drawn by two horses and carried twelve to fifteen passengers at a fixed fare over a fixed route. Because of high fares and low speeds commuting for more than ten miles from the city center was out of the question.[3] In the early 1850's a horsecar on rails appeared in New York. It cost less to operate and made more frequent stops. Until the end of the Civil War most of the larger cities had single routes which, if they ran more than a half mile beyond the built-up area, reached real estate developments owned by the transportation company. The more prosperous members of the middle class now tended to live in town houses arranged in rows: the terraced brownstone rows of the large eastern cities date from this period. After the Civil War horsecar routes were extended somewhat, and during the 1870's and 1880's, when deflation reduced costs, many of the lines were built out to about four miles from the city center — a journey of half to three-quarters of an hour. According to David Ward (whose account has been paraphrased in most of the foregoing), many of the extensions were initially designed to serve outlying hospitals, cemeteries, and parks. The weekend and holiday use of these lines sustained them until adjacent residential developments supported commuter services. Although separate single-family dwellings were now the dominant form of suburban housing, most new construction was confined to discontinuous ribbon development.[4]

Where land costs were relatively high — that is, not far from the city center — the housing near the horsecar routes often consisted largely of "three-deckers" (upper-story porches decking the front and rear of four-story tenements). Soon, however, it became feasible to build farther out. The first elevated steam railroads were built in New York in the 1870's, and twenty years later every sizable city had an electric trolley system.[5] Railroads and trolleys enabled more people to commute and to commute larger distances; the farther out they went, the cheaper the land was and the larger the lot sizes they could afford. One- and two-family houses became common.

Wherever this outward movement of the well-off passed beyond the legal boundaries of the city, it created special problems. As early as 1823, Cincinnati officials complained that people living on the edge of the town did not contribute their fair share of taxes, and a few years later the council of St. Louis, which had the same problem, petitioned the state legislature to enlarge the city to include the settlers just beyond its borders who had "all the benifits [sic] of a City residence without any of its burdens."[6] Many cities were enlarged, thus post-poning — in some instances indefinitely — the emergence of an acute problem of city-suburb relations. The motives that impelled people to move outward were essentially the same, however, whether the boundaries of the city were near in or far out, and the strength of the outward movement seems to have been roughly the same in every era and in every place. The "flight to the suburbs" is certainly nothing new.[7]

The movement of the well-off out of the inner city was always regarded (as it had been by the select committee in New York) as both portent and cause of the city's decline. The well-off were sure that without their steadying and elevating influence the city would drift from bad to worse and become "the prey of professional thieves, ruffians, and political jugglers."[8] As a committee of leading Bostonians explained in the 1840's:

An individual's influence is exerted chiefly in the place where he resides. Take away from the city a hundred moral and religious families, and there will be taken away a hundred centers of moral and religious influence, though the constituted heads of those families spend the greatest part of their time in the city, and hold in the metropolis the greatest proportion of their property. Those who remove their residence from the city, remove also their places of attendance on public worship, and the children of those families are removed from our primary and higher schools, public and private. . . . They are not here to visit the poor and degraded, and by their example and conduct to assist in resisting the tide of iniquity that is rolling in on us.[9]

People said that they moved because the city was no longer habitable: they could not stand its dirt, noise, and disorder, not to mention the danger to property values from the arrival of "undesirable" people. ("The settlement of an Irish family in one of our suburban neighborhoods," William Dean Howells wrote in 1888, strikes a "mortal pang" in the old residents, whose property values "tremble."[10]) Actually, they would have moved anyway, although not in all cases quite so soon, even if the inner city had been as clean and fresh as a field of daisies. They would have moved sooner or later because, as the city grew, the land they occupied would have to be used more intensively. Or, to put it another way, they would have moved because only the very rich could afford to forego the advantage of much cheaper land on the outskirts.

As the well-off moved outward, the "not well-off" (meaning here those who could not afford new houses or the time and money to travel half an hour to work) moved into the relatively old and high-density housing left behind. Indeed, it was in part the pressure of their demand for this housing that caused the well-off to move as soon as they did. The result in many places was to thin out the most over-crowded districts ("rabbit-warrens," the reformers of the 1880's called them) adjacent to warehouses, factories, stores, and offices.

Had the supply of the not well-off not been continually replenished by migration from abroad and from the small towns and farms of this country, the high-density tenement districts would have emptied rapidly at the end of the last century as incomes rose and more people moved outward. As it happened, however, immigration continually brought new workers who, for at least a few years — until they, too, could move on — were glad to take refuge in the housing that the others had left behind.

Heavy as it was, migration to the city seldom fully offset the decentralizing effect of the commuter railroad and the trolley and of the expansion of commercial and industrial land uses near the city's center. In many cities the densest slums were either displaced by stores, offices, and factories or drained to reasonable densities by improvement of transportation, or both. The Basin tenement area of Cincinnati, for example, lost one-fourth of its population between 1910 and 1930, a period of rapid growth for the rest of the city. In Chicago, New York, and Philadelphia much the same thing happened.[11] One-quarter of the population of the twenty-five metropolitan districts defined by the Census Bureau in 1910 lived in suburban zones rather than in central cities.[12]

In the first half of the twentieth century the process of growth was accelerated by changes of technology, although its character was not changed in any essential way. Invention of the mechanical refrigerator, along with a vast increase in the variety of inexpensive canned foods, reduced the number of boardinghouses and restaurants. Dispersal of factories was brought about by the use of heavy-duty power transmission cables and, even more, of the assembly line (horizontal processes required more land). Probably of equal importance was the introduction of cheap and rapid highway transportation.[13] By 1915 nearly 2.5 million automobiles were in use; five years later there were 1.1 million trucks. The automobiles facilitated the creation of residential neighborhoods still farther out from the central business district, and the trucks cut factories loose from railheads (and thus from the center of the city also). Stupendous sums were spent for automobiles and for highways, in effect subsidizing the development of the hinterland.

The federal government gave outward expansion a further push when during the Depression it created the Federal Housing Administration. As was noted in the previous chapter, FHA's assistance (and later the Veterans Administration's as well) went mostly to those who bought new homes. For the most part these were in outlying neighborhoods of the central city or in the suburban ring, the only places where vacant land was plentiful. Had it been disposed to do so, FHA might have stimulated the renovation of existing housing and thus the refurbishing of the central cities. If it had done this, it would have assisted many of the not well-off, a category that included most Negroes as well as other minority group members. In fact, it did the opposite: it subsidized the well-off who wanted to leave the central city, while (by setting neighborhood and property standards that they could not meet) refusing to help the not well-off to renovate their central-city houses.[14]

The Depression slowed down but — thanks to the FHA — did not stop the outward movement of the well-off. It did, however, interrupt and even reverse the flow into the city of the not well-off. In the 1920's more than four million immigrants had come from abroad, the great majority of them settling in the larger cities. There also had been a considerable movement of Negroes from the rural South to the large cities of the North, especially New York. (The Negro population of New York more than doubled in this decade, rising from 152,467 to 327,706, and Harlem, which had only recently been occupied by outward-bound, second-generation Jews and Italians, was suddenly transformed.[15]) When the Depression struck, people not only stopped coming to the city but left it in large numbers to go "back to the land" and back to the old country. Now, partially drained and no longer being replenished, the inner city began to stagnate. Neighborhoods that had been packed a few years before were more or less depopulated; people who lived in them no longer expected to follow the "tenement trail" out of the city. They seemed to have been left permanently behind and it appeared to some people that a new and serious problem had arisen. As Edith Elmer Wood explained in a bulletin written for the Public Works Administration in 1935:

The blighting effect of slums on human lives and human character was less acute during the period of immigration and rapid population growth than it is now. Newcomers sought the cheapest and therefore the worst housing, literally pushing out, and necessarily into something better, the last previous immigrant wave. They were able to afford the move because rapidly expanding population meant rapidly expanding jobs. . . . Living in the slums was a temporary discomfort, cheerfully endured, because of an animating faith that prosperity and comfort were just ahead. . . .
Since immigration stopped, all that has changed. The situation has become static. A superior family climbs out here and there, but it is the exception, not the rule, and for every one that goes up, another must come down. Discouragement or bitterness has taken the place of hope. It is only recently that we have seen a generation reach manhood and womanhood which was born and bred in our city slums, which has known no home but a dingy tenement, no playground but the city streets. And worst of all, it has little hope of attaining anything better except by the short-cuts of crime.[16]

The "defense boom" and then World War II quickly filled the inner city to overflowing once again. Now the well-off could not move away because of controls on residential construction; at the same time, large numbers of workers, most of them unskilled, came from small towns and farms until all the inner city housing that could possibly be used was occupied. A huge amount of new factory capacity was built in two or three years, most of it at the periphery of the city but within its borders. Had this expansion taken place under normal circumstances, most of the new factories would have been located in the suburban ring, beyond the borders of the city. The effect of the war, therefore, was to slow down somewhat the decentralization of the city.

As soon as wartime controls were lifted, the logic of growth reasserted itself. A huge pent-up demand on the part of the well-off, whose numbers had been swelled by formation of new families, wartime prosperity, and the home-loan provisions of the "G.I. Bill of Rights," burst forth in a mass exodus from the city to the suburbs: between 1940 and 1950 some 2.3 million persons moved out of the twelve largest central cities. Not all of these people went to the suburbs, of course, and 2.3 million was only 12 percent of the total population of these cities; nevertheless, the sudden outward surge was unprecedented in scale. As had happened before, when the well-off left, the not well-off moved into the housing left behind. The more prosperous among them took the best of it and left the housing that they vacated for those below them on the income ladder, who in turn passed their housing down to still others. Many of those in this housing queue — practically all those at the "far" end of it — were Negroes (in New York, Puerto Ricans also; in Los Angeles, Oakland, and some other cities, Mexicans also).[17]

The heavy, continued Negro migration to the city during and after the war changed the situation markedly. In 1940 more than three-quarters (77 percent) of the nation's Negroes lived in the South; by 1970 only a little more than half (53 percent) lived there. Whereas until recently the Negro was rural, now he was big-city: 58 percent of Negroes, as compared to 28 percent of whites, lived in central cities in 1970. The net out-migration of Negroes from the South slowed in the 1960's, but migration and natural increase together gave them by 1970 a little more than 20 percent of the total central city population and nearly 30 percent of the population of the dozen largest cities.[18]

Great as it was, the postwar movement into the larger, older central cities did not anywhere equal the movement out of them. This in itself tended to make housing more plentiful. The growing demand for low-cost housing also brought about an increase in the supply of it as the well-off found it advantageous to sell and move to the suburbs, leaving their houses to be converted for occupancy by two or three families of the not well-off and, in the case of those who were landlords, spending less than before on maintenance and improvements.[19] Much of the housing that came to the not well-off in this way was of good quality, built only thirty or forty years before and still structurally sound. All that was wrong with much of it was that it was out-of-date, aesthetically and otherwise, by the standards of the well-off — standards that had risen rapidly during the war and postwar prosperity. The not well-off very quickly occupied the better housing that came on the market. In the past, the least well-off had lived in compact, high-density districts. Now they spread out in all directions, leapfrogging neighborhoods here and there, covering miles and miles.[20] In the 1960's these movements were still strong: in that decade the white (read well-off) population of Chicago declined by more than half a million (nearly 20 percent) and there were even larger percentage declines in Detroit (30 percent), St. Louis (31 percent), and Newark (37 percent). As was remarked in the previous chapter, in 1970 relatively few families in the "poverty areas" of the large cities lived in crowded housing and many spent only a small part of their income on housing.

By no means all of the well-off left the city. Some who could afford any rent lived in luxury apartments, a gold coast along the central business district. The number of such people was bound to grow, but not enough to change the inner city fundamentally. In the outlying neighborhoods, heads of families often remained even when they could afford to move; people getting along in years saw no point in moving from neighborhoods in which they had lived so long and to which they had become attached. It was their children and their boarders who moved away to the suburbs. On the lower East Side of New York in the 1960's and early 1970's there were still some neighborhoods occupied mainly by remnants of the Jewish immigration of the early 1900's and the Puerto Rican immigration of the 1920's,[21] but the population of such neighborhoods was thinning out. The later migrants, mostly Negroes (and in New York, Puerto Ricans), had in most cases come to the city as young adults or children and were a remarkably fast-growing and fast-spreading population.

Looking at the neighborhoods they had left a decade or two before, suburbanites were often dismayed at what they saw — lawns and shrubbery trampled out, houses unpainted, porches sagging, vacant lots filled with broken bottles and junk. To them — and, of course, even more to the scattering of "old residents" who for one reason or another remained — these things constituted "blight" and "decay." To many commentators it appeared that the white middle class was "running away" from "blight" and also from neighbors whom they considered inferior or of whom they were afraid (although exaggeration was frequent, there was no doubt that in many districts the amount of street crime increased dramatically as the composition of the population changed). Allowing for exceptions, however, the "flight" of the middle class to the suburbs was not properly speaking flight at all. Most of those who left did so neither from fear of violence or of blight but simply because they wanted and could afford newer and more spacious houses and neighborhoods. In his study of Levittown, the huge new suburb that was built in New Jersey, Herbert J. Gans found that only 9 percent of those interviewed volunteered the inadequacy of their old neighborhood or community as their most important reason for leaving it. The desire to own a spacious, free-standing house was the most frequent and important motivation.[22]

To the people who moved from old tenements and shanties into the housing that had been vacated by the relatively well-off people who moved to the suburbs, what was happening to the central city neighborhoods did not appear as "decay."[23] Many of them cared little or nothing for lawns and had no objections to broken bottles; they knew, too, that the more "fixed up" things were, the higher rents would be. What mattered most to them was having four or five rooms instead of one or two, plumbing that worked, an inside bathroom that did not have to be shared with strangers down the hall, and central heating. To the least well-off, "blight" was a blessing. They were able, for the first time in their lives, to occupy housing that was comfortable.

Although the appearance of neighborhoods declined as they were occupied by lower-income groups, the quality of housing in the central city as a whole improved dramatically. Housing was repaired and improved on a wholesale scale during the postwar years, some of it by government programs but more of it through the normal processes of consumer spending. Although differences in Census definition make precise comparisons impossible, more than half the housing in metropolitan areas that was substandard in 1949 was put in sound condition during the next ten years through structural repairs or by plumbing additions. At the end of the decade, some families still lived in housing that was appallingly bad, but their number was small and getting smaller. As incomes rose, so did the quality of housing.[24] (Muth estimated that a 10 percent increase in average income is accompanied by a decline of about one-third in the amount of sub-

URBAN HOUSING NEEDS IN THE UNITED STATES AS REPRESENTED
BY SUBSTANDARD AND STANDARD OVERCROWDED UNITS UNDER
THREE DIFFERING ASSUMPTIONS

Millions
of Units

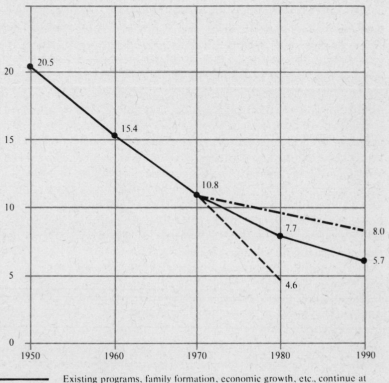

Existing programs, family formation, economic growth, etc., continue at
present rates.

If government assistance programs were discontinued.

If 500,000 low- and moderate-income units were built annually under
assisted programs for families with incomes of $5,000 or less, over a 10-
year period.

Source: Frank S. Kristof, *Urban Housing Needs Through the 1980's: an Analysis and
Projection,* Report prepared for the National Commission on Urban Problems,
Research Report No. 10 (Washington, D.C.: U.S. Government Printing Office, 1968),
p. 58.

standard housing.[25]) There was reason to believe that if government programs and other factors operating in 1968 were to continue (and in mid-1973 they *were* continuing) the number of urban housing units which were either substandard or overcrowded would be less than 5 million by 1980.

Data of the sort presented in the preceding paragraph and the chart must be viewed with a certain skepticism, however. For one thing, Census data on the quality of housing are hastily gathered by persons without much training and are therefore not very reliable.[26] For another, if — as is happening in the inner districts of many large cities — the quality of a neighborhood is going from bad to worse it is misleading to report, albeit correctly, that there is less substandard or overcrowded housing there. As Frank S. Kristof, the authority whose estimates are shown in the chart, has written, "If a neighborhood is no longer regarded as a good place to live, the condition and quality of its housing become almost irrelevant to its survival."[27] In New York, Newark, Philadelphia, Detroit, and many other cities some neighborhoods are being abandoned at a time when housing, looked at house-by-house and without regard to social conditions and attitudes, would lead one to conclude that there is no "housing problem" in the tracts where abandonment is occurring.[28]

By discarding housing that was still usable, the well-off conferred a great benefit upon the not well-off. Like many benefits, however, this one had hidden costs: in order to use the discarded housing, one had to live where it was; all too often this meant living where there were not enough jobs.

The central business district — and with it the central city as a whole — had long been losing its monopoly of accessibility. As the population at the periphery of the city grew, there was increasing support for large stores and other facilities that could compete with those of the central business district. People no longer had to go downtown for almost everything. At the same time, improvements in transportation, especially the building of expressways and of major airports that were some distance from the city, made it easier than before to get from one part of the metropolitan area to another without going downtown. Also, manufacturing always tended to move outward to cheaper land; beginning in the early 1930's, increases in

plant size and improvements in materials-handling techniques hastened this movement. More and more manufacturers wanted single-
story plants with horizontal material flows and aisles wide enough to
permit mechanical handling of materials. This usually compelled
them to move their operations to a less congested area close to a
center of long-distance truck hauling.[29] After the Second World War,
much manufacturing, and much retailing and wholesaling as well,
moved out of the city.

The central business district retained its advantage of accessibility
with respect to activities involving frequent face-to-face communication. Top executives had to be near to each other and to the bankers,
lawyers, advertising men, government officials, and others with whom
they dealt frequently; consequently, they kept their headquarters
downtown. The rest of their operations — factories as well as
record-keeping — they could send to the suburbs, where land was
cheaper and clerical help easier to find, or to other areas altogether. In
the 1950's the central cities stagnated economically, and it appeared
likely that they would decline drastically in the 1960's. In fact,
although most lost population and suffered some deterioration of
public facilities, the economies of the large central cities grew,
although at a slower rate than those of the suburban fringes. Between
1960 and 1968, the 30 largest central cities more than made up what
they lost in manufacturing and trade by gains in insurance, communications, tourism, and services, especially governmental services; in
those years the value of their production (in constant dollars)
increased by one-third. Employment in most large central cities
increased in the 1960's even though population decreased and the
quality of city services declined.[30]

The rapid growth of the service sector in the central cities has not
meant jobs for all, however. Most of the new service jobs are held by
relatively well-trained suburbanites rather than by the low-skilled
central city residents whose factory jobs have moved to the suburbs.
Oakland, Calif., is apparently a fairly typical example. According to
Pressman and Wildavsky, the East Bay economy is flourishing and,
although the suburbs are growing faster, Central Oakland is becoming
a service center. There are plenty of jobs in the city for the well-
trained, most of them middle-class white suburbanites who can con-

veniently commute. For the low-skilled black workers who live in the inner city the case is entirely different. They cannot follow their factory jobs to the suburbs and for lack of training and because of discrimination they do not get good jobs in the new service economy. "Oakland," the City Planning Department is quoted as saying, "is increasingly providing a home for blacks and a place of employment for *whites*."[31]

It should not be supposed that most central city workers have been left stranded by these developments, however. There are still more jobs for the unskilled in the central cities than elsewhere in the metropolitan areas, and, except in three or four of the largest metropolitan areas, a worker can travel from his inner city dwelling to a job anywhere on the outer perimeter of the metropolitan area in no more than half an hour. The radial pattern of highway and rail transportation, although not planned for the purpose, is ideal from the standpoint of workers, such as domestics and construction workers, who typically are employed for a few days in one suburb and then a few in another, the second perhaps being on the opposite side of the metropolitan area from the first. "Reverse commuting" — that is, traveling from an inner city residence to a job in the suburbs — was done by nearly 1,500,000 workers in 1970.

The increase in the number of new jobs — especially of ones suitable for the unskilled — has been much greater in the suburbs than in the central cities. Some economists think that this constitutes a very serious handicap for the poor and the black who, because of discrimination in the housing market and the absence in the suburbs of an adequate supply of low-cost housing, are obliged to live in the inner parts of the central cities. Nothing would contribute more to the welfare of these people, in the opinion of these economists, than the creation of a supply of housing enabling them to live where job opportunities are growing.[32] Other economists disagree, however. One found from a study of sixty-five large metropolitan areas no support for the view that the "suburbanization of jobs" significantly affected the employment of blacks.[33] Another found that although whites gained from living in or near a suburb (rather than in a central-city "poverty area") *blacks* did not. ". . . [O]ne cannot," he concluded, "react . . . with anything other than the deepest pessimism about the potential effectiveness of policies for 'suburbanizing' non-whites in the urban ghetto. The known costs of such policies would be very great, and the expected benefits very small, at least in terms of employment opportunity."[34]

At some future time — a very distant one perhaps — the logic of metropolitan growth will have to change. Conceivably, the urban population may stop growing, or technology may change so as to make it cheaper to build upward than outward, or government may redistribute income to such an extent that everyone can afford to buy a new house and to commute a considerable distance to work. If none of these changes occurs, the supply of vacant land into which the metropolis can expand will run out. None of these changes seems likely to occur in the foreseeable future, however. Essentially the same logic that shaped the growth of the city in the past may therefore be expected to shape that of the metropolitan area in the future. It is, in fact, already clear that the urban population will grow: the children of the postwar baby boom are already reaching adulthood, and a new, "second-generation" baby boom is in the making. Migration from the rural South will continue to decline and many migrants will avoid cities like Newark, which are known to be dead ends, in favor of ones like Seattle that hitherto have not been favored. Migration, however, has in recent years accounted for only about one-third of urban growth, the remainder coming from births. On the basis of "high fertility" and other assumptions, the Census projects increases in central city populations between 1970 and 2000 of as much as one-third, but on probably more realistic "low fertility" assumptions, a decrease of about 4 percent. Either way, the nonwhite population is expected to be about 40 percent of the total.[35]

Immigration will also contribute to the cities' growth. Under present law the anticipated level of about 400,000 immigrants per year will contribute about one-fifth of the nation's population gain from 1970 to 1985. Illegal entries, most of them from Mexico, may swell the total very substantially: according to some estimates, they may more than double it. The legal immigrants will be mostly skilled and semi-skilled and the illegal mostly unskilled; almost all will settle in urban places.

Not only will there be more city dwellers in the coming decades but their incomes will be higher. In the most conservative forecasts (a slower rate of population growth and a slower rate of economic expansion), Gross National Product per capita in 1967 dollars is expected to increase from $3,937 in 1970 to $7,218 in 2000.[36] As people become more prosperous, they will buy more housing. To the extent that this involves their discarding at a faster rate the housing that they already have (many may prefer to renovate what they have), it will give more and better housing bargains to the not well-off, encouraging them to move ever farther outward and thus eventually emptying the central city and bringing "blight" to suburbs that were new a decade or two ago. To the "pulling" effect of these bargains will be added two "pushing" ones: the physical deterioration of central city housing (which, being the oldest, has been in use the longest) and the clearance activities of urban renewal and public works programs, which are expected to displace between half a million and two million families between 1965 and 1975. Among those moving outward from the central city will be large numbers of Negroes. Efforts to keep them in the central city where their voting strength can be exploited are bound to fail, as are efforts to distribute them throughout white neighborhoods. In their quest for living space and jobs, relatively well-off Negroes, like the relatively well-off in other groups, are moving to the suburban ring. In the 1960's blacks doubled their numbers in the suburbs of Los Angeles and Washington, D.C., and increased by more than one-half in the New York area. In the country as a whole, the black suburban population grew by more than 1.1 million, bringing the total to more than 3.5 million. Of these, almost half live in neighborhoods that contain fewer than 1 percent Negroes, and only about 15 percent live in "substantially integrated" (more than 10 percent Negro) neighborhoods.[37] Most live in what have been called "mini-ghettos" lying between white residential districts.[38]

As better-off suburbanites make ready to move farther out into the suburban fringe in search of larger lots, they will relax zoning and other restrictions that have excluded the less well-off from suburban communities; as the need to find customers for their "downgraded" properties grows, less and less exhortation will be needed to convince them of the soundness of the principle of open occupancy. The pressure of court decisions against exclusionary zoning and similar practices is hastening this process.[39] Despite these influences, however, it is certain that large numbers of Negroes will live in the major central cities for at least several decades to come.

If there is any check on outward expansion, it is probably the limited supply of vacant land. This supply will be used up faster than ever, not only because more people will be able to afford land, but also because they will be able to afford larger lots. (In the New York metropolitan region, for example, the next six million people to move to new homes in the outlying suburbs are expected to take as much land as the previous sixteen million took. Two-thirds of the land in these suburbs is now zoned for single-family houses on lots of a half acre or more.) It will be many years before the frontier of vacant land is reached, however. (Even in the New York region, where the demand is greatest, the supply is expected to last for at least another generation.[40]) And when it is at last reached, the outward movement will not stop abruptly; instead, two- and three-acre lots will probably be subdivided into half-acre ones, permitting movement from the older, higher-density rings of settlement to continue for some time. As the supply of vacant land diminishes, however, the price of it will rise, and this will dampen the desire to use it lavishly. That the outlying suburbs of New York and other cities are zoned for large lots therefore indicates little about the density at which they will actually be built; the zoners there may not have anticipated how costly land would become and how sobering an effect this would have upon prospective buyers. In fact, the dampening effect of higher land prices in the suburbs has been operating for some time. Of the new housing units started in 1972, 42 percent were in apartment buildings for three or more families; in 1960 the comparable figure was 18 percent. As gasoline prices increase in response to the increased demand for oil in world markets suburbs will be built somewhat more compactly but it seems likely that the main adjustment will be initially to smaller cars and later to modes of transportation using other sources of energy. In short, the trend of development will be modified but not essentially changed by rising costs of transportation.

As the price of vacant land in the suburbs goes up, that of land and buildings in the central city will go down. As was pointed out earlier, the central business district — and with it the central city as a whole — has been losing the monopoly of accessibility that made its land so valuable. As the exodus of commerce, industry, and population continues, the value of real estate in the central city will decline. Urban renewal will tend to slow this down: so long as it appears likely that the government will buy deteriorating property at its present market value, that value is not likely to fall. In a few parts of a city, speculation arising from uncertainty about governmental policies and other developments may hold values steady or even cause them to rise. (Land in the Shaw ghetto of Washington, D.C., was selling for more than $640,000 an acre in 1972, a price which would make "low-income" town houses, some of which were only sixteen feet wide and twenty-nine feet deep, cost at least $52,200 each.)[41] But it is highly unlikely that such influences will prevent the decline of land values in large districts of most central cities. The amount of public subsidy that would be required is now, and seems likely to remain far beyond what anyone would consider tolerable, a condition which will probably discourage speculators.

If the populations of the inner cities are not again replenished by unskilled immigrants — something that, in view of the large flow of illegal entrants from Mexico and the potentially large legal flow from Puerto Rico, cannot be taken for granted — the time will eventually come when cleared land in the depopulated central city will be worth less than vacant land in the heavily populated suburbs. When this time comes, the direction of metropolitan growth will reverse itself: the well-off will move from the suburbs to the cities, probably causing editorial writers to deplore the "flight to the central city" and politicians to call for government programs to check it by redeveloping the suburbs.

Some tendencies toward recentralization have appeared.[42] First, advances in electronic data processing are making some offices into "paper-processing factories"; these employ unskilled workers at the bottom of the white-collar occupational ladder in jobs such as key punch operator. Second, "the computer and the recent technological advances in teleprocessing and time-sharing have also strongly reinforced the ability of a business enterprise to retain its head office and management in a centralized location in the face of ever wider decentralization of operations."[43] Third, huge expenditures are being made for scientific research and development. Much of this work does not require great land space, is independent of manufacturing and materials locations, and is best done in close proximity to universities.

The central city has lost its old monopoly on accessibility, however. At most, it will be one of several nuclei in a metropolitan area over which business activity and residential occupance are, as compared to the "old-fashioned" city, rather evenly and thinly spread. In the opinion of George Sternlieb, the older central cities, having lost their capacity to serve as effective staging areas for immigrants and other newcomers, no longer have any function except that of "sandbox" — they are places where the poor and the unskilled (the children) are left to occupy themselves with government social welfare programs (toys) while other people (the grown-ups) go about the serious business of making money.[44]

Presumably Sternlieb is exaggerating in order to make a point. But it is idle to talk of bringing large numbers of the well-off back into the central city. For the city to compete as a residential area with the suburbs, large districts of it would have to be completely rebuilt at very low densities. This is out of the question so long as people are living in these districts. To be sure, the government might build new housing somewhere else (where?) for the residents of the old neighborhoods and move them to it, forcibly if necessary. It might then tear down the existing structures and put up new ones, creating neighborhoods that would attract the well-off back from the suburbs. This plan would be fantastically expensive, of course, since it would mean destroying a great deal of useful housing, as well as stores, factories, churches, schools, and other facilities. Doing this would be insane if the purpose were nothing more than "civic patriotism" or the wish to confer benefits on the well-off.

A case might perhaps be made for a wholesale exchange of population between the central city and the suburbs on the ground that the preservation of democratic institutions requires it. But if such were the purpose, the redeveloped central city could not be occupied solely or even mainly by the well-off — rich and poor, black and white, would have to be settled in proximity to one another, sharing schools and other facilities, the object being to improve the quality of the community by their association. An undertaking of this sort would have the justification of aiming at an important public good. Whether it would, within reasonable probability, secure that good is doubtful, however. For one thing, it would be hard to give the well-off the space necessary to bring them back from the suburbs and still have room for the large number of the not well-off who would have to be accommodated. If, as is all too likely, one of the requirements of the well-off was that they be insulated from "undesirables," then obviously the reoccupation of the city by them could not be brought about on terms that would serve any public purpose. Even on the most favorable view of the possibilities — that is, assuming that stable, integrated neighborhoods could be created — the wisdom of, in effect, throwing a large part of the city's physical plant on the scrap heap may well be questioned.

To build "new towns" (actually small cities) when doing so involves abandoning or underutilizing existing facilities would be an even more costly venture since not only housing, schools, churches, and stores, but everything else as well — factories, streets, water and sewer lines — would have to be built new from the ground up. Here again, one may say that if the object is to create an integrated community, and if that object can be attained in this way and in no other that entails smaller costs (so that abandoning existing streets, sewer lines, and the like is unavoidable), the money is well spent. The undertaking would be enormously expensive, however. As Irving Hoch has remarked, in an inflationary age older cities have an advantage by virtue of possessing highways, utilities, and other elements of "infra-structure" that were cheap to build.[45] He acknowledges that there may be disadvantages where these were put in place before the automobile came into wide use but, noting that few American new towns have been developed since the Civil War and also that the European cities destroyed during the war were rebuilt on the same sites, he concludes that established cities probably have some net long-run advantage. Alongside of his view, that of an economist, may be placed that of a demographer, Peter A. Morrison, who thinks it likely that most people will eventually reside in a few megalopolises (large regions populated more or less contiguously but at widely varying densities) and that this will have advantages (the preservation of large, sparsely inhabited areas and increases in productivity due to economies of scale) but also dangers (concentration of the consumption of energy and water and of the generation of wastes may threaten the environment's absorptive capacity). The dilemma cannot be escaped by building new towns, however, for (Morrison says) they would have to be built at the rate of about one a month in order to accommodate even a small fraction of the increase of population that will occur by the end of the century and building one would require a construction camp half as large as the city itself. Worse still, the people who would be attracted to new cities would tend to be young and hypermobile — precisely the kind most likely to move on after a short stay. Using new cities to deflect growth away from congested metropolitan areas or to alter the distribution of population nationally, he concludes, "goes against the grain of demographic realities."[46]

The impracticability of attracting large numbers of the well-off back into the central city before land prices there have become competitive with those in the suburbs (and without the use of large subsidies) can be seen — in a very extreme form, to be sure, since Manhattan is a special case — from a newspaper report of a "seminar" on the problems of owning and occupying one of the old-fashioned brownstone houses of which there are about 2,500 on the city's crime-ridden West Side.[47] Prices start at $100,000 and go up to about $300,000, depending upon the condition of the building which in many instances must then be renovated. According to the report, about 1,500 of the brownstones have been renovated in the last ten years and about another 500 are "ripe" for renovation and available for purchase now. Presumably purchasers will be found, despite the prices and the hazards of the district. But the real problem, of course, is not to induce a few hundred very wealthy people to buy houses a few blocks from Lincoln Center or Columbia University but to bring tens of thousands of moderately well-off families back to such unglamorous places as Brooklyn and the Bronx.

The three imperatives listed at the beginning of this chapter — namely, rate of population growth, technology of transportation, and distribution of income — place stringent limits on policy. Except as it may relax one or more of them and so change the logic of metropolitan growth, government — even the wisest and most powerful government — must work within the limits set by these imperatives. It may hasten or delay the unfolding of the logic of growth and it may make such adaptations — very important ones sometimes — as are possible within it. But given the premises, it cannot prevent the conclusions from following.

Consider the case of New York City. The state legislative committee of 1857, whose report was quoted earlier, confidently asserted that "wise and simple laws," if only they had been adopted in time, would have checked or prevented the evils it deplored. With such laws, it said, "the city of New York would now exhibit more gratifying bills of health, more general social comfort and prosperity and less, far less expenditure for the support of pauperism and the punishment of crime." It blamed the authorities of an earlier time for not having passed the necessary laws; those authorities, it said, "were unmindful of the future public good, precisely as we, in our day and generation, are pertinaciously regardless of our posterity's welfare."[48]

Perhaps the authorities *were* unmindful of the future public good. Whether they were or were not does not matter much; they could not, in any case, have changed the imperatives of population growth, transportation technology, and income level, and it is these factors that account not only for their failure to change the pattern of growth but also for the failure of authorities in later times as well, including, of course, the committee of 1857 itself.

What, one wonders, are the wise and simple laws that would have saved the situation if only they had been made soon enough? The idea of controlling land use by a zoning ordinance is a recent one, but suppose that when Manhattan was first settled an ordinance had limited the spread of warehouses, factories, and other objectionable land uses. If such an ordinance had been made and enforced, the old Knickerbocker mansions would still be standing — but there would be no city. Nor, if *all* towns had made and enforced such ordinances, would there be cities anywhere. If towns are to grow into cities and cities into metropolises, old residential districts necessarily must decline and disappear.

Suppose, again, that in the city's earliest days the authorities had enacted a housing code requiring the demolition of all substandard dwellings. (The committee of 1857 did, in fact, propose a regulation against the renting of cellars.[49]) Such a code, if enforced, would have prevented the city from growing fast and from ever becoming a metropolis.[50] In order to grow fast, the city had to become a center of warehouses, shops, and factories, which meant that it had to have a plentiful supply of cheap labor, which meant that it had to have a plentiful supply of housing that such labor could afford. If all the housing had been decent by the standards of the time, some of the labor required for the city's growth could not have afforded to live in the city at all.[51]

It may be argued that if the city had insisted, adequate housing would have been provided and the extra cost in effect added to the wage bill and so passed on to the consumer. But no city could have added very much to its wage bill without worsening its competitive position vis-à-vis other areas. Had all places provided adequate housing, the city would have been under a cost handicap, and its development would have been impeded accordingly. The fundamental fact was that it would have cost more to provide adequate housing in the city than elsewhere. (To be sure, had the extra costs been imposed upon the affluent *regardless of where they lived*, the city would not have been handicapped, but because of political boundaries and other institutional arrangements this was not a real possibility.)

If society had been willing to accept a curtailment of the rate of economic growth for the sake of preventing overcrowding and bad housing in the city, it could have prevented people who could not support themselves properly from coming to the city at all. By restricting the supply of labor in the city, the authorities could have forced the price of it up. Keeping the farm boys on the farms and stopping immigration of all but skilled workers from abroad could have checked or prevented the evils that the committee deplored. But, of course, the growth of New York would also have been checked or prevented. The old Knickerbocker mansions might still be there, but the Statue of Liberty would not be.

It was impossible both to allow unrestricted immigration and to eliminate substandard housing. If free to do so, people would come to the cities from the rural backwaters of this country and from abroad and they would keep on coming until the opportunities in the city as they perceived them were no better than those in the places where they were. Since opportunities in much of the world were extremely poor, the movement into the city was bound to be massive and to continue almost indefinitely if allowed. Improving conditions in the city while allowing migration to continue freely could have no effect but to establish the final equilibrium at a different point — i.e., one at which *more* of the poor would have come to the city. As Jacob A. Riis wrote in *The Poor in Great Cities* (1895), if it were possible for New York to "shut her door against the immigration of the world and still maintain the conditions of today, I should confidently predict a steady progress that would leave little of the problem for the next generation to wrestle with. But that is only another way of saying, 'if New York were not New York.' "[52]

If the authorities had been able to find a miraculously cheap and fast means of transporting large numbers of people from the factory district to the outskirts of the city, the evils that the select committee deplored would easily have been ended. For a time, in fact, reformers in New York thought the subway might accomplish wonders. ("If the happy day ever comes when a poor man can be carried to the green fields of Long Island, New Jersey, or Westchester County for five cents, then a wonderful change will take place," one of them wrote.[53]) The subway and the trolley did put an end to "rabbit warrens," but, despite the new transportation technology, there were still many people in the large cities who either could not afford to move away from the old district close to factories, stores, and offices or did not wish to do so. In 1893 a member of the American Economic Association declared that the confident belief of a few years before that rapid transit would solve New York's housing problems had proved to be a vain hope.[54]

So long as large numbers of workers had to (or chose to) live near their jobs, it was impossible to avoid high rents and overcrowding in the large cities, a conclusion that the reformers of every generation fought manfully against but finally had to accept. It was impossible, a city commission concluded in 1900, to design a tenement house that was both adequate and commercially feasible; moreover, legislation to require the conversion of existing tenements to other uses was not practicable.[55] And in 1955 a mayor's committee estimated that about a million persons (268,000 families) would be displaced if the multiple-dwelling code were strictly enforced.[56]

Redistributing income was another possibility, and it, too, was tried. Subway and highway construction was subsidized, as was the purchase of new homes. Insofar as these and other measures put people who would otherwise not have gotten there so soon in the class of the well-off, they hastened the decongestion of the city. But since they had to be paid for by taxes — taxes that could not be raised solely from the rich — such measures would necessarily have had some contrary and offsetting effect as well. In any event, migration into the city always replenished at least partially what the New York legislative committee of 1857 had called the "class of tenantry living from hand to mouth, loose in morals, improvident in habits, degraded and squalid as beggary itself." Redistribution of income could not eliminate poverty in the city so long as opportunities in any part of the world were conspicuously worse than there and so long as people were free to move to it.

CHAPTER THREE

The Imperatives of Class

... the dominant aim of our society seems to be to middle-
class-ify all of its members.
— John Dollard, 1937

T HE logic of growth does not explain all that needs explaining. For one thing, it does not explain why the city expanded outward as fast as it did. When they moved, the well-off were strongly impelled by economic forces to move outward — first to the outlying neighborhoods of the central city, then to inlying suburbs, and later to outlying ones. But the well-off did not have to move as soon as they did or in such numbers. If the trolley car and then the automobile were causes of their moving, they were also effects of their desire to move. (Philadelphia was the "city of homes" long before rapid transit was invented, Adna F. Weber pointed out apropos of this in 1899.[1]) Also, the logic of growth does not explain why a considerable proportion of the well-off failed to move at all. In 1971, as previously noted, more than a quarter of a million families with incomes in excess of $15,000 a year lived in the "poverty areas" of fifty-one of the largest cities.[2] Obviously some people evaluate the advantages of central city versus suburban living very differently than do others. Furthermore, the logic of growth does not explain the existence of slums. Strictly speaking, a slum is not simply a district of low-quality housing; rather, it is one in which a squalid and wretched style of life is widespread.[3] The logic of growth *does* require that, in general, the lowest-income people live in the oldest, highest-density, most run-down housing, which will be nearest to the factories, warehouses, stores, and offices of the inner, or downtown, part of the central city;

however, nothing in the logic of growth says that such districts must be squalid or crime-ridden.

To account for these and certain other features of metropolitan development in the United States, a second explanatory principle must, so to speak, be placed over the first. This is the concept of class. The purpose of this chapter is to show how certain patterns of perception, taste, attitude, and behavior operate (within the limits set by the logic of growth) to influence the city's form and the nature of its problems. It is one of the main contentions of this book that these patterns, no less than the logic of growth, are constraints which the policymaker must take into account and which limit what he may accomplish.

American sociologists define social class in very different ways: by objective criteria (income, schooling, occupation), subjective criteria (attitudes, tastes, values), and position in a deference hierarchy (who looks up to whom), among others. Whatever criteria are used, it turns out that essentially the same pattern of traits is found to be characteristic of the class. "All who have studied the lower class," writes Lee Rainwater, one of those who has studied it most, have produced findings that suggest a "distinct patterning" of attitudes, values, and modes of behavior.[4] The same can be said of those who have studied the working, middle, and upper classes. Each class exhibits a characteristic patterning that extends to all aspects of life: manners, consumption, child-rearing, sex, politics, or whatever. In the United States over the past half century these patternings have been described — although never with the completeness that an ethnographer would want — in hundreds of books and articles. By and large these many accounts agree.

Various principles have been advanced by which to rationalize or "explain" the association of the many, heterogeneous traits that have been found to constitute each "distinct patterning." Probably no one of these is best for all purposes. For the purpose here — namely, analysis of social problems from a policy standpoint — the most promising principle seems to be that of psychological orientation toward the future. Consequently, in what follows in this and later chapters much will be made of the concepts "present-" and "future-orientation." The theory or explanatory hypothesis (it cannot be called a "fact," although there is some evidence to support it)[5] is that the many traits that constitute a "patterning" are all consequences, indirect if not direct, of a time horizon that is characteristic of a class. Thus, the traits that constitute what is called lower-class culture or life style are consequences of the extreme present-orientation of that class. The lower-class person lives from moment to moment, he is either unable or unwilling to take account of the future or to control his impulses. Improvidence and irresponsibility are direct consequences of this failure to take the future into account (which is not to say that these traits may not have other causes as well), and these consequences have further consequences: being improvident and irresponsible, he is likely also to be unskilled, to move frequently from one dead-end job to another, to be a poor husband and father. . . .

It is useful to employ the same principle — ability or willingness to provide for the future — to account for the traits that are characteristic of the other class cultures as well. The working class is more future-oriented than the lower class but less than the middle class, the middle class in turn is less future-oriented than the upper. At the upper end of the class-cultural scale the traits are all "opposite" those at the lower end.

It must be understood that the perfectly present- and future-oriented individuals are ideal types or constructs; the time horizon theory is intended as an analytical tool, not as a precise description of social reality.[6] In this it is like that familiar category of economic analysis, the "perfectly competitive market," in which all buyers and sellers have perfect information and none is able to influence the price at which anything is sold. In the real world, of course, there never was, and never will be, such a market; that markets are *more or less* competitive is enough, however, to make the concept indispensable in economics. It is pointless to inquire how many people are "perfectly" present- or future-oriented (lower or upper class) — undoubtedly there are none. If the concepts are useful, it is in helping one to think about behavior that approximately corresponds to the model.

The general agreement that exists as to the content of the several class cultures does not extend to the theories about the *causes* of cultural difference and of cultural change. On the one side, there are those who stress the importance of "social heredity." They think of the individual as largely formed in infancy and childhood by influences that reflect the collective experience of the group; by the time he has reached adolescence, his ways of thinking and feeling have been ineradicably marked by these influences. "[C]ertain possibly critical emotional, linguistic, and cognitive patterns associated with social background are already present at the age of three," writes Jerome S. Bruner, an educational psychologist. The young child's social background, he adds, influences the way he learns to set goals, mobilize means, and delay or fail to delay gratification.[7]

On the other side, there are those who consider these early influences relatively unimportant in shaping later behavior as compared to situational factors like income, schooling, and social standing that are either avenues to or obstacles in the way of opportunity. Elliot Liebow, for example, in *Tally's Corner*, a book about a group of Negro streetcorner men in Washington, D.C., after acknowledging that each generation provides "role models" for the succeeding one, goes on to assert that "of much greater importance for the possibilities of change, however, is the fact that many similarities between the lower-class Negro father and son (or mother and daughter) do not result from 'cultural transmission' but from the fact that the son goes out and independently experiences the same failures, in the same areas, and for much the same reasons as his father. What appears as a dynamic, self-sustaining cultural process is, in part at least, a relatively simple piece of social machinery which turns out, in rather mechanical fashion, independently produced look-alikes."[8] Thus, when Richard, one of the streetcorner men, squanders a week's pay in two days, it is not because he is unaware of or unconcerned with his future. "He does so precisely because he is aware of the future and the hopelessness of it all."[9]

Obviously from a policy standpoint it makes a great deal of difference whether one emphasizes "social heredity" or "social machinery." One who emphasizes the former will expect little from measures that are intended to change the individual by improving his opportunities; he will be inclined to think that one must first change the culture in which the individual is so largely formed — something that takes time — a generation or two at least — if it can be done at all. By an odd quirk of reasoning, the difficulty — perhaps impossibility — of bringing about change quickly and according to plan seems to some social scientists to justify giving the "social machinery" theory preference as an explanatory principle even though its truth value may be less.[10]

For the present it suffices to alert the reader to the difficulty — and the relevance — of the "social heredity" versus "social machinery" question. Clearly the subcultures that are described below are not fixed and unchangeable. Even cultures (as opposed to subcultures) sometimes change with remarkable speed. Witness, for example, the "cultural revolution" of China, during a stage of which once-venerated scholars were dragged through the streets by their Red Guard students. If, however, one takes at all seriously the principal insights of social science — represented by the concepts of culture, personality, and social structure — one must expect a high degree of continuity in most behavior. Indeed, one must expect behavior sometimes to persist in the face of conditions that offer powerful inducements to change.

The time-horizon theory does not prejudge this question. It merely asserts that the traits constituting a culture or life style are best understood as resulting from a greater or lesser ability (or desire) to provide for the future. Whether the time horizon of an individual is mainly passed on to the individual by cultural transmission, mainly an adaptation that he more or less rationally makes to the realities of his situation (poverty or racial discrimination, for example) or — by far the most likely possibility — the outcome of a complex interaction between *both* sets of forces, has to be decided (so far as it *can* be decided) in accordance with the facts of particular cases and not in the abstract.[11]

The reader is asked to keep in mind that members of a "class" as the word is used here are people who share a "distinct patterning of attitudes, values, and modes of behavior," *not* people of like income, occupation, schooling, or status. A lower class individual is likely to be unskilled and poor, but it does not follow from this that persons who are unskilled and poor are likely to be lower class. (That Italians eat spaghetti does not imply that people who eat spaghetti are Italian!) The reader is reminded also that the truth of the observations about class cultures that are summarized below does not in the least depend upon that of the time-horizon theory used to "explain" them. If it should be shown that Richard is not present-oriented, what is crucial for present purposes — namely, that he had others like him exhibit a distinct patterning of traits — would have to be accounted for in some other way.

Strong correlations exist between IQ and socioeconomic status, and some scholars have presented evidence tending to show that they are due in large part to genetic factors.[12] Ability (or willingness) to take account of the future does not appear to have much relation to intelligence or IQ; however, it is not implausible to conjecture that some genetic factor may influence it. The position taken here, however, is that time horizon is a social, not a biological, product.

The Upper Class.[13] At the most future-oriented end of the scale, the upper-class individual expects a long life, looks forward to the future of his children, grandchildren, great-grandchildren (the family "line"), and is concerned also for the future of such abstract entities as the community, nation, or mankind. He is confident that within rather wide limits he can, if he exerts himself to do so, shape the future to accord with his purposes. He therefore has strong incentives to "invest" in the improvement of the future situation — i.e., to sacrifice some present satisfaction in the expectation of enabling someone (himself, his children, mankind, etc.) to enjoy greater satisfactions at some future time. Future-oriented culture teaches the individual that he would be cheating himself if he allowed gratification of his impulses (for example, for sex or violence) to interfere with his provision for the future.

The upper-class individual is markedly self-respecting, self-confident, and self-sufficient. He places great value on independence, curiosity, creativity, happiness, "developing one's potentialities to the full," and consideration for others. In rearing his children, he stresses these values along with the idea that one should govern one's relations with others (and, in the final analysis, with one's self) by *internal* standards rather than by conformity to an externally given code ("not because you're told to but because you take the other person into consideration").[14] The upper-class parent is not alarmed if his chil-

dren remain unemployed and unmarried to the age of thirty, especially if they remain in school.[15] He does not mind being alone;
indeed, he requires a good deal of privacy. He wants to express
himself (he may carry self-expression to the point of eccentricity),
and, in principle at least, he favors self-expression by others. He takes
a tolerant, perhaps even an encouraging, view of unconventional
behavior in sex, the arts, and politics. He is mindful of the rights of
others and wants issues to be settled on their merits and by rational
discussion. He deplores bigotry (which is not to say that he has no
prejudices) and abhors violence in personal relations.

It will be seen that two features of this culture — the disposition to
postpone present satisfaction for the sake of improving matters in the
future and the desire to "express one's personality" — are somewhat
antagonistic. Upper-class (that is, future-oriented) culture permits the
individual to emphasize either theme. If he thinks that his means
(money, power, knowledge, and the like) are almost certainly adequate to maintain him and his "line" throughout the future he envi-
sions, the future-oriented individual has no incentive to "invest" (that
is, trade present for future satisfaction) and may therefore emphasize
self-expression.[16] If, on the other hand, he thinks that his means may
not be adequate (he will think this, of course, no matter how large his
means if his plans for the future are grand enough), he is likely to
emphasize self-discipline so that he may acquire the larger stock of
means that he thinks he needs. Insofar as he chooses the expressive
alternative, the upper-class individual's style of life may resemble the
present-oriented one of the lower class. But whereas the lower-class
individual is capable *only* of present-oriented behavior, the upper-
class one can choose. He may, for example, do some things that
require a high degree of skill, discipline, and judgment, living the rest
of the time from moment to moment. Even if he lives from moment to
moment all the time, he does so by choice — it is his "thing," his
mode of self-expression. By contrast, the "true" present-orientedness
of the lower class is both unrelieved and involuntary.

The upper-class individual feels a strong attachment to entities
(formal organizations, the neighborhood, the nation, the world)
toward which he stands, or wants to stand, in a relation of fellowship.[17] He sees the "community" (or "society") as having long-range

goals and the ability to shape the future. He tends to feel that it is one's responsibility to "serve" the community by assisting in efforts for its improvement — perhaps because, his own goals being long-range ones, he has a stake in the future of the community. At any rate, he tends to be active in "public service" organizations and to feel a strong obligation (which he does not always act upon, of course) to contribute time, money, and effort to worthy causes.[18] (In the South the upper-class attitude in these matters is different. As W. J. Cash remarked, the aristocratic ideal of the planter became corrupted by frontier individualism, which, "while willing enough to ameliorate the specific instance, relentlessly laid down as its basic social postulate the doctrine that every man was completely and wholly responsible for himself."[19])

The Middle Class. The middle-class individual expects to be still in his prime at sixty or thereabouts; he plans ahead for his children and perhaps his grandchildren, but, less future-oriented than the ideal typical member of the upper class, he is not likely to think in terms of "line" or to be much concerned about "mankind" in the distant future. He, too, is confident of his ability to influence the future, but he does not expect to influence so distant a future as does the upper-class individual, nor is he as confident about the probable success of his efforts to influence it. The middle-class individual's self-feelings are a little less strong than those of the upper-class individual; he is also somewhat less desirous of privacy. Although he shows a good deal of independence and creativity and a certain taste for self-expression, these traits rarely lead to eccentricity. He is less likely than the upper-class individual to have means that he considers adequate to assure a satisfactory level of goal attainment throughout his anticipated future. Therefore, "getting ahead" — and the self-improvement and sacrifice of impulse gratification that it requires — will be more likely to take precedence with him over "the expression of one's personality." In the lower middle class, self-improvement is a principal theme of life, whereas in the upper middle class, self-expression is emphasized. Almost without exception, middle-class people want their children to go to college and to acquire the kind of formal training that will help them "get ahead." In matters of sex, the middle-class individual is (in principle, at least) "conventional," and in art and politics, too, he is more ready than the upper-class individual to accept the received opinion. He has regard for the rights of others; he deplores bigotry and abhors violence. He does not, however, hold these attitudes as strongly as do members of the upper class.

The middle-class individual does not feel as strong a sense of responsibility to the community as does the upper-class one, and he defines the community somewhat less inclusively. He wants (in principle, at least) to "belong" to a community and to be of "service" to it, and accordingly he joins organizations, including "service" ones. (In the lower middle class, the taste for public service and reform is relatively weak: the individual usually votes against public improvements that will not benefit him directly.) The middle-class individual, however, is less willing than the upper-class one to give time, money, and effort for public causes.

The Working Class. The working-class individual does not "invest" as heavily in the future, nor in so distant a future, as does the middle-class one.[20] He expects to be an "old man" by the time he is fifty, and his time horizon is fixed accordingly. Also, he has less confidence than the middle-class individual in his ability to shape the future and has a stronger sense of being at the mercy of fate, a "power structure," and other uncontrollable forces. For this reason, perhaps, he attaches more importance to luck than does the middle-class individual. He is self-respecting and self-confident, but these feelings are less marked in him than in the middle-class individual and they extend to a somewhat narrower range of matters. As compared to the middle-class individual, he is little disposed toward either self-improvement or self-expression; "getting ahead" and "enlarging one's horizon" have relatively little attraction for him. In rearing his children, he emphasizes the virtues of neatness and cleanliness, honesty, obedience, and respect for external authority. (As David Riesman has observed, the problem in the working class is not, as in the upper middle class, to stimulate children; rather, it is to control them — "to teach them faith, respect, and obedience, rather than independence of mind and development of talents."[21]) If his children do not go to college, the working-class individual does not mind much. In his relations with others, he is often authoritarian and intolerant, and sometimes aggressive. He is not only a bigot but a self-righteous one. Violence and brutality are less shocking to him than to middle-class persons; indeed, he regards them — up to a point — as normal expressions of a masculine style. To the working class, the middle class appears somewhat lacking in masculinity, and the upper class — a male member of which may even weep under stress — appears decidedly feminine or "queer."

The working-class individual's deepest attachment is to his family (most of his visiting is with relatives, not friends). However, his relationship to his wife and children is not as stable or as close — for instance, does not involve as much companionship — as these relationships tend to be in the middle class.[22] Privacy is of less importance to him: he likes to have people around, and the noises and smells that they make seldom bother him (when he goes on vacation it is not to the country, which he finds too quiet and lonely, but to crowded resorts). The sense of sharing a purpose with others is not as important to him as it is to members of the upper classes, and when he joins an organization it is more likely to be for companionship and "fun" than for "service" or civic improvement. He may vote, especially if someone asks him to as a favor. His opinions on public matters are highly conventional (it does not seem to occur to him that he is entitled to form opinions of his own), and his participation in politics is motivated not by political principles but by ethnic and party loyalties, the appeal of personalities, or the hope of favors from the precinct captain.

The Lower Class. At the present-oriented end of the scale, the lower-class individual lives from moment to moment. If he has any awareness of a future, it is of something fixed, fated, beyond his control: things happen *to* him, he does not *make* them happen. Impulse governs his behavior, either because he cannot discipline himself to sacrifice a present for a future satisfaction or because he has no sense of the future. He is therefore radically improvident: whatever he cannot use immediately he considers valueless. His bodily needs (especially for sex) and his taste for "action"[23] take precedence over everything else — and certainly over any work routine. He works only as he must to stay alive, and drifts from one unskilled job to another, taking no interest in his work. As compared to the working-class individual, he "doesn't want much success, knows he couldn't get it even if he wanted to, and doesn't want what might help him get success."[24] Although his income is usually much lower than that of the working-class individual, the market value of his car, television, and household appliances and playthings is likely to be considerably more. He is careless with his things, however, and, even when nearly new, they are likely to be permanently out of order for lack of minor repairs.[25] His body, too, is a thing "to be worked out but not repaired"; he seeks medical treatment only when practically forced to do so: "symptoms that do not incapacitate are often ignored."[26]

The lower-class individual has a feeble, attenuated sense of self; he suffers from feelings of self-contempt and inadequacy, and is often apathetic or dejected. (In her discussion of "very low-lower class" families, Eleanor Pavenstadt notes that "the saddest, and to us the outstanding characteristic of this group, with adults and children alike, was the self-devaluation."[27]) In his relations with others he is suspicious and hostile, aggressive yet dependent. He is unable to maintain a stable relationship with a mate; commonly he does not marry. ("The evidence is unambiguous and powerful," writes Marc Fried, "that the lowest social classes have the highest rates of severe psychiatric disorder. . . ."[28]) He feels no attachment to community, neighbors, or friends (he has companions, not friends), resents all authority (for example, that of policemen, social workers, teachers, landlords, employers), and is apt to think that he has been "railroaded" and to want to "get even." He is a nonparticipant: he belongs to no voluntary organizations, has no political interests, and does not vote unless paid to do so.

The lower-class household is usually female-based. The woman who heads it is likely to have a succession of mates who contribute intermittently to its support but take little or no part in rearing the children. In managing the children, the mother (or aunt, or grandmother) is characteristically impulsive: once children have passed babyhood they are likely to be neglected or abused, and at best they never know what to expect next. A boy raised in such a household is likely at an early age to join a corner gang of other such boys and to learn from the gang the "tough" style of the lower-class man.[29]

The stress on "masculinity," "action," risk-taking, conquest, fighting, and "smartness" makes lower-class life extraordinarily violent. However, much of the violence is probably more an expression of mental illness than of class culture. The incidence of serious mental illness is greater in the lower class than in any of the others. Moreover, the nature of lower-class culture is such that much behavior that in another class would be considered bizarre seems routine.[30]

In its emphasis on "action" and its utter instability, lower-class culture seems to be more attractive to men than to women. Gans writes:

The woman tries to develop a stable routine in the midst of poverty and deprivation; the action-seeking man upsets it. In order to have any male relationships, however, the woman must participate to some extent in his episodic life style. On rare occasions, she may even pursue it herself. Even then, however, she will try to encourage her children to seek a routine way of life. Thus the woman is much closer to working class culture, at least in her aspirations, although she is not often successful in achieving them.[31]

In the chapters that follow, the term *normal* will be used to refer to class culture that is not lower class. The implication that lower-class culture is pathological seems fully warranted both because of the relatively high incidence of mental illness in the lower class and also because human nature seems loath to accept a style of life that is so radically present-oriented. This is not the main reason for using the word *normal*, however. Rather, it is that *some* word is needed to designate the sector of the class-cultural continuum that is not lower class, and no other word seems preferable on the whole.

From the beginning, the cities of the United States have had upper, middle, working, and lower classes. The relative strength of the various classes has varied greatly from time to time and place to place, although the nature of the class cultures has not. At the beginning of the nineteenth century, the free population of the United States was predominantly middle class. Most were descendants of English and American yeomen, artisans, and tradesmen, a stratum of society that had long had good opportunities to better its condition and had been confident of its ability to do so.[32] The Old Stock American inherited a culture that gave prominent place to the future-oriented virtues of self-discipline and denial, industry, thrift, and respect for law and order. He was sure that these virtues would be rewarded by success; he expected to "get on" and to "improve himself" in material and other ways. The Puritans had come to America with the intention of establishing ideal communities — "a city upon a hill" — and the millennial impulse, still powerful, took many forms in the first half of the nineteenth century. In the towns and cities, most early Americans, especially those of English origin, were skilled craftsmen or tradesmen. Of the few in New England who were day laborers, nearly all could read and write and nearly all voted.[33]

The number of working- and lower-class people was by no means insignificant, however, especially in the cities. In every sizable city there were transient laborers — and in the seaports, sailors, and in inland cities like Cincinnati and St. Louis, boatmen, wagoners, and drifters, who, like Huckleberry Finn's father, lived from hand to mouth, worked only when they had to, drank and fought prodigiously, felt no tie to the community, and left their women and children behind to fend for themselves or to be looked after at public expense once they had moved on.[34] In every city there also were unassimilated immigrants from countries — Catholic ones — in which "normal" behavior tended to be relatively present-oriented. It is safe to say, however, that transients and Catholic immigrants did not comprise the whole of the working- and lower-class population. In Boston, for example, which in 1817 had only about four hundred Catholics, the Old Stock American residents must have patronized the city's two thousand prostitutes (one for every six males above the age of sixteen), hundreds of liquor shops, and the gambling houses open night and day. It must also have been the Old Stock Bostonians who denied the mayor, Josiah Quincy, reelection after he waged a vigorous war on vice.[35]

Eventually, as immigration increased, the working and lower classes — especially the latter — did come to consist disproportionately of Catholic immigrants. In 1832, for example, the South Boston Almshouse held almost twice as many immigrants as natives. "To see anything like indigence or idleness," a visitor to New England from abroad wrote a few years later, "we must penetrate into the purlieus in the seaport towns, occupied by the Irish laboring population." The districts inhabited by the Irish and the Negroes formed, he said, "a painful contrast to the general air of cleanliness and comfort."[36]

After 1840 immigration increased rapidly, the immigrants coming mainly from peasant cultures — first Irish and then, after 1885, southern Italian and eastern European — that were more present-oriented than those of New England, Great Britain, and northern Europe. Coming from places where ordinary people had never had opportunities to rise by effort and enterprise, these immigrants, it is plausible to conjecture, tended to see the world as a place ruled by fate or luck. Most were probably more concerned with survival from day to day than with getting ahead, and the idea that one might get ahead by saving and investing — by some form of self-improvement — must have been unfamiliar to most and unintelligible to some. On the other hand, that they chose to emigrate strongly implies that they were not all present-oriented. According to the historian Timothy L. Smith, "Long before the ship on which he traveled touched the docks, many an immigrant had inquired carefully of those he met what conditions were that he must face, the lessons he must learn to make his venture a success."[37] Those who looked ahead were most numerous, one suspects, before the introduction of steamships reduced the duration of the voyage from several weeks to several days, among townsmen rather than peasants, and among those for whom the alternative to immigration was not the prospect of immediate starvation. "The emigrants of this year are not like those of former ones," the *Cork Examiner* noted during the peak of the Irish emigration, "they are now actually *running away* from fever and disease and hunger. . . ."[38]

Among the Old Stock Americans it was a rare day laborer who could not read, write, and cipher; among the peasant immigrants it was a rare one who could. The immigrants from present-oriented cultures were slow to see the advantages of education and of self-improvement generally. Even to some sympathetic observers it appeared that many of them would as soon live in hovels and shanties as not. Unlike the Old Stock Americans and the more future-oriented immigrants from England and northern Europe, the peasant immigrants seldom patronized the free mechanics libraries. Very few became skilled workers. In part, perhaps, this was because employers, most of whom were native-born, were prejudiced against them; in part also, however, it was probably because the present-oriented outlook and style did not suit the requirements of work and organization.

It was symptomatic of these different attitudes toward self-improvement and "getting on" that compulsory school attendance laws were adopted only after large-scale peasant immigration got under way. In Massachusetts, for example, the first such law was passed in 1852 and required all children between the ages of eight and fourteen to attend for twelve weeks each year. Until then it had been taken for granted that anyone able to go to school would not fail to do so.

The Jewish immigrants were very different from the peasant peoples. Like the Old Stock Americans, they were future-oriented. They believed, as had the Puritans, who were in many ways like them, that they were under a special obligation to assist in the realization of God's plan for the future. The idea of making sacrifices in the expectation of future rewards came naturally to them. Even more than the Old Stock American, the Jewish immigrant worked to acquire the capital (not only money and other material goods but also knowledge, skill, character, attachment to family and community, and so on), that would enable him to rise. Jacob A. Riis wrote:

The poorest Hebrew knows — the poorer he is, the better he knows it — that knowledge is power, and power as the means of getting on in the world that has spurned him so long, is what his soul yearns for. He lets no opportunity slip to obtain it. Day- and night-schools are crowded with his children, who learn rapidly and with ease. Every synagogue, every second rear tenement or dark back-yard, has its school and its school master, with his scourge to intercept those who might otherwise escape.[39]

The future-oriented ideal diffused rapidly throughout the population. In the latter half of the nineteenth century the whole nation seemed suddenly seized with a passion for self-improvement: in every city and in thousands of towns and villages there were lyceum discussions, Chautauquas, evening lectures, and the like. Self-improvement implied community improvement, and the Old Stock American (originally Puritan) idea that it was everyone's obligation to do what he could to bring the millennial hope to fulfillment and to create "a city on a hill" became the generally accepted doctrine of "service." To immigrants like the Jews, whose native culture was future-oriented, these tendencies were highly congenial, but to others — notably the Irish — they were alien and distasteful. Eventually, however, all the immigrant groups succumbed to the Old Stock American, future-oriented ideal. Even Negroes, whose isolation as slaves and then as Southern farmhands might, one would think, have excluded them from the culture almost altogether, were drawn toward the ideal. Although they traveled at very different rates of speed, all ethnic and racial groups were headed in the same cultural direction: from less to more future-oriented.

Movement upward along the scale of class culture tended to follow increases in income and opportunity. Those people sacrificed the present for the future who had reason to think that doing so would be in some sense profitable, and the greater the prospective rewards, the more willing they were to accept the discipline and to put forth the effort required. People generally had good grounds for believing that the future-oriented virtues would pay off. To be sure, not many rose from rags to riches, as the mythology claimed, but it was very common for the son of an unskilled laborer to become a semiskilled or a skilled one and for *his* son to emerge as a manager, teacher, or professional.[40]

It is not clear, however, whether those who moved up the occupational, income, and status ladders did so because they had absorbed a more future-oriented culture. It is possible, for example, that Patrick Kennedy, who came to this country a laborer in 1848 and was still one when he died, was present-oriented and that it was because his son, Patrick Joseph, was somehow affected by the future-oriented atmosphere of Boston that he (the son) became a leading saloonkeeper and ward politician and — *mirabile dictu* — had the foresight to send *his* son, Joseph P., to the Boston Latin School and then to Harvard College. But it is also possible that the original Patrick was just as future-oriented as his son and that he remained a laborer all his life because the circumstances of his time and place made rising too difficult for him. It makes a great difference whether one supposes that (1) the American environment instilled in the immigrant a more future-oriented view; (2) it merely gave scope to those individuals whose view was such to begin with; or (3) it produced both effects.

From every ethnic group, including, of course, the Old Stock American, some individuals were born into the lower class and others dropped into it from above. As the sociologist David Matza has written,

Each experience of ethnic mobility leaves a sediment which appears to be trapped in slum life, whether as a result of insistence on maintaining traditional peasant values, or as a result of family disorganization, relatively lower intelligence, more emotional problems, or just plain misfortune. These are the dregs who settle into the milieu of disreputable poverty and perpetuate its distinctive characteristics.[41]

It is plausible to conjecture that the more present-oriented the culture of an ethnic group, the larger the proportion of its members who became lower class (similarly, the more future-oriented a group's culture, the higher the proportion who entered the upper classes). The Irish, for example, contributed heavily to the lower class as compared to the Jews. From 1885 to 1890, persons born in Ireland comprised 12.6 percent of the population but accounted for 60.4 percent of the almshouse, 36.7 percent of the workhouse, and 15.5 percent of prison inmates; Jews from Russia and Austria-Hungary were 3 percent of the population but accounted for none of the almshouse, 1 percent of the workhouse, and 1 percent of the prison inmates.[42] Very likely, the present-orientation of the Irish and the future-orientation of the Jews had important indirect effects as well. The Anglo-Saxon Protestant elite, for example, probably discriminated against people who showed little disposition to get ahead and in favor of those who showed much (provided that it was not *too* much, which would have made them "pushing").

The lower the individual was on the cultural scale, the greater the obstacles in the way of his moving up occupationally or otherwise and the less his motivation to try. At the *very* bottom of the scale, the desire to rise was altogether lacking — and those who reached adulthood in the lower class rarely if ever climbed out of it. Moreover, the obstacles in the way of rising — many of which were due to the distaste future-oriented people had for the manners and morals of the extremely present-oriented — were all but insuperable. Some families doubtless remained lower class for many generations, but most probably died out within two or three.

Each class culture implies — indeed, more or less requires — a certain sort of physical environment. It follows that a city (or district within a city) which suits one culture very well is likely to suit another very poorly or not at all.

To an upper-class individual, having a great deal of space at one's disposal is important both practically and symbolically; the demand for space, a city planner-economist observes, "seems to be a deeply ingrained cultural value associated not only with such functional needs as play space for children, but also with basic attitudes toward nature, privacy, and the meaning of the family."[43] Being by oneself a good deal — and therefore having room enough for privacy — is essential to the development of a well-defined self; in the middle and upper classes, but not in the working class, it is thought essential that each child have a room of his or her own. The higher a family is on the class-culture scale, the wider the expanse of lawn (or in the case of an apartment house, the thicker the walls) that it wants between it and the neighbors. Similarly, the higher the commuter is on the scale, the more important it is to him to ride to work in solitary splendor. For the lower-middle-class person a car pool will do — it is better than the bus; the upper-middle-class person, however, finds even that distasteful.

In the middle- and upper-class cultures, one's house and grounds afford opportunities for self-improvement and self-expression.[44] To the upper-class individual, it is the latter value that is usually more important: the house is the setting for and the representation of his family line ("house"). The middle-class individual is more likely to value his house for giving scope to his impulse to improve things — not only physical things (the house and grounds) but also, and especially, his own and his family's skills, habits, feelings, and attitudes. (The do-it-yourself movement is at least in part an expression of the middle-class taste for mastering skills and "expressing one's personality.") The middle-class individual — particularly the *lower*-middle-class one — also regards the house as a means of improving his social status; having a "good address" helps one rise in the world.

In the upper- and middle-class cultures, the neighborhood and community are as important as the house and are hardly to be separated from it. It is essential to live where there are good schools, for otherwise the children might not get into good colleges. Other community facilities — parks, libraries, museums, and the like — are highly valued, as are opportunities to be of "service" by participating in civic organizations. The middle- or upper-class individual wants to feel that his local government is honest, impartial, and efficient. At the upper end of the scale, especially, he wants a sense of "belonging" to a "community" — that is, of standing in a fellowship relation to his neighbors (even though he may never see them) and thus of constituting with them a moral entity — not unlike the Puritan congregation of visible saints in the seventeenth century. This desire to belong to a community partly accounts for the exclusiveness of the "better" neighborhoods and suburbs. The exclusion of all who are not parties to the covenant (in the language of Puritanism) is a precondition of fellowship: a community, after all, consists of people who feel a sense of oneness. Where the principle of exclusion appears to be — and perhaps is — racial or ethnic, the neighbors are likely to see that in the pursuit of one of their values they have infringed upon another. Those who feel most strongly the obligation to be of "service" and to act "responsibly" — upper-middle and upper-class Jews, especially — often resolve the conflict by sponsoring a strenuous community effort to bring a certain number of Negroes (or whatever group is being discriminated against) into the neighborhood.[45]

To the working class, a different set of values to accord with its life style governs the choice of physical arrangements in the city. Space is less important to the working-class family than to the middle- or upper-class one. It prefers being "comfy" to having privacy; it is thought natural for children to sleep two or three to a room or perhaps even to a bed. Having neighbors — even noisy ones — down the hall or in a house that is adjoining or almost adjoining is taken for granted. The working-class individual has few deep friendships with his neighbors, but he likes knowing who they are and he likes seeing — and even hearing — their goings-on. (It was because the Italian working-class residents of Boston's West End took this interest in one another that Herbert J. Gans called his account of them *The Urban Villagers*.) From the working-class point of view, middle- and upper-class neighborhoods are dull and lonely. Riding to work by oneself is no fun either; the working-class person prefers a car pool but does not mind a bus or subway.

When he must choose between more and better community facilities on the one hand and lower taxes on the other, the working-class
individual usually chooses the latter. He will be satisfied if his children graduate from high school, and any school that is not a black-
board jungle will do. Parks and libraries matter to him even less than
schools. He has no desire to participate in community improvement
projects and no wish to feel himself part of a community, except
perhaps an ethnic one. If his neighbors are a mixed lot, some being
hardly sane and others less than respectable, that does not concern
him: he is likely to take the attitude that so long as they do not
interfere with him, they can do or be what they please.

To this last statement an important qualification must be attached.
The working-class individual is likely to become ugly and aggressive
if members of an ethnic or racial group that he dislikes begin to "take
over" his neighborhood. He is more apt to be prejudiced than are
members of the middle class and much less apt to conceal his prejudice. There is no talk in working-class neighborhoods about "responsibility for reducing racial tensions."

In some areas the movement of factories to the suburban ring has
led to the building of residential suburbs that are working class.
Physically, these look much like middle-class ones, but in style of life
the two differ sharply. The working-class suburbanite's house is not a
way station on the road to something better, as is often the case with
the middle class. He is also less likely than is his middle-class counterpart to forgo his favorite TV program in order to collect for the Heart
Fund or "serve the community" in some other way.[46]

The lower-class individual lives in the slum, which, to a greater or
lesser extent, is an expression of his tastes and style of life. The slum,
according to the sociologist Marshall B. Clinard, is a way of life with
its own subculture. The subcultural norms and values of the slum are
reflected in poor sanitation and health practices, deviant behavior,
and often a real lack of interest in formal education. With some
exceptions, there is little general desire to engage in personal or
community efforts for self-improvement. Slum persons generally are
apathetic toward the employment of self-help on a community basis,
they are socially isolated, and most sense their powerlessness. This
does not mean that they are satisfied with their way of life or do not
want a better way to live; it is simply that slum apathy tends to inhibit

individuals from putting forth sufficient efforts to change the local community. They may protest and they may blame the slum entirely on the outside world, but at the same time they remain apathetic about what they could themselves do to change their world.[47]

Although he has more "leisure" than almost anyone, the indifference ("apathy" if one prefers) of the lower-class person is such that he seldom makes even the simplest repairs to the place that he lives in. He is not troubled by dirt and dilapidation and he does not mind the inadequacy of public facilities such as schools, parks, hospitals, and libraries; indeed, where such things exist he may destroy them by carelessness or even by vandalism. Conditions that make the slum repellent to others are serviceable to him in several ways.[48] First, the slum is a place of excitement — "where the action is." Nothing happens there by plan and anything may happen by accident — a game, a fight, a tense confrontation with the police; feeling that something exciting is about to happen is highly congenial to people who live for the present and for whom the present is often empty. Second, it is a place of opportunity. Just as some districts of the city are specialized as a market for, say, jewelry or antiques, so the slum is specialized as one for vice and for illicit commodities generally. Dope peddlers, prostitutes, and receivers of stolen goods are all readily available there, within easy reach of each other and of their customers and victims. For "hustlers," the slum is the natural headquarters. Third, it is a place of concealment. A criminal is less visible to the police in the slum than elsewhere, and the lower-class individual, who in some parts of the city would attract attention, is one among many there. In the slum one can beat one's children, lie drunk in the gutter, or go to jail without attracting any special notice; these are things that most of the neighbors themselves have done and that they consider quite normal.

Although it is the lower class that gives the slum its special character, lower-class people are by no means the only ones who live in it. (Still less are they the only ones who live in the "poverty areas" of the largest cities, a fact abundantly evident from the 1971 survey, some findings of which were briefly summarized in Chapter One.) Some blocks may be occupied almost exclusively by the lower class, but in the district as a whole, the majority of residents may well be working-class and not a few middle-class. These are people whose incomes do not correspond to their class culture; in some cases they are the victims of bad luck — the death of a breadwinner, for example — but more often they are in the slum because racial discrimination, past or present, has deprived them of normal opportunities for education and employment.

For these working- and middle-class slum dwellers, life in the slum is a daily battle to preserve life, sanity, and self-respect. They must send their children to schools where little or nothing is taught or learned and where the children are in constant physical and moral danger; they must endure garbage-filled alleys and rat-infested halls; if they shop in nearby stores, they must pay high prices for poor selections of inferior goods (the prices are often high only for them — for the lower class, which demands credit even though its credit rating is very poor, the same prices may actually be low); they must suffer the risk of annoyance and even of serious hardship by being mistaken for members of the lower class by policemen, teachers, landlords, and others, who either cannot discern or do not trouble to look for the clues to class differences among the poor.

Although the lower-class *type* finds the slum convenient and even congenial, there are many lower-class individuals — especially women — who are ambivalent about it or who want to escape from it. By exceptional luck or enterprise now and then one does. Claude Brown, the author of *Manchild in a Promised Land*, is an example.

To the normal people who live in the slum, the worst feature of life there is fear. Many slum dwellers, Patricia Cayo Sexton writes, "live in a generalized state of fear — of being robbed, knifed, attacked, bullied, or having their children injured. This fear colors their whole lives: their ability to learn, to work, to stay sane and healthy, to venture out of their apartments or block, to live openly and freely, to be friends with their neighbors, to trust the world, outsiders, themselves."[49]

Within the limits set by the logic of growth, the mix of class cultures more than anything else determines the city's character and the nature of its problems. Almost everything about the city — population density, per capita income, the nature and quality of housing, the crime rate, the dropout rate, the level of public services, the tenor of race relations, the style of politics — depends in some way and to some extent upon the class composition of the population. When this changes, either in a neighborhood or in the city as a whole, almost everything else changes accordingly. And except as they are compatible with the realities of class culture in the city, the most carefully contrived efforts of public and private policymakers cannot succeed, for the mix of class cultures is a constraint as real as those of income, technology, or climate. It is necessary, therefore, to form the best estimate one can of the direction that change in the class system will take.

For at least a century there has been a general movement upward on the class scale from every class except possibly (a question that will be considered in Chapter Ten) the lowest. A century ago the urban population was heavily working class; now it is heavily middle class. The process of "middle-class-ification," as Dollard called it, is undoubtedly continuing at an accelerating rate and will in a few decades have reduced the working class to a very small proportion of the whole population. The upper middle class has meanwhile been increasing rapidly in its relative strength, especially since the Second World War. Eventually, the distribution of population along the class scale may be decidedly bimodal, the largest concentration being in the upper middle class and the next largest (much smaller than the first) in the lower class.

No hard data bear on these predictions. Census data on education, income, and occupation cannot be made to yield more than very approximate measures of the size of classes as defined here.[50] There are, however, many indirect indicators that are to some extent relevant. One can see evidence of the effects of the process of "middle-class-ification" in changes that have occurred in the occupational structure (at the turn of the century one in six persons in the work force was a white collar worker; in 1950, one in three, now, one in two); in the decline of the saloon, the poolhall, and the brothel, and the rise of the family television set (the 1880 Census counted 517 brothels in Philadelphia, and Jane Addams complained at about the same time that in some wards of Chicago, there was one saloon to every twenty-eight voters);[51] in the ever-greater sensitivity of the

public to brutality such as the beating of suspects by policemen —
commonplace even half a century ago — and wife and child beating
("If screams resounded through a tenement-house it was taken for
granted that the child deserved all it got and more");[52] in the growing
fear of violent crime on the part of people whose danger from it is less
than ever; in the unconcern of the same people about victimless crime
and their acceptance of "the sexual revolution" and of vice; in the
legalization of abortion, the illegalization of capital punishment, and
the growing unwillingness to inflict severe penalties on those who
commit serious crimes; in the greater concern for individual rights (of
racial minorities, women, person accused of crimes, the insane, juveniles, political extremists, homosexuals, and deviants in general); in
increased distress at inequalities of wealth, schooling, health care, and
political power (this last as evidenced by efforts to encourage "citizens' participation"); in the decline of a politics based on personal
material inducements and on ethnic and local attachments (the
"machine") and the growth of one based on national issues and
personalities (and accordingly the compulsion to find evidence of
national moral imperfections); and in the growth of a mass audience
for serious literature, music, and art (readers, listeners, and viewers
are counted now by the millions, whereas a generation or two ago they
were counted by the thousands).

The mass movement from the working into the middle class and
from the lower middle into the upper middle class accounts as much
as anything for the general elevation of standards that, as was contended in Chapter One, makes most urban problems appear to be
getting worse even when, *measured by a fixed standard*, they are
getting better. The new standards are those of a higher class. It is
because the process of "middle-class-ification" has given great numbers of people higher perspectives and standards that dissatisfaction
with the city is so widespread. The city that was thought pleasant
when most people were working class is thought repellent now that
most are middle class, and it will be thought abhorrent when, before
long, most are upper middle class.

The ascendancy of the middle and upper middle classes has
increased feelings of guilt at "social failures" (that is, discrepancies
between actual performance and what by the rising class standards is

deemed adequate) and given rise to public rhetoric about "accepting responsibility" for ills that in some cases could not have been prevented and cannot be cured. The dropout, for example, in turning his back on education "is telling us that we never really connected with him, that in our preoccupation with others we never gave him enough time or attention."[53] This is typical. In the upper-middle-class view it is always society that is to blame. Society, according to this view, could solve all problems if it only tried hard enough; that a problem continues to exist is therefore proof positive of its guilt.

In this tendency to find society responsible for all ills, including those that are a function of rising standards, two dangers appear. One is that the allegation of social guilt may lead the individual to believe that he can do nothing to help himself. The dropout, for example, may feel himself excused from all effort once it has been established that he was never given enough time or attention, just as the juvenile delinquent may excuse himself when it has been established that he is the product of wrong social conditions. The other danger is that many people will take the talk of social guilt seriously and conclude that the society is one for which they can have no respect and in which they can place no trust. Such condemnation is mainly to be expected in those sections of society — the upper classes, especially their youth — that are most alive to moral issues, and in those other sectors — notably the poor and the minority groups — that have obvious grounds for thinking themselves victims of social injustice. To the rhetoricians, the guilty society will be "not worth saving." To those who have known all along that it is society's fault that they are at the bottom of the heap, the case will be that much clearer and their righteous anger that much hotter.[54]

CHAPTER FOUR

Race: Thinking May Make It So

. . . Being from America made me intensely sensitive to matters
of color. I saw that people who looked alike drew together and
most of the time stayed together. This was entirely voluntary;
there being no other reason for it. But Africans were with Africans. Pakistanis were with Pakistanis. And so on. I tucked it
into my mind that when I returned home I would tell Americans this observation; that where true brotherhood existed
among all colors, where no one felt segregated, where there was
no "superiority" complex, no "inferiority" complex — then
voluntarily, naturally, people of the same kind felt drawn
together by that which they had in common.
                                                    — Malcolm X

THE most conspicuous fact of life in the city is racial division. A
hundred times a day there are confrontations between black and
white, and almost every day an explosion turns part of some city into
a battleground. The residential suburbs are mostly white — often
"lily-white"; the central cities, especially their older, more deterio-
rated parts, and above all their slums, are predominantly or entirely
black. Many observers see little reason to hope for improvement. The
city, they say, has always exploited, humiliated, and degraded its
immigrant groups. But whereas all the others eventually have been
able to escape their oppressors by joining them, the Negro, marked as
he is by skin color, can never do so. For him, in this view, the city is
degradation without hope. "The dark ghettoes," writes Kenneth B.
Clark, "are social, political, educational, and — above all — economic colonies. Their inhabitants are subject peoples, victims of the
greed, cruelty, insensitivity, guilt, and fear of their masters."[1]
The view to be developed here is altogether different from this one.

The existence of racial prejudice is a fact too painfully evident to require assertion. There is no denying, however, that — widespread as it still is — racial prejudice today is of a different order of magnitude than it was prior to the Second War; the change of attitudes in the last two decades alone has been so widespread and profound as to make meaningless comparisons between the two periods. Moreover, as Thomas Sowell has emphasized, the advancement of ethnic groups in this country, far from depending upon the absence of prejudice and discrimination, has been most rapid when opposition was strongest: "periods of advancement have coincided with increasing group animosity."[2] Discrimination was not the *main* obstacle in the way of the Irish, the Italians, the Jews, and other minorities that have "made it." Nor is it the *main* one of the Negro — not to mention the Puerto Rican and the Mexican — today. The other minority groups once lived in the oldest parts of the inner city — and the Negro lives in them now — not so much because they were looked down on (although, of course, they *were*) as because they had low incomes. It was because they were poor that they had to come to the city, and being poor they could not afford good housing on the outskirts of the city or in the suburbs, nor could they afford to commute to the factories, stores, and offices where they worked. Similarly, the neighborhoods in which the other groups lived were often squalid and vicious — as the Negro slum is now — not because they were subject people, victimized and degraded by the city (although there was an element of that, too), but because every wave of migration, whether from rural America or abroad, brought with it some who were, or soon became, lower class.

Today the Negro's *main* disadvantage is the same as the Puerto Rican's and Mexican's: namely, that he is the most recent unskilled, and hence relatively low-income, migrant to reach the city from a backward rural area. The city is not the end of his journey but the start of it. He came to it not because he was lured by a cruel and greedy master but because he was attracted by job, housing, school, and other opportunities that, bad as they were, were nevertheless better by far than any he had known before. Like earlier immigrants, the Negro has reason to expect that his children will have increases of opportunity even greater than his.[3] If he lives in a neighborhood that is all-black, the reason is not white prejudice simply, and in some instances it may not be that at all. This physical separation may arise from any or all of various causes — his having a low income, his being part of a wave of migration that inundated all of the cheap housing then available (had more been available, more migrants might well have come to take it), his having class-cultural characteristics that make him an undesirable neighbor, his inclination to live among his own kind. That physically distinguishing racial characteristics do not necessarily stand in the way of acceptance and upward mobility is evident from the example of Orientals. The median family income of urban Japanese-Americans in 1969 ($12,794) was considerably higher than that of urban whites ($11,203) and their unemployment rate (2.1 percent) was considerably lower (4.7 percent).[4] The same was true, although not in the same degree, of Chinese-Americans.

The misfortune, amounting to a tragedy, is not that Negroes got to the city but that they got there so late and then in such great numbers in so short a time. Although in the 1830's the great majority of Negroes living in cities were extremely poor (as of course were many whites as well) there were substantial numbers of Negro craftsmen and professionals. Instead of growing in size and influence after the Civil War, these middle-class Negro communities shrank. They were handicapped by the unending flow of poor and backward immigrants from the rural South, but it was the growth and spread of racial hostility that, by depriving the skilled of the opportunity to use their skills, all but destroyed the middle class. The flood of European immigration followed shortly by the Great Depression left the mass of Negroes with worsening prospects.[5] Had these forces over which the Negro had no control not existed — had he been allowed to enter urban labor markets and to compete on equal terms with whites from the end of the Civil War on — there is no reason to suppose that he would not have long since been fully assimilated into the working, middle, and upper classes. The slums of the cities today would not be black and their suburbs white. What is more important, problems that are essentially economic or class-cultural would not be so easily misperceived as essentially racial.

Almost everything said about the problems of the Negro tends to exaggerate the purely racial aspects of the situation. (The same is true of what is said of the Puerto Rican, the Mexican, and other groups, but discussion here will be limited to the Negro.) "Purely racial" factors mean, first, prejudice on racial grounds (not only prejudice against but also prejudice *for* — that is, racial pride) and, second, whatever cultural characteristics pertain to a racial group *qua* racial group. The importance of these factors is exaggerated implicitly by any statement about the Negro that fails — as almost all do — to take account of the many other (nonracial or contingently racial) factors that are at work along with the purely racial ones. These nonracial factors include, especially, age, income, class, education, and place of origin (rural or urban, Southern or not). Unquestionably the effect of these factors on the Negro has been increased by the operation of racial ones in the background: for example, the lack of education that in large measure accounts for the Negro's handicaps is itself to be explained largely by racial discrimination past and present. (On the other hand, there are groups — rural Southern whites, for example — whose handicaps are much like the Negro's and must be explained entirely by nonracial factors.) In any case, there is no a priori reason to assume (as is too often done) that the causes operating in the *evolution* of a problem over time ("historical" causes) must be identical with those operating to *perpetuate* that problem at any given time ("presently operating" causes). The concern here is with the presently operating causes of the Negro's problems, which, it will be argued, are seldom mainly racial and very often have little or nothing to do with race. In order to have measures that include only the effects of presently operating racial factors (such as discrimination) what will here be called the Comparable Negro — that is, the Negro when nonracial as well as historically racial causes have been controlled for — will replace the Census Negro.[6] As will presently appear, the two are very different fellows. The Comparable Negro always more closely resembles the white and sometimes he is indistinguishable from him.

The table on page 81 illustrates how the Census Negro is turned into the Comparable one. The average income of the Census white in 1962 was $7,070 and that of the Census Negro $3,280. By the technique of regression analysis, the sociologist O. D. Duncan finds

DIFFERENCES IN AVERAGE INCOME LEVELS FOR NEGROES AND WHITES AND THE AMOUNTS OF THESE INCOME DIFFERENCES ATTRIBUTABLE TO SUCCESSIVELY CHANGING LEVEL OF INDICATED VARIABLES.[a]

White income	→	Family background	→	Number of siblings	→	Educational level	→	Occupational prestige level	→	Unexplained	→	Negro income
$7,070		6,130		6,060		5,540		4,170				3,280
Decrement		940		70		520		830		1,430		

[a] *Source:* O. D. Duncan, "Inheritance of Poverty or Inheritance of Race," in Daniel P. Moynihan, ed., *On Understanding Poverty* (New York, Basic Books, 1969, pp. 85–110). Family background is occupation and education of head of family as a child. The amounts accounted for by each variable are after the effects of the variables to the left of it are accounted for. The estimates were obtained by successive regression equations for whites, then substituting in each equation the values of the relevant variables held by average Negroes; for example, the number 940 is obtained by use of a regression equation including only family background, whereas the 70 obtained for number of siblings uses a regression equation that includes family background as well as number of siblings. Reprinted from James S. Coleman, *Resources for Social Change* (New York: Wiley-Interscience, 1971), p. 46.

that $940 of the difference is attributable to differences in "family background" (that is, when whites and Negroes alike in this respect were compared that much of the income difference disappeared); controlling for "number of siblings" reduced the difference by another $70, for "educational level" by still another $520, and for "occupational prestige level" by yet another $830. (These four variables were not nonracial in an *historical* sense, of course: racial injustice in the past may explain all of the Negro's disadvantage in, say, a "family background." But the object is to measure *presently operating* factors that cause income differences). If one assumes — most implausibly — that the four variables treated by Duncan are the *only* nonracial ones of importance, then the "unexplained" residue ($1,430) represents the effect of racial factors, presumably discrimination. The difference in average income between the Comparable Negro and white is then $1,430 as against $3,790 for the Census Negro and white.[7]

The Census Negro has a birthrate about one-third higher than does the white. If, however, in both groups women who have lived on Southern farms are left out of account, the Negro birthrate does not differ significantly from that of the white. If, in addition, in both groups women with less than a high school education are omitted, the Negro rate is actually a little lower than the white.[8]

The school dropout rate among Census Negro adolescents is almost twice that among whites. But when the occupation of parents is controlled for, this difference is much reduced, and with children of white-collar parents it almost disappears.[9] When many factors (sex, family status, family income, wage and employment conditions in the metropolitan area, and residence in a poverty tract) are controlled for, the effect of race on the amount of time spent in school by youths is too small to be statistically significant.[10]

Unemployment rates are persistently higher for Census Negroes than for whites. About half the differential in rates is to be accounted for by differences between the two groups in their distribution by occupation, education, age, and region, however. These differences are largely the result of historical discrimination, of course, but the fact is that *present* discrimination by employers on the basis of color accounts for much less unemployment than the gross figures would suggest.[11] One important factor behind unemployment differentials is place of residence: boys and girls who live in districts where there is a relative surplus of unskilled workers are at a manifest disadvantage whatever their color. Occupation and income of parents are other factors: boys and girls whose parents own businesses or "know people" have an advantage in finding jobs. Class culture is still another factor: lower-class youths are less likely than others to look for jobs, and the lower their class culture the less acceptable they are to employers. Even after correcting for everything possible, something is left that must be explained on racial grounds, especially job discrimination. Still, considering all these other factors, white prejudice and any specifically Negro characteristics account for much less of the difference in employment rates than would otherwise appear.

The Census Negro spends as much as a third more for housing than do whites at a given income level but, in Chicago at least, the Comparable Negro has been found to pay about the same rent and live at about the same density as the white. Discrimination in housing, in the opinion of Richard Muth, does not contribute to the poverty of the Negro "to any practically significant extent."[12]

The proportion of Negro children in households without a father present is very high. Whether it is higher than among whites of the same income, education, rural-urban origin, and class culture is not clear, however. An investigation conducted just before the First World War in the then predominantly Irish Middle West Side of New York found that about half the families there were fatherless.[13]

Sexual promiscuity in the Negro slum is notorious. This is in part a class characteristic, however. In another report on the predominantly Irish Middle West Side of half a century ago, mention is made of "the hopelessly unmoral attitude of the neighborhood," where "boys as young as seven and eight actually practice sodomy."[14]

The arrest rates of Census Negroes are very much higher than those of whites, but when such factors as age and income are taken into account the difference is reduced but apparently by no means eliminated. Although the evidence is conflicting, there is reason to believe that the Comparable Negro commits a disproportionate share of most types of crimes.[15]

That the Comparable Negro is in all respects less injured (or otherwise affected) by currently operating racial factors than is the Census Negro does not mean that these factors are of little or no importance. It is all too obvious that racial prejudice enters into every sphere of life. Cultural differences (apart from *class*-cultural differences) — and conceivably even biological ones as well — also account in some degree for the special position of the Negro, as they do for that of every ethnic group.[16] If there is something about Jewish culture that makes the Jew tend to be upwardly mobile, there may be something about Negro culture that makes the Negro tend not to be. Strangely (considering the great number of sociologists and social anthropologists produced by American universities in the last two or three decades and considering the interest of the subject), very little is known about the personality and culture of the Negro or of other racial and ethnic groups in the city.[17] Eventually, systematic study may reveal deep cultural differences among ethnic groups. It is very unlikely, however, that any differences in racial (or ethnic) culture will have as much explanatory importance for the matters under discussion here as do differences in income, education and class culture.

Under favorable conditions Negroes can be expected to close the gap between their levels of welfare and those of whites much faster than most people would probably imagine. This is strongly suggested by the experience of the last decade or so, a period which although more favorable to Negro progress than earlier ones was, of course, far from optimal. Looking at the rates of white and nonwhite progress in certain aspects of life in the years 1960 to 1968, Michael J. Flax of the Urban Institute has tried to answer the question: If these rates were to remain constant, when, if at all, would nonwhites reach the level whites had attained in 1968? Here are some of his findings:[18]

The figures are not predictions, of course, and it is highly unlikely that the rates of change for both races will remain constant. They are nevertheless suggestive of the possibilities.

Without any doubt, blacks would make faster progress in overtaking whites if it were not for the racial discrimination to which, albeit in gradually lesser degree, they are still subject. (Working from

Indicator of welfare	Year white 1968 levels might be reached
% men (age 25–29) completing high school	1973
% families with incomes over $8,000	1974
% in clerical occupations	1974
Median family income	1978
% in professional and technical occupations	1978
Fertility rates	1979
% unemployed	1982
% completing at least four years of college	1987
% housing that is substandard	1988
% teenagers unemployed	1989
% persons below poverty level	1992
Infant mortality	1994
Life expectancy at 35 years	2019
% female-headed households	never
% illegitimate births	never
% children living with two parents	never

1960 Census data, Barry R. Chiswick found support for his hypothesis that white male workers act as if they have a "taste" for not working with blacks to overcome which employers pay them what is in effect a bonus when they do work with blacks; the amount of this bonus, he estimates, increases average white income inequality by 2.3 percent over what it would be if the white workers did not have this "taste."[19]) Insofar as it is discrimination that prevents Negroes from having the same distribution as whites among the major occupational categories and, when they are in the same occupations, from receiving equal pay, that, far more than unemployment, accounts for their lower incomes.[20]

Even in the complete absence of discrimination, however, the situation of most Negroes would not be changed very dramatically or at once. One can see this if one asks how matters would change if overnight all Negroes turned white (or, if one prefers, all whites turned black), thus making discrimination on racial grounds physically impossible. If this were to happen, most of the New Whites would continue working at the same jobs, living in the same neighborhoods, and sending their children to the same schools for at least a decade or two.

There would be no sudden, mass exodus from the neighborhoods — many of them blighted and some of them slum — in which most Negroes now live. For some time to come New Whites would constitute the largest part of the low-income group and would therefore occupy a large share of the cheapest housing, which is to say the oldest, most run-down housing in the highest-density districts of the inner city. After a few years many would be living on the same blocks with Old Whites of the same (low) income level as themselves, but this change would be of slight importance, since the neighborhoods would be about as poor as before. In the very worst sections, New Whites would be an overwhelming majority for a long time to come, the reason being that Negroes constitute most of the poorest of the poor. Stores, schools, churches, and other community institutions and facilities there would still be segregated. For example, New White children would go to school only with New White children, and the slum school would remain a slum school.

With the end of racial discrimination, some New Whites would quickly climb the job and income ladder and then leave the slums and blighted areas. Unfortunately, however, the end of racial discrimination would not very greatly improve the job situation of most New Whites. Those who, because of discrimination in the past or for other reasons, were unskilled would still be at a disadvantage. As for the well-trained, most of them would gain by the end of discrimination, but some would lose by it. At present, most Negro professionals and politicians (the latter meaning all who act in representative capacities qua Negroes) have an advantage in not having to compete with whites; of the middle-class Negroes who do compete with whites, some receive a premium for being black. By putting them into competition with Old Whites, the end of racial discrimination would, in the short run at least, hurt perhaps as many New Whites as it would help.

One circumstance that would tend to hold the New White back in many cases is the size of his family. The mean number of children in below-the-poverty-line black families in 1971 was 3.24, almost the same as in 1967 (3.64), and considerably more than in above-the-line black families (2.32) and white ones (2.95) in 1971. Having more children and a lower income, the poor New White's disadvantage would be compounded: that is, the amount of capital *per child* that he would invest in its education and training would be relatively small.

Finally, it must be said that many New Whites would suffer indignities and humiliations not so different from those to which the Negro now is subject. The treatment that the lower-class white receives is in many ways like that of the victim of racial prejudice — and a larger proportion of New Whites would be lower class. In one respect their new (class) status might be harder to bear than their former (racial) one; for the victim of race prejudice can take some comfort, however small, in the knowledge that he is being treated unjustly.

Much of what appears (especially to Negroes) as race prejudice is really *class* prejudice or, at any rate, class antipathy. Similarly, much of what appears (especially to whites) as "Negro" behavior is really lower-class behavior. The lower class is relatively large among Negroes; it appears even larger than it is to those whites who fail to distinguish a Negro who exhibits outward signs — lack of skill, low income, slum housing, and so on — which in a white would mark him as lower class, from one whose culture is working, middle, or even upper class but whose opportunities have been limited by discrimination and whose income is low.

How much outward resemblance there is between class antipathy and racial prejudice may be seen from sociologists' accounts of the treatment often accorded to the white lower class. A. B. Hollingshead, for example, describes in *Elmtown's Youth* the social structure of a "typical" Midwestern county seat, the population of which in 1940 was white (there was only one Negro family) and consisted mostly of native-born Protestants, many descended from "old American stock." In this all-American community, nearly a quarter of the population had the status of pariahs. Class V (lower-class) families "are excluded from the two leading residential areas. . . . Employers do not like to hire them unless labor is scarce or they can be induced to work for low wages. . . . Class V persons are almost totally isolated from organized community activities. . . . They knew that their children were discriminated against in the school system by both the teachers and the pupils. . . . The Class V's get the bad jobs, such as helping in the junk yards and hauling garbage and ashes. . . . Class V persons give the impression of being resigned to a life of frustration and defeat in a community that despises them for their disregard of morals, lack of 'success' goals, and dire poverty."[21]

Hollingshead summarizes the community's view of the lower class — "the scum of the city" — as follows:

They have no respect for the law, or themselves.

They enjoy their shacks and huts along the river or across the tracks and love their dirty, smoky, low-class dives and taverns.

Whole families — children, in-laws, mistresses, and all — live in one shack.

This is the crime class that produces the delinquency and sexual promiscuity that fills the paper.

Their interests lie in sex and its perversion. The girls are always pregnant; the families are huge; incestual relations occur frequently.

They are not inspired by education, and only a few are able to make any attainments along this line.

They are loud in their speech, vulgar in their actions, sloppy in their dress, and indifferent toward their plight. Their vocabulary develops as profanity is learned.

If they work, they work at very menial jobs.

Their life experiences are purely physical, and even these are on a low plane.

They have no interest in health and medical care.

The men are too lazy to work or do odd jobs around town.

They support the Democratic party because of the relief obtained during the depression.

This group lives for a Saturday of drinking or fighting. . . .[22]

The community's view of the lower class is not, apparently, based entirely on prejudice. Class V parents, Hollingshead says, are "indifferent to the future":

They will leave a job casually, often without notice . . . 8 percent of the mothers and 46 percent of the fathers had been convicted once or more in the local courts. . . . Serial monogamy is the rule . . . one-fifth to one-fourth of all births are illegitimate. . . . The mean [number of children] is 5.6 per mother. . . . Disagreements leading to quarrels and vicious fights, followed by desertion by either the man or the woman, possibly divorce, is not unusual. . . . The burden of child care, as well as support, falls on the mother more often than on the father when the family is broken. . . . Before the sixteenth birthday is reached . . . 75 percent of the class V's have left school. . . .[23]

If something like one-quarter of the population of a typical Midwestern town is (more or less correctly) perceived in this way, it should not be surprising that a sizable part of the population of a large city is perceived (also more or less correctly) in the same way. Racial and ethnic prejudice obviously do not account for the low status of so many Elmtown people. Why, then, should the same attitudes be attributed to racial prejudice when the Class V's are Negroes (or Puerto Ricans or Mexicans or whatever) rather than white, Protestant, native-born Americans?

Obviously, racial prejudice is manifested when, as often happens, the Negro is automatically regarded as lower class simply on the basis of his skin color or when he is treated as if he were lower class even though it is clear that he is not. But to treat the lower-class Negro exactly like the lower-class white is not, on the face of it, to show racial prejudice.

Although, in principle, it is easy to distinguish racial prejudice from class prejudice as well as prejudice ("an irrational attitude of hostility on the basis of supposed characteristics," according to the dictionary) from justifiable antipathy (a rational attitude of hostility on the basis of objective characteristics), in practice to do so would usually require a wisdom greater than Solomon's. Concretely, racial and class prejudice are usually inextricably mixed, and so are prejudice and justifiable antipathy. Consider the following:

A Negro drifter not long ago was arrested for breaking into a liquor store and swiping a bottle. He smashed the neck, took a swig and was caught with the goods, so to speak inside him. Two policemen carted him off to the station house for booking. He was a moderately difficult prisoner, swaying around as they tried to fingerprint him. But he had joshed them into a good mood and all three were making something of a joke about the fingerprinting. The Negro then shoved a bit, saying "C'mon you m____r f____ers." The cops immediately turned upon him and beat him up. The word he had used is not a word to which lower-middle-class Irishmen or Italians take kindly — even in jest, and especially from a Negro (although that particular epithet is a common-place of lower-class Negro speech).[24]

In a case like this, it is impossible to say what part was played by "racial prejudice." Negroes may be convinced that the drifter would not have been beaten if he had been white. On the other hand, readers of *Elmtown's Youth* may conclude that a white, Protestant, "old-stock American" of Class V would have gotten exactly the same treatment.

Obstacles of many kinds, some insuperable, are placed in the way of Negroes who want to move into white neighborhoods. This fact, however, does not adequately explain the existence of neighborhoods that are wholly or almost wholly black. In many inner-city areas Negroes now constitute the main body of low-skilled, low-paid labor; this in itself would account for their being the main body of residents in the poorer parts of the city. No doubt, also, many Negroes *prefer* black neighborhoods and would live in them even if their opportunities to live in white ones were excellent (which, to repeat, they generally are not). The evidence of recent public opinion polls on this is somewhat contradictory. One large survey found that 85 percent of the black respondents either preferred neighborhoods that were about one-half Negro or said that the composition of the neighborhood made no difference to them (only 1 percent wanted to live in predominantly white neighborhoods).[25] Another, made in 1967 among Negroes living in the North and the West, found that almost two-thirds preferred neighborhoods that were mostly or entirely Negro. Whatever their preferences with respect to the racial composition of the neighborhood, the adequacy of the housing, the survey makers write, is of more concern to Negroes, as it is to whites.[26]

The practice of calling all Negro neighborhoods "segregated" and "ghettoes" misrepresents the situation seriously and perhaps dangerously. In the technical language of many sociologists, a Negro neighborhood would be called segregated even if every family in it had recently turned down an excellent opportunity to live among whites; it is "unevenness in the distribution of white and Negro households" within a neighborhood, whatever the motive or cause of the unevenness, that constitutes segregation for the sociologist.[27] The lay reader, unaware that the word is used in a Pickwickian sense, supposes that the "ghetto" studied by such sociologists and described in the newspapers must be the result of white prejudice. That it *may* be, partly or wholly, the result of circumstances (namely, that large numbers of unskilled Negro workers came all at once to the inner city and occupied all the low-cost housing then available) or of the Negroes' own preference is not likely to occur to him. Negroes, hearing incessantly that they are "segregated" and that they live in "ghettoes," are given additional grounds for supposing that they are in all cases "forced" to do what they would sometimes — perhaps often — do of their own accord as a matter of course. One can only conjecture, but it seems plausible that the universal practice of using "ghetto" and "segregated" in reference to any Negro neighborhood tends to condition Negroes to the idea — which is usually a half-truth at most — that white prejudice "forces" them to live in poor housing and among other Negroes. If this is so, the semantic confusion goes a long way toward making bad matters worse.[28]

There would be residential segregation in the city even if there were no Negroes in it. Class prejudice (or, more generally, differences of taste associated with class cultures) would give rise to some of it. In the Chicago metropolitan area, Anthony H. Pascal found, white households with 1959 incomes between $2,000 and $4,000 were not distributed among other whites in the way that one would expect judging from housing characteristics alone: this unevenness of distribution he attributed to class prejudice.[29] In the New York metropolitan area, Nathan Kantrowitz constructed indexes of segregation in 1960 for eleven ethnic groups plus Negroes and Puerto Ricans. Segregation as between whites of southern and northern European origins was such, he found, that slightly more than half of the population of southern European origin would have to be redistributed in order to achieve full integration with the population of northern European origin. Even *within* these two populations of European origin there was residential segregation: the index between Norwegians and Swedes, for example, was 45.4.[30]

It is also possible for a neighborhood to become almost completely segregated even if none of its residents favors segregation. This could happen, Thomas C. Schelling has shown, if people have a "moderate urge" to avoid neighborhoods in which they would be members of a small minority.[31]

Obviously it makes a world of difference from a moral and therefore a policy standpoint whether in a concrete case segregation is voluntary or involuntary and what motives (if any!) lie behind it. These are matters about which it is usually extremely difficult, and sometimes quite impossible, to reach reliable judgments in particular circumstances. Do the Norwegians live apart from the Swedes because they *like* Norwegians or because they *dislike* Swedes? What, exactly, is the mixture of motives on both sides? And at what precise point do the constraints upon a Swede become such as to make his living apart from Norwegians "involuntary"?

One of the few studies to shed light on *why* Negroes live apart from whites was published in 1964 by a team of researchers from Brandeis University.[32] They made the study for the Boston Urban Renewal Administration, which wanted to know how many of the families in the Washington Park neighborhood — a middle-income "ghetto" — were likely to remain there if the neighborhood was rehabilitated. When interviewers first talked to the families, they assumed that most of them would want to move to predominantly white neighborhoods. There was nothing to stop them from doing so. The renewal agency had given them lists of housing that they might rent or purchase in white neighborhoods at prices they could afford. Moreover, most of them were very dissatisfied where they were; they strongly criticized the neighborhood schools and they complained also of inadequate shopping facilities, insufficient police protection, and noise and disorder in the streets. Since they could easily leave the "ghetto," it was reasonable to expect them to do so.

In fact, only thirty-three of the families (13 percent) did leave, and of these only nine left the Negro community. A large majority of the families did not even look at the housing listed as available. Some did not look at it because they were sure that they would be turned down on one pretext or another if they decided that they wanted it, but most were just not interested. (Incidentally, the few who inspected the listed housing encountered no prejudice.)

The main reason why the Washington Park people did not move, the researchers finally concluded, was that they had good housing at bargain prices where they were. They were paying a median rent of $85 per month, which was only 12 percent of their income. The carrying charges on a house in the suburbs would be between $125 and $150. Most of the families could afford this much — two-thirds of them had incomes of over $7,800 — but they preferred to use their money for other things. As the researchers put it, "One might describe them as having been 'spoiled' by their current low costs of housing."[33] In this respect the Negroes were just like the Italians in the West End of Boston whom Gans had studied a few years before. "People were so used to paying low rents," Gans found, "that their whole mode of life was adjusted to them. Any apartment that rented for more than $50 for five or six rooms was thought to be outrageously expensive."[34]

Another reason why most of the Washington Park people chose not to move was that they wanted to be near friends and relatives. This also was a motive of Gans's Italians; indeed, it was what made them "urban villagers."

In a more recent study families were asked what were the chief advantages that caused them to move to their present homes. Whites and blacks gave pretty much the same answers, and this whether they had moved into segregated or integrated neighborhoods. The four most important advantages listed were: convenience to work, appropriateness of the size of the dwelling, certain special features of the dwelling (such as a garage, fencing, or architectural style), and financial gains.[35]

Behind the reasons people give when they are asked such questions there are doubtless unconscious motives that are also of importance. Without being aware of what they are doing, the members of an ethnic or racial group may impose physical separation on themselves as a means of maintaining their collective identity and values. As Ralph Ellison has explained:

. . . it is a misunderstanding to assume that Negroes want to break out of Harlem. They want to transform the Harlems of their country. These places are precious to them. These places are where they have dreamed, where they have lived, where they have loved, where they have worked out life as they could. . . . it isn't the desire to run to the suburbs or to invade "white" neighborhoods that is the main concern with my people in Harlem. They would just like to have a more human life there. A slum like Harlem isn't just a place of decay. It is also a form of historical and social memory.[36]

Even if more "segregation" is voluntary than most people realize, the fact remains that a great deal is *not* voluntary. There are many neighborhoods into which it is all but impossible for a black family to move and many more in which blacks are, to put it mildly, unwelcome. By no means all of this hostility represents *racial* prejudice, however. Some of it is simply snobbery (it is safe to say that, if the Washington Park Negroes had been blue-collar rather than white-collar, the white neighborhoods would have been less open to them), and some of it is the more or less justifiable distaste and fear that working- and middle-class people feel toward lower-class ones. (If a Negro is assumed to be lower class simply because he is black and not because of anything he does, that, of course, is prejudice pure and simple.) This distaste and fear is probably as common among Negroes as among whites: the lower-class Negro is usually as unwelcome in or near a middle-class Negro neighborhood as in or near a middle-class white one. Still, even when these motives are added to voluntary "segregation," there is no doubt that much segregation based on race prejudice remains.

As the Washington Park case shows, it is not the absence of white faces that makes the "ghetto" objectionable to the Negro. Rather, it is the feeling that he is not perfectly free to live wherever he pleases and, also, the inadequacy of the stores, schools, playgrounds, and other facilities of his neighborhood. Once it is established, as in Washington Park, that he can live in a white neighborhood if he wishes, and once the facilities of the neighborhood are brought up to a standard of adequacy, the Negro very often prefers to live among other Negroes.

Like everyone else, too, he prefers to live among people whose class culture is not very different from his own. From the standpoint of those who live in it the "ghetto" is not so much that many of its residents are poor as that a relatively small number of them are lower class. The poverty of the many accounts for the absence of super-markets (these depend upon rapid turnover of goods to break even) and for the generally low quality of the goods in the stores. But it is the style of life of the small lower class that accounts for black-board jungle schools, garbage-strewn and rat-infested alleys, and disorderly and dangerous streets.

The middle- and upper-working-class Negro, then, if he is to be anywhere near his friends and relatives and in a community to which he feels he "belongs," must live among people whose style of life he finds repugnant. His situation differs fundamentally from that of, say, the Italian described by Gans in that the Italian belongs to a group that is predominantly working and lower middle class. The middle-class Italian can live in comfort and without annoyance or embarrass-ment in the midst of an all-Italian neighborhood because the Italian lower class is too small to be noticeable. By contrast, the middle-class Negro who lives in an all-Negro district can rarely avoid contact with the slum. The choice open to him is painful: he may move to a white neighborhood, paying more for housing than he is used to, cutting himself off from relatives and friends, and risking insult and even injury from prejudiced neighbors; or he may suffer the inconve-niences, annoyances, and hazards of living in or near a slum. The working-class Negro who lives in a housing project has a problem that is no less awkward; as Gerald D. Suttles has pointed out, he must find out which of his neighbors are dangerous and which are not and he must do so in the absence of the cues that nonproject housing nor-mally provides.[37]

Such problems do not exist either for the lower-class Negro, who typically feels very much at home in the slum, or for the upper-class one, who can insulate himself from it by living in an expensive apartment house, working and shopping downtown, and sending his children to private schools. The problem is acute, however, for middle- and upper-working-class people whose incomes and work routines do not permit much insulation, and who are often distressed at the possibility of slipping — psychologically if not physically — into a state from which they have only recently managed to emerge. This thought, one suspects, is what lies behind Kenneth B. Clark's call for a struggle "to prevent decadence from winning over the remaining islands of middle class society."[38] His rhetoric has to do entirely with the hatefulness, callousness, and brutality of whites, but what he seems to mean by "decadence" is lower-class culture. The "dark ghetto" is, in the last analysis, the lower-class one.

The movement of the Negro up the class scale appears as inexorable as that of all other groups. The number of middle- and upper-class Negroes is in many areas already large enough to allow the formation of predominantly middle- and upper-class neighborhoods and suburbs — places large enough to support stores, churches, restaurants, and local public services of the sort that middle- and upper-class people desire. Between 1951 and 1971 the percentage of Negro families earning more than $10,000 jumped from 3 to 30 (the figures are in constant 1971 dollars), which means that the time has come when many Negroes who find the slum intolerable can leave it without at the same time having to leave the society of other Negroes.

Differentiation along income and class lines is occurring within the Negro areas of the large cities. It tends to follow the normal pattern, people settling farther from the city center the higher their income. A more or less conflicting tendency is also at work, however: neighborhoods that are relatively new (in terms of the length of time that they have been occupied by Negroes) being preferred by upper-status families to those that are relatively old. The consequence of this is (one investigator has reported) that high-prestige Negro neighborhoods are frequently located as close to the city center as are low-prestige ones.[39]

The "upgrading" of some neighborhoods will often mean the "downgrading" of others. As more and more Negroes withdraw into middle- and upper-class communities, the concentration of the lower class in the slum will necessarily increase. Very probably the "worsening" of the slum will be seen not as a consequence of the improved position of Negroes generally, but rather as further evidence of callousness and neglect by the "white power structure." "We have absentee leadership, absentee ministers, absentee merchants," a resident of Watts complained after the riot there.[40] Apparently, he thought that this was a problem that someone — presumably the government — should do something about. The increasing isolation of the lower class is a problem, to be sure, but it is hard to see what can be done about it. The upper classes will continue to want to separate themselves physically from the lower, and in a free country they probably cannot be prevented from doing so.

"Whatever their origin," writes sociologist Urie Bronfenbrenner, "the most immediate, overwhelming, and stubborn obstacles to achieving quality and equality in education now lie as much in the character and way of life of the American Negro as in the indifference and hostility of the white community."[41] This observation also is true of areas other than education. Prejudice against the Negro has declined sharply since the Second World War, making his other handicaps relatively more important. It is not likely, however, that the Negro man-on-the-street will fully recognize the changes that have occurred; he still has the lowest-paid and most menial jobs, he still lives in the worst neighborhoods, and he still sends his children to inadequate and mostly-black schools. Naturally, he concludes that the same old cause — "Whitey" — is still producing the same old effects. That these effects are now being produced largely (not entirely, of course) by other causes, especially differences of education, income, and — in the case of those who are lower class — class culture is something that he cannot be expected to see for himself or to believe if it is pointed out to him, especially when the pointing out is done by a white.

Negro leaders cannot be expected to explain that prejudice is no longer *the* obstacle. Those of them who understand that it is not are bound to pretend otherwise. Like every specialist, the Negro leader is prone to magnify to himself as well as to others the importance of his specialty, seeing every problem in terms of it. Even when he recognizes that the situation of most Negroes would be very far from satisfactory if there were no racial prejudice at all, the logic of his position as a leader prevents him from saying so. To acknowledge that nonracial factors have become more important than racial ones would cool the zeal of his supporters, give aid and comfort to the enemy, and destroy his very reason for being. So long as there is *any* racial prejudice at work, the leader cannot risk seeming to tolerate it, as he would if he emphasized those other (nonracial) aspects of the situation which from a practical (but not a moral) standpoint are now vastly more important. For the race leader, there is everything to gain and nothing to lose by treating all problems as if they derived solely from the racial one. "Why," asked Ben J. Wattenberg and Richard M. Scammon in 1973, "have the data of black advancement been kept secret by those who presumably have an interest in making them known?" The answer, they said,

is of course that civil-rights leaders do know what has happened, and even acknowledge it in private; but they have elected as a matter of policy to mute any public acknowledgment or celebration of black accomplishments in order to maintain moral and political pressure on the administration and on public opinion.[42]

Whites, too, find prejudice a peculiarly satisfying explanation for the troubles of the Negro. As was observed in the last chapter, it is characteristic of upper- and middle-class culture not only to try to improve oneself and one's society but also to blame oneself for not doing more and succeeding better. Members of these classes are prone to see all social problems in terms of their own moral shortcomings — to say, for example, that the Negro is "forced to live in a ghetto" even when it is clear that he *chooses* to live among other Negroes.[43] The Brandeis researchers, for example, refer to Washington Park as a "ghetto" even though their main finding is that most families live there by choice. Another study reports that the question "Do you think Puerto Ricans can live anywhere they want to if they can afford the rent?" was answered "yes" by 87 percent of a sample of New York Puerto Ricans, but calls the *barrio* a "ghetto" nevertheless.[44]

The motives that produce this overemphasis on prejudice are understandable. It is graceless of the white, to say the very least, to run any risk of underemphasizing it. There is the feeling, too, that it can do no harm — and may do some good — to err on the side of seeing more prejudice than is really there. Besides, even if prejudice is not important causally, it is very important morally.

There are, however, at least two serious dangers in widespread overemphasis on prejudice as a cause of the Negro's troubles. The first is that it may lead to the adoption of futile and even destructive policies and to the nonadoption of others that might do great good. It is clear, for example, that if improving the housing of Washington Park Negroes is the goal, programs built on the assumption that the main problem is prejudice will lead nowhere.

The other, perhaps more serious danger in the overemphasis of prejudice is that it raises still higher the psychic cost of being Negro, a cost cruelly high under the best of circumstances. It is bad enough to suffer real prejudice, as every Negro does, without having to suffer imaginary prejudice as well. To refer once more to Washington Park, it is worth noting that some of the people there who did not look at the housing listed as available in white neighborhoods "knew" that Negroes could not buy it and that they would only be humiliated if they tried. In short, the overemphasis on prejudice encourages the Negro to define all his troubles in racial terms. Driving it into him that he is forced to live in a ghetto, the victim of the white man's hate and greed, and so on, makes it all the more difficult for him to feel that he is a man first and a Negro second.

CHAPTER FIVE

The Problem of Unemployment

They keep telling you about job opportunities, this job opportunity, and that, but who wants a job working all week and bringing home a sweat man's pay?
— Man, aged eighteen, quoted in *Youth in the Ghetto*

Maybe we are going to have to accept that many able-bodied people are never going to be engaged in economically productive employment.
— Welfare Commissioner of New York City, 1964

MANY people seem to think that the employment prospect in the city is dismal, especially for the unskilled. Technological change in general and automation in particular are said to be eliminating jobs at an unprecedented rate, and it is predicted that before long there will be permanent, mass unemployment, especially of the unskilled. Historian Constance Green describes a case in point: "Where 200 hands had run the looms in a Holyoke, Massachusetts, mill in the 1930s fifteen years later the great weave shed contained two people watching the automatic machines turn out the fine fabrics. . . ."[1] Nathan Glazer, a sociologist, makes the same observation in general terms: Our society "has less and less work for people with only hands."[2] And Paul Goodman, essayist and novelist, puts it even more bluntly: "For the uneducated there will be no jobs at all."[3] Pointing out that the baby boom of a few years ago is about to produce a big increase in the work force, demographer Donald Bogue writes that unless the new workers are kept in school and trained to hold down skilled jobs, "the economy of the entire metropolitan area [of Chicago] can literally drown in a sea of unemployment and under-employment."[4] Thomas F. Pettigrew, a social psychologist, having in mind that Negroes are concentrated in unskilled sectors of the labor force, concludes that broadening of minimum wage legislation and other measures are desperately needed "not just for national prosperity but for improved race relations as well."[5] John Kosa, a sociologist, thinks that cybernetics, "a sophisticated form of increasing mechanization," eliminates "many unskilled jobs in services and industrial production" and "regularly dislocates a great number of laborers whose chances to find new jobs on a shrinking market are in proportion to their educational and industrial skills," the "under-educated" among them being "likely to face chronic unemployment."[6]

These authorities — all first-rate in their fields — have been quoted in order to suggest how widely and seriously the nature of the unemployment problem in the cities is misunderstood. This chapter will contend that automation and technological change are not creating a serious unemployment problem and are not likely to; that the unskilled, far from facing a hopeless future, will probably maintain and improve their position relative to the skilled (which is not to say that the relatively small number who are lower class will therefore adopt a different style of life) and that the Negro will benefit from this trend; and that some of the measures recommended by the quoted authorities — increasing the minimum wage, for example — would make matters worse for the least employable workers, while others — keeping them in school, for example — would probably do more harm than good in most cases. The conclusion reached is not that there is no unemployment problem in the cities, but that the problem is of a different nature than is generally supposed.

It will be noted that none of the persons quoted above is an economist. Most economists find nothing new or fearsome in a high rate of technological change and in the substitution of new methods and machines for labor (the term *automation* is used in various senses, but it always refers to some special case of this general phenomenon). Indeed, they say that the enormous and increasing productivity of the economy is the best possible evidence that technological change leads to economic progress.

No one denies, however, that automation has caused a net loss of jobs in *particular* plants, cities, and industries. Steel, coal, and oil refining have been cited as industries in which employment has declined (by 10 or 20 percent in the 1960's) largely from this cause.[7] Some — but not all — of the cities heavily dependent upon these industries suffered from these changes. Pittsburgh, for example, was hard hit; on the other hand, Detroit produced as many cars in 1963 as in 1955 while using 17 percent fewer employees, and had an unemployment rate below the national average in 1964.[8]

To be sure, one can always find instances, like that in Holyoke, Massachusetts, where two people now do the work formerly done by two hundred. Such instances are misleading, however, since they ignore the fact that other technological changes (as well as other factors altogether) may at the same time have been *creating* jobs (although not in the same industries or cities) and that what is relevant is the number of jobs in total. According to Robert M. Solow, an M.I.T. economist who was a member of the National Commission on Technology, Automation, and Economic Progress, the question whether automation creates or destroys more jobs is unanswerable; he doubts, he says, that anyone could make a good estimate of the net number of jobs created or destroyed merely by the invention of the zipper or of sliced bread. The question is irrelevant anyway, he adds, because the total volume of employment is not determined by the rate of technological progress; a modern mixed economy "can, by proper and active use of fiscal and monetary policy weapons, have full employment for *any* plausible rate of technological change within a range that is easily wide enough to cover the American experience."[9]

Even if it should turn out that the society has less work for the unskilled, the consequences would not necessarily be undesirable from their standpoint and they might be beneficial. It must be remembered that the price of unskilled labor, like that of other commodities, is a function of supply as well as demand. Therefore even though the demand for unskilled labor decreases the price of it will rise if the supply decreases even more. This in fact has happened over the long run. Before the Civil War the unskilled worker earned only about one-third as much as the skilled; at the turn of the century he earned about one-half as much; now he earns two-thirds as much.[10] Conceivably, the time will come when he will earn *more* than the skilled worker. As James Tobin has observed, "When there are only a few people left in the population whose capacities are confined to garbage-collecting, it will be a high-paid calling. The same is true of domestic service and all kinds of menial work."[11]

The interaction of supply and demand also determines the price of *skilled* labor, of course. It follows, then, to paraphrase Tobin, that when almost everyone is a skilled computer programmer, programming will be a low-paid job. In other words, it cannot be assumed that raising the skill level of workers will result in either higher wages or reduced unemployment. In states where college graduates constitute a relatively large proportion of the work force the percentage difference between their earnings and those of other workers is less than in states where they constitute a relatively small proportion of the work force. The same is true with respect to high school graduates as compared to elementary school graduates.[12]

Changes in technology do not, on the whole, either favor or retard the employment of Negroes. Indeed, Negroes, because they are concentrated near the bottom of the occupational ladder, have obtained far greater *relative* advances in income than have whites.[13]

Among noneconomists the belief is widespread that automation reduces the demand for unskilled labor more than for other labor. On a priori grounds, there is no reason to expect this, however, and empirically it does not appear to be so. The impact is mixed: in some cases automation does eliminate unskilled jobs, but in others it enables unskilled workers to do things formerly done by skilled workers. In the manufacturing and service industries, many jobs done by the unskilled and the semiskilled have proved harder to automate than those done by more skilled workers.[14]

It is not true that unskilled workers cannot get jobs. In 1972, 90 percent of nonfarm unskilled laborers and nearly 98 percent of farmworkers were employed. These, incidentally, were the highest unemployment rates for these groups in ten years.[15]

The crucial factor is not automation but the aggregate demand of the economy for goods and services. If demand is high enough, everyone who wants to work can find a job no matter how lacking in skills he or she may be. To assure full employment, aggregate demand will have to grow constantly, however, for the number of persons wanting jobs is increasing along with the population as a whole, and the average output per man-hour of work is increasing too. According to the National Commission on Technology, Automation, and Economic Progress, aggregate demand must grow by more than 4 percent a year just to keep the unemployment rate from rising; to decrease the unemployment rate, it must grow by even more. In the past, the economy has seldom, if ever, grown at a rate faster than 3.5 percent for any extended time; however, it can be made to do so, the Commission said, by positive fiscal, monetary, and manpower policies.[16]

If the labor market is kept tight, employers will find it necessary to employ people previously thought undesirable or even unemployable. On the other hand, if the labor market is allowed to become slack, they will pick and choose. The labor market, the Commission said, can be viewed

as a gigantic "shapeup," with members of the labor force queued in order of their relative attractiveness to employers. If the labor market operates efficiently, employers will start at the head of the line, selecting as many as they need of employees most attractive to them. Their choice may be based on objective standards relating to ability, or on dubious standards of race, sex, or age; wage differentials may also be important; and formal education may be used as a rough screening device. The total number employed and unemployed depends primarily on the general state of economic activity. The employed tend to be those near the beginning and the unemployed those near the end of the line. Only as demand rises will employers reach further down the line in their search for employees.[17]

Those near the far end of the line — that is, those considered least desirable by employers — tend to be teen-agers and other young people with little education and little or no job experience, members of the lower class (who cannot be depended upon from one day to the next), and victims of racial and other prejudice. At the very end of the line, of course, are those who have *all* these handicaps — lower-class-Negro-teen-age dropouts. In 1972 when the general unemployment rate was 5.6 percent, the rate among adult men 25 years and older was only 3.1 percent, but that among eighteen- and nineteen-year-old white males was 12.4 percent and that among eighteen- and nineteen-year-old white females was 12.3 percent. The rates for nonwhite males and females of these ages were 26.2 percent and 38.7

percent, respectively. Among still younger teen-agers and dropouts, the rate was even higher.

As is apparent from these figures, a small reduction in the general unemployment rate would make a big difference to those near the end of the hiring line. If the general rate were brought down to about 2 percent (which must be close to the absolute minimum, since some workers are always in the process of moving from one job to another), even those at the end of the line would, in a well-functioning labor market, receive job offers. In the United States the general yearly unemployment rate has never, except in wartime, fallen below 3.2 percent. Therefore, the rate of unemployment among the least-wanted workers is normally high.

For some people — especially teen-agers and women who are not the main support of a family — a job is more a convenience than a necessity. For obvious reasons, people in this position are more likely than others to leave a job casually and to be slow and "choosey" about finding another. Changes that increase the proportion of such people in the labor force — for example, larger numbers of teen-agers in the population, fewer small children to be looked after by mothers, wider acceptance of the view that women should compete on equal terms with men — all tend to raise the unemployment rate, over what it would otherwise be. Insofar as it reflects these causes, the higher rate does not have the same significance as the old, for many of those now counted as unemployed are really people who have chosen not to work for the time being; even for those teen-agers and married women who are anxious to work, unemployment does not as a rule involve the degree of hardship that it often does for men and women who are the main support of families. In the past decade or two the proportion of workers who are only weakly attached to the labor force has grown substantially, as can be seen from the fact that the percentage of teen-agers and women in the labor force rose from 36 in 1956 to 44 in 1972. Largely because of these changes, unemployment is now more a matter of turnover than of shortage of jobs. (In 1972, less than half of the unemployed had been fired or laid off, about half were unemployed for less than five weeks, and about one-fourth were young people, many of whom were other students or graduates seeking their first job).[18] In view of the changed situation, the goal of "full employment," some authorities think, should be moved from 4 percent unemployed to five.[19]

Economists disagree as to why we do not come closer to achieving the full employment goal. One reason, some say, is that public opinion does not give the President or anyone else the authority to carry a fiscal and monetary policy into effect. A President can only recommend actions needed to maintain the necessary high level of aggregate demand; other bodies, especially Congress and the Federal Reserve System, pursue frequently unrelated and perhaps contradictory policies of their own. Even without these bodies to contend with, public opinion might prevent a President from taking the necessary steps. Strange as it may seem, Presidents have on occasion failed even to propose tax cuts thought urgently necessary for fear of the reaction from righteously indignant taxpayers.

A second reason why we do not reduce unemployment to the barest minimum, some economists say, is that the measures required would worsen the nation's international balance of payments problem.[20] This fear arises from a widespread and perhaps not wholly rational concern about the value of the dollar in relation to other nations' currencies.

The third reason that economists give to explain an unnecessarily high rate of unemployment refers not to mythology but to interests that are real. A reduction in unemployment, they say, would require monetary and fiscal policies that would raise the consumer price level. In effect, a 4 percent unemployment rate would have to be paid for by accepting at least a 4 percent rate of inflation. To get the unemployment rate down further, say to 3 percent, would entail more inflation than the public would stand for. There is, in other words, a fundamental conflict of interest between those at the end of the hiring line and the much larger number of people (ones on fixed incomes, especially) who would lose by inflation.

Some economists go so far as to assert that there is *no* steady rate of inflation that would reduce the average level of unemployment. This position was taken by Milton Friedman in his 1968 presidential address to the American Economic Association.[21] He acknowledged that by speeding up inflation one may reduce unemployment, but he pointed out that it is impossible to keep on speeding it up forever and he maintained that whenever the rate stabilizes people will grow accustomed to the new rate and unemployment will return to its old level or to an even higher one. Some other economists, while not entirely disagreeing with this, have since taken a somewhat more optimistic view. Martin S. Feldstein, for example, has concluded from his calculations that the average long-run unemployment rate can be lowered to — but probably not below — 4 percent by expansionary fiscal and monetary policy.[22]

At first glance it may appear that the people near the end of the hiring line are there solely because they are young, unskilled victims of racial prejudice, and so on. On reflection, however, it will be seen that, except in a recession, when skilled workers bid for unskilled work, there is no reason to expect a higher rate of unemployment among the classes of labor that are the least capable (the inexperienced, the unskilled, and so on) than among those that are the most capable. This is because the attractiveness of a class of labor to an employer depends not solely upon its capability (real or imagined) but also upon its *price*. A lazy worker, for example, is more attractive to an employer than an energetic one, provided that his wages (and the other costs involved in using him) are low enough to more than compensate for his lesser productivity. To state the matter generally, those at the end of the hiring line are there not because of an absolute incapability (real or imagined) but because *the price of their services makes it unprofitable to employ them.* If their price were low enough, they would move to the head of the hiring line, forcing some more "attractive" (i.e., more attractive in all but price) workers to the rear. In practice, the price of the least capable (real or imagined) would have to be very low indeed in order for this to occur; it might even have to be negative, employers being paid to take the workers they found least attractive, but this does not invalidate the principle involved.

One reason why low-quality labor is overpriced is that numerous laws and institutional arrangements, all supposed to benefit the worker, make it so. Minimum-wage laws are among the worst offenders. Enacted by the federal government[23] and by thirty-three states, Puerto Rico, and the District of Columbia, these laws forbid an employer to pay a worker in a covered occupation less than a certain wage ($1.60 an hour under the federal laws[24]) even though the alternative may be not to employ him at all. Originally, minimum wage was an approach to curbing prostitution: the laws applied only to women and were passed by some states shortly after the federal government adopted the Mann Act (1910). ("Economic needs," a reformer explained, "impel many a girl toward a personally degrading life."[25]) Later, northern textile manufacturers joined with labor unions to support federal minimum-wage legislation in order to reduce southern competition by raising the price of its labor. Although the minimum is redefined upward from time to time, it is never set high enough to affect most wage workers.[26] Those who *are* affected are the previously low-paid and low-productivity ones, but not all of them; many of the very lowest-paid are in occupations — agriculture, for instance — not covered by the laws.

A principal effect of the minimum wage is to "injure some of the lowest-paid workers by forcing them into even lower-paid occupations exempt from the act, one of which is unemployment."[27] An employer who does not have to compete with other employers for labor may pay his workers less than their labor is worth in production; in his case the effect of the minimum wage may be to raise wages without creating unemployment. But the number of such employers is negligible: workers today move around by car and otherwise and usually have a variety of job alternatives. This being the case, the effect of the minimum wage is not to cause an employer to raise wages (except as he may have been about to do so anyway); rather, it is to cause him to eliminate all labor that will cost more than it is worth in his productive process. Some work that would be done if the price of this labor were lower is left undone. Other work is done in ways that economize on low-productivity but high-cost labor; labor-saving methods are tried, machines are substituted for labor, and a somewhat higher quality of labor is hired at the somewhat higher wage set by law, leaving the least productive with fewer and worse opportunities than before. "What good does it do to a black youth," asks Paul A. Samuelson, "to know that an employer must pay him $1.60 an hour — or $2.00 — if that amount is what keeps him from getting a job?"[28]

That youths *are* kept from getting jobs by the minimum wage is a view supported by theory and by much, but not all, empirical evidence. In 1973, after reviewing recent empirical studies, Andrew Brimmer, a Negro economist of distinction (he is a member of the Board of Governors of the Federal Reserve System), concluded that although the issue could not be regarded as settled ("it is difficult to draw firm conclusions from these empirical studies unless one is willing to play one methodology off against another"), it would be well to allow employment of youths at less than the minimum wage. This, he thought, might preserve some jobs, particularly for sixteen- to seventeen-year-olds, that would otherwise be lost, although it was not likely to lead to an expansion of the teen-age share of employment.[29]

Feldstein has criticized the minimum wage on quite different grounds. It works to the disadvantage of many young people who get jobs, he says, because those with few skills and below-average education are often not productive enough to permit the employer to pay them the minimum wage *while also providing on-the-job training and opportunity for advancement* that they desperately need. Lowering the minimum wage for such workers might help, he thinks, but it would not be sufficient: the government should give youth employment scholarships to supplement earnings temporarily and allow the young workers to "buy" more and better on-the-job training.[30]

In some labor markets trade unions doubtless have more effect than do minimum wage laws in fixing the price of low-productivity labor above its value to employers, thus making its employment unprofitable. In New York City's highly unionized construction industry, for example, the union scale for unskilled building laborers as of July 1, 1971, was $6.82 an hour for a thirty-five-hour week, plus pensions and insurance. (Incidentally, this compares to $7.79 for skilled workers.) One effect of overpaying the unskilled workers is to cause fewer of them to be employed; the construction industry is vigorous in its effort to find techniques — for example, diamond drills that will go through concrete — by which it can economize on labor. Another effect is to restrict the jobs to a favored few, mostly workers in a relatively good position to get jobs elsewhere. Negroes, for example, have great difficulty getting into apprenticeship programs.

The job security and seniority provisions now common in union

UNEMPLOYMENT RATES FOR MALE TEEN-AGERS (AGES 14-19),
WHITE AND NONWHITE,
COMPARED WITH INCREASES IN THE MINIMUM WAGE

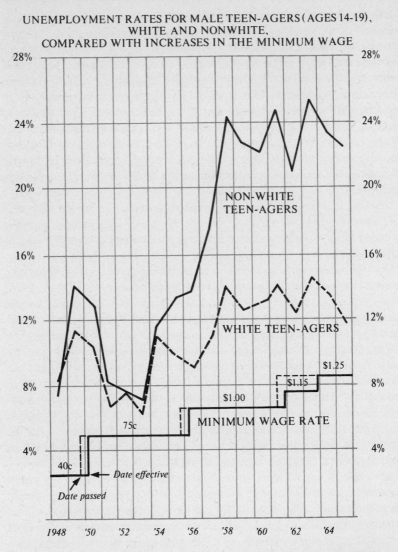

Source: The Free Society Association, Inc., *The Minimum Wage Rate; Who Really Pays?—An Interview with Yale Brozen and Milton Friedman* (Washington, D.C., April 1966). *Source of chart data:* Bureau of Labor Statistics, U.S. Department of Labor. Reprinted by courtesy of The Free Society Association, Inc.

contracts also tend to cause discrimination against low-productivity workers and probably also against Negroes. Knowing that he will incur large costs if he cannot discharge, or must eventually promote, a worker who is incompetent, an employer is likely to reject job applicants about whose future competence he cannot be reasonably certain. Therefore the worker who is perfectly capable of pushing a brush around the factory floor but not of doing much else will not get a job when promotion by seniority is mandatory: the employer cannot risk some day having to put him in charge of an expensive machine or in a supervisory position. Some portion of what appears to be racial discrimination may be generated by job security requirements in the opinion of Doeringer and Piore. "Race," they say, "is an inexpensive screening criterion. Where two racial populations differ significantly in terms of the proportion of persons possessing certain desired characteristics, the most efficient hiring policy may be simply to reject all members of the one racial population."[31]

Occupational licensure is another way in which the law says that some labor must either be overpaid or else not employed. By restricting entry into certain occupations to those who have passed a course of training — by requiring, for example, that in order to cut hair one must graduate from a barbering school that provides at least one thousand hours of instruction in "theoretical subjects" and then go through an apprenticeship,[32] or that a television repairman or garage mechanic pass a rigorous examination and post a bond[33] — the cities and states reduce employment opportunities for the workers whose possibilities are most limited.

Local, state, and federal agencies are all under pressure to "set an example of enlightened wage policy," that is, to pay labor more than it is worth. This policy injures workers at the bottom of the heap by giving others not at the bottom an incentive to take jobs they otherwise would avoid. Early in 1965 some three thousand persons took examinations for 125 jobs as coin collectors for Boston's metropolitan transit system. The jobs could have been done by workers who were not capable of doing much else, but because the wages were set higher than need be — $3.00 an hour plus various fringe benefits — low-capability workers had to compete for them against workers who could have been better employed. Naturally, the low-capability workers lost out; they remained unemployed while those who got the jobs wasted ability doing what less-able people could have done as well.[34]

After the Watts riots it was pointed out that the city's civil-service system had contributed to the Negroes' employment problem. Operating on "merit" alone, it had established such high education qualifications for employees that most Watts residents could not get civil-service jobs even as common laborers. This outcome would have been impossible had the city not been overpaying its employees; the Watts residents would have had little or no competition for the jobs if the only qualification had been ability to perform the task and if the wage rate had not been above the market.

Opinion is another factor that often causes overpricing of — and therefore unemployment of — low-value labor. In every locale people have a common idea of the lowest wage it is "reasonable" to expect workers to accept even if the alternative is to remain unemployed. Frequently, this "informal" minimum wage is higher than the legal one. And frequently it calls for paying wages only a philanthropist could afford. In Detroit, for example, auto companies pay unskilled production workers a very high wage — $5.17 an hour in 1973 (as compared to $6.61 for the skilled worker) — and this high rate is taken by unskilled workers in all industries as the model of what is "fair" and "decent." The auto workers' wages are high not because unskilled workers are more valuable in the auto industry than elsewhere, but because the power of an aggressive union (the UAW) has forced them up. Unskilled workers not lucky enough to get one of the small number of good union jobs — especially workers in low-paying enterprises, such as laundries and car parking lots — earn less than half as much as the auto workers. Naturally they are angry at the injustice of it all. They suppose that they are being underpaid, not that the others are being overpaid.

Working for less than the informal minimum — "for peanuts" — destroys a man's standing in whatever circle he moves in and undermines his self-respect. Some men prefer to go on welfare. In the summer of 1965, when a federal youth employment project in Detroit proposed paying seventy youths the legal minimum wage while training them for better-paying jobs, it could find only thirty who would accept its offer.[35] The legal minimum, then $1.25 an hour, was "peanuts." Three years later, the Labor Department made a $3,104,044 grant to train and find jobs for 970 "hard-core" unemployed in Detroit, but there was some question whether enough men could be found to accept training. The city had about thirty thousand eligibles, about ten thousand of whom were considered extreme cases. However, the trainees were to receive only $1.60 an hour during training and $2.30 an hour afterward. A laid-off auto worker, it was pointed out, would receive from the state and the company more take-home pay than a man putting in forty hours a week at $2.30 an hour.[36]

Illicit enterprises, too, tend to have the effect of setting an informal minimum wage for unskilled labor that has no relation to the market value of such labor and that other employers cannot afford to pay. As a result, the young "dropout" loses face and self-respect unless he is either a "hustler" or an idler; the suggestion that he be paid what his work is worth is tantamount to an insult. Asked why he did not go downtown and get a job, a Harlem youth replied:

Oh, come on. Get off that crap. I make $40 or $50 a day selling marijuana. You want me to go down into the garment district and push one of those trucks through the street and at the end of the week take home $40 or $50 if I'm lucky? Come off it. They don't have animals doing what you want me to do. There would be some society to protect animals if anybody had them pushing those damn trucks around. I'm better than an animal, but nobody protects me. Go away, mister. I got to look out for myself.[37]

In the final analysis, it is middle-class opinion that sets the informal minimum wage for low-value labor, and it does so, of course, on the basis of its own notion of what is reasonable. Unemployment compensation and other welfare programs explicitly recognize an informal minimum: no applicant for assistance may be required to accept "unreasonable" offers of employment, which is to say that no one may be required to work for what he is worth to his employer if this is much under what the general (middle-class) opinion considers "fair."

One important reason, then, why the number of jobs for very low-value labor is declining — why, for example, fewer shops make occasional deliveries, fewer part-time messengers are hired, fewer people are paid to mow lawns and shovel sidewalks — is not, as Paul

Goodman contends, that the system is "tightly organized and highly urbanized,"[38] but rather that those who might do these jobs have been told by parents, welfare departments, and the ever more affluent middle class generally that the small amounts they could earn by doing them are "peanuts" — too little for a self-respecting person to bother with.

Racial prejudice and discrimination are surely partly responsible for the very high rate of unemployment among black youth. Even when they have had as good schooling as whites, blacks often lack self-confidence and feel that they will not be treated fairly. This "background effect" of prior discrimination is an important handicap in itself. But in addition there is likely to be discrimination — both real and imagined — on the job. Some discriminatory practices not motivated by racial animus lead to racial responses of a kind which seem to justify the practices. For example, employers, knowing that blacks are twice as likely as whites to quit their jobs, may for purely business reasons be loath to hire, train, or promote them. In these circumstances the black employee, seeing himself discriminated against, becomes frustrated and sour; this leads to absenteeism, to recalcitrance in taking orders from foremen, to impatience in dealings with older co-workers (some of whom are manifestly racist), and to early quitting.[39] The employer's initial judgment, a correct one, is in this way reinforced in the manner of a self-fulfilling prophecy. Exactly the same can be said of the employee's judgment, of course.

Real though it undoubtedly is, racial discrimination is probably a less important cause of the high unemployment rate among Negro teenagers than the manifold opportunities that the Negro district offers for "action" of the sorts that many young people live for. This is suggested by the fact that the unemployment rate declines precipitously between ages 16–21 and 21–24 and also by the fact that once they have "settled down" as family heads black men are at least as likely to be employed as whites of the same age and schooling. That male black teenagers do not expect to be discriminated against is implied (although other interpretations are possible) by the fact that they give as their lowest acceptable wage a figure almost the same as that given by their white counterparts.[40]

Another cause of unemployment among the low-skilled is the tendency of some employers to set hiring standards that are unreasonably high, thus screening out applicants who could perform satisfactorily if given the chance. A study of the practices of a national sample of 280 employers, public and private, showed that even in the employment of laborers (as distinguished from "service" and "blue-collar" workers) 14 percent required a high school diploma, 17 percent required that applicants pass a test, 45 percent required references, and 57 percent attached importance to "good personal appearance." Even when the laborer job was a "dead-end" one a record of alcoholism was a disqualification with 46 percent of the employers, "other health problems" with 46 percent, garnishment with 18 percent, and an arrest record with 18 percent.[41] Insofar as such standards really are unrelated to work requirements, employers (acting against their own interest) in effect price many workers out of the market.

"Credentialism," as it has been called, is illegal when racially discriminatory. In March 1971 the United States Supreme Court found in favor of black employees who, in a class action suit, sought to prevent an employer from requiring a high school diploma and a "satisfactory intelligence test score" for certain jobs which had previously been given only to whites. In a unanimous opinion, the Court held that the intent of Congress in passing Title VII of the Civil Rights Act of 1964 was "to achieve equality of employment opportunities" and that the burden rests upon an employer to show that a "given requirement has a manifest relation to the employment in question"; the absence of discriminatory intent, the Court ruled, does not justify requirements or tests that do not have this manifest relation.[42]

Ironically, one form of credentialism — the evaluation of applicants on the basis of diplomas and degrees — may recently have begun to operate *in favor of* minority groups. According to Christopher Jencks, blacks now seem to be getting slightly more schooling than whites with comparable test scores.[43] If one assumes, as it is plausible to do, that test scores are better predictors of job performance than years of schooling, then whites are at a disadvantage with employers who take only the latter into account. A further irony arises from the fact that employers who rely solely upon interviews, ignoring credentials of all sorts, may, consciously or not, be more discriminatory than those who give weight to diplomas or test scores. If only interviews were used, Jencks suspects, "upward mobile men from low status homes would find themselves at more of a disadvantage than they do now."[44]

Thomas Sowell makes an extremely important point when he writes that "the net effect of any institutional arrangement which sets the rate of pay above that required to attract the number of qualified workers needed is to make it cheaper to discriminate in deciding who *not* to hire."[45] In other words, the employer who passes over the job applicant whose work would contribute most to his profit in favor of one whose race, sex, age, or other characteristics are more to his liking pays a price for indulging his tastes or prejudices. An employer, however, who is in one way or another prevented from using the profit criterion — as, for example, by formal or informal minimum wage, union practices, licensure laws, or politically determined wage rates — pays no price. Indeed, since he cannot use the businesslike criterion of "low bidder gets the job," he *must* find some other (unbusinesslike) criterion by which to choose among equally qualified applicants. This may help to explain the facts alleged in a suit filed in a federal district court by several Puerto Ricans who said that although Puerto Ricans and other Spanish-speaking persons make up 16 percent of New York City's population they have only 1.9 percent of the sanitation men jobs.[46] For unskilled workers these are very good jobs indeed: the starting salary is $9,690, there are many fringe benefits, and great job security; needless to say, then, the number of applicants far exceeds the number of jobs. Since one person can toss a bag of garbage into a truck about as well as another, there is no purely job-related basis for choosing among the many qualified applicants. Under these circumstances it is almost inevitable that criteria unrelated to performance or very weakly related to it — in the case of the sanitation men, height and fluency in English — will be introduced. If some of these criteria reflect the tastes or prejudices of the people who make them up, no one should be surprised. The surprising thing would be to find an underrepresentation of Puerto Ricans in a sanitation bureau which paid its workers no more than the market required.

Even if the total supply of jobs is large, there is likely to be (except perhaps in the very long run) some chronic unemployment among the unskilled workers who are concentrated in the inner city. For one thing, factories have long been moving from the inner to the outer city and from the city to the suburbs and beyond. Also, since the Second World War, large numbers of unskilled workers have moved into the inner city. (In 1929 two-thirds of all production jobs were in central cities; now well under half are there. The number of unskilled workers in the central cities, meanwhile, has risen.) As the previous chapters have pointed out, economic, class-cultural, and racial factors tend to prevent some factory workers from following their jobs out of the city. Of particular importance are the relative abundance of cheap housing in the central city as compared to the suburbs and the inability or unwillingness of some workers to commute to jobs in the suburban fringe.

Next to high transportation costs and the need for space, the overpricing of low-value labor explains why factories have left the inner city so rapidly. In many instances employers have gone to the suburbs in order to build new plants that would enable them to take advantage of labor-saving methods and devices.

In almost all of the large central cities the loss of jobs in manufacturing and trade was more than offset in the 1960's by increases in service activities — finance and insurance, communications, business services, recreation and tourism, personal services and, especially, government. This shift raised the value of the cities' product, but it was disadvantageous to unskilled workers. Service activities do not offer as much job-training as does manufacturing and for the unskilled most service jobs are "dead end."[47] Moreover, the criteria for selecting service workers tend to be more subjective and therefore more often unfair to — or at any rate unfavorable to — persons whose attributes are deemed undesirable. No one cares if a factory worker speaks crudely, scratches himself in the wrong places, or is physically unattractive; if he can read signs like DANGER — NO SMOKING and if he keeps his part of the assembly line moving, little else matters. In many service jobs, on the other hand, it is essential that the service worker "make a good impression" on the middle-class people he serves. If ethnic, racial, class, or other characteristics render him unattractive in their eyes, he is for that reason unemployable. The problem is not that he is unskilled, but that he is aesthetically objectionable — he spoils the decor, so to speak.[48] (In the survey of hiring standards cited above, employers were almost twice as likely to require "a good appearance" of white-collar and service workers as of blue-collar workers and laborers.[49])

It would appear that the way to solve the employment problem in the city is to allow the price of all labor, including the least valuable, to fall to a level at which it will all be purchased. If a ditchdigger's work is worth no more than $1.00 an hour to anyone and if a fifteen-year-old dropout's work is worth no more than 50 cents an hour, these should be their wages. The point is that low-value labor must be priced no higher than it is worth if those who can use it are to have an incentive to do so.

It will be objected that to require the low-value worker to work for what he is worth to an employer is to condemn him and his family to poverty. This does not follow. Much low-value work is done not by breadwinners but by persons, especially married women and teenagers, who want to supplement an income already above the poverty line. But even if this aspect is disregarded, the objection is not a weighty one. Theoretically, at least, there is no reason why a family (or unattached person) earning too little could not be subsidized from public sources so as to bring its total income up to a level deemed adequate.[50] This arrangement has an obvious advantage to the public: whatever the worker earns, however little, reduces the cost of his support.

The main beneficiaries, however, would be the workers themselves. A job can be much more than a source of income. It can be an opportunity to learn things, to test one's ability to stand up to strains, to get out of the house and away from home, and to feel that one is a part, however small, of a worthwhile undertaking. Especially for a male, the job (along with other things) helps establish one's identity and supports one's self-respect. Obviously, a job that pays "peanuts" is no aid to self-respect; on the contrary, having such a job entails a loss of it. Other, nonmonetary advantages accrue even from a poor job, however, and if everyone were expected to work for what his work is worth, the lowest paid would have at least somewhat less cause for embarrassment than they have now.

The idea of pricing low-value labor into the market is not worth serious consideration, however; it is hopelessly Utopian. Trade unions are not about to stop trying to get their members paid more than their work is worth. Minimum-wage laws will not be repealed; instead, the minimum rate will be pushed steadily upward (Bayard Rustin, the Negro leader, said that he would gladly trade the whole war on poverty for an increase to $2.00 in the minimum wage). Occupational licensure will not be dropped so long as various occupational groups can gain by restricting entry and raising prices. Nor is the idea that one should not work for "peanuts" (even if that happens to be all that one's labor is worth) likely to lose its hold. On the contrary, the informal minimum is likely to rise at an accelerating rate: as the standard of living of the affluent goes up, more and more low-pay, no-future jobs will be thought to be beneath the dignity of even the poorest and the least able.

If low-value labor cannot be priced into the market, what can be done to make the best of a bad situation? One familiar suggestion is to train the unskilled, the idea being that if the price of low-value labor cannot be brought down to its value-in-production, then its value-in-production should be raised up to its price. In practice, however, this can seldom be done simply by teaching the worker new skills. What makes the kind of labor here under discussion valuable to the employer is usually not so much possession of skills (the ones needed are mostly manual and can be learned on the job by almost anyone who will try); rather, it is possession of certain qualities — reliability, motivation to learn, and adaptability to the demands of the work situation. Perhaps this fact helps to explain why the federal government's Manpower Development Training program has not achieved more.[51] Of course, even if training programs succeeded in making employees more productive, they would not make them more employable if their wages were made to rise even faster than their productivity; as was emphasized before, it is overpricing of labor that is the principal obstacle to its employment, and skilled labor, too, can be overpriced.

Another possibility — one that has natural appeal to small-city mayors and Chambers of Commerce — is to offer tax exemptions and other subsidies to induce factories to stay in the city or to move back to it from the suburbs. For this approach to work, the subsidies offered must be quite large — large enough, at least, to offset the added costs to the employer of using the overpriced labor and to make up for the loss of accessibility and the other advantages that would be gained by moving. As a practical matter, city governments are very rarely able to offer subsidies large enough to have much effect, which may be just as well anyway, since in the long run the city must adjust to becoming a center for services and exchanges rather than for the production of goods. To race for manufacturing jobs, says Wilbur R. Thompson in his *A Preface to Urban Economics*, is to swim against the current, especially if it is unskilled and semiskilled jobs that are sought.[52] Even so, it might cost the public less to subsidize the return of factories to the city than to support workers who are permanently unemployed. There is an important danger, however, that a job-creation program may attract more migrants from the rural South. Indeed, it is possible, as Kain and Persky have pointed out, that more migrants might come than there are jobs created, and unemployment in the city would actually increase.[53]

If there is a surplus of unskilled workers in the big cities, perhaps the thing to do is to assist them to move to places where their long-run prospects are better — from Harlem, say, to rural areas upstate or to the centers of space-age industry in Southern California. This idea seems plausible until one considers that in many places employment opportunities for the unskilled are even worse than they are in the big cities. It is hard to justify moving workers from Harlem until other workers whose job situations are even worse have been moved from, say, Appalachia. As a practical matter, moreover, it is often impossible to persuade workers to leave the city even when doing so would be to their material advantage.[54] People who have lived in a big city all their lives are apt to find a small one intolerably dull, and if, as is usually the case, they are accustomed to a neighborhood with a certain class and ethnic character, then another — even a "better" one — lacking this character may not suit them at all. Finally, an unpleasant fact must be taken into account: places to which the government might propose moving the workers would fight the idea tooth and nail, for the workers usually would be people whose income, class, and race (they would be Negroes in most cases) would make them unwelcome. Considering that the number of persons who might need relocation runs to many hundreds of thousands, government programs of this kind offer little hope.

A more practical approach is to make it easier for the unskilled or semiskilled worker living in the inner city to get to the suburban ring, where the new jobs are. At present, bus and train schedules are often better arranged to carry suburbanites to the city than to carry city workers to the suburbs. Most low-income city dwellers do not own automobiles, while public transportation to the suburbs is sometimes poor and frequently expensive. The study of employment in the "poverty areas" of fifty-one of the largest cities made in 1971 by the Census showed that about 20 percent of the employed persons worked outside of the city; of these, nearly 40 percent spent forty minutes or more getting to work. Of the workers who used public transportation, about 20 percent paid fares of fifty cents or more each way.[55]

Another way to improve the job situation of the unskilled (as was pointed out in Chapter Two, economists disagree as to its importance) would be to eliminate the barriers that discourage them from moving from the inner city to the suburban ring. The inner city is the focus of radial transportation lines extending in almost all directions to the outer perimeter of the metropolitan area. Therefore, casual workers — domestics, for example — generally find it the most logical place to reside. There are, however, some suburban areas where it would be advantageous for these workers to live, and if free to do so, many workers would move there from the inner city. They seldom are free to do so, however; in the name of health, safety, and the maintenance of local property values, suburban building codes and zoning regulations commonly set housing standards so high as in effect to exclude low-income people. If such standards were relaxed to allow use of the cheapest housing that can reasonably be called safe — mobile homes, for example — some unskilled workers would move to the suburbs rather than commute or (the only alternative for some) be unemployed or underemployed. All interferences with the freedom of workers to live where they please, whether in the inner city or in the suburban ring, tend to contribute to unemployment.

It must be recognized, however, that where there exists a large stock of relatively cheap housing in the inner city, and where it is relatively easy to commute from the inner city to the suburban ring, most unskilled workers will prefer to live in the inner city. Apart from housing and transportation, there is another consideration: Negroes (like members of other minority groups) will not in general move to places where they will be cut off from the social life of their group. Once enough families to constitute a "critical mass" have moved to a particular place, the growth of population there may be very rapid; establishing the critical mass presents a real difficulty, however.

Eventually, the logic of metropolitan growth will of itself cause the low-earner to move to the suburban ring. As always, he will replace the well-off, who themselves will be moving still farther out, leaving behind housing better than that which the low-earners presently occupy. As was pointed out in Chapter Two, many suburbs built after the war will be "downgraded" and ready for occupancy by the not well-off in the next decade or two. In the meantime, of course, the older housing in the central city will be wearing out. That low-earning workers will eventually reach the suburban ring does not necessarily mean that they will find jobs, however. By the time they arrive, some factories will have moved still farther out. Moreover, many jobs will have been eliminated altogether by suburban employers who could not wait for workers to arrive.

The discussion so far has proceeded on the assumptions of the "queue" theory that was introduced on page 104. The remainder of the chapter will be based upon an alternative theory, developed by Michael J. Piore, the policy implications of which are altogether different.[56]

The "dual market" theory distinguishes a "primary" from a "secondary" labor market. In the primary market wages are high, working conditions are good, employment is stable, employees have chances to advance, and work rules are administered equitably. In the secondary market, by contrast, wages and working conditions are poor, workers are always in danger of being laid off, there are few if any chances of advancement, and work rules are administered arbitrarily. "Disadvantaged" workers find jobs only in the secondary market.

Insofar as the exclusion of secondary workers from the primary market is based on something other than race, class, or sex discrimination, the cause is usually their inability to show up for work regularly and on time. Lack of work skills may be a contributing factor, but the essential problem is that the life style of the worker is not compatible with the requirements of the primary market. "Leisure time in low-income neighborhoods," Doeringer and Piore explain, "is frequently dominated by street-corner life, a life-style widely prevalent among low-income people in general and the black ghettos in particular. For the individual attached to the street, status and position in the world are defined by his group. His life has reality only in a group context; divorced from the group he is lonely and lost. The goal of group life is constant excitement. Its behavior is episodic; an endless period of 'hanging around,' punctuated by short adventures undertaken by the group as a whole or by individuals. Life thus tends to be immediate and sensational; past adventures are continually recalled, and the future is not anticipated."[57]

Workers who have the traits implied by this life style are not acceptable in the primary market. Those who come to work late, talk back to foremen, are careless with equipment, or pilfer supplies lose their jobs: there is no place in the primary market for workers who cannot, or will not, accept the discipline of the shop. In the secondary market, however, such behavior is taken for granted. The employee need accept very little discipline. He may get away with being late for work, tipsy on the job, and even with a certain amount of pilferage. Because he is less productive and more costly, he is, of course, paid less than he otherwise would be. And because the employer does not expect him to stay long, he makes no investment in his training.

As this suggests, the instability of both worker and job interact and, in doing so, reinforce one another. The job has been adapted to the life style of the worker, but the life style of the worker has also been adapted to the job. Knowing that he will be poorly paid and have no job security and knowing too that he can get away with being late and otherwise undependable, the worker is encouraged in — or at least not discouraged from — the pattern of behavior that confines him to the secondary market.

The "dual market" theory explains — what the "queue" theory does not — why, even in periods of high employment, many workers are not offered steady and well-paying jobs. It also explains something about the nature of unemployment among the "disadvantaged."

There is no lack of jobs in the secondary market; unemployment among secondary workers is mostly voluntary and temporary; they frequently move from one job to another, from work to public assistance or "the hustle," and then back to work. Their problem is not inability to find a job but inability to find — and keep — a "good" job, meaning one in the primary market.

From the standpoint of policy, there are two possible approaches to the situation. One is to change the secondary worker — or the employer's perception of him — so as to make him employable in the primary market. The other is to improve the secondary job — raise wages, give training, offer chances of advancement.

Federal manpower programs have followed the first approach. Some have tried to change workers' traits and others to increase their skills, but none has had much success with secondary workers. Allowing for exceptions, these workers have merely been circulated from one secondary job to another.[58]

The other approach — conversion of secondary jobs into primary ones — has not been attempted. Doeringer and Piore say that it is "probably possible to stabilize most — but not all — secondary jobs and build into them the career ladders, skill levels, and wage rates characteristic of primary jobs."[59] (This in fact happened to a considerable extent, they say, with longshoring and unskilled construction work since the Second War). Raising the minimum wage, although objectionable on other grounds, would contribute to this, but the most successful instruments, Doeringer and Piore believe, would probably be ones that would operate indirectly — for example, changes in social security and workmen's compensation laws, a tax on labor turnover, and the enforcement of anti-discrimination legislation.

In *Education, Training and the Urban Ghetto*, Bennett Harrison contends that "planned job development" should be "the central program element in a strategy to reduce urban blight, poverty, underemployment, and pathology."[60] The focus of effort, he says, should be to get employers to offer good wages, training, and chances of advancement to workers in the secondary labor market. He would have the federal government give capital subsidies to secondary employers in order to facilitate the "upgrading" of jobs and he would also have a much-enlarged program of public employment. The large cities, he says, could employ hundreds of thousands more of the poor, especially if they relaxed unreasonable hiring standards such as those which make persons with arrest records ineligible for jobs. Local government jobs, he points out, pay from one to three times more than "ghetto" families earn in the secondary market.[61]

Such policy prescriptions overlook, or take little account of, the characteristics of both the secondary worker and the secondary job — characteristics that (as Harrison observes) seem to benefit both workers and firms.[62] If the undesirable features of the job are part of an adaptation to the life style of the worker, it is hard to see how they can be much changed unless the life style of the worker is changed first. Even under favorable circumstances this is likely to be a slow process, uncertain in its outcome. "The problem of instability and poor work habits among adult workers," Doeringer and Piore write, "has generally evaded solution."[63]

To such objections it may be responded that if sufficiently good jobs are offered by employers who make a serious and sustained effort to recruit from the secondary market and who allow the recruits a reasonable period of time in which to adapt to the requirements of their new situation, a considerable number of the workers — although of course not all — will make the transition successfully. This is certainly plausible, but problems remain. Even though subsidized, an employer may not be able to meet his competition (perhaps from a "tertiary" labor market abroad) if the habits of the workers recruited from the secondary market change too slowly. Presumably public employment would impose a looser discipline than private and would also allow the worker a longer period to adjust. It is far from clear, however, that the political reality in most places is such as would permit employment of a considerable number of additional workers who, by the standards applied to incumbents and by comparison with other applicants, did not qualify for "good" jobs. It may be indicative of these realities that the unreasonable hiring standards which Harrison deplores are more common in public than in private employment.[64]

If local governments, acting as employers of last resort, were to offer jobs considerably better than those now available to secondary workers, many primary as well as secondary workers would want them. If all applicants were employed, the costs would be huge and the transfer of workers from private to public employment would exert a strong inflationary pressure.[65] As a practical matter, however, appropriations would never suffice to employ *all* applicants, and in all likelihood many, if not most, of the jobs would go to workers whose opportunities were relatively good to begin with. The most "disadvantaged," it is safe to say, would stand jobless at the end of the public queue.

Nevertheless, a case can be made for subsidized employment on a limited scale.[66] The special task force of the Department of Health, Education, and Welfare which prepared *Work in America*, while acknowledging "the sad truth . . . that for some we can expect nothing more than low-level employment," concluded that a guaranteed job program would do more to strengthen the family and reduce dependency than a guaranteed income program. Assuring opportunity for the central provider to work full-time at a living wage, the report says, "should be the first goal of public policy."[67] William Fellner, in a paper published just before his appointment to the Council of Economic Advisers, recommended subsidies for workers (presumably heads of families) whose prolonged unemployment would entail hardship. Subsidized employment, he remarked, is preferable to subsidized idleness by means of 'welfare' type payments.[68] John Kain, in testimony before the Joint Economic Committee, proposed that employers hiring workers certified by the employment service to have been unemployed for a long period receive an hourly cash subsidy — the longer the period of unemployment the larger the subsidy.[69] The reader will recall that, according to a Census report cited in Chapter One, there were in 1970 only 82,000 persons in the "poverty areas" of the 51 largest cities who had been unemployed as long as six months. That this "hard core" unemployment problem in the cities is small in terms of numbers of people does not mean that it is easily solved, however. Quite possibly many of the workers in question would remain unemployed even if employers were enabled to pay them high wages at public expense.

CHAPTER SIX

Several Kinds of Poverty

A condition of chronic poverty is developing in the Jewish community of New York that is appalling in its immensity. Forty-five percent of our applicants, representing between twenty thousand and twenty-five thousand human beings, have been in the United States over five years; have been given the opportunities for economic and industrial improvement which this country affords; yet, notwithstanding all this, have not managed to reach a position of economic independence.

— United Hebrew Charities,
Annual Report for 1901

T HE city, far from being a cause of poverty, has proved to be a remarkably efficient machine for transforming it into prosperity and even affluence. For many generations the world's "wretched refuse" (as the inscription on the Statue of Liberty puts it) has been coming to live in the city. One would expect that after so many years of immigration, incomes in the city would be much lower than anywhere else. In fact, the median money income of families and unrelated individuals is about the same in the central cities of the large (over one million population) metropolitan areas as in the United States as a whole ($10,100 as against $10,285 in 1971), although considerably less, of course, than in the suburban fringes ($12,696 in 1971).

The city's remarkable performance would be even more clearly evident if, so to speak, the books were kept on a more meaningful basis — if the city were credited with the incomes of all persons brought up in it and not debited with those of persons who grew up elsewhere. By counting the millions of suburbanites who attended city schools and got their feet on the first rung of the occupational ladder in the city and by omitting the other millions of persons of farm and rural origins, whose earning capacity was already largely fixed when they migrated, the city's role as destroyer of poverty and creator of wealth would be dramatically revealed.

The city attracts the poor — especially poor parents with numerous children — by offering better conditions of life — better food, clothing, shelter, health care, schools, and treatment from employers and officials; this is why it always has so many poor.[1] The problem of poverty in the cities is seldom of the cities' own making; it is essentially a problem made elsewhere and then brought to the city. Rural migrants who move to cities, especially large ones, reap substantial economic gains. Typically the migrant's earnings are much less before his move than are those of city-born persons of the same race, age, sex, and education, but it takes him only about five years to catch up.[2]

A federal interagency committee in 1969 adopted a "poverty index" reflecting various consumption requirements of families based on family size, sex and age of family head, number of children, and farm-nonfarm residence. Each year, after taking into account changes in the Consumer Price Index, a poverty line ("low income threshold") is derived from the index. In 1972 the poverty line was $4,275 for a nonfarm family of four and 24.5 million Americans were considered poor. Of these, 3.8 million lived in central cities where they comprised 16 percent of the population and 2.3 million lived in suburbs (strictly speaking, outside of central cities but within metropolitan areas) where they comprised 8 percent of the population. Poverty was disproportionately frequent among Negroes, the old, and persons not members of households ("unrelated individuals," in Census terminology).[3]

There is no doubt that these figures considerably exaggerate both the number of persons having low incomes and the lowness of their incomes. People in general have a tendency to underreport their incomes either because they do not remember accurately what they receive or do not tell the truth about it. (The Current Population Survey finds public assistance payments underreported by at least one-fourth and income from property by more than one-half. Also, there is reason to believe that if income from illegal activities were reported, a considerable percentage of the "poor" in some of the large cities would turn out to be well-off).[4] Even when properly reported, the official figures misrepresent the situation, for only *money* income is counted and most of the poor now receive substantial amounts of income in kind — for example, food stamps, housing, and Medicaid. Moreover, every survey catches some people when they are receiving less than their normal income. (Thus, in 1960 it was found that in the large cities consumers with incomes under $1,000 were spending $224 for every $100 of income and those with incomes from $2,000 to $3,000 were spending $116.)[5] If incomes were measured over a two-year period there would be many fewer poor. Turnover among the poor is rapid: one-third per year.

There are also sizable differences in the cost of living from one city to another: an income of $3,000 will buy as much in a small city as will, say, $2,500 in a large one, which means that the number of the poor may be understated in large cities and overstated in small ones. Most people who live in large cities would prefer to live in smaller ones; therefore some of what they earn is really compensation not for work but for putting up with the unpleasantnesses that they find in big-city life.[6] Obviously the drawing of a poverty line involves making a good many rather subjective judgments. One economist, using the same figures as the Council of Economic Advisers, cut its estimate of the amount of poverty in half — from 20 percent of the population to 10 percent.[7]

A more fundamental question concerns the *definition* of poverty. According to the dictionary, "poverty" is lack of money or material possessions. But how severe a lack? *How* poor is "poor"?

For present purposes, it will be useful to distinguish four degrees of poverty: *destitution,* which is lack of income sufficient to assure physical survival and to prevent suffering from hunger, exposure, or remediable or preventable illness; *want*, which is lack of enough income to support "essential welfare" (as distinguished from comfort and convenience); *hardship*, which is lack of enough to prevent acute, persistent discomfort or inconvenience. In addition, a term will be used to designate a kind, as opposed to degree, of poverty: *relative deprivation* is lack of enough income, status, or whatever else may be valued to prevent one from feeling poor in comparison to others.

The official poverty line obviously does not refer to destitution, although even half a century ago destitution was not uncommon. (It was estimated that in New York at the turn of the century, one person in ten was buried in Potter's Field — an indication of widespread distress, since "lying in a pauper's grave" was a disgrace most people would make almost any sacrifice to avoid.[8]) Today, however, it is probably safe to say that no one in the city is destitute. Many persons still suffer from hunger, exposure, or illness but lack of income is not the cause, or at any rate not the proximate cause, of their suffering. A cultural (or other) incapacity to make use of income is a different matter from lack of income, and destitution (as defined here) has to do with income.[9]

One might suppose, then, that the poverty line refers to want. The Council implies this by characterizing the poor as "those who are not now maintaining a *decent* standard of living — those whose basic needs exceed their means to satisfy them."[10] It is very difficult to specify, even for food, the minimum "bundle" of goods necessary to support essential welfare. It is impossible to state precisely the indispensable material prerequisites of individual happiness and social well-being. However, although the contents of the bundle might vary a good deal from one country to another and from one age to another, within a given culture and a given age the variations would not be very great. "Basic needs" do not change much from one generation to the next (if they do, they are not "basic"!); neither does a culture's idea of what constitutes a "decent," worthy, respectable, etc., mode of life. Therefore, want can be defined by a standard that changes so slowly as to be for all practical purposes fixed. One laid down by Alfred Marshall almost a century ago will serve rather well today:

The necessaries for the efficiency of an ordinary agricultural or of an unskilled town laborer and his family, in England, in this generation, may be said to consist of a well-drained dwelling with several rooms, warm clothing, with some changes of underclothing, pure water, a plentiful supply of cereal food, with a moderate allowance of meat and milk, and a little tea, etc., some education, and some recreation, and lastly, sufficient freedom for his wife from other work to enable her to perform properly her maternal and household duties.[11]

Measured by this standard, or by one anything like it, the amount of want in the city has been steadily reduced decade by decade for at least a century. There was still considerable want twenty or thirty years ago, but today there is very little. Within another few decades there will almost certainly be none. If no one goes hungry, very few have (for reasons of income) diets that are nutritionally inadequate; as long ago as 1955 the poorest third of city dwellers' average consumption exceeded the National Research Council's recommended dietary allowances for eight of nine nutrients:[12]

	Recommended allowance per adult male [a]	Nutritive value of diets of lowest income third in cities, per person per day, 1955 [b]
Energy value — cals.	2,900	2,910
Protein grams	70	94
Calcium grams	.8	1.00
Iron (milligrams)	10	16.4
Vit. A value I.U.	5,000	8,700
Thiamine	1.2	1.42
Riboflavin	1.7	2.04
Niacin	19.0	17.4
Ascorbic acid	70.0	94.0

[a] National Research Council, Food and Nutrition Board, *Recommended Dietary Allowances*, 6th revised edition, 1964.

[b] U.S. Department of Agriculture, *Dietary Evaluation of Food Used in Households in the United States* (Household Food Consumption Survey, 1955), Report #16, Table 19, p. 30.

Almost everyone has enough warm clothing; few people live in housing that is greatly overcrowded, structurally unsafe, or otherwise injurious to essential welfare; all children can have not only a high school education but (assuming that the Basic Opportunity Grant program passed by Congress in 1972 is fully implemented) higher education as well; books and records are easily obtainable (one can buy almost any book of general interest, including all the classics, for the price of a couple of packages of cigarettes); every city has a public library and the larger ones also have museums, art galleries, adult-education classes, and so on.

About health in the city it is somewhat harder to generalize.[13] The distribution of most important diseases seems to have nothing to do with income. Occupationally caused injuries are probably more frequent on lower-paid jobs; these tend to result from conditions not obvious to an observer, such as stress or repetitive work, rather than from well-defined hazards like dust, presumably because safety precautions are normally taken when hazards are identified. Probably because their ailments more often interfere with their daily activities, the poor more often than others perceive themselves as ill, something that probably results in a higher rate of reporting of their illnesses. But although the poor are more aware of their ailments, they are also more likely to delay going to a physician or hospital until a condition has become serious, the result being that their chances of complete recovery are poorer. Neither income nor education has more than a very minor role in the likelihood of disability (however, factors correlated with income, especially the characteristics of jobs, have an important influence); the single most important factor in determining the overall disability rate is residence in a rural area.[14]

In general the amount and quality of health care received by the poor are good. Even before the establishment of Medicaid, the publicly financed program of health care for the poor, low-income families were getting as much hospital care as higher income ones, and there is now hardly any relation between income and use of physician's services. A national survey in 1970 for the Department of Health, Education, and Welfare showed that in central cities low-income residents aged 18 to 64 were slightly more likely to have seen a physician in the survey year than were others in that age group. Low-income children and the low-income aged in the central cities saw physicians somewhat less often than did higher income persons in their age groups, but this reflected household demand rather than inability to obtain the service.[15]

The poor make more use of public clinics than do others, and most clinics give competent diagnoses and treatment for specific complaints, although their atmosphere — hurried, impersonal, and bureaucratic — tends to discourage treatment that goes beyond a specific complaint.[17] Clinic treatment, however, is a minor part of the total received by the poor: three-fourths of their contacts are with private physicians at home or in the physician's office — the same

Persons Hospitalized per 1,000 Population, 1968[16]	
Low income (under $5,000)	114.5
Middle income ($5,000–$9,999)	95.4
High income (over $10,000)	81.8

Physician Visits per Capita, 1969	
Low income (under $5,000)	4.6
Middle income ($5,000–$9,999)	4.0
High income (over $10,000)	4.3

proportion, incidentally, as among the well-off. About the quality of the care provided for the poor it is of course hard to judge. Measured by one indicator — the use of specialists — the poor are less well served; however, there is reason to believe that schooling has as much to do with this as does income. Another indicator — infant mortality — shows no consistent relationship between income and mortality in white families when parents' schooling is taken into account; in black families, *both* income and schooling appear to make a difference.

Contrary to what one might expect, the health of the poor does not show a marked improvement when as much, or even more, is spent on it than on the health of the better-off.[18] This may be explained in part by the fact that even good medical care has less effect on health than is generally supposed. (Environmental factors have more influence on mortality rates than does medical care; if education and expenditure on medical care are held constant, the higher the income the higher the mortality rate.[19]) Life styles associated with income — and probably more significantly with schooling — profoundly influence health. Diet, number and spacing of children, and accident proneness, for example, are all affected by life style and all in turn affect health. "Health services, no matter how effective," an authority concludes, "cannot solve the problems of the impoverished slum dweller."[20] By way of illustration he cites the inability of visiting public health nurses to persuade Puerto Rican mothers to bring their preschool children to child-health clinics. Another observes that a high proportion of indigent Negro mothers are "walk-ins" who have babies — often underweight and retarded — without having availed themselves of prenatal instruction or care.[21]

Although the poor are in better health and receive more and better health care than is generally supposed, the consequences of serious illness are clearly much worse for them than for others. Medicare, Medicaid, and other federal medical benefits to people in families with incomes under $5,000 amounted to about $6.5 billion in 1970 (somewhat less than half of the total of all such benefits),[22] but although these benefits cover most out-of-pocket costs of illness, loss of work days and restriction in work activities entail a larger proportional loss to the poor than to the well-off. With all out-of-pocket costs met from public subsidies, illness or premature death may nevertheless impoverish a family. In view of this, health programs may be less useful in relieving the consequences of poor health among the poor than would vocational rehabilitation or cash transfers of income.

If one is willing to live just above the level of want — that is, having enough for essential welfare but not enough to avoid hardship — one can do so now with little effort. In Marshall's time the unskilled laborer had to work from dawn to dusk merely to escape destitution. Today, because of economic progress, technological improvement, and various welfare measures, an unskilled laborer is not likely to suffer want if he works only a few hours a day and he may not suffer it if he does not work at all.

Most of those classified by the Council of Economic Advisers as poor do not experience want. Their poverty may entail hardship, but it does not entail serious injury. They can afford nutritionally adequate diets but not the better cuts of meat; their clothing is warm and plentiful but not "the latest thing"; their housing keeps out the rain and the cold, but the bath is down the hall; their children can finish high school, but they cannot go to college unless they are good scholars or athletes; they will usually be adequately cared for in case of illness — especially in case of *serious* illness — if they are willing to avail themselves of the services and facilities that are available to them.

Most of those who report incomes below the poverty line are not undergoing hardship — not, at any rate, because of poverty. Among households with incomes under $5,000 in metropolitan areas in 1971, 42 percent owned their homes, half owned at least one car, nearly 90 percent at least one television set (11 percent of the sets being color ones), 75 percent had a washing machine, 27 percent a clothes dryer, 22 percent a freezer, and 21 percent air conditioning in at least one room.[23]

Discomfort and inconvenience, real as they are for a great many people, are probably not the most frequent or important elements in what is generally experienced as poverty. Having less than others may make one appear — and feel — poor even if one is well-off by any objective standard. This sort of poverty is not new, of course. Karl Marx remarked upon it: "A house may be large or small; as long as the surrounding houses are equally small it satisfies all social demands for a dwelling. But if a palace arises beside the little house, the little house shrinks into a hut."[24] To a considerable extent, the present-day "poverty problem" is of this sort; houses have shrunk into huts and other things have shrunk also. In short, the problem is less one of income *level* than of income *distribution*. As Victor R. Fuchs explains:

> By the standards that have prevailed over most of history, and still prevail over large areas of the world, there are very few poor in the United States today. Nevertheless, there are millions of American families who, both in their own eyes and in those of others, are poor. As our nation prospers, our judgment as to what constitutes poverty will inevitably change. *When we talk about poverty in America, we are talking about families and individuals who have much less income than most of us. When we talk about reducing or eliminating poverty, we are really talking about changing the distribution of income* [italics added].[25]

Fuchs goes on to define as poor "any family whose income is less than one-half the median family income." By this standard, which refers to relative rather than absolute deprivation, the number of poor people — 36 million — was the same in 1971 as in 1963.[26] It should be kept in mind, however, that *in principle* the number of poor so defined could actually increase even if everyone were well above what is usually meant by the poverty line. That the *relative* position of the lowest-income group has not improved is a significant fact, but it is to be accounted for not by the continued distress of some so much as by the rapid rise of others into the larger proportion of skilled and demanding jobs that are an inevitable accompaniment of rapid economic growth.

On first impression the poverty problem may not seem very difficult to solve. Even if no special measures are taken, the amount of poverty (in the sense of incomes below the poverty line as now officially defined) will gradually decrease until twenty-five to fifty years hence there will very likely be none at all.[27] If one is unwilling to wait that long, all that is necessary (so it may seem) is to redistribute income: in a society as affluent as ours there will be enough for everyone if the total is distributed properly.

There are essentially two ways of redistributing income. The first, which is altogether preferable so far as it goes, is to increase the productivity and earning power of those who are poor. This might be done by measures some of which have already been discussed — maintaining a very high level of employment, pricing labor at what it is worth so that all of it will be employed, improving workers' skills, health, and geographical mobility, and ending discrimination in jobs (and, of course, in housing) on grounds of race, age, sex, class, amount of schooling, or whatever.

These measures, however, would not eliminate poverty no matter how far they were carried; their direct and main effect is on *employable* persons and, although nearly three-fourths of all poor families have at least one earner, many cannot possibly be affected by changes in the job market. The poor always include disproportionate numbers of the old, young, disabled, mothers with dependent children, and members of certain minority groups. The amount of poverty at any given time therefore depends to a considerable extent upon the proportion of dependent people in the population — which is to say, upon the operation of long-term demographic trends. From 1900 to 1940, for example, the dependency ratio (persons under age fifteen or over sixty-five per hundred of all others) fell sharply (from 62.6 to 46.8), in the next twenty years rose sharply (to 67.6), and has since declined and is expected to remain fairly constant (at 55 to 60) to the year 2000.[28]

The other way of redistributing income is by "transfer payments" — that is, by taxing some and giving to others. This, of course, is done on a large scale: federal spending on social welfare programs amounted to an estimated $101.7 billion in 1973, almost 40 percent of all federal expenditures. Most transfer programs, however, were not intended to relieve poverty (unemployment insurance and old-age retirement, for example, were enacted on the assumption that most people would normally earn enough to keep out of poverty), and in 1966, the year for which figures are most nearly up to date, only about half of all benefits went to the poor. These brought slightly more than half of the aged (over sixty-five) poor above the poverty line but only 19 percent of the others; of families headed by non-white women, 62 percent remained poor after the transfers.[29]

A method of transferring income that is simpler and would reach the poor and only the poor is the "negative income tax." This plan, which economists all along the political spectrum have endorsed, calls for all families ("income units") to file federal income tax returns; those reporting incomes below the poverty line would then receive a payment from the government to make up part or (if the rate schedule were sufficiently generous) all of the deficiency. In the view of Milton Friedman, the first active promoter of the idea, all the poor could be brought above the poverty line with total transfer payments much smaller than those presently made, provided that few people stopped working once they were assured of some minimum income and provided that the negative income tax were regarded as a substitute for, not an addition to, most existing welfare programs. In his opinion, the savings would amount to more than twice the cost of the negative income tax itself. The plan has the added advantages, he argues, of minimizing interference in the allocation of resources by the market and of making explicit the cost of transfers to any particular income group.[30]

In 1969 the Administration proposed a Family Assistance Plan (FAP) which was to begin with (complications were introduced in the course of the effort to get it through Congress) essentially a negative income tax, albeit one limited to families with children.[31] Under the plan as first proposed, a family of four would be guaranteed an income of $1,500 per year; this would increase with family size ($450 per adult and $300 per child) up to a family of seven, which would be guaranteed $2,400. For every $1 of earnings or other income that the family received, its payment would be reduced by 50 cents. Thus a family of four with an income of more than $3,000 would get no payment whereas one of seven with an income of $4,000 would get $700. Although the House accepted FAP, the Senate did not. A revised proposal was reintroduced in the Ninety-second Congress, but it also failed in the Senate. In 1972 Congress did, however, enact a guaranteed annual income for the disabled, the aged, and the blind.

All methods of redistributing income by transfer payments are open, although not in the same degree, to the objection that they may weaken (or destroy) incentives that are desirable in the interest of the individual and of the society and may strengthen (or create) others that are no less undesirable. No one knows, for example, what the effect of a guaranteed family income may be on the willingness of people not only to work but also to save, to learn new skills, and in general to make provision for the future. Even the most carefully controlled experiments will not yield reliable predictions of these effects if for no other reason because the effects will not all be apparent until a new generation has grown up under the new circumstances. As Michael K. Taussig has pointed out, the United States has had more than thirty years of experience with the programs enacted in the Social Security Act of 1935; two of these, Aid to Families with Dependent Children and Old Age Assistance, have, he remarks, "apparently financed a dramatic revolution in the American family structure" and have led to the "isolation of new, virtually separate subsocieties" (he refers to persons aged sixty-five or more and to mothers with dependent children, most of whom are black). Is it likely, he asks, that well-designed experiments before 1935 would have predicted these effects? Taussig's answer is: No.[32]

On theoretical grounds, one would expect the disincentive effects of a guaranteed family income to be of increasing importance as one moves from the high to the low end of the class-cultural scale. Upper- and upper-middle-class people often find intrinsic satisfaction in their work. To them work is a means of self-improvement, self-expression, and "service"; sometimes it is "exciting," "fun," "a game." Such satisfactions exist, but to a relatively small degree, in the work of the lower-middle and the upper-working classes. For the lower-working class they amount to very little: in this subculture, one works only because one has to. In the lower class, work is most dissatisfying because of the discipline it entails; the lower-class person prefers near-destitution without work to relative abundance with it. The evidence (such as it is) seems to confirm these expectations. High-income earners have been found not to be — up to now at least — much deterred by the prospect of higher taxes.[33] On the other hand, some low-income earners seem to be very sensitive to disincentives. That they will not work when welfare payments are as much or more than they could earn is to be expected, of course. However, it also appears that many poor persons will not put forth effort to get "extras" once they have been assured of a level of living which, while extremely low, seems to them to be "enough."

The higher the floor that is put under incomes, the greater the number of workers who will see no reason to work.[34] A minimum income at or slightly above the present poverty line might induce many working- and middle-class people to lower substantially their level of living for the sake of not working. To the extent that living standards are thus reduced, the cost of eliminating poverty will be tremendously increased; conceivably, it may be more than even a very rich society can afford.

It may seem possible to avoid the disincentive problem merely by refusing to give a minimum income to anyone able to work. Most of the poor would still qualify, since a large majority are in families headed by mothers, or by persons disabled or too old to work. The difficulty, however, is that it would be outrageously unfair to give generous support to dependent families while supporting meagerly or not at all families — including about 30 percent of the poor — in which the head works full time. There is, as a recent Brookings Institution report points out,

the problem of balancing work incentives for those who are able to work against the needs of those who cannot. A guarantee level that is adequate to the needs of those who cannot work may tempt some workers to drop out of the labor force or at least to reduce their effort. Allowing people to keep a sizable fraction of their earnings should encourage work, but it also means that benefits go to people with substantial earnings, which sharply increases the cost of the program. For example, if the guarantee was $4,000 and benefits were reduced only by one dollar for each three dollars earned, families with incomes up to $12,000 would get some benefits.[35]

Why, it may be asked, should anyone care — so long as society can afford it — if many able-bodied people are supported at some minimum-acceptable level of living without their having to work or to worry about the future? That it is unfair for some to "ride free" at the expense of others is one answer to this question but a rather minor one. (It must be remembered, too, that if it is unfair for the poor to live without working, it is also unfair for the rich to do so — more so, in fact, since they live better.) Another answer is that the level of living of those accepting the minimum will almost certainly be lower than it otherwise would be and lower than is socially desirable.

The major lesson in the British experience seems to be that flatrate schemes, whatever the original intention, end up at the subsistence level, forcing the system to depend on a combination of insurance and welfare.[36]

Still another consideration is that, generally speaking, the experience of not working and not taking responsibility for oneself and for one's family's welfare weakens not only personal character and happiness but also the family itself and perhaps other institutions upon which the welfare of society depends.[37] Indeed, it is arguable that *any* income maintenance scheme will offer incentives both to have more children[38] and to split up families.[39]

A serious difficulty exists insofar as it is relative deprivation that constitutes poverty. It is usually assumed that only *great* inequalities of income make people feel poor in this sense. Victor R. Fuchs, in the article that was cited above, assumes that if all incomes were brought up to at least half the median income no one would be thought poor. It is certainly conceivable, however, that even then people with incomes below, say, three-fourths of the median might seem — to themselves or to others — as poor as those with incomes under half the median used to seem. In principle, the subjective significance of income differences may increase steadily while the objective size of the differences decreases; this process may continue right up to the point (assuming that there is one in some meaningful sense) of income equality. In other words, it is at least possible that the closer they come to income equality the more acutely dissatisfied people with relatively low incomes may feel on account of such differences as remain.

This possibility is not as remote as it may seem. The poor today are not "objectively" any more deprived relative to the nonpoor than they were a decade ago. Few will doubt, however, that they *feel* more deprived — that they perceive the gap to be wider and that, this being the case, it *is* wider in the sense that matters most. By constantly calling attention to income differences, the War on Poverty probably engendered and strengthened feelings of relative deprivation. This subjective effect may have more than offset whatever objective reduction occurred in income inequality.

Finally, it may be that poverty in the sense of relative deprivation is only incidentally related to a lack of material things, and that therefore even "equality" of income (whatever that may mean) would leave as many people "poor" — i.e., feeling deprived — as before. This conclusion is implied by some of David Caplovitz's comments on the behavior of the low-income consumers he studied. They bought console phonographs, color television sets, and so on, he says, in order to "embellish" their social status; having failed to move up the social ladder, they "compensated" by climbing symbolically through consumption of such things.[40] If he is right, no amount of income redistribution can reduce, much less eliminate, their poverty: it consists not of lack of income, but of lack of *status*. Indeed, the more far-reaching the income redistribution, the more painfully apparent it may become that such symbols as color television sets cannot provide "real" status. If what the poor really want is a reduction of the extremes of status inequality, then income redistribution, however comprehensive, cannot help much. If they want the elimination of *all* status differences, then nothing can help. "Poverty," writes Lester C. Thurow, "is a dispersion or variance, problem; thus, it falls into the category of economic problems for which there is no known solution."[41]

There is another kind of poverty, however. Robert Hunter described it in 1904:

> They lived in God only knows what misery. They ate when there were things to eat; they starved when there was lack of food. But, on the whole, although they swore and beat each other and got drunk, they were more contented than any other class I have happened to know. It took a long time to understand them. Our Committees were busy from morning until night in giving them opportunities to take up the fight again, and to become independent of relief. They always took what we gave them; they always promised to try; but as soon as we expected them to fulfill any promises, they gave up in despair, and either wept or looked ashamed, and took to misery and drink again, — almost, so it seemed to me at times, with a sense of relief.[42]

In Hunter's day these were the "undeserving," "unworthy," "depraved," "debased," or "disreputable" poor; today, they are the "troubled," "culturally deprived," "hard to reach," "chronically," or "multiproblem."[43] This sort of poverty reflects not only lack of money but also, and especially, the pattern of tastes, attitudes, and habits that, according to the hypothesis advanced in Chapter Three, results from extreme present-orientation and is the life style of the lower class.

Outside of this lower class, poverty in the sense of hardship, want, or destitution is nowadays almost always the result of external circumstances — involuntary unemployment, prolonged illness, the death of a breadwinner, or some other misfortune. Even when severe, such poverty is not squalid or degrading. Moreover, it ends quickly once the (external) cause of it no longer exists. Public or private assistance can sometimes remove or alleviate the cause — for example, by job retraining or remedial surgery. Even when the cause cannot be removed, simply providing the nonlower-class poor with sufficient income is enough to enable them to live "decently."

Lower-class poverty, by contrast, has as its proximate (but, as has been stressed, not its remote or ultimate) cause ways of thinking and behaving that are, in the adult, if not elements built into personality, at least more or less deeply ingrained habits. In large degree it is "inwardly" caused, and improvements in external circumstances are likely to affect it gradually if at all.[44] Poverty of this type tends to be self-perpetuating: one problem of a "multiproblem" family is no sooner solved than another arises. In principle, it is possible to eliminate the poverty (material lack) of such a family, but only at great expense, since the capacity of the radically improvident to waste money is almost unlimited. Raising such a family's income would not necessarily improve its way of life, moreover, and could conceivably even make things worse. Consider, for example, the H. Family:

Mrs. H. seemed overwhelmed with the simple mechanics of dressing her six children and washing their clothes. The younger ones were running around in their underwear; the older ones were unaccounted for, but presumably were around the neighborhood. Mrs. H. had not been out of the house for several months; evidently her husband did the shopping. The apartment was filthy and it smelled. Mrs. H. was dressed in a bathrobe, although it was mid-afternoon. She seemed to have no plan or expectations with regard to the children; she did not know the names of their teachers and she did not seem to worry about their school work, although one child had been retained one year and another two years. Mrs. H. did seem to be somewhat concerned about her husband's lack of activity over the weekend — his continuous drinking and watching baseball on television. Apparently he and she never went out socially together nor did the family ever go anywhere as a unit.[45]

If this family had a very high income — say, $50,000 a year — it would not be considered a "culture of poverty" case. Mrs. H. would hire maids to look after the small children, send the others to boarding schools, and spend her time at fashion shows while her husband drank and watched TV at his club. But with an income of only moderate size — say 100 percent above the poverty line — they would probably be about as badly off as they are now. They might be even worse off, for Mrs. H. would be able to go to the dog races, leaving the children alone, and Mr. H. could devote more time to his bottle and TV set.

Such families constitute a small proportion both of all families in the city (perhaps 5 percent at most[46]) and of those with incomes below the poverty line (perhaps 10 to 20 percent). The problems that they present are out of proportion to their numbers, however; in St. Paul, Minnesota, for example, a survey showed that 6 percent of the city's families absorbed 77 percent of its public assistance, 51 percent of its health services, and 56 percent of its mental health and correction casework services.[47] Moreover, their misery is (or at least seems) far greater than that of the other poor — the garbage-strewn, rat-infested hovels with toilets out of order are now almost exclusively theirs. Giving them income or services, even in rather larger amounts, is unlikely to reduce and may even increase their poverty.

Welfare agencies, recognizing the difference between "internally" and "externally" caused poverty, have long been trying first by one means and then another to improve the characters or, as it is now put, to "bring about personal adjustment" of the poor. In the nineteenth century, the view was widely held that what the lower-class individual needed was to be brought into a right relation with God or (the secular version of the same thing) with the respectable (that is, middle- and upper-class) elements of the community. The missionary who distributed tracts door to door in the slums was the first caseworker; his — more often, her — task was to minister to what today would be called "feelings of alienation."

The stranger, coming on a stranger's errand, becomes a friend, discharging the offices and exerting the influence of a friend. . . .[48]

Secularized, this approach became the "friendly visitor" system under which "certain persons, under the direction of a central board, pledge themselves to take one or more families who need counsel, if not material help, on their visiting list, and maintain personal friendly relations with them."[49] The system did not work; middle- and upper-class people might be "friendly," but they could not sympathize, let alone communicate, with the lower class. By the beginning of the twentieth century the friendly visitor had been replaced by the "expert."[50] The idea now was that the authority of "the facts" would bring about desired changes of attitude, motive, and habit. As it happened, however, the lower class did not recognize the authority of the facts. The expert then became a supervisor, using his (or her) power to confer or withhold material benefits in order to force the poor to do the things that were supposed to lead to "rehabilitation" (that is, to a middle-class style of life).[51] This method did not work either; the lower class could always find ways to defeat and exploit the system. They seldom changed their ways very much and they never changed them for long. Besides, there was really no body of expertise to tell caseworkers how to produce the changes desired. As one caseworker has remarked in a book addressed to fellow social service professionals:

> Despite years of experience in providing public aid to poor families precious little is yet known about how to help truly inadequate parents make long term improvements in child care, personal maturity, social relations, or work stability.[52]

Some people understood that if the individual's style of life was to be changed at all, it would be necessary to change that of the group that produced, motivated, and constrained him. Thus, the settlement house. As Robert A. Woods explained early in the present century:

> The settlements are able to take neighborhoods in cities, and by patience bring back to them much of the healthy village life, so that the people shall again know and care for one another. . . .[53]

When it became clear that settlement houses would not change the culture of slum neighborhoods, the group approach was broadened into what is called "community action." In one type of community action ("community development"), a community organizer tries to persuade a neighborhood's informal leaders to support measures (for instance, measures for delinquency control) that he advances.[54] In another form of it ("community organization"), the organizer tries to promote self-confidence, self-respect, and attachment to the group (and, hopefully, to normal society) among lower-class people. He attempts to do this by encouraging them in efforts at joint action, or by showing them how to conduct meetings, carry on discussions, pass resolutions, present requests to politicians, and the like. In still another form ("community mobilization"), the organizer endeavors to arouse the anger of lower-class persons against the local "power structure," to teach them the techniques of mass action — strikes, sit-ins, picketing, and so on — and to show them how they may capture power. The theory of community organization attributes the malaise of the poor to their lack of self-confidence (which is held to derive largely from their "inexperience"); community mobilization theory, by contrast, attributes it to their feelings of "powerlessness." According to this doctrine, the best cure for poverty is to give the poor power. But since power is not "given," it must be seized.[55]

The success of the group approach has been no greater than that of the caseworker approach. Reviewing five years of effort on the part of various community action programs, Marris and Rein conclude:

... the reforms had not evolved any reliable solutions to the intractable problems with which they struggled. They had not discovered how in general to override the intransigent autonomy of public and private agencies, at any level of government; nor how to use the social sciences practically to formulate and evaluate policy; nor how, under the sponsorship of government, to raise the power of the poor. Given the talent and money they had brought to bear, they had not even reopened very many opportunities.[56]

Later observations support these judgments. The Economic Opportunity Act of 1965 might require "maximum feasible participation" in the planning and conduct of programs financed under it, but the poor rarely cared to participate even to the extent of voting.[57] In Philadelphia, for example, there was a polling place in each of the twelve "poverty areas," and the Gas Works contributed twelve trucks and drivers to carry additional voting machines from block to block; the turnout, however, was only 5.5 percent of those eligible in 1966.[58] In five San Francisco Bay Area communities, those who were employed in the Community Action Program "gained experience and skills and many of the CAP participants improved their understanding, but there was widespread recognition among both groups in all communities that the hardcore and unaffiliated poor had really not been reached, nor did they benefit in any substantial way from the programs and services of the war on poverty."[59]

Even community mobilization, despite the advantages of a rhetoric of hate and an emphasis on "action," failed to involve lower-class persons to a significant extent.[60] Gangsters and leaders of youth gangs were co-opted on occasion; they did not suffer from feelings of powerlessness and were not representative of the class for which mobilization was to provide therapy — and what they did, in Chicago and New York, for example — was to terrorize and destroy.[61]

CHAPTER SEVEN

Schooling versus Education

DEAR ABBY: I took my freshman year over again and I am still a freshman. In other words, I failed everything again. I admit I fooled around the first time, but I really tried to make it this time, but the work was too hard for me. My parents don't believe me. They think I let them down, but I really tried my best.

I would like to quit school and go to a trade school, but my father says I have to graduate from high school if it takes me 10 years. What can I do?

— ASHAMED

T HE most widely recommended "solution" to the problems of the city is more and better schooling. There is almost nothing that someone does not hope to achieve by this means. City planners see it as a necessary and perhaps sufficient condition for bringing the middle class back into the city from the suburbs. Almost everyone (except economists) thinks that the unschooled will be unemployable in the automated society of the future and — a non sequitur — that schooling will prevent unemployment. Since it can be shown statistically that the least schooled have the lowest incomes, schooling is also thought to be a cure for poverty and thus, indirectly, for the slum and the "ghetto." A proper system of education, the HARYOU manual says, is "an inescapable foundation for the reality of respect and self-respect . . . and the basis for the type of vocational and academic adjustment essential for an effective life. . . ."[1]

Education is, of course, a good thing, and no society can have too much of it. What must be questioned, however, is whether "schooling" and "education" necessarily imply one another and, more particularly, whether the kind of schooling possible under existing circumstances — for instance, the intelligence of children, their class culture, the state of the art of teaching, the character of the teaching profession, and so on — is capable of producing the desired effects. The view to be taken in this chapter is that the possibilities for improving the city by reforming its schools are sharply limited. Even if the schools were to do much better those things that it is possible for them to do, the result would not change the main features of the situation in the city. Nothing that can be done in the schools of the central city can significantly affect the movement of the well-off to the suburbs or much reduce the amount of poverty or teen-age unemployment. Nothing done in them can provide that "inescapable foundation of respect and self-respect" which, according to the HARYOU manual, would reduce racial unrest and social disorganization in general. On the contrary, the reforms most likely to be made in the name of "education" — especially requiring more children to spend more time in school — may be expected to produce results exactly the opposite of those intended; that is, hasten the movement of the well-off from the city, increase unemployment and poverty, widen the chasms of class and race, and plunge deeper into apathy, or stir into fiercer anger, those already angry or apathetic.

There is little doubt that, in general, boys and girls who graduate from high school find better jobs and find them faster than do boys and girls who do not graduate from high school, or that those who have two or three years of high school find better jobs than those who have only one.[2] The more high school one has, the less unemployment one is likely to suffer in later life and the greater one's lifetime earnings are likely to be. Economists have calculated that on the average the individual who finishes high school gets a very high rate of return on his investment of time (represented by what he might earn if he went to work). Reviewing the growing body of economic studies, Theodore W. Schultz of the University of Chicago concludes that the private (as opposed to social) rate of return on investment in elementary and secondary schooling has been rising for several decades and is now "upwards of 100 percent" for elementary and close to 30 percent for secondary schooling (the high school data are for white, male graduates after personal taxes); for higher education (these data, too, are for white males), the rate of return has been constant over time at about 15 percent.[3] He points out that the figures are all biased downward in that they do not take any account of the personal — that is, nonincome-returning — satisfactions that people get from their schooling over the course of their lives.

Early studies along these lines dealt only with whites. When the 1960 Census made comparisons possible, it was reported that black males with very little schooling earned about one-fourth less than comparable whites and that black college graduates earned less than half as much as whites. Subsequently, a more discriminating analysis of the data by Finis Welch showed that while returns from schooling were indeed significantly lower for blacks who had entered the labor force in the 1930's and 1940's they were significantly *higher* for those who had entered it in the 1960's.[4] In Welch's view, this "vintage effect" could not be explained as the result of a sudden decrease in racial discrimination; for one thing, the relative return to black schooling had begun to improve in the mid-1930's, long before the civil rights revolution, and for another, the "vintage effect" extended to whites. His conclusion — the only one that seemed to him to fit these facts — was that the quality of schooling has been improving and that the improvement has been most striking in the schools attended by blacks.

That earnings rise sharply with years spent in school does not prove that schooling *causes* them to rise. Other factors, such as IQ or family background, might account largely or even wholly for differences in earnings. In recent years many analysts have struggled to get rough measures (the best that could be hoped for) of the importance of nonschool factors. Apparently "ability" (except for mathematical ability) accounts for no more than 10 percent of the returns that are associated with schooling;[5] on the other hand, "family background" (socioeconomic status) seems to account for between 25 and 50 percent of them; the schooling of the mother is a "family background" factor of particular importance.[6]

Whatever the contribution of schooling to later earnings, the question arises as to how much of it is attributable to learning the subject matter which the school is endeavoring to teach ("cognitive" learning) and how much to learning something else. Herbert A. Gintis, an economist, has concluded from his empirical studies that students are penalized for creativity, autonomy, initiative, tolerance for ambiguity, and independence and are rewarded for docility, industry, and ego control. The function of the school, he thinks, is both to inculcate these traits and to habituate the student to a system which separates rewards (grades and the like) from the intrinsic satisfaction of work (learning) "thus reproducing rather faithfully the capitalist work-environment."[7] One may, of course, agree that the inculcation of these and other attitudes is indeed the main effort of the school and yet place an entirely different valuation on the outcome. In *Race and Economics* Thomas Sowell remarks that "in many cases education — as such — is not crucial for doing the job, but the general set of *attitudes* and habits [his emphasis] exhibited in behavior toward education may be very important factors in one's capability and reliability as a worker."[8]

Employers, Christopher Jencks writes in *Inequality*, favor more educated [schooled?] workers over less even when there are no significant differences in their productivity because the employers "need a legitimate device for rationing privilege." Wage differentials "could" meet this need, but, for reasons Jencks does not explain, employers use educational credentials which "serve the purpose quite well."[9] Although it is *private* ones that Jencks seems to be discussing, his analysis has much more application to public employers. As was pointed out in Chapter Five, the pay scales of public bodies are affected by political considerations; rationing by noneconomic criteria is therefore usually unavoidable for them. It is not surprising, therefore, to find that a laundry Bennett Harrison complains of for requiring beginning, inexperienced workers to have high school diplomas is publicly operated and pays not an hourly wage but an annual salary of $3,600 (plus substantial pension and other fringe benefits, no doubt). Rather than impose a pointless educational requirement of this sort, a privately operated laundry would surely "ration privilege" by paying less.[10]

Among private employers, "credentialism" is most likely to exist where there is monopoly (enabling the employer to indulge his prejudices without loss of profit) or where the scale of the enterprise makes credentials a cheap screening device. As Daniel E. Diamond, a labor economist, explains, the tests used are sometimes useless or even worse as indicators of performance, but — as the example he cites shows — the private employer is not likely to rely upon them exclusively. (If he makes that mistake, his place may shortly be taken by a more efficient competitor — something that would not happen to a public employer who did the same thing.) According to Diamond:

There is evidence that employers often fail to test whether a particular requirement or set of requirements are justified by the actual job to be performed. For example, one of our graduate students, utilizing statistical analysis, studied the relationship between hiring requirements and job performance of bank tellers in a large New York City bank. The bank gave each job applicant a battery of psychological tests. High test scores were interpreted as evidence of potential success as a teller and low scores as evidence of potential failure. Fortunately for the bank, the test scores were not used as an automatic screening-out device; although some applicants undoubtedly were denied employment because of low test scores. Discriminate analysis showed that there were no significant relationships between test scores and success on the job. Indeed, some of the test scores correlated negatively with job performance.[11]

If the job market is slack, private employers may give an automatic preference to high school or college graduates. Even if the work — e.g., in a laundry — could as well be done by a "functional illiterate," an employer will probably prefer a graduate *when he can have him at little or no extra cost.* Such a choice is not, as Jencks is inclined to think, "capricious rather than rational;"[12] a diploma may reasonably be regarded as evidence of some sort of achievement; or — more realistically perhaps — lack of one, at a time when almost all young people finish school, may give the employer cause to wonder if there may not be "something wrong" with the boy or girl who dropped out.

Presumably, the enormous amount of propaganda directed at actual and potential dropouts by school authorities and by officialdom in general proceeds from the assumption that jobs require more formal education now than they did a generation or two ago and that every additional year of schooling will make a boy or girl that much more employable. The conclusion makes sense for students who are going into such work as medicine, which does require more technical training. But much work does not require more, and investment in a high school diploma *can* result in an economic loss to those who enter certain occupations.[13]

There is every reason to try to persuade the would-be — or to-be — manual laborer to get as much education as he can for his own enjoyment later on. But there is no reason to encourage him to stay in school on the pretext that he will acquire skills valuable to him as a laborer. As Arthur Stinchcombe remarks in *Rebellion in High School:*

Is there anything that a high school can teach which employers of manual labor would be willing to pay for, if it were learned well? In general, the answer is no. Neither physical abilities nor reliability, the two main variables of interest to employers of manual labor, are much influenced by schooling. Employers concerned with securing reliable workers may require high school diplomas as evidence of good discipline. Otherwise they can train workers better and cheaper than a high school can, on the job.[14]

It seems clear that "success" in later life does not require as much achievement in school (not to mention time spent there) as is generally supposed. Jencks is certainly correct in remarking that students who leave school reading at the eighth or ninth grade level are "by no means unemployable" "nor are they excluded from the main stream of American life."[15] This can be seen from the careers of people of such low intelligence that they cannot have learned much in school. Such people often do about as well as "normal" ones in the job market. A sociologist in Connecticut compared the job experience of a group of "mentally deficient persons who had graduated from the special class for slow learners in the regular public schools" with that of a control group consisting of persons who had started first grade at the same time and had passed through the school system in the regular way. The two groups were approximately matched as to age, sex, nationality, religion, and father's occupation, but the subjects' IQ's ranged from 50 to 75, whereas those of the controls ranged from 75 upward. After interviewing each subject in 1948 and again in 1960, the investigator concluded: "The overwhelming majority of both subjects and controls had made acceptable and remarkably similar adjustment in all three areas: personal, social, and economic." The median weekly earnings of the subjects were $88.50, those of the controls $102.50. More than a fourth of both groups had been on the same job for twelve years. None of the subjects earned exceptionally large salaries; a few of the controls did. Employers rated the subjects somewhat less favorably than the controls on almost all criteria. The subjects also were less likely to have savings accounts, checking accounts, or telephones, or to own their own homes. *"In most respects, however,"* the investigator concluded, *"the differences in . . . economic measurements between subjects and controls are insignificant. . . ."*[16]

It is safe to say that if the subjects in this study had been known to the employers as "mentally retarded" they would not have gotten their jobs in the first place. Indeed, "mentally retarded" persons are generally to be found in institutions, and the reason in most cases is not that they are innately incapable of working but that public opinion simply takes it for granted that the "retarded" cannot work and should be institutionalized. "Normal" employees suffer loss of self-esteem when they work alongside known retardates; knowing that the retardate can do what they do — perhaps almost as well as they can do it — makes it hard for them to take pride in their work. But if the retardate is not known as such, the problem does not arise. There are societies in which more than half the population would be "retarded" if retardation were defined in the usual way by an IQ score. They manage quite well, however, because they lack a concept of retardation; in the nature of the case, the percentage of those seriously handicapped by lack of intelligence in competition with others is small. But when, as in our society, retardation is defined in terms of an objective test and the retardates' alleged incapacity is made known to all, the number of retardates is thereby enormously increased and their chances of leading normal lives enormously decreased.[17]

It is because our society is rich and wasteful — and because it is too much on the lookout for ways of "doing good" — that it defines millions of people with IQ's between 50 and 70 as "retarded" and "needing help" (thereby implying that they are not employable and probably ought to be institutionalized) and hundreds of thousands who have not seen fit to spend twelve years in school as "dropouts" (thereby implying that they, too, need help and will be of little use to society and to themselves unless they get it).[18]

Contrary to popular opinion, the tendency of the economy is to require less rather than more knowledge and intellectual ability of most people. As Thomas Sowell remarks in *Black Education*, many jobs "are becoming *simpler* to the point of boredom." There is certainly no indication, he says, "that most jobs are beyond the intellectual range of anyone above the level of mental retardation. Indeed, for many jobs the trainable mentally retarded have been found to do not only a competent job but often a better job than persons of average intelligence. Some firms which use mental tests to screen job applicants have secretly established upper limits for those they will hire, having learned from experience that individuals above a certain intellectual level are more likely to become bored and careless."[19]

Measures to reduce unemployment and poverty by increasing the skills of workers through schooling can have only a very limited success. They cannot change the situation fundamentally; probably the best they can do is to hasten somewhat the movement up the job and income ladder of people who would move up it anyway.

A distinction should be made between a "trained" worker and an "educated" one. The trained worker has learned how to perform certain tasks of more or less complexity — to operate a machine, say, or to keep accounts. Training may mean acquiring certain manual dexterities, mastering some body of facts, or learning to apply a set of rules or to exercise discretion within some well-defined limits. The educated worker, by contrast, (1) possesses the kind of general knowledge, especially of reading and mathematics, that will help him to solve various new problems, and (2) has certain traits of character — especially motivation to achieve, ability to accept the discipline of a work situation, willingness to take the initiative and to accept responsibility, and ability to deal fairly with employers, fellow-employees, and others.

Training may be given entirely in school or on the job. Education, on the other hand, cannot be wholly acquired in either place. Some of what it takes to make a worker educated (especially in reading and mathematical knowledge) can only be learned from books and is usually best learned in school — or perhaps one should say would be best learned there if the school is, in fact, a place where boys and girls generally try to learn; but the traits of character that are equally a part of education are not learned in school — or at any rate not there more than elsewhere. For the most part, they are acquired in childhood.

The lower-class person cannot as a rule be given much training because he will not accept it. He lives for the moment, but learning to perform a task is a way of providing for the future. If the training process is accompanied by immediate rewards to the trainee — if it is "fun" or if he is paid while learning — the lower-class person *may* accept training. But even if he does, his earning power will not be much increased, because his class outlook and style of life will generally make him an unreliable and otherwise undesirable employee. Besides, the ability to perform tasks (that is, to do what he has been trained to do) is seldom a very rare or valuable commodity. He *would* increase his earning power greatly if he became educated (as opposed to trained); to have in high degree and in combination both general education and the traits of character mentioned above is rare and valuable. Unfortunately, however, the lower-class person acquires in childhood an outlook and style of life completely antithetical to education.

The lower-class person presents the extreme case: it is all but impossible to increase his employability by training. With the lower working class the difficulties are the same in kind but less in degree. There are also many persons who, because of racial prejudice or other externally imposed handicaps, are taken to be lower or lower working class when in fact they are not. Their abilities, motivation, and traits of character are such that they can be trained to perform tasks and perhaps educated to hold down skilled jobs. Most such people would find ways of getting the training or education somehow even if there were no schools, but not all of them would, and in any case there is much to be said for measures that may speed up the process. That the problem of the low-capability worker can be solved in this way is too much to hope for, however.

Much more might be accomplished by altering jobs to fit the limitations of workers than vice versa.[20] The principle of specialization could be applied so as to make the low-intelligence and even the lower-class worker much more employable than he is at present. Cutting meat, for example, need not involve dealing with customers: the two activities could be organized as separate jobs. If employers would program work for low-capability workers in the manner that they program it for computers, the workers' job opportunities would be vastly increased. They are not likely to do so, however, so long as minimum-wage laws, union practices, and social prejudices compel them to pay more for low-value labor than it is worth. Instead, they will do the opposite — find ways to replace low-capacity workers with high-capacity ones and with machines.

To say that the school cannot change the child's class culture is to deny that it can serve what many believe to be its principal purpose. The schools, many people think, exist to liberate the child from the confines — moral and emotional as well as intellectual — of his earliest environment and to open higher horizons for him. (". . . [A]wakening the child to cultural values" and "helping him to adjust normally to his environment," the Supreme Court said in the famous *Brown* v. *Board of Education* decision.) No child is more in need of liberation than the lower-class one, and therefore it is thought that the schools are — or at any rate should be — instrumentalities for drawing this child into the larger, freer, more productive world of normal culture as well as for encouraging and facilitating the movement of the working-class child into the middle class and the middle-class child into the upper class. This seems to be what is meant when it is said that schooling provides an "inescapable foundation for the reality of respect and self-respect . . . and the basis for the type of vocational and academic adjustment essential for an effective life." This is why it is generally held that, both from the standpoint of the individual and of the society, it is impossible to have too much schooling. And this is why the inability of the schools to prepare thousands of boys and girls for skilled (or even semiskilled) work and for responsible citizenship and adulthood is counted against them as a failure and is taken as a portent of social decay and collapse.

This idea of what the schools should do contrasts strangely with the account sociologists give of what they do in fact.[21] According to this account, the school does not liberate the child from his class culture but instead confines him in it even more securely — it thickens the walls that separate him from the rest of society. The child has absorbed the elements of his class culture long before reaching school; what the school does is to "socialize" him into it more fully and to make him more aware of the differences that separate him and his kind from others. The child has "picked up" from parents and playmates an outline map of his universe, and the main features of it — the continents, so to speak — cannot be changed by anything that is said or done in school. At best, teachers can only help the child to fill in certain empty spaces on the map he brings with him to school. If the map is extremely crude or wildly inaccurate, teachers and textbooks can be of little help. Nor can they help very much if it is drawn in symbols that are incomprehensible to them. (Working-class Italian-American children studied by Gans in Boston's West End were not adept at manipulating concepts or at handling the reasoning processes in texts and lessons; instead, they were sensitive to people, used words not as concepts but to impress people, and stressed the anecdotal and the episodic — all of which led to learning difficulties in school.[22]) In extreme cases (that is, those presented by lower-class children) not much filling-in of the map is possible, and the little that is possible must take place in the street rather than in the school.

How, it may be asked, can this claim that the school furthers the socialization of a child into his class culture be reconciled with the familiar fact that in America the schools are and always have been a principal vehicle of upward mobility? The answer is that the children who are stimulated into mobility in school are ones whose initial class culture permits or encourages — perhaps even demands — mobility. The more nearly upper class the child's initial culture, the more susceptible he is to being "set in motion" by the school. At the other end of the continuum, the lower-class child's culture does not even recognize — much less value — the possibility of rising or, rather, of doing those things, all of which require some sacrifice of present for future gratification, without which rising is impossible. The lower-class child's conceptual universe lacks the dimension of time; in such a universe people rarely try to change things.

Even if he does not enjoy it, a middle-class child, Jencks remarks, expects that he will have to stay in school for a long time. By contrast, "children with working-class or lower-class parents evidently assume that if they dislike school they can and should drop out."

Those who plan to drop out "usually assume they will have to take low-status jobs. But such jobs evidently seem more acceptable to working-class students than to most upper-middle-class children. This suggests that if we want to equalize the educational attainment of children from different economic backgrounds, we will probably have to change not only their test scores and financial resources, but also their attitudes and values."[23]

The circumstances that prevent the lower-class child (and in lesser degree the lower-working-class one as well) from acquiring in school the traits of character that contribute to education also prevent him from learning how to read, write, and compute adequately. The inadequacy of his preparation in the earliest years imposes a handicap that schools cannot overcome later on. By the age of fourteen, according to Basil Bernstein, many such children are "unteachable." Keeping them in school does not add to their knowledge; it only damages their self-respect, which is already small.[24] For the child whose class culture *does* encourage upward mobility, schooling very often has the broadening and liberating effects that it is supposed to have. But even for these children, ". . . education is but one of many factors influencing mobility, and it may be far from a dominant factor."[25]

Class-cultural factors largely account for the conspicuous difference between the slum and the suburban school. Each school has a class character imposed upon it by the social setting in which it exists; this, and not staff inefficiency, racial discrimination, or inequitable provision of resources, is the *main* reason for the virtues of one and the defects of the other. The implication is one that reformers find hard to accept — to wit, that no matter how able, dedicated, and hardworking the teachers, no matter how ample the facilities of the school or how well-designed its curriculum, no matter how free the atmosphere of the school from racial or other prejudice, the performance of pupils at the lower end of the class-cultural scale will always fall short not only of that of pupils at the upper end of the scale, but also of what is necessary to make them educated workers.

It is tempting to suppose that even when the pupils' class-cultural or other disadvantages are severe they can be overcome by a school whose resources are ample and which employs the best practices in the right combination. Some efforts have indeed been followed by better pupil performance and presumably caused it. None has proved to be generally applicable, however, and even the most comprehensive programs have yielded little or no measurable benefit. Consider, for example, what happened in a typical lower-income school in central Newark — the Cleveland school.[26] In a period of about six years the Victoria Foundation added $1 million to its regular budget and the Board of Education also gave it extra funds. Innovations were planned largely by the teachers. They included supplementing the regular staff with "project teachers" in subjects like science, speech, and remedial reading and with "helping teachers" to assist the less experienced; starting a prekindergarten program; placing heavy emphasis in all grades on reading ability and using a variety of approaches to the teaching of reading; continually examining and refurbishing the curriculum; giving students practice at taking standardized tests; tripling the capacity of the library and adding a full-time librarian; providing comprehensive medical and dental services; enlarging the cultural horizons of the children by field trips, an after-school club, an Afro-American program, assemblies dealing with black history and other efforts to build the self-esteem of the children, almost all of whom were black; establishing a Social Service Center with five full-time professional social workers to provide services for children who needed them; starting parent groups to encourage their involvement; and employing a school psychologist.

Such a program might be expected to work if anything would, but after six years an evaluation revealed that the children were doing little if any better than before. Tests made each year in the third and sixth grades of the Cleveland school and in the same grades of two very similar Newark schools showed that the program had little or no effect on reading or IQ score. The Cleveland students did get slightly higher grades (the difference was about one-third of a grade) than the controls when they reached junior high school. This, the evaluators speculated, might mean that they had gained not academic but "social adjustment skills" — cues for successful classroom behavior (e.g., deference to teachers, discipline, orderliness, and so on) — a hypothesis that was supported by the fact that the Cleveland students did no better than the controls in math, a subject likely to be graded purely on the basis of performance.

Whether anything was accomplished with all the money, time, effort, and dedication appeared doubtful to the evaluators. Even with the assumption that the small differences in junior high school grades indicated gains in "social adjustment skills," it was questionable whether these skills would last and, if they did, whether they would help much in the larger world.

The lack of success (to put it mildly) of almost all such compensatory efforts does not by any means prove that "the problem of the slum school" is insoluble. It does strongly suggest, however, that no amount of tinkering with present arrangements is likely to produce any significant results.

The conclusion is supported (and, so far as the author is aware, not contradicted) by a vast outpouring of studies. The best known of these and the largest (it involved some 645,000 pupils in 4,000 public schools) was made by James S. Coleman and several associates for the U.S. Office of Education and published in 1965 under the title *Equality of Educational Opportunity*.[27] To his own and everyone else's surprise, Coleman found that not only were differences in school resources (facilities, curricula, and staff) within school districts not as great as had been supposed but — more important — they explained relatively little of the wide variations in pupils' achievement. As compared to "family background," the school was unimportant. And of the several variables constituting "family background," one, "pupils' attitudes," accounted for more of the variation in achievement than all of the others together and also more than all of the school-related variables together. Among the three pupil attitudes measured was sense of control over the environment ("Good luck is more important than hard work for success." "Every time I try to get ahead, something or somebody stops me." "People like me don't have much of a chance to be successful in life"); pupils in the groups having the lowest average achievement — Negro, Mexican-American, Puerto Rican, and American Indian — related more strongly to this variable than to any other, a circumstance which Coleman found "particularly impressive because this attitude has no direct logical relation to achievement in school or to ability."

Coleman's data have since been extensively reanalyzed by other investigators,[28] and numerous new studies, some of them very elaborate, have been made of factors influencing achievement in school.

Two separate groups have subjected this avalanche of research (as one report calls it) to critical scrutiny. One, led by Harvey A. Averch of the Rand Corporation, prepared a report for the President's Commission on School Finance on *How Effective Is Schooling?*[29] The other, led by Christopher Jencks of the Graduate School of Education at Harvard University, covered some of the same ground in a more ambitious inquiry into the causes of inequality in American society. The first half of the book by Jencks and his associates, *Inequality*, is essentially a review and analysis of others' findings about the effects of schools on pupils' achievement.

It is not possible here to summarize systematically the principal conclusions of these two works, still less to note the ifs, ands, and buts that they attach to many of them. It will be useful, however, to paraphrase (in some instances actually to quote without quotation marks) some of their conclusions that are of special interest in the present context. It should be emphasized that this is a winnowing from two works each of which is a winnowing from hundreds of other works.

Jencks

Children with affluent parents want more education than children with poor parents, even when we compare those with the same test scores and grades (p. 140).

Perceived pressure from home seems to explain most of the difference between working-class and middle-class students' aspirations (p. 140).

If we want to equalize the attainment of children from different economic backgrounds, we will probably have to change not only their test scores and financial resources, but also their attitudes and values (p. 141).

Averch

The socioeconomic status of a student's family — his parents' income, education, and occupation — invariably prove to be significant predictors of educational outcome (p. 148).

Student attitudes and motivation are undoubtedly major determinants of achievement level (p. 88).

There is little doubt that major determinants of learning style and ability are fixed in the early life of the individual and that environment plays a dominant role (p. 91).

If all elementary schools were closed, white middle-class children might still learn much of what they now know (p. 87). But most poor black children would probably not learn to read without schools (p. 88).

If all elementary schools were equally effective, cognitive inequality would decline less than 3 percent among sixth graders; if all high schools were, it would hardly decline at all among twelfth graders (p. 255).

There is no correlation between what a high school spends and its impact on students' attainment (p. 148).

The evidence does not suggest that doubling expenditures would raise students' performance on standardized tests (p. 93).

Desegregation is associated with higher test scores only if it involves socioeconomic as well as racial desegregation (p. 100).

We can find no convincing evidence that racial desegregation affects students' eventual attainment (p. 155).

If we compare ninth graders with similar aspirations, test scores,

There is no strong evidence for or against the proposition that the characteristics of his peers affect a student's performance (p. 43). In particular, there is no evidence that the racial composition of a student body affects the student's performance (p. 43).

Teachers' experience and advanced degrees, two basic factors determining salaries, are not closely related to student achievement (p. 155). Reduction in class size does not seem to be either (p. 155).

Increasing expenditures on traditional educational practices is not likely to improve outcomes substantially (p. 155).

The large surveys of the large compensatory education programs (ESEA Title I, Headstart, and Follow Through) have shown no beneficial results on the average (p. 125). Two or three smaller surveys tend to show modest and positive effects in the short run (p. 125).

There is little probability of significantly improving classroom performance through the development of new instructional techniques, more educational ex-

and economic backgrounds, we find those who got the most education attended high schools which spent less money than average, had worse paid teachers, and had larger classes (p. 149).

penditures, or changes in the bureaucratic structure of the schools, given the present limitations of knowledge and current institutional constraints of the school system (p. 146).

Trial and error seem to be the only way to answer most practical questions about the causes and cures of cognitive inequality (p. 76).

Research offers little guidance as to what educational practices should be adopted (p. 155).

The "avalanche" of research appears to support the view that what the pupil brings to school in the way of attitudes and motivations (class culture, in large part) influences his success there, as measured by standardized tests, more than do the practices of the school. If this is indeed the case, so long as present practices are followed increased investment in schools will do little or nothing to help the low achievers. Indeed, unless an increase is made only in the classes attended by the low achievers — something that is probably politically impossible — it may be expected to benefit mainly the children of the middle and upper classes because by and large it is they who are most disposed to learn.

How hard it is to get around this problem may be seen from the experience of *Sesame Street*, the educational television program begun in 1969 which reaches seven million preschool children for one hour a day. The intention of the program was (and is) to help offset the handicap of "disadvantaged" children in the poverty areas of the cities by teaching certain skills. When the Educational Testing Service made a survey, it found that about half of the children in its sample watched the program four times a week or more. The children who watched it often showed improvement in the skills that it was designed to improve, and the amount of the improvement was about equal for "disadvantaged" and "advantaged" children. However, the "advantaged" children (who, of course, had more of the skills in question to begin with) were much more likely to watch it often than were the others. When infrequent viewers were compared, the "advantaged" were found to have gained more from watching than the "disadvantaged." There was no way of telling whether the effects on any of the children will be lasting, but, if they are, *Sesame Street*, instead of decreasing inequalities, may increase them.[30]

It is plausible to suggest that the attitudes and motivations which have been found associated with pupils' achievement (or lack of it) are related to the time horizons of the class cultures. One would expect a present-oriented person not to have as much sense of control over his environment as a future-oriented one, for example; similarly one would expect him to be more likely to trust "luck" rather than "hard work." (Coleman mentions, as a striking result of his study, that ninth-grade Negroes who gave the "hard work" response scored higher on the verbal achievement test, both in the North and the South, than whites who gave the "good luck" one, and this although the average Negro scored (in different regions) from 2.7 to 3.8 years behind whites.[31]) As Alan B. Wilson remarks in *The Consequences of Segregation: Academic Achievement in a Northern Community,*

> For some students the future is real for the very reason that they have a future, a fact repeatedly brought home to them by the school system. This link to the future strengthens the bond to the present, because those with a future have something to lose by deviant activity. This orientation to the future is reflected in concern for present academic performance. Students who think good grades are important, for example, are likely to be future oriented. They are also less likely to commit delinquent acts.[32]

If the view taken here is correct, there would seem to be a fundamental incompatibility between the outlook of the lower-class pupil, who is present-oriented, and that of the school, which is (as Bernstein has written) "an institution where every item in the present is finely linked to a distant future, and in consequence there is no serious clash of expectations between the school and the middle-class child." The lower-class child, by contrast,

> is concerned mainly with the present; his social structure, unlike that of the middle-class child, provides little incentive or purposeful support to make the methods and ends of the school personally meaningful. The problems of discipline and classroom control result not from isolated points of resis-

tance or conflict but from the attempt to reorient a whole pattern of perception with its emotional counterpart.[33]

Cloward and Jones describe the American situation in much the same terms:

Our system of education places a strong stress upon doing rather than being, upon a future orientation rather than an orientation toward the present or the past, upon the notion that man is superordinate to nature rather than in harmony with it or subjugated by it, upon the notion that man is flexible and plastic and capable of change rather than that he is essentially, and perhaps immutably, evil. A child who has not acquired these particular value orientations in his home and community is not so likely to compete successfully with youngsters among whom these values are implicitly taken for granted.[34]

The implication is that the school must adapt to the mentality of the lower-class child if it is to be of use to him. *"The methods and problems of teaching need to be thought out almost as though middle-class children do not exist,"* Bernstein says.[35] Others think that it is unfair to offer the lower-class child a choice between a middle-class education and no education at all. Cloward and Jones, for example, say that the system should not be organized "to favor children who are socialized in one rather than another part of the social structure."[36] However, the only way to avoid this is to organize some schools to give what may be called a lower-class (in contradistinction to a middle- or upper-class) education — an education for those who want to be rather than to do, whose verbal ability is very low, and who are not motivated to learn. This notion of fairness, presumably, is the basis for complaints about the fact that teachers are almost all middle-class and for objections to the efforts of the schools to teach correct (middle-class) English to children who will never have occasion to speak it. Apparently, the idea is that to be fair to the lower-class child, the schools should give him teachers, books, and subject matter appropriate to a lower-class education.[37]

The trouble with this idea, however, is that a lower-class education is a contradiction in terms; lower-class culture is the attitudes and behavior patterns of people who have not been educated at all. To be sure, a child "learns" this culture in the sense that he learns to be improvident, undisciplined, and so on. But what he learns is not knowledge that could be taught in school even if everyone agreed that it should be. No one would write it down in books (for to do so would require a large measure of "middle-class" knowledge), no one would teach it (a lower-class teacher would not come to work regularly and would not have anything to teach in a classroom if he or she did), and no one would learn it (for the lower-class pupil is poorly disposed toward learning anything).

Giving a "lower-class education" can only mean giving no education at all, and this, one would suppose, can be done better on the street than in school. If, for example, it is pointless to try to teach the child correct English, it is pointless to try to teach him English at all. The only system that will not favor the child at the upper end of the class-cultural scale is one that frees the lower-class child from having to go to school at all. *All* education favors the middle- and upper-class child, because to be middle- or upper-class is to have qualities that make one particularly educable.

Perhaps critics who attack the school for its middle-class character really mean that if a strenuous enough effort were made to avoid confusing and humiliating the lower-class child, it might be possible to get him to try climbing the educational ladder. On this view, the school should not only avoid the unconscious snobbism of the middle class but ought also to make some pretense of being lower-class in order to put the child at his ease and to establish contact with him. This approach is not really to change the school's class character but only to seem to do so. The question that must be asked is: Will it work, and not merely with a few gifted teachers but with most teachers? That it is highly desirable not to offend or humiliate the child goes without saying. But whether the school, which in the nature of things must be an expression of normal (as opposed to lower-class) culture, can pretend not to be that, or could accomplish anything by so doing, may well be doubted. Such evidence as there is suggests that by the time he reaches school, the lower-class child's handicap is too firmly fixed to allow of its being significantly reduced by anything the school might do.

There is much evidence that children learn fastest in the earliest years of life. By the age of four, according to one account, general intelligence has developed as much as it will in the next fourteen years; a poor start in these first years means that the child is likely to fail throughout his school career no matter what the school may do later on to help him.[38]

These findings make it plausible to suppose that if the school is to educate the lower-class child as well as the others who make up the ill-defined category "disadvantaged," it must start very early in his or her life. Preschool programs (which in 1971 enrolled 44 percent of children aged three to five in metropolitan areas) apparently do not start early enough; at any rate, whether for this reason or for some other, the initial gains of those who participate in them are soon lost. Indeed, children who participate in Headstart and other compensatory programs frequently make *slower* progress than those who do not. According to the U.S. Office of Education's fourth annual report (published in 1971) on the huge ($1 billion annually) program under Title I of the Elementary and Secondary Education Act of 1965, "Participants in the compensatory programs [not many of which were nursery schools, to be sure] continued to show declines in average yearly achievement in comparison to nonparticipants who included advantaged and nondisadvantaged pupils. . . ."[39] It was not possible from the data, the report adds, to tell whether the decline in average achievement was greater or less than in previous years.

It would be premature to conclude that efforts to overcome the handicap of "disadvantaged" children must start almost from birth if the children are to succeed in school. This will be discussed at some length later (in Chapter Ten), albeit only in reference to the lower class. It will be seen that on this question, as on most others of importance, experts disagree.

Since the schools are not teaching much to many children after ninth grade, it would make sense to lower the normal school-leaving age to fourteen, giving a diploma on completion of nine rather than twelve grades and (as a comment by Jencks suggests) allowing a child of any age to earn a diploma by passing an equivalency examination.[40] This would not reduce the amount of free schooling available to those who are able and willing to learn, but it would eliminate the efforts — almost wholly futile — to stop truancy, which in some schools runs as high as 50 percent, and it would enable nonlearners to leave without being stigmatized as dropouts.

There are at least three compelling reasons for getting nonlearners out of school. The first is to stop what one educator has called the process of "anti-education" in school and thus to prevent further injury to the nonlearners' self-respect and further lessening of their regard for the institutions of the society. As matters now stand, the pretense of the school — one that must be ridiculous to boys who will be manual workers and to girls who will soon start having babies — that it and it alone offers "opportunity" is surely one cause of youth unrest. The boy who knows that he has learned nothing since the eighth grade but that he must nevertheless sit in boredom, frustration, and embarrassment until he is sixteen or seventeen (in a few states, eighteen), when finally he will be labeled "dropout," must be profoundly disaffected by the experience. He senses that the school authorities and the whole apparatus of middle- and upper-class opinion that confine him there neither understand nor even care about the most palpable realities of his situation: that he will very likely work with his hands all his life, that he is not learning anything, that for such work he would not be helped by learning any more, and that one who works with his hands had better start early because he will be "old" by the time he is forty. To tell such a boy that he must stay in school anyway because in the future there will be no jobs for people with only hands is to tell him something that is both untrue and irrelevant. If he cannot learn, staying in school will not help, and if there are no jobs for people with only hands, supporting him will be society's problem, not his.

Rebellious behavior, Stinchcombe concluded from his study of a high school, "is largely a reaction to the school itself and to its promises, not a failure of the family or community."[41] The suggestion is that much juvenile delinquency originates in the adolescent's anger at the stupidity and hypocrisy of a system that uses him in this way. The later the school-leaving age, the more involved with delinquency the school will be. As Martin Trow has written:

The growth of educational opportunity threatens to make the greater part of terminal education in high schools coincidental with the social problems of juvenile delinquency. This is not to say that every classroom full of non-college-going students is or will be a "blackboard jungle." It does mean that the hostility toward the school characteristic of the juvenile gangs, but much more widespread than their membership, will be an increasing part of the educational problem faced by schools and teachers dealing with terminal students.[42]

The school's involvement with delinquency may become greater as the school-leaving age is delayed, not simply because there are then more students of an age to be delinquent (which is what Trow seems to mean) but also because having to stay in school after learning has stopped is itself a cause of delinquency. In Britain, the Crowther Committee reported that when (in 1947) the school-leaving age was raised from fourteen to fifteen ". . . there was an immediate change over in the delinquency record of the thirteen-year-olds (who until then had been the most troublesome age group) and the fourteen-year-olds, who took their place in 1948 and have held it consistently ever since."[43] Presumably what happened was that fourteen-year-olds, upon confinement in school, became more delinquent than fourteen-year-olds had been before. If so, one may conjecture that if they were to be confined still another year or two or three (as they are in most states of this country), they would become even more troublesome.

Boys, especially working-class ones, frequently want to leave school for the very practical reason that changing their status from "schoolboy" to "worker" will give them independence and even a certain prestige at home. If not permitted to leave, the boy who finds the "schoolboy" role intolerable may replace it with membership in a youth gang or other delinquent subculture. Indirectly, then, the school may be a factor generating delinquency.[44]

The frustration, anger, and contempt for authority engendered by the school may possibly enter into the personality of the individual, coloring his attitudes in adulthood and leading him to take a cynical and resentful view of the society and all its works. Conceivably, the practice of forcing the incapable and unwilling to waste their adolescent years in schoolrooms further weakens the already tenuous attachment of the lower classes to social institutions. The discovery that the school consists largely of cant and pretense may prepare the way for the discovery that the police and the courts, for example, do too.

That many lower-class pupils are also black complicates the school problem in a tragic way. Increasingly since 1960 the ideology of the civil-rights movement has tended to justify and thus reinforce the Negro's resentment of the white; this has had a subtle but pervasive effect on the attitudes of the black working and lower classes, even though those classes have little or no interest in the ideology of equality or of anything else. Since 1964 (the year of the first riots) the growing "black power" movement, by accusing the "white" school system of practicing "mental genocide" against black children and by forcibly demanding "community control" of schools, has dramatized for black pupils the idea that whites are to blame for everything and that they, the pupils, ought to show their resentment by learning nothing while making life as miserable as possible for their white teachers. Not all black schoolchildren have been infected by the contagion of these ideas, but enough have been to make it doubtful that whites — even those sympathetic to the militant point of view — can in the future be even moderately successful in the inner-city schools.[45]

A second reason for getting nonlearners out of the school is — paradoxical though it may seem — to give them opportunities and incentives to learn. Not everything worth learning must be (or indeed can be) learned from books and teachers, and not everyone — not even everyone with a first-rate mind — learns better from books and teachers than from other sources. Educators tend to overlook this, since they have a professional interest in booklearning and have been self-selected into their occupation on the basis of an aptitude for it. To be sure, some of the boys and girls here in question are not likely to learn much from *any* source. But if they leave school and go to work, they will learn more than they would if they stayed in school. There are additional reasons, apart from the fact that some people learn otherwise than from books, for supposing this to be so: one is that on a job a worker is usually rewarded at once if he learns something that improves his performance; the job, that is, gives incentives to present-oriented people, whereas the school gives them only to the future-oriented. Another is that in some jobs (but, alas, not in all by any means) the thing to be learned is "fun" — even a radically present-oriented person has an incentive to learn under these circumstances. As Howard S. Becker has written (in an essay titled "School Is a Lousy Place to Learn Anything"),

> On-the-job training is often effective because someone does have time to do a little teaching, because the enterprise allows enough leeway for the apprentice to make some mistakes without costing others too much, because the things that can interfere with his learning are fortuitous occurrences rather than structural necessities.[46]

The third reason for getting nonlearners out of school is to improve the situation of the learners. Although research studies have shown that in general high-achieving pupils are not adversely affected by the presence in the classroom of low-achieving ones, it seems obvious that a class composed largely or predominantly of bored and frustrated nonlearners will be far less stimulating for both teachers and pupils than one in which there are few or none such. The low achiever is, after all, frequently diligent and interested. By contrast, the nonlearner, as he has been called here, is one who has ceased to try, if indeed he ever did try. Because he is bored if for no other reason, he is likely to be a troublemaker. Even a few like him can distract and intimidate a whole class of serious students and wear almost any teacher down to the breaking point. In one slum school it was found that even the best teachers had to devote half the school day to discipline and to organizational detail.[47]

It should be emphasized that lowering the school-leaving age to fourteen need not mean giving less education to anyone. In the case of the nonlearners it is only to acknowledge what already exists. The more able and willing students would in almost all cases go on to college. Four years of high school is too much for those who will do manual work; it is not enough for those who will do work that requires education. These need at least fourteen years of schooling, and ending high school at the ninth grade would enable them to start college or other advanced training that much sooner.

An able pupil under the present system is usually ready for college after the tenth or the eleventh grade. (In one experiment, such "dropouts" did as well or better in college than classmates who spent four years in high school; moreover, "their interest in their studies is often greater than that of their contemporaries who have been exposed to the boredom which frequently accompanies high school education."[48]) The system should be changed to speed up the process of education. It is evident from European practice, as well as from that of the better schools in this country, that with proper curricula and teaching methods almost as much can be learned in a nine-year school as in the present twelve-year one. Fritz Machlup, whose conclusion this is, has remarked, "Most people *can* learn what they ever learn in school in eight years, and if they are kept there for ten, twelve, fourteen, or sixteen years they will merely learn it more slowly."[49]

It is hard to say whether "Ashamed" (whose letter to "Dear Abby" is quoted at the head of this chapter) would be well advised to go to a vocational ("trade") school. In the 1960's a research group concluded that in most cases students having the capability and motivation to take a serious vocational course could do satisfactory work in an "academic" one and would be better served by it.[50] Recently the HEW task force whose report was published under the title *Work in America* remarked that although vocational high school education is very expensive, costing 60 to 75 percent more than other, few entry-level jobs require the specific skills that it might provide; that more often than not vocational graduates take jobs for which they were not trained; and that vocational graduates are no less likely than other graduates to be unemployed or (except for a particular category) to earn more.[51] Presumably in recognition of these limitations, the U.S. Office of Education has since 1971 given priority in the awarding of grants to school systems that agree to switch from the traditional vocational training to something called "career education" a combination of technical training and academic study that begins in the early grades and offers a wide variety of courses of increasing difficulty in order to prepare the student for a choice of occupations when he or she graduates.

One stray fact suggests that just as it is about to be replaced by "career education" the traditional form of vocational training may have a clientele whose needs it can serve well. In Philadelphia, the vocational schools had the highest rate of pupil absenteeism in the 1940's (when the city's middle class was much larger than it is now); since the middle 1960's, however, they have had the lowest.

Although without a doubt "Ashamed" received her diploma on schedule (the usual practice is now to give them to all who have served their time, whether they have learned anything or not), the presence in a school of large numbers of such children assures what Trow has called "a second-class program for second-class students." And, as he adds, ". . . they will know it, and that knowledge will feed their bitterness and resentment."[52] In other words, "Ashamed" is very likely to end up being "Angry" or even "In Open Rebellion."

If large numbers of boys and girls are to be let out of school after eight grades, which in most cases would be at the age of fourteen, the question arises of how their time is to be occupied. One could argue that, even if they learn nothing in school, it is, on the whole, better to keep them there than to let them lie around in idleness or roam the streets. The young require a certain amount of looking after. Who is to look after them if not teachers?

In principle, the answer to this question is easy. At whatever age they finish school, boys and girls should go to work. The discipline of the job will more than take the place of that of the school. Moreover, it is a better discipline. One *chooses* one's job, and therefore one's boss and fellow workers, in that (at the very least) one can always quit and look for another; the boss knows this and therefore has some incentive to make the conditions of work pleasant or at least tolerable. But if the discipline of the job is in some ways less confining than that of the school, in other ways — ones that are on the whole beneficial to the individual — it is more confining. The employee must do or produce something of value if he is to keep his job. He is not permitted, or at any rate not encouraged, to waste his time and that of others. Having to work is not really the disadvantage it is often made out to be, for nothing is so demoralizing in the long run as to know that one's energies and abilities are of no use to anyone.

To a society as wealthy as this one, the loss of income from having nonlearners in school rather than at work is not of very great moment. But neither is it trivial. Except in the elementary grades, the biggest items of cost are not buildings or teachers' salaries but the earnings forgone by students. The importance of these forgone earnings is greater than the dollar amounts might suggest because (as was explained in Chapter Six) there are obstacles — perhaps insuperable — in the way of *giving* income to the people in question without thereby reducing their incentives to provide for themselves and thus in the long run making them worse off.

The main reason for encouraging boys and girls who leave school to go to work, however, is not to increase their incomes but to hasten their growing up — to bring them sooner into the adult world, where they will have the satisfactions of being taken seriously, of being on their own, of being responsible for themselves and indeed very soon for others as well. Stretching out childhood and adolescence is characteristic of the upper classes, and for them doing so makes good sense: the individual anticipates a long life and therefore an extended period of preparation is both a luxury he can afford and a good investment as well.[53] In the lower classes the individual's situation is very different: his earning power and his capacity to enjoy what for him are the good things of life are greatest in his twenties and thirties and diminish rapidly thereafter. To force the lower classes to adapt to the practice of the upper classes in these matters is both pointless and harmful: it does not give their youth the advantages that the upper class youth enjoy. Instead, it creates problems — loss of self-confidence, boredom, unrest, loss of income — for the boys and girls whose urge to grow up is frustrated and thus, of course, problems for the society as well.

As a matter of biology, youth is a time when one seeks a good deal of hard physical exercise, preferably accompanied by excitement and even danger. It is also a time when one wants and needs opportunities to find out who and what one is, and therefore to test one's qualities — endurance, skill, courage, and the rest — against those of adult models. These needs are especially strong in the lower classes and they are more urgent among boys than among girls. (Youth culture is in some ways similar to lower-class culture: being present-oriented, it places high value on excitement, danger, and thrills — being "where the action is" — and low value on providing for the future.)

To be sure, the jobs that teen-agers might get would in most instances be far from exciting, like pushing a broom around a factory. Even a dull job, however, would be exciting as compared to sitting in a classroom where the subjects discussed are boring if not incomprehensible. The factory, unlike the school, is the "real" world; it is a world of adults, usually male, and of lower- or working- (as opposed to middle- or upper-) class types. In such a world even dull work has satisfactions for a youth: one stands in line with men (not "kids") to punch the time clock, one takes orders from a foreman who talks one's own language (instead of from a middle-class lady), and one learns from the boss and from fellow workers that it makes a difference whether one does one's job or not. Not all jobs for the young need be as simple and unexciting as pushing a broom, however. There is no reason why a healthy boy of fourteen or fifteen should not do work that calls for considerable strength, endurance, and bravery. Indeed, it is only in the upper classes of an affluent society that any doubt about this could arise. If, as the military asserts, eighteen to nineteen is the optimal age for a combat soldier, it is safe to say that nothing but prejudice prevents the employment of boys of that age as lumberjacks, long-distance truck drivers, longshoremen, construction workers, taxicab drivers, and the like, and of even younger ones as helpers in these occupations.[54]

It will be objected that, whether because of prejudice or something else, employers will not hire boys and girls in their early teens; even at the high wartime employment level of 1967 the unemployment rate among teen-agers was 13 percent. This figure need only be turned around to answer the objection: if 13 percent of the teen-agers wanting jobs had not found them, then 87 percent *had* found them. The fact is that a great many boys and girls are employed: in New York City 106,494 aged fourteen to seventeen had jobs in 1970.[55] These young people, moreover, were able to get jobs despite many institutional obstacles in their way and in the way of potential employers — state and federal child labor laws (the Fair Labor Standards Act prohibits employment of anyone under sixteen for general work and under eighteen for hazardous work; fourteen- and fifteen-year-olds may take nonhazardous, nonmanufacturing jobs after school hours and for short periods), compulsory school attendance laws (the leaving age is sixteen in New York), licensing and union restrictions, and minimum-wage rates that overprice low-productivity labor. If these obstacles were removed, many boys and girls who are now last in line for jobs, as well as many who are not permitted to get in line at all, would move to the head of the line. Indeed, the real danger may be not that the young would be unable to find jobs but that they would find them too readily by displacing the no-longer-young. Middle- and upper-class bias in favor of education and prolonged adolescence is one reason why the young are kept in school longer than necessary; another is that unskilled adult workers prefer not to compete with them for jobs.[56]

Even with no prejudice against the young and the unschooled, with the fullest of full employment, and with realistic pricing of low-productivity labor, there would remain some boys and girls — perhaps a considerable number — who either would not take a job or could not get one. These youths would require enough supervision to keep them "out of trouble" until they got a job or reached an age at which they would be entitled to do exactly as they pleased so long as they broke no laws. Although publicly supported institutions would have to meet this need, such institutions need not be in any sense schools. The function of supervising the activities of nonlearners simply cannot be performed well by the same institution (namely, the school) that educates the learners. The combination means poor education for learners and antieducation for nonlearners. If the schools were limited to their proper business, other institutions might be developed to meet the needs of those boys and girls who are too old to learn but too young to work.

High school, it seems fair to conclude, cannot possibly "educate" those young people who are strongly disposed not to learn. In the case of lower-class youth, enforced attendance tends to undermine what little self-respect the individual has and to aggravate his feeling, already strong, of being victimized by forces beyond his control. It must be acknowledged, however, that the alternative of allowing the lower-class youth to receive his diploma at the age of fourteen and then expecting him to go to work presents serious difficulties, too. The same class culture that stood in the boy's way in school will stand in his way elsewhere. He may not be willing to take a job even if good ones are available. Indeed, it is more than likely that he will prefer the "action" of the street to any job that he could possibly fill. If the choice is between idleness and demoralization in school and idleness and demoralization on the street, then doubtless the former is the lesser evil. It may be possible to avoid these alternatives, however, by — as James S. Coleman has suggested[57] — moving high school training out of schools and into factories and offices: that is, by giving students the option of combining work and learning. In order to do this it would be necessary for governmental bodies (in effect, school districts) to enter into contracts with private firms, specifying the kind of training to be given and the amount to be paid for it by the public. This would certainly entail a great many practical difficulties (for example, firms would tend to demand payment for giving training that their own business interest would prompt them to give anyway), but so much is at stake and the alternatives are so dismal that even serious difficulties should not be regarded as prohibitive.

CHAPTER EIGHT

Several Kinds of Crime

... let the policeman's club be thrown down or wrested from
him, and the fountains of the great deep are opened, and
quicker than ever before chaos comes again. Strong as it may
seem, our civilization is evolving destructive forces. Not desert
and forest, but city slums and country roadsides are nursing the
barbarians who may be to the new what Hun and Vandal were
to the old.

— Henry George

Warring on poverty, inadequate housing and unemployment, is warring on crime. A civil rights law is a law against
crime. Money for schools is money against crime. Medical,
psychiatric, and family-counseling services are services against
crime. More broadly and most importantly every effort to
improve life in America's "inner cities" is an effort against
crime.

— The Crime Commission

THEORIES about the causes and cures of crime tend to be variations of ones about the causes and cures of hard-core poverty.
One theory asserts that the criminal suffers from some malaise (such
as "alienation") and must be brought into a right relation with the
Deity, or — nowadays — with Society or with Self. According to
another, he is frustrated by lack of opportunity; the cure is to enable
him to earn by socially acceptable means the rewards (largely material) that society declares to be the indispensable marks of success.[1]
Still another theory holds that if only he had an adequate income and
a proper physical environment — good housing, schools, hospitals,
transportation, clean air and so on — his outlook and style of life
would improve, and he would cease to commit crimes. That efforts

to apply these theories have not led to the reduction of crime in the city is painfully apparent. Indeed, it is possible that they may somehow have led to an increase in crime.

In this chapter it will be maintained that crime, like poverty, depends primarily upon two sets of variables. One set relates mainly to class culture and personality (but also to sex and age) and determines an individual's *propensity* to crime. The other relates to situational factors (such as the number of policemen on the scene and the size of the payroll) and determines his *inducement*. The probability that he will commit crimes — his *proneness* to crime — depends upon propensity *and* inducement. A city's *potential* for crime may be thought of as the average proneness of persons in various "sex-age-culture-personality" groups times their number.

This view does not deny all causal importance to alienation, poor housing, inferior schools, and the like. Such factors help to shape class culture and personality (and therefore propensity), and may also influence the situation (and therefore incentive). However, the more "subjective" factors (such as alienation) can seldom be defined and related to crime with much precision, while the connection between crime and more "objective" factors (such as housing) can almost never be determined for the reason that countless such factors influence culture and personality on the one hand and the situation on the other.

As was remarked in earlier chapters, the policymaker usually must take certain cultural and psychological traits as given. If he is to change a city's potential for crime it must be by manipulating situational factors, which is to say inducements. It cannot be taken for granted that the measures commonly recommended for this purpose — raising incomes, improving housing and schooling, and the like — will in fact tend to reduce crime. The reason why crime rates tend to be higher in large cities than in small ones *may* have something to do with the fact that in the larger city the individual has more schooling, more income, and more opportunity.[2]

Before entering into a discussion of substantive matters, it is necessary to give some further account of the analytical framework just outlined.[3]

The individual will be thought of as perceiving various action possibilities; he chooses from among them the one that he thinks will yield him the most utility. He estimates the benefits and costs to himself of acting on each alternative and chooses that which promises the largest net benefit. He counts as benefits whatever money or other material goods he expects to gain by the action, any satisfaction that he expects to take in its performance (he may, for example, enjoy hurting someone), and any indirect returns that he expects to accrue from it (for example, a gain in reputation by virtue of having performed it). Similar considerations enter into his estimation of costs (for example, he may feel displeasure at having to hurt someone or may fear loss of reputation). He counts as a cost any work required in the performance of the action or in preparation for it (for example, acquiring information about how to do it).

It may seem far-fetched to describe human behavior — above all criminal behavior — in such rationalistic terms. In fact they cannot be applied either to the behavior of the insane (who commit only a negligible proportion of all crimes) or to that of narcotics addicts when they are in desperate need of a "fix" (addicts do not often become desperate; usually they "feed their habits" by routine "hustling").[4] But except in these rather rare cases, there is an element of calculation — indeed, a very considerable one — in practically all criminal behavior.[5] To be sure, impulse characteristically enters into some types of crimes more than into others, but an element of rationality is hardly ever absent. ("Crimes of passion" are rarely committed in the presence of policemen or against persons who are in a good position to defend themselves, and the juvenile who steals "to punish his father" almost always steals something he wants and almost always takes some account of his chances of being caught.) Criminologists generally agree that there is no such thing as a "criminal type"; presumably, they mean that people decide whether or not to do illegal things in essentially the same way that they decide whether or not to do other things.

The present scheme implies that when probable costs exceed probable benefits, an individual will not commit the crime. Indeed, he will not commit it even when probable benefits exceed probable costs if another (noncriminal) action promises to be *more* profitable.

It should not be supposed that everyone responds in the same way to the same inducements. Class-cultural and personality factors enter into the individual's cost-benefit calculus, making him more or less ready to accept one or another type of criminal opportunity (or criminal opportunity in general). The influence of these factors may be such that situational ones will never induce him to commit a crime. Commonly, however, this is not the case; situational factors are often decisive even with persons who have little propensity toward crime.[6] One who would "never think of stealing" steals when the temptation becomes great enough; that is, when the situation promises great enough benefits at small enough cost. Similarly, one who thinks nothing of murder may be checked by the presence of a policeman.

The elements of propensity seem to be mainly these:

Type of Morality.[7] This refers to the way in which an individual conceptualizes right and wrong and, therefore, to the weight he gives to legal and moral rules in making choices. One whose morality is *"preconventional"* understands a "right" action to be one that will serve his purpose and that can be gotten away with; a "wrong" action is one that will bring ill success or punishment. An individual whose morality is preconventional cannot be influenced by authority (as opposed to power). One whose morality is *"conventional"* defines "right" action as doing one's "duty" or doing what those in authority require; for him, laws and moral rules have a constraining effect even in the absence of an enforcement apparatus. One whose morality is *"postconventional"* defines "right" action as that which is in accord with some universal (or very general) principle that he considers worthy of choice. Such an individual is constrained by law as such only if the principle that he has chosen requires him to be; if it requires him to obey the law only when he thinks that the law in question is just, he is, of course, not under the constraint of law at all.

Ego Strength. This refers to the individual's ability to control himself — especially to his ability to adhere to and act on his intentions (and therefore to manage his impulses) and to his ability to make efforts at self-reform. One who is radically deficient in ego strength cannot conceive or implement a plan of action; he has a succession of fleeting resolves, the last of which eventuates in action under the pressure of circumstances.

Time Horizon. This refers to the time perspective an individual takes in estimating costs and benefits of alternative courses of action. The more present-oriented an individual, the less likely he is to take account of consequences that lie in the future. Since the benefits of crime tend to be immediate and its costs (such as imprisonment or loss of reputation) in the future, the present-oriented individual is ipso facto more disposed toward crime than others.

Taste for Risk. Commission of most crimes involves a certain amount of risk. An individual who places a very low (perhaps even a negative) value on the avoidance of risk is thereby biased in the direction of crime.

Willingness to Inflict Injury. Most crimes involve at least the possibility of injury to others and therefore a certain willingness on the part of the actor to inflict injury. It may be useful to distinguish among (a) individuals with a distaste for inflicting *any* injury ("crimes without victims" would still be open to them, of course); (b) those with a distaste for injuring specifiable individuals (they might steal from a large enterprise, but they would not cheat the corner grocer); (c) those with a distaste for doing bodily (but not necessarily other) injury to people; and (d) those with no distaste for inflicting injuries, along with those who positively enjoy inflicting them.

These several elements of propensity tend to exist in typical combinations. In general, an individual whose morality is preconventional also has little ego strength, a short time horizon, a fondness for risk, and little distaste for doing bodily harm to specifiable individuals. The opposites of these traits also tend to be found together.

It also happens that individuals whose propensity toward crime is relatively high — especially those with high propensity for *violent* crime — tend to be those whose situation provides the strongest incentive to crimes of the common sorts. The low-income individual obviously has much more incentive to steal than does the high-income one. Similarly, a boy has much more incentive to "prove he is not chicken" than does a girl. In general, then, high propensity and high inducement go together.

With respect to both propensity and inducement, there are very important differences between: (1) males and females, (2) persons of different class cultures, and (3) the young and the not-young.

Although their arrest rates for serious offenses have risen sharply in recent years (from 10 percent of all arrests in 1960 to 18 percent in 1972), females have much less propensity toward crime, especially violent crime, than males. (Among girls, running away from home is the most common offense, but females in general account for from 25 to 30 percent of arrests for forgery, fraud, and embezzlement.) In general, women seem to be more future-oriented than men, better able to control their impulses, more adverse to risk, and less disposed to inflict physical injuries. Be this as it may, in all class cultures their *inducement* to most kinds of crime is clearly less than that of men. Far from being under pressure to be "tough" and to prove that they have "been around," they are, even in the lower class, expected to be frail and "domestic." (It is safe to say that the women's liberation movement has had no influence upon the working and lower classes.) In recent years large numbers of women have entered the labor force (however, relatively few in the lower-working and lower classes have done so), but women are still much less likely than men to be in the role of provider — a role that increases both motive and opportunity for the most common crime, stealing. Moreover, their relative lack of physical strength disqualifies them from heavy criminal work as it does from other heavy work, and no doubt it has much to do with their distaste for risk and for inflicting bodily injury.

The difference in propensity and inducement is hardly less striking among classes than between sexes. For the lower-class individual, high propensity coincides with high inducement. As a child he may have been punished physically rather than psychologically, and therefore it may seem natural to him that aggression take the form of a physical attack.[8] He has little ability to control impulses. His behavior is "decided upon" from moment to moment.

Now without havin' any intention of robbin' this guy I was crossin' the street. Actually I was crossin' the street to rob him, but it actually wasn't on my mind. If someone had asked me why I had crossed the street I couldn't a told him. I just doin' this unconscious.[9]

The morality of lower-class culture is preconventional, which means that the individual's actions are influenced not by conscience but only by a sense of what he can get away with.[10]

The general attitude toward stealing is one in which the individual feels some type of "right" to do so. It is not perceived strictly in terms of "stealing" but instead of "taking."[11]

Apparently everyone has this conception of stealing at a stage of his childhood. Most persons grow out of it, pangs of conscience making it hard for them to steal; the lower-class person, however, continues to "take" things all his life.

As the child grows older, there is a gradual change in the type of things stolen and their relative worth. There is a graduation from the candy bar to stealing from the rummage shop sale, to stealing from downtown department stores, to stealing, signing and cashing welfare checks.[12]

Infliction of bodily injury is also sanctioned — often inculcated — by lower-class culture.

The lower classes not uncommonly teach their children and adolescents to strike out with fist or knife and to be certain to hit first. Both girls and boys at adolescence may curse their father to his face or even attack him with fists, sticks, or axes in free-for-all family encounters. Husbands and wives sometimes stage pitched battles in the home; wives have their husbands arrested; and husbands try to break in or burn down their own homes when locked out. Such fights with fists or weapons, and the whipping of wives, occur sooner or later in most lower-class families. They may not appear today, nor tomorrow, but they will appear if the observer remains long enough.[13]

The rapist, according to Amir, tends to be a member of a lower-class subculture in which masculinity is expressed in general aggressiveness, including sexual exploits. Boys brought up in this subculture "learn overt and direct aggressive attitudes and conduct from their families, as well as from peers."[14] Exploitive behavior toward women becomes part of their motivational systems: they do not conceive it "as wrong or as a deviation from the normal."

Because the lower-class style of life involves an unremitting search for sex and for relief from boredom, it tends to bring the individual into situations in which he is likely to violate a law. Moreover, he has little or nothing to lose — no job, no money, no reputation — by being charged with a crime. In the lower-class world it is taken for granted that everyone "gets in trouble" and may go to jail now and then. Being known as vicious and violent may give one a certain prestige in the slum, as it does in a prison. Finally, since he is unwilling or unable to keep a job or to acquire a skill, the lower-class individual's opportunities for income are relatively poor. Even if the "wage rate" for "hustling" were low (in fact it is often very high) that might be the best "job" open to an unskilled youth, especially one who prefers the "life of action" to regular work.[15]

Higher up on the class-cultural continuum — in the upper-working and lower-middle classes — the situation is very different as regards both propensity and inducement. As compared to the lower class, members of these classes have little taste for violence or for risk; they are also much more able to take the future into account and to control their behavior. But what most distinguishes them from those "above" as well as from those "below" them on the class-cultural continuum is their respect for authority. They tend to accept unquestioningly whatever the authority of law, custom, religious teaching, or even "public opinion" declares. Of course, the individual sometimes does what he knows to be wrong, but when he does he feels guilty about it. The prickings of conscience weight his calculus heavily, if not always decisively, toward what he considers right and proper.

In these classes, too, inducement tends to reinforce propensity. Once he has married and settled down, such an individual can usually earn more at honest work than he could get by crime. In addition, his job, family, and circle of friends and neighbors insulate him from many temptations. He knows also that if he "got in trouble," he would lose his job and bring disgrace upon himself and his family.

It might be expected that those "highest" on the continuum — the upper-middle and upper classes — would be least prone to crime. They have the greatest ability to take account of the future and to control themselves. They tend to be more adverse to risk, and, whereas the lower class has learned in childhood to be violent, they have learned to be nonviolent — "to hammer on the Playskool Cobbler Bench but not on their brothers and sisters."[16]

There is, however, another tendency within the upper- and upper-middle-class culture that works in an opposite direction. The individual has a strong sense of self, and he attaches great importance to "developing his potentialities to the full." Insofar as he thinks that his future is sufficiently provided for (that he "has it made"), he tends to emphasize self-expression rather than self-improvement and, accordingly, present gratification rather than saving and investment; his style of life may then resemble that of the present-oriented individual, except, of course, that whereas he *chooses* to live in the present, the lower-class one lives in it because he must. In order to develop or express his personality, the upper- or upper-middle-class person seeks out new and "rewarding" "experiences." He "owes it to himself" to try dried grasshoppers with his martinis and the equivalent with his sex, his politics, his child rearing, and all else. He feels obliged "as a responsible person" to decide for himself what is right and wrong; simply to accept the dictates of authority, including that of law, appears to him demeaning: one ought to assert oneself as an "individual" by deciding (on "rational" grounds, of course) what rules to follow. Having done so, one ought to have "the courage of one's convictions."

Such an individual is apt to try illegal as well as other "experiences." He is especially apt to do so if he thinks that the law proscribing them is "stupid" or inappropriate to the circumstances of his particular case. If he breaks the law, he is unlikely to feel guilty; on the contrary, he may take virtuous satisfaction in the thought that he has performed a public service by helping to bring a "stupid" law into disrepute.

How upper- and upper-middle-class attitudes can lead by this different route to behavior that is concretely indistinguishable from that of the lower class may be seen in the matter of drug use. According to Dr. Norman E. Zinberg, there are two contrasting motivations behind the use of drugs. One group of users, drawn mainly from the lower socioeconomic strata, are "like children" in that they "want nothing but the immediate satisfaction of pleasurable desires." The other group, drawn mainly from the middle and upper socioeconomic strata, consists of "experience seekers": "Drugs give them a sense of liberation from convention, a feeling that a level of genuine experience which is closed to them by their culture is opened for them by the drug."[17]

As with drug use, so with many crimes: the "same" act has very different meaning for the experience-seeker and the pleasure-seeker. If it is characteristic of the upper- and upper-middle-class individual to express his personality and to seek experience, it is also characteristic of him not to want to hurt others — indeed, to want to do them good if possible. This attitude also influences the kinds of crime that he may commit. For murder, assault, and rape — violence in general — he has no stomach. He may commit an act of violence in order to further a political principle; this, after all, is what doing the "right" thing or the "just" thing may require. Euthanasia and suicide are the only kinds of killing that are really compatible with his style, however — the latter because it injures no one but the doer and the former because it is a way of doing good. Whereas rates of aggressive (i.e., nonaccidental) homicide decrease the higher one goes on the class-cultural scale, those of suicide increase.[18]

The same principle applies to other kinds of crime. Vice, for example, may attract the upper- or upper-middle-class individual both because it is "experience" and because (in his view) no one is injured by it. Under some circumstances he may steal with a clear, or almost clear, conscience. If he is a teen-ager he may "borrow" an automobile (much — some think most — auto theft is by middle-class youths), expecting that the owner will suffer nothing more than a certain amount of inconvenience on account of the theft. If he is a grown-up, he may embezzle from an organization (the larger the better) knowing that no specifiable individual will be much injured by his action. If the organization is a very large one, he may steal in the knowledge that no one will be injured at all. Who suffers if he cheats a little on his income tax?

In every social class, children, adolescents, and youths, most of them male, commit far more than their proportionate share of most crimes. In 1972, 27 percent of all serious ("index") crimes solved involved persons under eighteen years of age, although the age group ten to seventeen accounted for only about 16 percent of the nation's population.[19] Of the arrests for violent crimes (murder, forcible rape, aggravated assault, and robbery), 7 percent were of children under the age of fifteen. (These figures, it should be noted, include only *arrests* for *serious* offenses. In 1972, 1,271,000 juveniles were "taken into custody" by the police, nearly half being released without having been arrested.)

Change in the age composition of the population — meaning for all practical purposes, increase in the proportion of young men — accounts for 13 percent of the difference in the number of serious crimes committed in 1970 as against 1960, an amount equal to that caused by mere increase in the number of the population.[20]

By far the most common offense of the young — girls as well as boys — is stealing. They steal things that they "need," such as cigarettes, candy, bicycles, and presents for girl and boy friends and mothers.[21] When they "need" something and do not have the money to pay for it, they "take" it. Stealing is also a way in which boys "prove" themselves by displaying qualities that they believe (not altogether mistakenly) to be manly — boldness, stamina, willingness to accept risk — in a word, "heart." Unusual achievement along these lines earns a boy prestige among his fellows. "You stole eight cars! Jeez!"

The younger the individual, the greater (other things being equal) his propensity toward crime. Children, of course, have very little ability to control their impulses or to take account of the future. Even teen-agers are typically improvident in the extreme.

Whatever money meant to them, the boys never kept it very long. When they had money, they stopped stealing and started spending. Very often they bought things they did not need, and sometimes things they did not want. They would perhaps plan in rather meticulous detail how much money they would save for what, but the money seldom lasted long enough to be spent even the next day.[22]

If ego strength and awareness of the future develop slowly, so does moral understanding. A boy has passed the stage of preconventional morality (if he is ever going to pass it) long before reaching his teens; the hold of conventional (or postconventional) morality on him is less than firm, however. Moreover, the disturbance, partly biological and partly sociopsychological, arising from the sudden eruption of sexual impulses and the compulsion to find an answer to the question: Who am I? frequently leads to confused and irrational behavior.

In the case of boys, especially, one is struck by a resemblance between the adolescent and the lower-class styles. Both emphasize the present, action, risk, defiance of authority, and the display of "masculinity." What sociologist David Matza says of the juvenile — that for him delinquency is (among other things) a way of "making things happen" and so of escaping a "mood of fatalism"[23] — is probably true also of the lower-class adult.

It is to be expected, then, that when male adolescence and lower-class culture meet in the same person, they will interact, reinforce each other, and produce an extraordinarily high propensity toward crime. At the other end of the class-cultural continuum, the situation is not altogether different: upper- and upper-middle-class people — those of them who are oriented more toward self-expression than toward self-improvement — encourage their children to "experiment" and "find themselves," a process that is likely to reinforce the natural restlessness of the adolescent and to heighten his desire to "make things happen." Describing the "cult of the present" among middle- and upper-middle-class youths, psychologist Kenneth Keniston writes:

Indeed, among the defining characteristics of American youth culture — the special world of American adolescents and young adults — are a concentration on the present, a focus on immediate experience, an effort to achieve "genuineness," "directness," "sincerity," in perception and human relations. We see this cult in both forms — as a search for external stimulation and for internal transformation — in many of the deviant behaviors of our society: in the search for adventure among delinquent gangs, in the use of drugs to break through the gates of perception, in the "beat" quest for "kicks." And in less extreme form, a similar emphasis on the present exists in the increasing American stress on consumption rather than saving, on the "rich, full life" in the present rather than the deferred goals and future satisfactions of an earlier society.[24]

Except as they may be lower-class participants in "the subculture of violence" (which a high proportion of chronic and serious offenders are), young delinquents do not enjoy hurting people. When they employ violence, it is as a means rather than as an end in itself. Youth gang members, according to Walter B. Miller, see it as a means of winning "honor and glory."

Gang members fight to secure and defend their honor as males; to secure and defend the reputation of their local area and the honor of their women;

to show that an affront to their pride and dignity demands retaliation. Combat between males is a major means for attaining these ends.[25]

It is sometimes supposed the "fighting gang" of the 1950's succumbed to drug addiction in the 1960's and then, toward the end of that decade, having been politicized by the spirit of the times, reestablished and (for reasons never explained) took to intergang violence with unprecedented ferocity. This, according to Miller (upon whose forthcoming work this paragraph is wholly based), is myth.[26] The "fighting gang" is itself a product of police and journalistic misperceptions. *All* street gangs engage in criminal activities — although never as more than a small part of their total activity — and the average gang's repertoire of illegalities is both large, including various forms of assault, theft, property destruction, drug abuse, and drinking, and also highly susceptible to changes of fashion and to variations by place: thus the "rumble" was "in" in some cities (but not others) in the 1950's and it is again "in" in some (but not others) in the 1970's. No gang has been politicized and, plausible as it is to expect it, interracial hostility is not a frequent basis of intergang conflict. In Philadelphia, for example, most clashes are between black gangs. It is the recurrent changes in style that attract the attention of the media, but from a sociological standpoint the nature of the underlying reality is remarkable for its stability. Although they used many Yiddish phrases, the Jewish gangs of the 1910's did not differ basically from the black and other gangs of today. More than anything else, it is the size of a city's lower class that determines the number and size of its gangs.

In the large majority of cases, delinquent boys and girls cease their delinquencies when (typically in the late teens for the girls and middle twenties for the boys) they marry and settle down to jobs and to looking after children. Then things that were "fun" all of a sudden become "kid stuff." The few whose delinquency continues in adult life probably come disporportionately from the lower class. In these cases, class culture, rather than the confusions that attend rapid physical and psychological development, may have been the real cause of trouble all along.

One would expect the process of middle-class-ification which has been going on for at least a century to have brought about a gradual decrease in the rate of violent crime (but not of victimless crimes, including the violent one of suicide). As the population moves upward on the class-cultural scale, the proportion of people able to control their impulses — especially impulses which if acted upon would produce a flow of blood and gore — increases as does the proportion whose families and friends would be horror-struck by such crimes. Although long time-series of crime rates exist for only two cities, Boston and Buffalo, these tend to support the impression that, taking urbanized areas as wholes and allowing for changes in the age composition of their populations, the rate of violent crime in the cities has declined by something like one-third in the last century.[27]

Although the rate of crimes of violence reported to the police has increased dramatically since the early 1960's, it is not certain that this represents a departure, or even a significant deviation, from the long-term trend. Fuller reporting of crimes accounts for some part of the increase. But the changed age, class-cultural, and racial composition of the large cities accounts for most of it. (In 1972, nearly half of all reported crimes of violence were in the twenty-seven cities of 500,000 or more population and two-thirds of all reported robberies were in cities of 250,000 or more.) For reasons discussed in previous chapters, the class-cultural composition of the large cities came to be, in the 1960's, not very different from what it had been half a century or more ago. Two other changes interacted with this one: the rapidly increasing proportion of blacks in the large cities (as was pointed out in Chapter Four, judging from arrest rates, Negroes, even when income, schooling, and other such factors are controlled for, commit far more than their proportionate share of violent crimes) and the even more rapidly increasing proportion of the cities' population that is in the crime-prone years of adolescence and youth (because the black population was a relatively young one, the proportionate increase of black youths in the 1960's was about twice that of whites).

One who knew in advance that these demographic changes would occur in the large cities could have predicted *most* of the "breakdown of law and order" in the 1960's. Other factors, however, made some contribution to it. Improvements in health services, Roger Starr has suggested, may have lowered the death-rate (which must have been extraordinarily high a century ago) among the most violence-prone people.[28] The sudden spread of drug addiction doubtless increased the amount of violence somewhat, although probably not as much as is widely supposed. (Except in Harlem, there was little addiction before about 1965; moreover, contrary to the widespread belief, addiction does not "drive" many people to crime, least of all violent crime — those addicts who *do* commit crimes are in most cases persons who would commit crimes anyway.[29])

Crime rates have risen in small cities, including middle-class suburbs, as well as in the large cities. To some extent this reflects the greater ability of lower- and lower-working class people to find housing and jobs in the fringe areas; to some extent also it is a result of the development of urban expressways. In pre-expressway days motorists had to stop frequently for lights, and police officers had good opportunities to look them over and to spot those who appeared suspicious. Now motorists drive back and forth between the central city and the suburbs without stopping and at such speeds that no one can tell whether they are suspicious-looking or not.

The greater proportion of youths and lower-class persons in the city's population probably does not entirely explain the increase in the rate of common crime of the last few years, however. It seems likely (the data do not allow of very confident statements on any of these matters) that upper-working- and lower-middle-class persons are considerably more crime-prone than they were a generation or more ago. If this is really the case, the reason probably is not that the "wage" of crime has increased relative to other (honest) work. A more plausible explanation is that these classes have come to have less respect for authority, including the authority of the law. It may be that their conventional morality has been weakened and partially destroyed by the example of the upper classes and by the efforts of these classes to "liberate" them by the process of "education." One wonders what may be the effect on boys and girls brought up to respect authority of the advice (given by an ex-nun in the magazine *Seventeen*) to "hold always the openness of questioning the president of the college, of questioning the dean of students, of questioning the policy of the United States in Vietnam, of questioning fair housing, divorce laws and birth control"[30] or of the view (attributed by the *New York Times* to a nun photographed "holding a semiofficial late evening session at

Clancy's Bar on Third Avenue") that the Pope and Bishops "ought to be charismatic types who see their job as turning us on and supporting us in doing our things."[31] Conceivably, the effect of such words on working- and lower-middle-class persons may be to undermine their moral foundations rather than (as the speakers intend) to renew and strengthen them. The alternative to respect for external authority is not necessarily respect for internal authority: it may be no respect at all.

Other changes in public opinion have also made it easier for working- and lower-working-class people to commit crimes. Perhaps the most important of these changes is the wide acceptance during the 1960's of the view that individuals belonging to groups that have suffered injustice or are severely disadvantaged (for example, Negroes and the poor) have a kind of quasi right to have their offenses against the law extenuated or even to have them regarded as political acts reflecting a morality "higher" than obedience to law. Even crimes that were formerly regarded as wholly unpolitical and immoral — rape, for example — were in the 1960's invested with political and moral meaning, and hence with some justification, when committed by one who (whether this meaning was in his mind or not when he committed the crime) belonged to a group that possessed this special license to have its violations of law extenuated or even approved. Eldridge Cleaver, for example, in his autobiographical *Soul on Ice* explains the apparently numerous rapes that he committed, some of them against black women, on the grounds that racial injustice had created in him a powerful attraction-repulsion to white women.[32] It is plausible to suppose that many of his hundreds of thousands of readers accept the view that a rape that can be interpreted as a gesture of social protest is not wholly without justification and may even be in some way admirable.

In the 1960's the Negro crime rate appears to have increased far more than can be accounted for by changes in the age distribution of the population. Robbery arrests, for example, more than doubled and Negroes account for nearly four-fifths of the difference between the number of arrests at the beginning and at the end of the decade. It is plausible to suggest that the rhetoric of the civil-rights movement and of the Great Society (including the much-publicized emphasis given to "white racism" by the Kerner Commission) encouraged many blacks to blame the social system for all their problems and to feel that racial injustice, past as well as present, somehow justified not only "denial of responsibility" on their part but also "condemnation of the condemners" in acts of aggression.[33] In other words, the atmosphere of the 1960's may have spread the impression, especially among the young, that, as victims of oppression, Negroes had, if not a license to break the law, at least reduced responsibility for breaking it. Although the overwhelming majority of their victims continued to be other Negroes, there seems to have been a decided increase in the proportion of attacks on whites. The number of law enforcement officers killed by Negroes has increased in recent years. (In 1963–1967 there were 298 such killings; of the 398 offenders identified, 38 percent were Negro. In 1968–1972 there were 488 killings; of the 686 offenders identified, 55 percent were Negro.) Impressionistic and fragmentary evidence suggests that explicitly racial elements may in the last few years have become more important in the motivation of some Negro offenders — as, for example, in the case of two youths who, when they held up a Philadelphia trolley in the Spring of 1973, announced they would rob *only* white passengers.[34] "I am increasingly convinced," writes Marvin Wolfgang, the criminologist, "that among many black teen-agers and young adults there is a systematic diffusion of the *Soul on Ice* ideology that ripping off whites as a kind of compensatory behavior is acceptable, tolerated and even encouraged. Raping white women, stealing from white commercial establishments, mugging whites in the street and burglarizing white residential quarters are all increasingly viewed by many black juveniles especially as behavior that is Robin Hood in style and another mark of victory for the black community."[35]

Although, as this suggests, policymakers have probably increased the propensity of certain groups to crime (without, of course, intending to do so or even being aware of having done so), it does not follow that by pursuing a more enlightened policy they could significantly reduce it. Certainly in the short run, and probably in the long run as well, the main factors influencing both the propensity of various groups to crime and the size of these groups — in short, the city's potential for crime — must be taken as given. As a later chapter will contend, it is very doubtful whether in a free country, or indeed in *any* country, either the size or the culture of the lower class can be changed according to plan. With respect to the other factors that are most significant for crime — sex and age — the constraints are at least as great. The policymaker must take both the number of boys in the city and the fact that "boys will be boys" as given. Conceivably, he might in effect reduce their numbers by shortening the period of their sociological and psychological (as opposed to biological) adolescence and youth — for example, by reducing the school-leaving age and by improving their opportunities to work — but even this would not change the situation fundamentally.

What the policymaker *can* do (in principle, at least) is reduce inducements to crime. These, it will be recalled, are the benefits and costs entering into the individual's calculus in consequence of the situation in which he is placed. Even though his propensity toward crime is great, he will not commit a crime if situational factors make some noncriminal action appear more profitable. Similarly, even if his propensity is very small, he will commit a crime if the situational benefits of doing so are sufficiently great.

The implication is, of course, that efforts to deter crime should concentrate on increasing the inducements to noncriminal behavior, especially those offered to persons who are near the margin between crime and noncrime — that is, who do not need to be moved very far one way or the other. In principle, this may be done either by raising the costs of crime or by raising the benefits of noncrime.

One way of raising the benefits of noncrime is by lowering its relative cost. Thus, for example, it has been suggested that if some public or quasi-public organization were to make usable, second-hand cars available on a loan basis, or at very low cost, to poor youths, perhaps also helping them to learn to drive and to get drivers' licenses, fewer cars would be stolen.[36] Another way would be to introduce the individual to new and preferred action possibilities. Parachute jumping, skiing on fast slopes, and "golden gloves" boxing, for example, may offer slum boys better opportunities to display "heart" than does stealing cars. The practical difficulty is, however, that some of these alternatives may be more costly in life and limb or in money than the actions for which substitutes are needed. Juvenile delinquency is not as destructive as is generally supposed. The number of boys and girls killed or seriously injured in acts of delinquency is probably small compared to the number killed or seriously injured in football and skiing accidents and it is certainly trivial compared to the number who lose life or limb — their own or someone else's — seeking thrills on the highway;[37] the stealing that the young do is not of enormous economic importance either (about 90 percent of all stolen cars are recovered). Moreover, there are some offenses for which no socially acceptable substitutes can be found. If a boy must defy authority, he obviously must do so in a way that the authorities do not approve.

Another way of raising the benefits of noncrime is by increasing the relative rate of return from it. In the view of some economists lack of job opportunities caused the rise in crime in the middle and latter 1960's; therefore "a successful attack on rising crime rates must consider the employment problems facing young people."[38] This argument, however, can be turned around: the availability of easy money in the "hustles" (or, as some economists are now calling it, the "irregular economy") may have caused withdrawals from the labor force which have been wrongly perceived as lack of job opportunities. This view receives some support from Stanley Friedlander, who, after studying unemployment and crime rates in 30 cities in 1960 and 1966, concludes that "contrary to the literature, the more property crimes in a city, the lower the unemployment rate for nonwhites in both time periods." People engaged in crime or supported by it, he writes, "had means of support that allowed them not to work and not to be counted in the labor force. The dramatic result is less unemployment [among nonwhites] in cities with high property crime rates."[39]

Impressionistic evidence from the social anthropologist Elliot Liebow in his book *Tally's Corner* suggests that some workers move freely back and forth between the "irregular" and "regular" economies depending upon the opportunities of the day. In a recent year, the crime rate in Washington for the month of August jumped 18 percent over the preceding month. A veteran police officer explained the increase to David L. Bazelon, Chief Judge, U.S. Court of Appeals for the District of Columbia.

It's quite simple. . . . You see, August was a very wet month. . . . These people wait on the street corner each morning around 6:00 or 6:30 for a truck to pick them up and take them to a construction site. If it's raining, that truck doesn't come, and the men are going to be idle that day. If the bad weather keeps up for three days . . . we know we are going to have trouble on our hands — and sure enough, there invariably follows a rash of purse-snatchings, house-breakings and the like. . . . These people have to eat like the rest of us, you know.[40]

Most stealing is done by persons who want small amounts *now*. For them a job that must be worked at regularly and that pays *only at the end of the week* is not a real alternative to stealing. Even if the wage rate is high, such a job is of no interest to one who wants only a few dollars — enough, say, to buy a couple of six-packs of beer and a carton of cigarettes — but wants them now — this very day, perhaps this very hour. What is needed to reduce stealing, then, is not so much high employment and rising incomes as it is greater opportunity for people who live in the present to get small sums when they want them. Paying unskilled workers by the day instead of the week would help matters some. So would paying them for days that they are prevented from working by weather, the illness of a family member, or some other good reason. So far as employment levels are concerned, the need is not so much for more "good" jobs as it is for more casual ones — jobs that, although not high paying, are readily available to persons who want to "make a few bucks" when, and only when, the spirit moves them. Boys, especially, need such job opportunities; perhaps there is no more economical way of reducing juvenile delinquency, and thus crime in general, than by repealing the minimum wage and relaxing the child-labor and school-attendance laws. The main effect of these laws, it is probably safe to say, is to make stealing the boy's easiest, if not his only, way of getting the money and other things he thinks he needs.

If making it easier to earn money is one way of influencing the outcome of the individual's calculus of profit and loss when he contemplates crime, increasing the probability both of his being caught and of his being severely punished is another. Obviously, one way of doing the former with respect to the kinds of crimes that occur in public places is to put more policemen on patrol. From the standpoint of the calculating individual, the greater probability of a policeman's appearing represents a cost; the higher this cost, the less likely (other things being equal) the individual is to commit a crime. "Operation 25," an experiment tried all too briefly by the New York Police Department in 1954, gave indications that rather dramatic results can be obtained by "saturating" an area with patrolmen.[41] For a four-month period the force in a high-crime district of Manhattan was doubled. Muggings fell from 69 to 7, auto thefts from 78 to 24, and assaults from 185 to 132. Murders, however, increased from 6 to 8. (Since it generally takes place in private, murder is not likely to be deterred by the presence on the street of any number of policemen.) To what extent the drop in crime reflected not deterrence from crime altogether but rather deterrence from crime *in that particular precinct* (that is, its displacement to a less heavily patrolled one) there is, of course, no way of knowing.

Attaching a stiffer penalty to an offense sometimes, but by no means always, raises the cost of the action significantly. In the first place, the penalties most likely to deter a middle- or working-class person — the disgrace that his arrest and conviction will bring upon his family and the prospect of losing his job — are not penalties at all to those whose families would not feel disgraced (and to whom it would not matter if they did) and whose chances of getting a job in the secondary labor market would not be affected by any number of arrests. So far as those who commit most of the common crimes are concerned, it is normally only *legal* penalties — fines and imprisonment — that enter into the calculus at all. These sometimes make a difference: when the penalty for prostitution was drastically reduced in New York City, the number of prostitutes in the city increased very quickly, some coming from cities hundreds of miles away in order to take advantage of the lower costs of doing business there.[42]

The opportunities to deter crime by threatening penalties — especially to deter *serious* crime by threatening *severe* penalties — are sharply limited. In part, this is because the probability of being caught is negligible for minor offenses.[43] (Of the *serious* crimes committed in 1972, only one-fifth were solved by arrests.) But it is also, as James Q. Wilson has pointed out, because severity of punishment is subject to rapidly diminishing returns (the difference between a one- and a five-year sentence appearing large and that between a twenty- and a twenty-five year one small) and because the more severe the penalty the less likely it is to be imposed. "To insure conviction, to avoid an expensive trial, to reduce the chances of reversal on appeal, and to give expression to their own views of benevolence, prosecutors and judges will try to get a guilty plea, and all they can offer in return is a lesser sentence. The more severe the sentence, the greater the bargaining power of the accused. . . ."[44]

Several recent studies have found that increasing the probability of punishment generally has more deterrent effect than increasing the severity of it.[45] Antunes and Hunt, taking as their measure of probability the number of persons sent to prison each year in each state for a given crime divided by the number of those crimes reported in those states in the previous year, showed that where a crime was most likely to lead to imprisonment it was least likely to be committed. There was no such association between severity of punishment, as measured by the median length of prison sentence, except in the case of murder. (Capital punishment was left out of account.[46]) In an earlier study, Tittle found that for all offenses except murder the rate of crime decreased as the probability of punishment increased no matter what the level of severity. Curiously, the association was weakest in more highly urbanized areas.[47] In still another study, Ehrlich found that much depends upon the offender's attitude toward risk: one who is averse to risk is deterred more by an increase in the severity of punishment than by an equal increase in the probability of it whereas with one who prefers risk the opposite is the case.[48]

The policy significance of these findings may change, however, as Reynolds has pointed out, if one takes into account the *costs* of the two methods.[49] Increasing the severity of punishment is very much less costly than increasing the probability of it, and the difference in cost — for some crimes at least — is so great as to make the latter method appear nothing short of extravagant despite its greater effectiveness. He has worked out the following table which compares the cost of deterring a marginal property crime by each method.

As a practical matter, even for serious crimes (murder being a partial exception) the probability of being caught is small, that of

	Burglary	Robbery	Larceny
Final cost per crime deterred by increasing probability	$7,050	$5,900	$8,400
Final cost per crime deterred by increasing sentence	$3,175	$3,450	$ 675

being convicted smaller, and that of being severely punished smaller still. If the accompanying diagram, from the 1969 report of the Violence Commission, were brought up to date, there is no doubt that the small circles would shrink considerably. It is indicative of this that despite the rapidly rising crime rates, the number of persons in prison has declined steadily and in 1970 (the latest year for which figures are available) was 23,720 (10 percent) less than in 1961.[50]

The threat of even very stiff future penalties would not have a deterrent effect upon radically present-oriented individuals. It is likely that even to a normal person a punishment appears smaller the farther off in the future it lies. With the radically present-oriented, this distortion of perspective is much greater: a punishment that is far enough off to appear small to a normal person appears tiny, or is quite invisible, to a present-oriented one. His calculus of benefits and costs is defective, since benefits are in the present where he can see them while costs are in the future where he cannot. Accordingly, even if he knows that the probability of his being caught is high and that the penalty for the crime is severe, he may commit it anyway; no matter how severe, a penalty that lies weeks or months away is not a part of reality for him.

The implication is that in order to deter juveniles and lower-class persons (the present-oriented classes of offenders), penalties must follow very closely upon the commission of crimes. Speeding up court processes so that fines will be imposed or jail sentences begin hours or days, rather than weeks or months, after arrest would probably reduce somewhat the rate of common crimes even if the probability of arrest and conviction remained as low as it now is.

As a practical matter, it is probably impossible to arrange a court procedure that would bring punishment within the time horizon of the most present-oriented. In order to deter these, the judge and jury

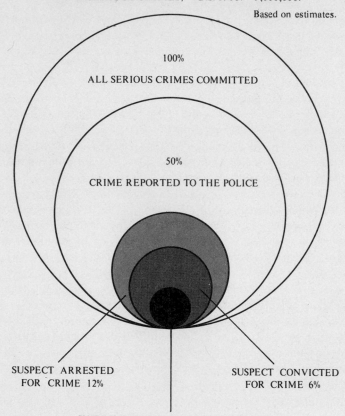

CRIME AND LAW ENFORCEMENT
TOTAL SERIOUS CRIMES, [a] U.S. 1968: 9,000,000.

Based on estimates.

100%
ALL SERIOUS CRIMES COMMITTED

50%
CRIME REPORTED TO THE POLICE

SUSPECT ARRESTED
FOR CRIME 12%

SUSPECT CONVICTED
FOR CRIME 6%

SUSPECT IMPRISONED FOR CRIME 1½%

[a] Aggregate of homicide, forcible rape, robbery, aggravated assault, burglary, larceny over $50, auto theft.

Source: Final Report of the National Commission on the Causes and Prevention of Violence (Washington D.C.: G.P.O., December 1969), p. xviii.

would have to be on the scene, or just offstage, at the time the action was being contemplated. This suggests that "curbstone justice" — punishment meted out on the spot by a policeman — is what is needed. This does not necessarily imply that the policeman should also *administer* the punishment. (The prospect of being "roughed up" would probably not deter many lower-class persons; among boys and young men, especially, this sort of punishment might actually increase crime by making it a surer way to display "heart.") The prospect of punishment would probably be brought within the time horizon of present-oriented persons if a policeman could issue a ticket that was tantamount to a fine. He can do this, of course, with traffic offenses. But with the common nontraffic offenses of present-oriented people, especially stealing and assault, he must go to court (often on his own time) to testify, and the disposition of the case is entirely in the hands of the judge or magistrate. Because in these cases the policeman is not the de facto judge, as he is in the traffic ones, penalties lie in the future rather than in the present.

There are, of course, reasons why policemen have de facto authority to set punishments in one kind of case but not the other. One is that the policeman *witnesses* a traffic violation but only *suspects* a theft. Another is that traffic offenses are morally neutral, whereas other offenses usually are not. One who values his good name has vastly more at stake if accused of stealing than if accused of speeding. With traffic offenses, then, there is an inherent safeguard against any very damaging error from the exercise of police discretion, whereas with other offenses there is no such safeguard. This may well be a decisive consideration against giving policemen de facto authority to punish the kinds of crimes that present-oriented people typically commit. If so, it should be noted in passing that it is the present-oriented who suffer from this. They have little need to be protected against any moral onus (the distinction between offenses against law and offenses against morality being unknown to them), and they are the ones who would most surely benefit by arrangements that brought deterrents within their time horizon.

One form of deterrence that *does* work with present-oriented people (in fact no less well with them than with others) has been called "hardening the target." The individual is deterred by measures that make it difficult or impossible for him to commit the crime. For example, a 167-acre subdivision containing sixty-seven high-cost residences near Washington, D.C., is surrounded by two fences with guardhouses at two entry points. The fencing is watched by closed-circuit television and supplemented by hidden sensors. Residents carry ID cards, and visitors are permitted beyond the guardhouses only after a resident has telephoned approval. This, of course, is the extreme.

Architectural features — stairways built on the exterior of a building and enclosed with glass, proper placing and trimming of trees and shrubbery, elimination of potential hiding places, windowless walls on ground floors — may make criminal action more troublesome, inconvenient, or risky enough (in some sense more costly) to deter it.[51] Even such simple devices as well-made locks, burglar alarms, powerful streetlights, clocks to turn on lights and radios, and new kinds of glass that take ten or fifteen minutes to break may raise costs enough to make a criminal undertaking appear unprofitable. As was remarked above, most crimes are committed opportunistically by youths who want small amounts of money right away and will not go to much trouble, or take much risk to get it. A target need be hardened very little to protect it from them.

Obviously "hardening the target" is not a task for law enforcement agencies. The ordinary citizen, by installing a good lock on his door and taking the trouble to use it, can do more to deter burglary than could any number of policemen. Similarly, by displaying his goods in one way rather than another, the merchant can do more than the police to reduce shoplifting. Institutions acting in behalf of individuals or public — architects and builders, city planners, and lawmakers — can take the initiative in some matters (and may on occasion go further than their clients, customers, or constituents would wish). Thus, for example, Congress, by requiring automobile manufacturers to install antitheft devices on the steering columns or transmissions of cars built after January 1, 1970, caused — or helped to cause — a decline of about 4 percent in the number of cars stolen in 1972, the first decline in history. Thus, also, city agencies may plan the use of space, distribute facilities (street lighting, for example), and set "minimum security" standards for buildings so as to further the creation of what is being called the "defensive city."

If the potential criminal responds rationally to deterrents, why does not the potential victim act rationally by offering them? The answer is that the potential victim usually *does* act rationally, but the structure of the situation in which he is placed is such that he seldom has much incentive to take preventive measures even when they are simple in their nature and effective in their application. Locking one's car is a nuisance, and the probability of its being stolen on any one occasion is small. If the motorist counts the nuisance of having to lock the car at no more than a fraction of a cent, it may very well be cheaper for him to run the risk of his car's being stolen than to take the trouble to lock it.

In the case of shoplifting, the appropriate deterrent measures — displaying goods differently and making less use of self-service — although simple and effective may be costly in terms of profit. From a business standpoint, measures to deter theft are likely to be inefficient.

One large chain of bookdealers reported less than .5 percent loss. Instead of regarding this minuscule loss as a cause for rejoicing, it was regarded as the result of "old fashioned" merchandising methods including much personal service by a large staff of sales clerks. "Certainly," said the security representative, "we have a small inventory shortage, but our payroll for sales personnel cuts our profit to almost nothing. We could be ahead by accepting the inevitability of shoplifting. Self-service plus all the losses it will bring will net us more profit in the long run than individualized service with almost no loss at all."[52]

Petty pilfering by white-collar employees, in the view of some employers, improves their morale and is an alternative to higher wage rates.[53]

Another reason why a potential victim does not go to more trouble and expense to deter crime is that he often knows that if the worst happens and he becomes a victim, he can shift most — perhaps all — of his loss to an insurance company or to some other institution. If the motorist were not insured against theft, he would be more likely to lock his car. And if in addition the police charged a proper fee for recovering stolen cars, he would be still more likely to lock it.

It will be seen that some crimes are not deterred because the potential victims lack a sufficient incentive to do so or may even have an incentive *not* to. This may occur even in those instances where the collective benefits from deterrence would far exceed the collective costs, for the profitability of anyone's incurring costs for deterrence may depend upon everyone's (or almost everyone's) incurring them. One way of getting around this is to organize entities so large that it will pay them to invest in preventive measures whether others do or not — so large, that is, that the gain to them from the preventive measures, even though not the whole gain (that is, even though others "ride free") is nevertheless large enough to make the investment profitable. This is what economists call "internalizing the externalities."

It is of course a function of government to act where a collective advantage can be secured only by the exercise of an authority — that of the tax collector — able to compel people to pay for a good or service (reduction of crime) whether they want it or not. This is the theory that justifies public support of law enforcement agencies and presumably it is the one that justified Congress in requiring manufacturers of automobiles to equip all new cars with antitheft devices and certain cities in requiring builders to install locks of a kind specified in a "minimum security code."

There is much to be said for governmental measures to reduce or remove the disincentives that tend to prevent people from taking simple measures to deter crime. Insurance companies could be forbidden to reimburse owners for loss of cars that were left unlocked (two-fifths of all those stolen, according to one report). Shoplifters could be arrested by the police, rather than by store detectives, and the cost of their arrest, detention, and trial charged against the merchant in whose store they were caught. The bad-check collecting services that the police perform could be charged to the storekeepers who accept bad checks. A strong argument for doing these things is that the cost to the individual of deterring crime is trifling as compared to the cost to the public of dealing with it after it has been committed. A California study showed that the average "career cost" of a forgery and check offender is $16,900, as compared to $5,800 for an adult homicide offender.[54] ("Career cost" is what the authorities spend on an average offender over his entire lifetime.)

One must take into account, however, that certain benefits are more or less incompatible with deterrence, and the loss of these must be weighed against the gains to be had from it. Millions of people are convenienced by the ease with which checks can be cashed, and millions are served by having the goods in department stores and supermarkets displayed so that close inspection of them is possible. These benefits to the consumer are worth something; possibly they are worth all the billions that they cost in the higher prices that must be charged to cover losses by theft, in the taxes that are required to support police forces, courts, jails, and in the welfare payments to the dependents of persons who are in jail.

One must also take into account that the costs of collectively required deterrents may exceed their benefits. It is not obvious, for example, that Congress got much for the consumer's money by requiring him to purchase antitheft devices with his new car. (Car thefts decreased by 6 percent — about 61,000 cars — from 1971 to 1972. If we assume that the devices were solely responsible for the decrease and that they cost $30 per car, or $330,000,000 for the 11 million cars produced, the per theft cost of prevention was $5,410.) Nor is it obvious that cities which require home builders to install locks that cost an extra $50 to $100 per dwelling thereby secure public benefits large enough to justify the added burden on the home buyer.

It is arguable that intangible benefits to the public from the reduction of crime will outweigh almost any dollar-and-cents cost to consumers or taxpayers. Neither convenience nor money, some will say, ought to count for much, or perhaps for anything at all, against the value of lawabidingness.

Even if legal penalties were brought much closer to the present, and even if potential victims took all reasonable precautions, it is safe to say that some people — mostly young, lower-class males — would continue to commit a great many serious crimes. There are individuals whose propensity to crime is so high that no set of incentives that it is feasible to offer to the whole population would influence their behavior. They may be compelled, but they cannot be deterred. The only entirely effective way of *compelling* someone not to commit crimes is to lock him up — in the most extreme case, in solitary confinement. Society does this even if the individual has not committed a crime when it is considered almost certain that he cannot be prevented in any other way from committing very serious crimes. No one would doubt the wisdom or justice of confining indefinitely a madman who, if released, would rush to attack anyone he saw — and this even if he had not as yet seriously injured anyone. The case is very different, however, if — as may be with most of those who might be found undeterrable (say, those who are very present-oriented and have little ego strength and a preconventional conception of morality) — the probability of their committing serious crimes is, although high, by no means a certainty. Even if one could be sure — which, of course, one cannot — that a particular boy now aged sixteen has a .5 probability of committing several robberies over the next ten years, one would not lock him up for that period as a preventive measure.

If there is any acceptable way of dealing with this problem — and there may not be — it would appear to be by abridging the individual's freedom in a degree that corresponds to the expected costs in crime to society of his being free (that is, to the probability of his committing crimes times a measure of their seriousness). Thus, for example, the boy with a .5 probability of committing several robberies might be kept under the surveillance of a parole officer, whereas one with a .9 probability of committing murder might be confined.

The principle implies, of course, that the law provide a gradation of abridgments of freedom, more or less onerous ones to be imposed upon the individual as his behavior raises or lowers the probability of his committing serious crimes.[55] The knowledge that his freedom would be further abridged if he misbehaved would doubtless have some deterrent effect in many cases, but it must not be forgotten that the reason for the abridgments of freedom is not deterrence (it being *undeterrables* who are here under discussion) but the reduction of the individual's opportunities to commit crimes. In other words, he is not threatened with some partial loss of freedom in order to make the criminal action relatively unattractive; rather, he is deprived of some freedom in order to prevent him from taking the criminal action that he prefers.

Such a scheme might employ successive levels of abridgment, as follows:

   1. The individual would be required to keep in touch weekly with a probation officer, to observe a 10 P.M. curfew, to post a

"peace" bond; he might not possess firearms or ride in private automobiles, and he would be liable to search at any time.

2. In addition to the above, he would be sequestered in a small town.

3. He would be confined to a penal village or work camp where he might receive visitors and support a family but which he might not leave.

An arrangement of this sort might be justified both on grounds that it is more humane than imprisonment (a consideration that ought to have special weight in dealing with people who are not able to control themselves to the normal extent and whose moral responsibility is accordingly less) and on grounds that, being more humane and also fairer, judges would be more willing to make use of it and it would therefore be more effective in reducing crime.[56] As a practical matter, however, it might prove unworkable. If, as seems likely, the undeterrables could not be deterred from breaking the rules of such a system, the authorities would be forced to abridge their freedom wholly — by imprisoning them — in order to abridge it at all. If this effect were general, the scheme would not work: it would lead to the imprisonment of all the undeterrables, including, of course, those who would never have been imprisoned but for the scheme iteslf. It may be doubted, too, whether the least onerous abridgments (Level 1) would be very effective in preventing crime. Conceivably, their chief effect would be to sort out rather quickly those who required more stringent abridgments.

The scheme is, of course, open to objection on the ground that *any* abridgment of an individual's freedom on the ground that he *may* commit a crime is incompatible with the essential principles of a free society.[57] But, of course, unless it is for retribution, the imprisonment of persons who have been convicted of crimes is on the assumption that they *may* commit more; the grounds of this probability judgment, although different, are not necessarily any better and under certain conditions may even be worse than those of judgments regarding persons who so far as is known have not committed *any* crimes. In any event, if abridging the freedom of persons who have not committed crimes is incompatible with the principles of free society, so, also, is the presence in such society of persons who, if their freedom is not abridged, would use it to inflict serious injuries on others. There is, therefore, a painful dilemma. If some people's freedom is not abridged by law-enforcement agencies, that of others will be abridged by law breakers. The question, therefore, is not whether abridging the freedom of those who may commit serious crimes is an evil — it is — but whether it is a lesser or a greater one than the alternative.[58]

CHAPTER NINE

Rioting Mainly for Fun and Profit

"Picketing and marching ain't getting us anywhere, man," said Byron Washington, a 16-year-old 11th-grader who was arrested during this week's riots for having a rock in his hand.

"The whites got to face it, man, this is a new generation. We aren't going to stand for the stuff our mamas and fathers stood for.

"Look at me, I've got a B average, but I can't get a summer job. And if you don't work, you can't afford to go to college."
— *New York Times* report from
Waterloo, Iowa, July 14, 1967

In the law of most states a riot is a lawless act engaged in by three or more persons and accompanied by violence or breach of the public peace. If the rioters are Negroes it is usually taken for granted that the riot is in some sense racial. Probably the most widespread view is that Negroes riot because they can no longer contain their pent-up fury at the mistreatment they receive from whites. The Watts riot, we are told "was a manifestation of a general sense of deep outrage, outrage at every aspect of the lives Negroes are forced to live, outrage at every element of the white community for forcing (or permitting) Negroes to live such lives."[1]

On this view it follows that the way to end rioting — the *only* way to end it — is to stop mistreating the Negro and, so far as possible, to repair the damage already done him. "Doing such things as punishing police misconduct, providing decent housing and schooling, ending job discrimination and so forth are essential, but the problem goes deeper than that. The ghetto itself, with all the shameful economic, social, political, and psychological deprivation it causes, must be done away with once and for all. The riots have 'let America know' that this is what must be done. Now America must do it."[2]

This is not the view that will be taken here. The assumption that if Negroes riot it must be *because* they are Negroes is naive. So is the assumption that if people who are poor, or who have long been treated unjustly, riot it must be *because* they are poor or have long been treated unjustly. If one rejects these starting places and looks at the facts instead, one sees that race, poverty, and injustice, although among the conditions that made the larger riots possible, were not *the causes* of them and had very little to do with many of the lesser ones. Indeed, it is probably not too much to say that *some* of the riots would have occurred even if (other things being the same) the people in the riot areas had all been white and even if they had all had incomes above the poverty line. The possibility of a riot exists wherever there are crowds of people,[3] and an "explanation" of the Negro riots which fails to take account of the generality of the phenomenon of civil disorder is inadequate. Distinctions should be drawn along analytical lines so that they will provide "building blocks" from which an account of all sorts of riots in all sorts of places may be constructed.

(1) Two thousand juveniles break windows after an amusement park closes early, leaving them without transportation.

(2) A gang of hoodlums robs a clothing store and smashes the display windows of three other stores, stealing watches, cameras, and rings.

(3) A young man has been shot and killed by the police during a burglary, and a crowd, shouting "This is for Willie," pelts the police with rocks, bottles, and fire bombs.

(4) Following an inflammatory speech by a racist politician, a mob overturns automobiles and assaults motorists.

To that strict behaviorist, the man on the moon, all four of these events probably look alike: all are "riots" and, if the rioters are Negro, presumably "racial." But to an observer able and willing to take motives into account (that is, to take note of the meaning of an act to the actor) the events are very different and some are not in any sense racial. The first is a rampage by frustrated teen-agers who happen to be black. The second is a foray for pillage by young toughs who find "taking" things the easiest way of getting them. In this case, too, race is not a motive and is in fact irrelevant to behavior: the toughs are Negro, but they could as well be white. The third event is an outburst of righteous indignation on the part of people who have witnessed what they think is an act of gross injustice. The young man who was killed was black and the policeman who killed him was white, but it is possible that the indignation the crowd feels is mainly or even entirely against the police rather than against whites as such. (In September 1962, Negroes in the all-Negro village of Kinlock, Missouri, rioted when a Negro policeman shot a Negro youth.) Indeed, some members of the crowd may be indignant at whites, others at the police, and still others at both whites and the police, and so it might be impossible to say whether or not the riot was "mainly racial," even if one had full knowledge of the subjective states of all rioters. In the final case, the event is a demonstration carried on for the express purpose of calling attention to a political position; since the position is a racist one, the riot can properly be called racial.

Each of these four motivations implies a riot of a certain character. As a basis for the analysis of more complicated events, it will be useful to describe four "simple types" of riot as follows:

The rampage. This is an outbreak of high spirits. Young men, especially, are naturally restless, in search of excitement, thrills, "action." Also, as David Matza has explained, they are apt to feel "pushed around"; one who is caught in this mood of fatalism (as Matza calls it) wants dramatic reassurance that he can "make things happen," and breaking the law is one of the few actions open to him that immediately and demonstrably makes things happen.[4] Rioting (which Matza does not mention) is a way of making them happen on a wholesale scale. "These young people, to whom a voter registration campaign, a picket line, or an economic boycott means very little, have found that they can stun an entire community by engaging in rioting. They can mobilize entire police forces and National Guard companies, keep mayors at their desks through the night, and bring representatives of the news media from all over the country."[5]

A rampage may start either with an incident — for example, an argument or an arrest — or "out of the blue." If it starts with an incident, the incident is more in the nature of a pretext than (as in a riot of the outburst of indignation type) a provocation; that is, the rampage begins not because the incident made the rampagers angry (although they may pretend that) but because they were "looking for trouble" or at least were in a mood to seize upon an excuse (signal?) to rampage. There is no pattern to the violence once it starts: it involves destruction for the sake of destruction and fighting for the sake of fighting. The police are frequently attacked by rampagers; this is not because they are hated (although they may be) but because they are at hand and will put up a good fight. Rampaging by teen-agers has always been a problem in the cities. From the very earliest times, harassing the watch, vandalism, and arson have been favorite pastimes of the young.[6] In Pittsburgh in 1809 an editor proposed satirically that the city establish a "conflagration fund" from which to buy twelve houses, one to be burned each month in a civil celebration.[7] Until the middle of the last century fire companies in the large cities were manned by volunteers, mostly boys and young men, and were in many cases what today would be called conflict gangs. Whether they put out more fires than they started is a question. In Philadelphia, for example, firemen used to riot almost every Sunday, using bricks, stones, and firearms, apparently with intent to kill.[8] In the slums of the large cities there were also street gangs, some claiming more than a thousand members, which fought each other and the police almost constantly.[9] Usually the authorities did not try very hard to interfere with these activities, which were regarded as in the nature of sporting events.[10]

Youth rampages occur today not only in the slums but elsewhere. Thousands of college boys rioted at Hampton Beach, New Hampshire, and at Seaside, Oregon, in 1964, the year the inner-city riots began, and there have been large rampages of white boys on the Sunset Strip of Los Angeles, in Atlantic City, and elsewhere since. It is not only American boys who behave this way, but boys almost everywhere. In Stockholm, for example, hordes of teen-agers hang around the subway stations committing acts of vandalism and harassing the police. "The police say that if a constable has to arrest a drunk who is disturbing the peace, the youngsters will often set upon the policeman, and a major riot looms before reinforcements can be called."[11] Probably many of the student "political demonstrations" reported in this and other countries are actually rampages.

In the upper classes the norms of culture tend to restrain the restlessness of youth and to encourage its sublimation. In the lower classes, on the other hand, cultural norms reinforce feelings of restlessness and the "mood of fatalism." Accordingly, lower-class youths are more apt than others to be caught up in frenzies of mob activity, and even adults of the lower class are, by comparison with those of the other classes, highly susceptible to the same influences.

The foray for pillage. Here the motive is theft, and here also boys and young adults of the lower class are the principal offenders. Stealing is ordinarily most conveniently done in private, of course, but when disasters — earthquakes, fires, floods, power failures, blizzards, enemy invasions, police strikes — interrupt law enforcement it may be done as well or better in public. On these occasions, when "Everyone is doing it" and "If I don't take the stuff it will just go to waste," upper-working- and middle-class adults who, under normal circumstances, would not steal, are likely to join the looters. (In 1711 the selectmen of Boston passed an act to punish persons "taking advantage of such confusion and calamities [as fire] to rob, plunder, embezzle, convey away and conceal the goods and effects of their distressed neighbours."[12]) From the standpoint of the youth or of the lower-class adult who makes a practice of stealing, it would be convenient to have a riot every day. Riots are seldom started by thieves merely to facilitate stealing, however. One reason is that the culture of the lower class renders it incapable of the planning and organization that would ordinarily be necessary to start a riot by design. Another and perhaps more important one is that although all thieves would benefit from a riot, no one thief would benefit enough from it to justify his taking the trouble and running the risks of starting it. (As an economist would put it, the riot is, from the standpoint of the thieves, a "collective good."[13]) But if thieves rarely start riots, they are always quick to join ones that are under way, and their presence in sufficient number may transform one from, say, a rampage to a foray for pillage. "I really know of no instance of a riot occurring in New York, or in any other large city, during which robbery did not play a prominent part," New York's Police Chief Walling wrote toward the end of the last century.[14]

The outburst of righteous indignation. Here the rioters are moved by indignation at what they regard, rightly or wrongly, as injustice or violation of the mores that is likely to go unpunished. Their indignation is partly at the wrongfulness of the act and partly at the wrongfulness of its going unpunished. A riot of this type is always spontaneous — people do not become indignant according to plan. Indignation is aroused by an incident of some sort (which may, of course, have been contrived by someone for the purpose), and in the nature of the case, the indignant people are without leaders. The incident itself may help to make up for this lack by serving a coordinating function; as Thomas C. Schelling has pointed out, "Without something like an incident, it may be difficult to get action at all, since immunity requires that all know when to act together."[15]

A righteously indignant mob usually consists mainly of working-class people. The lower-class individual is too alienated to be capable of much indignation, especially in a matter that he thinks does not affect him personally and directly; middle- and upper-class people are usually confident of their ability to get wrongs righted by making appeals through proper channels, and, besides, they abhor violence. The working class is not under any of these limitations: it has a capacity for righteous indignation, distrusts lawyers, public relations people, and "channels" generally, and does not greatly mind — indeed, sometimes very much enjoys — a good brawl and the spilling of some blood.

Under favorable circumstances, that is, where the working class is large and consists of people who have enough in common so that they will respond with indignation to the same provocation, an outburst of righteous indignation may involve a great many people — far more, certainly, than a rampage or a foray, both of which by their nature ordinarily draw upon relatively small "constituencies." All the large riots of the nineteenth century were mainly outbursts of righteous indignation. Some of them were very large indeed. For example, the Boston riot of 1837 (an American-born working-class attack on Irish immigrants) is supposed to have involved more than 15,000 persons, roughly one-sixth of the city's population.

In an outburst of righteous indignation the pattern of violence and destruction reflects the mob's wish to end, and also to redress or avenge, the wrong that aroused its indignation. As Rudé says in his account of popular disturbances in preindustrial France and England, the mob imposes a conception of "natural justice": "Strikers tended to destroy machinery or 'pull down' their employers' houses; food rioters to invade markets and bakers' shops and enforce a popular price control or *taxation populaire*; rural rioters to destroy fences and turnpikes or threshing machines and workhouses, or to set fire to the farmer's or landlord's stacks; and city rioters to 'pull down' dissenters' meeting houses and chapels, to destroy their victims' houses and property, and to burn their political enemies in effigy."[16]

The demonstration. Here the motive is to advance a political principle or ideology or to contribute to the maintenance of an organization. The riot is not a spontaneous, angry response to an incident. Rather, it is the result of prearrangement by persons who are organized, have leaders, and who see it as a means to some end. The word "demonstration" is descriptive, for the event is a kind of show staged to influence opinion. Those who put it on are usually middle or upper class, these being the classes from which the people who run organizations and espouse political causes are mostly drawn. Demonstrations characteristically involve breach of the public peace rather than violence (if they involve neither they are by definition not riots); the middle- and upper-class cultural style favors the use of mock violence (for example, the spraying of slogans with paint and the throwing of steer's blood), "happenings" (for example, halting traffic with police whistles), and behavior calculated to make the demonstrator the object, or the apparent object, of violence inflicted either by himself (as when he chains himself to something) or by the authorities (as when he "goes limp"). The middle and upper classes' abhorrence of violence is so great that techniques like these, which trade upon it without requiring the demonstrator to hurt anyone but himself (and usually not himself either), are often effective as a means of putting "the other side" at a moral disadvantage in the eyes of the middle- and upper-class television viewers for whose benefit the demonstration is staged.

These four types of riots are presented as analytical models. Some concrete riots very closely approximate a "pure" type, but what a historian has said of mob violence in early Boston — ". . . too many types of people took to the streets for too many reasons for any single formula to apply"[17] — can be said of most riots. All large ones, it seems safe to say, are compounds of at least two of the types. The New York Draft Riot of 1863, for example, was a compound of at least three. It was a rampage of young toughs from the slums (three-fourths of those actively engaged in violence were boys and men under twenty years of age who were not subject to the draft, a *Times* writer estimated; it was a foray for pillage (houses and places of business were ransacked all along Eleventh Avenue); and it was also — and perhaps mainly — an outburst of righteous indignation on the part of the Irish working class at the prospect of having to compete with freed Negroes for jobs and against the alleged injustices of the draft law.[18] Large riots tend to be compound, if for no other reason, simply because they attract looters. But it is likely that the fact of their being compound also tends to make them larger: that is, that interaction among types of rioters tends to reinforce the motives and heighten the activity of each type. For example, the looters and rampagers in the Draft Riot no doubt got some moral support from having all about them rioters motivated by righteous indignation; at the same time, the presence of the looters and rampagers, most of whom were not clearly identifiable as such, must have added to the general sense of confusion and frenzy and by so doing must have helped sustain the fury of the righteously indignant. That these latter had *two* objects of indignation — Negroes and the draft law — must also have increased the interaction. One may conjecture that the greater the variety of motivational elements appealed to, the larger the number of rioters who will be recruited and — what is more important — the more interaction tending to sustain and escalate the riot there will be among the rioters.

Looking from this perspective at the series of inner-city riots, one is struck by the fact that for twenty years prior to July 18, 1964, there had been very few riots by Negroes, and that these few, with only one exception, had been protests against racial injustice. In 1961, for example, white mobs in six cities attacked Negroes, but there were no riots by Negroes. In 1962 there were four Negro riots — one was a demonstration by Black Muslims, two seem to have been outbursts of righteous indignation provoked by incidents of alleged police brutality, and the fourth, the exception, was a rampage by high school students after a football game in the District of Columbia stadium. In 1963 and the first half of 1964 there were eleven Negro riots, all apparently outbursts of righteous indignation and all but three occurring in the South. In none of these years was there a major Negro riot — one involving several hundred rioters and lasting more than a day.[19]

On July 18, 1964, a riot began in Harlem that proved to be a turning point. Two days before, an off-duty white police lieutenant had shot and killed a fifteen-year-old Negro youth whom he said had attacked him with a knife. A mixed jury exonerated the police officer of wrongdoing, but the incident created widespread anger. After the youth's funeral there was a mass meeting; as the crowd poured out of it "someone apparently shoved someone who shoved back," "the mounting tension of weeks and months snapped, and in an instant the melee was on." "In the chaos," the writer continues, "the junkies, the winos, and down-and-outers and the plain lawless ones with little interest in politics or human rights gathered from Seventh Avenue and its shabby tributaries to make what profit they could in looting. . . ."[20] The next evening there was another mass meeting. A Black Nationalist "priest" made an inflammatory speech and then led a group of youths in a march on a nearby police station. A crowd pelted the station with bottles and stones. After three days in Harlem, the riot moved to the Bedford-Stuyvesant district of Brooklyn and six days later, for no apparent reason, to Rochester. (The incident — an attempt by a policeman to arrest a drunk and disorderly adolescent at a street dance — seems to have been a pretext rather than a provocation.) A few days later the rioting spread, also for no apparent reason, to three New Jersey cities, an industrial suburb of Chicago, and Philadelphia.

In Harlem, when it first broke out, the rioting was mainly an outburst of righteous indignation at the police. There was little looting; the mob was chiefly occupied in bitter fighting with the police. As the rioting continued and moved to other cities, however, its nature changed. Looting and rock throwing became the mob's principal activities, with attacks on the police sporadic and incidental. In Rochester, the city manager said later, the riot had "racial overtones" but was not actually a race riot.[21] In Philadelphia, the first policeman attacked was a Negro. Nowhere did a Negro mob invade a white neighborhood or assault whites as such.

Opinion leaders and publicists did not at this time see the riots as manifestations of deep unrest or anger on the part of Negroes. Roy Wilkins, the executive director of the NAACP, said that the riots and "brazen looting" had "brought shame upon the civil rights movement of a whole people": the suspicion was widespread, he added, that "people have been paid to start and keep them going." CORE Director James Farmer and Urban League Director Whitney Young, Jr., agreed that this was a possibility. Young thought that the riots would benefit Communist and right-wing groups by "sowing confusion and creating hostility between whites and Negroes."[22] At the end of the summer, J. Edgar Hoover, whose views were probably close to one end of the spectrum, reported to the President that although racial tensions had been a factor, none of the disorders — not even the Harlem one — was a race riot in the accepted meaning of the term (that is, race against race); they were, he said, "purposeless attacks" in which youths were responsible for most of the violence, and he classed them with the college-boy riots that occurred about the same time.[23] Others made similar assessments. Most civil rights leaders dismissed the idea that the riots were conscious protests; that was not merely an after-the-fact rationalization, Kenneth B. Clark said, it was an "independent of the fact" one.[24] Bayard Rustin was applauded by an audience of New York planners when he explained that the violence was caused by "merely a few confused Negro boys throwing stones in windows or a Molotov cocktail at a cop who was perfectly capable of ducking."[25] The police commissioner of New York said in effect that they were rampages and forays. "They riot either out of sheer cussedness or for criminal reasons, and in some instances because mob action seems to be taking on the aspects of a fad. . . . Bedevil the police, strip stores, shout and yell, crush anyone who opposes you . . . and if the police try to stop it, just yell 'brutality.' This is the pattern. . . ."[26] Speaking that winter at a symposium on new varieties of violence, Allen D. Grimshaw, a sociologist, explained that the Negroes who had fought the police and looted were not the same ones who had been engaging in peaceful demonstrations: they were, rather, "the lower-class apathetics, the new-style indifferents. . . ."[27]

The opinion that the riots did not reflect attitudes that were widespread among Negroes was consistent with the findings of an elaborate survey of Negro opinion made late in 1964 by Gary T. Marx. It showed that most Negroes were neither sunk in hopelessness nor consumed with anger. Only about a third were in any sense militant, and the proportion of Negroes who were strongly antiwhite was much smaller. Most thought that things were getting better for the Negro (81 percent of a sample in non-Southern metropolitan areas thought this), that America was worth fighting for (87 percent), that a day would come when whites would fully accept Negroes (70 percent), and that the police treated Negroes either fairly well or very well (59 percent). "The overwhelming majority of those questioned," Marx concluded, "felt that progress is being made and that integration is being pushed by the government at the right speed and were optimistic about the future."[28] That most Negroes held these opinions does not necessarily mean that the rioters held them, of course; in fact, however, there is some reason to suppose that most of them did.[29]

The 1964 riot pattern was repeated the following August in the Watts district of Los Angeles. This was not a slum in the usual sense (it was an area of single-family, detached houses, most of which were in good condition), and Los Angeles was a city in which the Negro fared better than in most places (the Urban League rated it first among sixty-eight cities on the basis of a "statistical portrait" drawn in 1964). In this case, too, the incident that supposedly set off the riot could hardly have aroused a great deal of righteous indignation (a drunken Negro motorist unable to produce a driver's license had been arrested in what seems to have been a proper manner). Apparently, the incident was mainly important as a pretext for a rampage by teen-age Negro boys and young men who began throwing whiskey and beer bottles and pieces of asphalt and cement at motorists on Avalon Boulevard.[30] Two hours after the incident the mob, which then numbered about fifteen hundred, consisted mostly of these boys and young men. There was nothing "racial" about what they were doing. "One thing that impressed me was that these Negroes who were hurling stones were throwing them right into their own people. That's why I believe this didn't start out to be a race riot. These were just young hoodlums working off their frustrations. They were out to do destruction. They just wanted to hurt anybody, black or white."[31] "The riot," Oberschall has written in what is probably

222 / THE UNHEAVENLY CITY REVISITED

the best sociological analysis of any of the large riots, "was a collective celebration in the manner of a carnival, during which about 40 liquor stores were broken into and much liquor consumed. It was also a collective contest similar to that between two athletic teams, with the supporters cheering and egging on the contestants. One could settle old scores with the police, show them who really controlled the territory, humiliate them and teach them a lesson. . . . [M]any Negroes saw it as a victory for their side and derived a sense of pride and accomplishment from this public demonstration of their collective power."[32]

WATTS RIOT

The statistics on arrests at Watts provide some slight basis for inferences about the motives of the rioters. About 15 percent of those arrested were juveniles. (The percentage would have been much higher, it has been suggested, were it not for the fact that the police, being short-handed, arrested the people who were easiest to catch.) Of the 3,438 adults arrested, nearly one-third had been convicted of major crimes (that is, crimes for which they had received sentences of more than ninety days) and fully one-third had minor records (that is, arrest or conviction with a sentence of ninety days or less).[33] Since the police may be quicker to arrest Negroes than whites, it is hard to say what significance should be attached to the proportion having minor records. It is more noteworthy that one-third had never been arrested. The riot, according to Oberschall, drew participants from all social strata in the area and cannot be attributed to the lawless and rootless minority, although doubtless members of this minority were active in it. It is best seen, he writes, "as a large scale collective action, with a wide, representative base in the lower-class Negro communities, which, however much it gained the sympathy of the more economically well-off Negroes, remained a violent lower-class outburst throughout."[34]

Although the Watts rioters, like those in New York the year before, proclaimed no aims, put no demands before the authorities or the press, and made no effort to organize their resistance to police and firemen, Negro spokesmen this time at once declared that the event was political — it was, they insisted, a revolt, not a riot.[35] Bayard Rustin wrote that it was carried on for an "express purpose" and was "the first major rebellion."[36] No one gave a very clear or convincing account of what the rioters were revolting against, however. The facts did not support the view that they were expressing hatred for the white man; even Rustin said the rebellion was against the Negro's "own masochism." Nor did the facts support very well the view that the rioters were asserting that (in Rustin's words) they "would no longer quietly submit to the deprivation of slum life"; after all, most Watts people lived comfortably in fairly good housing. It was somewhat more plausible to claim that they were angry about mistreatment by the police, but even this view did not fit the facts entirely, for the rioters had shown themselves more interested in burning and looting than in fighting the police.

However unjustifiably, Watts was regarded by many Negroes as something to be proud of — a kind of black Bunker Hill. This definition tended to make the rioting of the year before appear in retrospect as a kind of black Concord and Lexington and to establish a moral basis for any battles that might yet be fought in a black Revolution. The view now fast gained acceptance, among white as well as black opinion leaders, that the riots were spontaneous expressions of anger and frustration at continued injustice — that in the main they were politically motivated and therefore not riots at all but "disorders" (if one wished to express solidarity with the black masses). Very possibly this change of view was in some degree self-justifying: the more widely and authoritatively the riots were described as political, the more they became so in fact.[37]

As this interpretation would lead one to expect, the frequency of rioting increased after Watts. In 1966, there were eleven major (that is, two-day or more) and thirty-two minor riots, and in 1967 there were twenty-five major and thirty minor riots. In most instances, the rioting began either without any precipitating incident, boys and young men simply smashing windows, starting fires, and assaulting passers-by for no apparent reason, or with an incident that was a pretext rather than a provocation. Only two of the major riots in 1966 (those in Jacksonville, Florida, and San Francisco) seem to have started from a provocation and only eight (six of which were in Southern cities) of those in 1967 seem to have started from provocations.

The Detroit riot of 1967, although vastly more destructive, was in many ways typical. Like Los Angeles, Detroit was a city of relative prosperity and opportunity for the Negro; it had no real "ghetto" and its police had for several years been under very enlightened and determined leadership. The incident with which the riot started seems to have been a pretext rather than a provocation: when the police raided a speakeasy early one Sunday morning, a crowd began pelting the policemen with stones. This might not have led to a riot were it not for the fact that at that particular time very few policemen could be mustered. (Early Sunday morning was a "low crime" period and the stronger daytime shift was not scheduled to report for duty at precinct stations until 8 A.M.) For several critical hours the police were conspicuous by their absence. It was well known, too, that the police would not use their guns except in the most extreme circumstances. For five or six hours after the speakeasy raid Negroes and whites mingled on the streets and looted amicably side by side. On the second day of the riot Governor Romney said that it was "not primarily a civil rights disturbance but rather lawlessness and hoodlumism by Negroes and whites," an opinion with which Mayor Cavanagh agreed.[38] Almost all the arrests made were for looting, and of those arrested nearly half were aged nineteen through twenty-four. The pattern of destruction was what one would expect in a foray for pillage. Stores having things that could be consumed directly — liquor, cigarettes, drugs, clothing, television sets, appliances, furniture — were looted no matter who owned them. Stores having things that would have to be "fenced" — jewelry — were usually left untouched, as were all buildings symbolic of the "white power structure" — banks, public offices, and schools. As one of the rioters, a child, explained, "There was nothing to steal in the school. Who wants a book or a desk?" "This is not a riot," one of the rioters was later quoted as saying.

A lot of people have a misconception of it. This is nothing but — like the man said — pure lawlessness. People was trying to get what they could get. The police was letting them take it. They wasn't stopping it, so I said it was time for me to get some of these diamonds and watches and rings. It wasn't that I was mad at anyone or angry or trying to get back at the white man. They was having a good time, really enjoying themselves until them fools started shooting.[39]

It would appear, then, that what requires explanation is not so much rebellion by Negroes (whether against the whites, the slum, their "own masochism," the police, or something else) as it is outbreaks of the "carnival spirit" and of stealing by slum dwellers, mostly boys and young men and mostly Negro.[40] (A few non-Negroes participated, mostly as looters, in the Detroit riot and possibly in some of the others, and one major riot, a rampage-foray for which there seems to have been no precipitating incident, was carried on entirely by Puerto Rican youths in Perth Amboy, New Jersey, at the end of July 1966.)

In framing an explanation, it will be useful to begin by listing certain events ("accelerating causes"), each of which independently increased the probability of such riots occurring. This listing will be followed by a description of a set of states ("background causes"), the concurrent existence of which established *some* probability of their occurring.[41]

Accelerating causes. Without attempting to pass on their relative importance, several such causes may be listed.

1. Sensational television coverage enabled rioters to watch the movements of police and so move to evade them,[42] and, what was probably more important, recruited rampagers, pillagers, and others to the scene. As the mayor of Plainfield, New Jersey, explained, "The sensational coverage of the Newark riot showed persons looting stores while the police took no action to halt them. This view of looting appealed directly to the criminal and susceptible element."[43] Prior to the advent of television, it would have been very difficult for the authorities to have brought the possibilities for fun and profit in rioting to the attention of the lower class even if they had wanted to do so. Lower-class people do not read newspapers, but nearly all of them have at least one television set.[44] (To be sure, the lower class was only one element among the rioters. It is safe to say, however, that it was responsible for more than its proportionate share of the most reckless and destructive acts.)

2. By carrying vivid accounts of rioting to cities all over the country, television not only eliminated the necessity that would otherwise have existed for the independent discovery of certain techniques of rioting (for example, the use of fire bombs) but also, and especially,

it established the *possibility* of it. That by throwing rocks, smashing windows, and setting fires one can throw a great city into turmoil is something that the ordinary person does not recognize until it happens. Once the possibility of an action has been established, the probability of someone's taking it is very much increased. "Some cats come in the bar and talk about how they are going to start burning again next month — down about Broadway. Mostly, it is just talk, but they know that they could do it."[45] The main point here is that, thanks to television, knowledge that "they could do it" was widely disseminated to people who otherwise would have been slow to discover it for themselves. In 1935 and 1943 Harlem had riots, but for lack of television coverage these did not provide a model that was known and imitated in cities all over the United States.

3. The rioters knew that they had little or nothing to fear from the police and the courts. Under the pressure of the civil rights movement and of court decisions and as the result of the growing "professionalism" of police administrators (these developments, in turn, being consequences of "middle-class-ification" of the population), the patrolman's discretion in the use of force declined rapidly after the war. At the same time courts were lenient with juvenile offenders. "Tough kids" had always attacked policemen when they got the chance, but by the 1960's the amount of toughness required was not very great, for in most cities it became more and more apparent that a policeman who shot a boy would be in serious trouble. Not being able to use force, the police could not effectively use the *threat* of it. It was not uncommon for a gang of boys to disarm and beat a policeman who, following orders, would not use his gun against them. During a riot, the police were especially ineffective — because their offenses were not very serious, most rioters could not be successfully threatened; the only thing that could be done with them was to take them into custody, and this was something the police were seldom numerous enough to do. Sometimes the police had to stand by and allow looting to go on before their eyes. This, of course, increased the tempo of the rioting.

"Those first hours, when the cops pulled out, were just like a holiday," recalls one young man who joined in the looting of shops on 12th Street that morning. "All the kids wandered around sayin', real amazed like, 'The fuzz is scared; they ain't goin' to do nothin'.' I remember one day me and another kid, we was locked in the school and there wasn't any teachers around and we had a ball, we did all the things we'd been wantin' to do for a long time. We set some fires in the baskets and we emptied the teachers' desks and we stuck a whole mess of toiletpaper in the principal's mailbox. Well, that's what it was like out on the Street."[46]

4. The probability of rioting was increased by several factors that tended to give it legitimacy in the eyes of potential rioters. One was a feeling on the part of many people that they were not getting what they deserved when compared to whites or even to affluent Negroes.[47] Despite — or, more likely, because of — relatively large recent improvements in income and status, many Negroes were frustrated and angry that their progress was not as fast as they believed it would be if they were treated fairly. There was also a belief, widespread and in general amply justified by the facts, that Negroes were frequently harassed and insulted and sometimes brutally beaten by the police. (Police brutality had recently been brought to the forefront of public attention by vivid television portrayals of outrages against civil-rights workers in the South.[48]) Another factor was a barrage of statements by leaders of both races that represented the Negro's problems as entirely, or almost entirely, the result of racial injustice, implying that only white racism stood between the Negro and affluence. Another was the discovery that rioting was possible; as David Matza points out with reference to juveniles, learning through experience that an infraction *can* be done leads, by an illogic characteristic of childish thought, to the conclusion that it *may* be done.[49] Another factor was the spread of the rioting to several cities; the knowledge that "everybody is doing it" tended, by more childish illogic, to the conclusion that doing it could not be very wrong. "If they can do it in Detroit, we can do it here," Milwaukee teen-agers cried as they began smashing store windows. But what probably did most to make rioting seem legitimate was acceptance of the claim that the Watts riot was a "revolt" and that the rioting everywhere had some political purpose. Byron Washington, the Waterloo, Iowa, youth whose words appear at the head of this chapter, doubtless threw his stone with the strength of ten because he knew (having heard it over television perhaps) that he was not a boy out raising hell but a victim of injustice fighting for a college education. Whether correct or not, explanations that find the cause of rioting in the rioters' environment are bound to be taken as

justifications, or at any rate extenuations, of their behavior and there-fore tend to reinforce the irresponsibility that is characteristic of the age and class culture from which rioters are largely drawn.[50] Rustin may have been right in saying that the looters were "members of a deprived group who seized a chance to possess things that all the dinning affluence of Los Angeles has never given them."[51] But, right or wrong, the effect of such statements was to make it easier for the potential rioter to justify his behavior, and therefore the statements were themselves a contributing cause of rioting.[52] One can see this process clearly enough in something a twenty-year-old Watts rioter said to a reporter: "The white power structure looks on us as hood-lums when actually we are deprived people."[53]

If explaining the riots tended to justify them, so did predicting them. One who said that if drastic measures were not taken to end injustice riots could be expected might be correct, but correct or not his words would help form an impression in the public mind that rioting is a natural and perhaps even laudable response to the continu-ance of an injustice. From the very beginning of the civil rights movement its leaders have been wont to predict that violence will occur if reforms are not accepted at a faster pace; the riots, of course, made these predictions much more credible and therefore gave the civil-rights leaders more incentive than ever to make them.[54] At the end of 1966, Dr. Martin Luther King, Jr., after acknowledging that "a prediction of violence can sometimes be an invitation to it," went on to predict that "failure to pursue justice" would result in more riots.[55] Rustin, at about the same time, told a Senate subcommittee that if the President asked for only a small increase in funds for the poverty program, the Negro leadership "can no longer be responsible for what happens"; and Senator Robert Kennedy said that unless "major steps" were taken "we will reap a whirlwind that will be completely uncontrollable."[56] Even if these predictions had been based on actual knowledge, and even if by making them — and *only* by making them —it had been possible to secure the needed reforms, one would have to say that making the predictions increased the probability of there being riots; obviously, it was impossible for the reforms to achieve their effect in time to prevent what was being predicted. Realistically, however, those who made the predictions could not be at all sure that the measures they were proposing, some of which — for example, "pursue justice" — were so vague as to be almost meaningless, would have any tendency to prevent rioting; moreover, they had little or no reason to believe that their making the prediction would bring about the adoption of the measures they advocated. Rustin, for example, could not have supposed that his words to the Senate subcommittee would cause the President to ask for a larger increase in the poverty program. The one thing the predictions *were* likely to do was to make rioting appear more natural, normal, and hence justifiable.[57] (Even so, in fairness to Rustin and others it must be pointed out that civil rights leaders had a duty to press hard for change.)

Background causes. For there to be *any* probability of rioting of the kind here under discussion, several conditions had to exist concurrently.

1. Without a large supply of boys and young men, most of them lower-working or lower class, to draw upon, major riots would be impossible. One may not share McPhail's opinion that there is no compelling reason to think persons "more impetuous because of their youth, more daring because of their gender, more disenchanted because of their race, or less rational because of their educational level" to agree with him that it is important that such persons are "more available for participation by virtue of the large amount of unscheduled or uncommitted time which results from being young, black, male, and without educational credentials in the urban ghettos."[58] In the 1920's and 1930's (as was explained in Chapter Two) the number of such people in the inner cities was very much reduced from what it had been in the previous century because of the aging of the immigrant population and the movement of the relatively well-off to outlying neighborhoods and suburbs. During the Depression it looked for a while as if the inner-city slums and semislums might be permanently depopulated. During and after the war, however, these districts were filled or nearly filled once again by a new migration, this one from the rural South (and, in New York, from Puerto Rico). Being a young population with a very high birthrate, the newcomers quickly put more boys and young men on the streets than had been there before. The new (black) generation of inner-city youth was also more prone to violence than the earlier (white) ones.

2. The lower- and lower-working-class people who now comprise much of the inner-city residential population are largely cut off from participation in institutions that in times past regulated and restrained the behavior of people whose class culture and situation were similar to theirs. Racial discrimination, although obviously a factor, is not the main thing that cuts them off from these institutions; rather, what cuts them off is the changes that have occurred in the nature of the institutions because of the "middle-class-ification" of the population of this country. In the last century, for example, the volunteer fire company gave boys and young men of the lower classes opportunities to express high spirits under conditions that were to some degree controlled: the firemen fought *each other*, usually for the "honor" of their companies. Today, of course, fire departments are run on a professional basis and are open only to mature men who have placed well in an examination. More or less the same thing has happened in politics. Not so long ago party machines labored to establish claims on even the lowest of the low; the trading of jobs and favors in return for loyalty tended to create some sort of bond between the individual and the government. Now that the machine, precinct captain, and corner saloon have been replaced by the welfare bureaucracy, the nonpartisan election, and the candidate who makes his appeal on television, the lower classes no longer participate in politics and are therefore no longer held by any of the old ties. Even in criminal activities there has been the same trend. Like fire-fighting and politics, the money-making kinds of crime (as opposed to "kid stuff") are organized in such a way as to exclude — and therefore to exert no discipline upon — the irresponsible and incapable.

This exclusion from institutions of those who are not able or willing to participate on the terms set by the now predominant middle class has the effect of reducing the influence within the lower classes of those persons who, although not able to perform according to the standard set by the middle class, could nevertheless lead and set an example for — and thus place some restraint upon — less able members of their class. The situation is strikingly like that which, when it occurs in prisons, is said to cause riots. "It is the cohesively-oriented prisoner committed to the values of inmate loyalty, generosity, endurance, and the curbing of frictions who does much to maintain the prison's equilibrium. When the custodians strip him of his power — when the custodians destroy the system of illicit privileges, of preferential treatment and laxity which has functioned to increase the influence of the cohesively-oriented prisoner who stands for the value of keeping things quiet — the unstable elements in the inmate population have an opportunity to capitalize on the tensions of prison life and to rise into dominance. The stage has been set for insurrection."[59]

3. A considerable number of upper-working-class, middle-class, and upper-class people who have made large income and status gains in recent years and are impatient to make even larger gains lives in the inner city in close physical proximity to the lower classes. Upwardly mobile members of earlier slum populations very quickly left not only the slum but the inner city as well, and usually the neighborhoods they vacated were occupied by some different newly arrived ethnic group. In the case of the Negro, the outward movement has been rather slow, partly because of job and housing discrimination and partly because many Negroes want to live near other Negroes; moreover, in the case of the Negro, the places of those who *have* moved away have usually been taken by newly arriving Negroes. Upwardly mobile Negroes who for one reason or another live in or near the slum tend, of course, to be very sensitive to the dangers and unpleasantnesses of slum life and to blame them not on conditions common to the white and the Negro (for example, lower-class culture, low income, and so on) but on racial injustice past and present, real and imaginary. If, like the upwardly mobile members of earlier groups, these Negroes lived in suburbs far from the inner-city slums, they would not be available physically (and perhaps psychologically) for participation in riots. As it is they do not participate in them actively in large numbers. They do provide enough politically motivated rioters, however, to make possible the interaction effect that, it was argued earlier, tends to escalate a rampage-foray into a major riot. Even those who do not participate in the rioting tend to help legitimate it in the eyes of potential rioters by putting forward or concurring in the claim that it has a political purpose.

Several conclusions bearing on policy may be drawn from this analysis. One is that there is likely to be more rioting for many years to come, and this no matter what is done to prevent it.[60] So long as there are large concentrations of boys and young men of the lower classes on the streets, rampages and forays are to be expected. Without some support from righteously indignant members of the working class and from politically minded members of the middle and upper classes, such outbreaks probably will not reach the scale that was reached in Los Angeles, Newark, and Detroit, but even so some of them will probably be well beyond the ability of local police forces to deal with. Eventually, much of the inner-city population will move to the suburbs; this change, which is already under way, will reduce the potential for very large riots by physically separating the lower class from the working class and the working class from the middle and upper classes and thus (1) curtailing the number of persons available in any one place as recruits for a riot and (2) making interaction between rioters of different motivational types (for example, rampagers and demonstrators) less likely. For at least another twenty years, however, there will be enough potential rioters of all types in the inner cities to produce frequent rampage-forays and some major riots.[61]

Six years after the holocausts in Detroit and Newark no one any longer worried at the prospect of another "long, hot summer." Like the Beatles and their music, riots were remembered as a "craze" that had come and gone. In fact after 1967 there were many small riots and one or two that would have been called major before 1964–1967. That riots on the scale of those years did not occur and did not seem likely to was sometimes explained on the grounds that the earlier ones had been cathartic (with one possible exception, no city that had a major riot had a second one). There were other explanations to supplement this one. Television and news coverage of small riots had become extremely circumspect (in 1968 a major riot in New York City went almost unreported). Police forces were known to have become equipped and trained to act effectively at the first signs of trouble.

It is naive to think that efforts to end racial injustice and to eliminate poverty, slums, and unemployment will have an appreciable effect upon the amount of rioting that will be done in the next decade or two. These efforts are not likely to be very serious or, if they are, very successful. But even if they are both serious and successful they will not significantly affect the factors that produce riots. Boys and young men of the lower classes will not cease to "raise hell" once they have adequate job opportunities, housing, schools, and so on. Indeed, by the standards of any former time, they had these things in the 1960's. It may be that in time good opportunities and a high standard of living will bring about the assimilation of the lower classes into the middle and by so doing will make them less violent. But this will happen over the long run — say, from one generation to the next — if it happens at all, and, besides, even middle- and upper-class boys riot sometimes. As for the upwardly mobile and politically minded Negro who has a potential for outbursts of righteous indignation and for demonstrations, even serious and successful efforts at reform are likely to leave him more rather than less angry.[62] The faster and farther the Negro rises the more impatient he is likely to be with whatever he thinks prevents his rising still faster and still farther. As the HARYOU manual, "Youth in the Ghetto," remarks: "The closer the Negro community gets to the attainment of its goals — the closer it gets to the removal of the determinants and manifestations of racial exploitation and powerlessness — the more impatient individual Negroes will become for total equality."[63]

It is not only the Negro who will become more disaffected as his situation improves. The process of "middle-" and "upper-class-ification" is making the whole society more sensitive to departures, both real and imaginary, from the ideal, inherently unrealizable, of how things ought to be. As the economy becomes more productive and social arrangements more decent, the well-off — and among them youth especially — become more restless and more intolerant of the continued failure to achieve social perfection.[64] Demonstrations, confrontations, protests, dialogues, and so forth, are bound to be more frequent as the middle and upper classes grow and more and more people have the leisure to act upon what the Judeo-Puritan tradition tells them is a positive obligation to make society over. No doubt most of the blood spilled by the middle and upper classes will be steer's blood carried for the purpose in plastic containers. The effect on the lower classes of this sort of behavior by the upper classes may be incendiary, however.

CHAPTER TEN

The Future of the Lower Class

> If the children of the degraded classes could be taken in
> infancy, before their bad habits have had time to form, and
> trained to earn a livelihood, a certain proportion of them would
> be redeemed. If those who could not be so trained were allowed
> to starve, the number to grow up a burden on society would be
> diminished. The greatest difficulty in the way of such a policy is
> to organize charitable effort in such a way that it shall be intelli-
> gently directed to this end. The natural tendency of such effort
> is the very opposite of that here pointed out.
> — Simon Newcomb, 1886

> Let us take the little child in the future from its possibly
> ignorant, filthy, careless mother, as soon as it can walk . . . and
> give it three hours daily in the kindergarten, where during that
> time it will be made clean, will enjoy light, color, order, music
> and the sweet influence of a loving and self-controlled voice.
> — Annie Adams (Mrs. James T.) Fields,
> 1886

So long as the city contains a sizable lower class, nothing basic can
be done about its most serious problems. Good jobs may be offered to all, but some will remain chronically unemployed. Slums
may be demolished, but if the housing that replaces them is occupied
by the lower class it will shortly be turned into new slums. Welfare
payments may be doubled or tripled and a negative income tax insti-
tuted, but some persons will continue to live in squalor and misery.
New schools may be built, new curricula devised, and the teacher-
pupil ratio cut in half, but if the children who attend these schools
come from lower-class homes, the schools will be turned into black-
board jungles, and those who graduate or drop out from them will,
in most cases, be functionally illiterate. The streets may be filled with

armies of policemen, but violent crime and civil disorder will decrease very little. If, however, the lower class were to disappear — if, say, its members were overnight to acquire the attitudes, motivations, and habits of the working class — the most serious and intractable problems of the city would all disappear with it.

As the last several chapters have contended, the serious problems of the city all exist in two forms — a normal-class and a lower-class form — which are fundamentally different from each other. In its normal-class form, the employment problem, for example, consists mainly of young people who are just entering the labor market and who must make a certain number of trials and errors before finding suitable jobs; in its lower-class form, it consists of people who prefer the "action" of the street to any steady job. The poverty problem in its normal-class form consists of people (especially the aged, the physically handicapped, and mothers with dependent children) whose only need in order to live decently is money; in its lower-class form it consists of people who would live in squalor and misery even if their incomes were doubled or tripled. The same is true with the other problems — slum housing, schools, crime, rioting; each is really two quite different problems.

The lower-class forms of all problems are at bottom a single problem: the existence of an outlook and style of life which is radically present-oriented and which therefore attaches no value to work, sacrifice, self-improvement, or service to family, friends, or community.

Despite all that was said to the contrary in the earlier chapters of this book, some readers may suspect that when the author uses the words "lower class" what he has in the back of his mind is "Negro." They may suspect, too, that the "real" purpose of the rather pessimistic account of the possibilities of reducing the size of the lower class that follows is to lay the basis for the conclusion that nothing should be done about any of the city's serious problems. There is, of course, no arguing with a reader who is determined to mistake one's meaning. All the author can do is to repeat once more that there are lower-class people, as defined here, in *all* ethnic groups, including the Anglo-Saxon white Protestant one, and to point to the obvious fact that most Negroes are not improvident, do not live in squalor and violence, and therefore are plainly *not* lower class. As for the suspicion that the argument of this chapter will be used to justify a program of inaction, the reader is advised to wait and see.

Whether lower-class outlook and style of life will change — or can be changed — and, if so, under what circumstances and at what rate — are questions of great interest to policymakers. As was pointed out when the concept of class culture was introduced (early in Chapter Three), social scientists differ as to the relative importance of "social heredity" and "social machinery" in forming class patternings of attitudes, values, and modes of behavior. As was said before, both sets of influences are undoubtedly at work and interact in complex ways; undoubtedly, too, the relative importance of these forces, as well as the nature of their interaction, differs from one group to another and from one individual to another.

Whether because (as Walter B. Miller has insisted in a brilliant essay)[1] they have been caught up in an ideological movement or for some other reason, since the late 1950's most social scientists have discounted heavily the view that the lower-class person has been permanently damaged by having been assimilated in infancy and early childhood into a pathological culture and instead have come to view the lower-class life style as an adaptation to the realities of poverty, racial and class discrimination, bad schooling, poor or nonexistent job opportunities, and, in general, "blocked opportunities."

From the standpoint of its theorists, the War on Poverty of the 1960's represented an effort to eliminate the lower class. (That "poverty" was not to be regarded as solely, or even mainly, a matter of low income was stressed by Michael Harrington in *The Other America*, a book which did much to create in the public opinion that made possible the War on Poverty. His "most important analytic point," Harrington wrote, was that *"poverty in America forms a culture, a way of life and feeling."*[2]) few social scientists supposed that raising incomes would of itself bring about the desired changes in the life style of "the poor."[3] Higher incomes were a necessary but not a sufficient condition for this. It was crucial to change the "opportunity structure" in many ways: by ending racial discrimination, providing job training, improving schools, housing, and health care, and enabling and encouraging "the poor" to participate in the making of neighborhood and community decisions. A "service strategy," as it was called, would lead to higher incomes, but, what was of fundamental importance, it would change the individual's attitudes and habits, cause him to gain self-confidence and self-respect, and thus render him able and willing to move out of lower-class and into normal ("mainstream") culture.[4]

Whatever its achievements in other directions, the War on Poverty did not change the style of life of "the poor." The reason for its failure to do so, many of its proponents have contended, was insufficient funding (this although federal spending for major Great Society programs increased from $1.7 billion in fiscal 1963 to $35.7 billion in fiscal 1973)[5] together with (at most) half-hearted support in crucial matters, such as citizen participation, on the part of the politicians and administrators who ran things. If these complaints had some validity as applied to the national scene, they had none at all in certain places where the failure was no less. New Haven, for example, embarked upon an elaborate effort to change the life style of "the poor," especially that of the young among them (the young being thought most amenable to change), as early as 1959; large sums were expended ($7,700 per poor family in the peak year); the effort was enthusiastically backed and promoted by a powerful, energetic, and able mayor, and the programs were designed and run (albeit without citizen participation) by talented administrators. Nevertheless, after eight years a careful scholar concluded that their contribution to any decline in the amount of poverty in New Haven "can at best have been marginal and indirect."[6]

A variant of the "blocked opportunity" theory asserts that stable employment is sufficient to bring the lower class to "mainstream" ways. Providing full-time jobs at a "living" wage "*should be the first goal of public policy*," a Special Task Force of social scientists reported to the Secretary of HEW in *Work in America*.[7] If all men could count on such jobs, they said, "and if all women could therefore look forward to marrying men who could serve them in the provider role and for whom they could serve in the homemaker role, then it is likely that fewer girls would become pregnant before marriage, that lower-class couples would marry at a somewhat later age, that relationships in lower-class marriages would be less tense, that fewer marriages would break up, and for those that did, remarriage would take place more quickly.")

The "employment strategy," like the "services" one, assumes that the tastes of the lower class are not very different from those of the "mainstream": that they want to be "successful" by the standards of the larger society and accordingly will accept real "opportunities" if they are offered. Rainwater is very explicit on this. Lower-class people, he writes, "know what they would like if only they had the resources of the average working class man — they would want a quiet, rather 'square' life in a quiet neighborhood far from the dangers, seductions, and insults of the world in which they live."[8] This may be true of many, especially among women, but for others the dangers and seductions (if not the insults) of the lower-class world are life itself.

Pondering why welfare workers have not had more success in luring men "away from a life of irresponsibility, sensuality, and free-wheeling aggression," Alvin Gouldner, a sociologist, concludes that many men may simply judge that the bargain offered them — " 'give up promiscuous sex, give up freely expressed aggression and wild spontaneity . . . and you, or your children, may be admitted to the world of three square meals a day, to a high school or perhaps even a college education, to the world of charge accounts, of secure jobs and respectability' " — is not a very attractive one.[9] Certainly there is reason to believe that many lower-class men, especially young ones and those profitably engaged in illicit activities, would not be attracted to regular work — and thus induced to change fundamentally their style of life — by any inducements that an employer, public or private, could be expected to offer.

Even where such differences of values and tastes are not crucial, measures implied by the "blocked opportunity" theory encounter an obstacle the seriousness of which is not often fully realized. This is that attitudes, habits, and modes of behavior change slowly — so slowly, in the case of adults at least, as to much reduce, if not altogether eliminate, the practical significance of the distinction between "social machinery" and "social heredity." On this the further testimony of Rainwater is of special interest. "Even with the best possible policies, vigorously pursued and properly funded," he writes, "it will take at least a generation for the poor to acquire the kind of experience they need if they are to sustain themselves through employment to produce equality of opportunity in our society."[10]

That most people — including the "disadvantaged poor" — eventually respond to situational inducements ("opportunities") in ways that, although they may not conspicuously affect their own life styles, profoundly affect those of their children or grandchildren appears very likely. T. W. Schultz, Gary Becker, and other economists have developed and partially tested theories about "investment in human capital" that strongly support this idea. In an interpretative summary of this work, Schultz conjectures, with reference to changes that have taken place in the Western world over the last half-century, that the introduction of various forms of new and useful knowledge has been the impetus to far-reaching transformations.[11] The effect of the new knowledge, he and others think, has been to increase the value of people's time both absolutely and relative to that of physical capital, and, in particular, to put a premium on the skill and "quality attributes" of individuals. This premium has caused — and is causing — millions of parents to have fewer children both in order that they (the parents) may acquire and use the skills and attributes so much in demand and in order to give their children better opportunities to acquire them also. The investments people are making to improve their own and their children's "quality" take many forms — more learning both in and out of school, greater concern for health and safety, increased geographical mobility in response to job opportunities — and the total amount being invested is unprecedented.

It is plausible to suggest that time horizons change, although perhaps not without a considerable lag, in response to changes in the objective situation. One's time horizon, it may be hypothesized, is whichever point in future time is closer to the present: (1) that beyond which "nothing matters" — that is, beyond which one's goals have no concrete implications for action, or (2) that beyond which one cannot influence events in accordance with one's intentions. On this hypothesis, not only the introduction of new knowledge but various other changes in the situation — for example, the acceptance of goals that have implications for a more distant future, a reduction of uncertainty about future possibilities, or an increase in ability to exert political or other influence — would extend time horizons thereby (as was suggested in Chapter Three) producing changes in the traits that constitute a culture or life style.

Even on the most optimistic assumptions as to the inducements offered them and their willingness and ability to respond to them, it is safe to say that lower-class persons will not disappear in the foreseeable future. Although a very small part of the population, they are nevertheless numerous enough to generate social problems — violent crime, for example — of great seriousness in the eyes of the society and there is at least the possibility that their numbers will increase rather than decrease in the future. It is necessary, therefore, to consider further the future of that portion of the lower class — a small one, perhaps — which will persist no matter what changes are made in "social machinery."

It is convenient to begin a discussion of the future of the lower class by considering its probable rate of natural increase. This is not on the assumption that there is a "lower class gene pool"; on the contrary (as was explained in Chapter Three), class is here regarded as a cultural, not a biological, phenomenon. Since there is a high probability that children born to lower-class parents will be socialized into the culture of the lower class, it is necessary to consider how many such children there are likely to be.

No data exist on the deathrate in the lower class as defined here. However, such data as do exist suggest that, in the last century and in the early decades of this one, it may have been high enough nearly to offset the birthrate (which also can only be guessed at). In 1864, Boston's crusading Unitarian minister, Theodore Parker, exclaimed in horror that three-fifths of the children born there to Catholic parents "die before the sun of their fifth year shines on their luckless heads."[12] The infant and child mortality rates among *lower-class* Catholics were no doubt even higher, which means that the sun could have shone on very few lower-class heads indeed. Although death took its heaviest toll in infancy and childhood, adult deathrates among the poor were also high (and among the *lower-class* poor they were certainly highest of all). Probably the lower-class poor died from want more often than did the other poor; certainly they died more often from syphilis, excessive drinking, accidents, and homicide. It is probably indicative of differences in class culture that, at the turn of the century, the life expectancy at age ten of the Irish immigrant was only thirty-eight years, whereas for the Russian Jew (who did not brawl or drink and whose religious observances probably had some hygienic value), it was a little more than fifty.[13]

Fifty or more years ago, the Malthusian checks of poverty and vice may have been operating so strongly on the lower class of the largest cities as to cause it nearly to die out every generation or two. There is no "hard" evidence to support this proposition, however.

Whatever was the case half a century or more ago, the lower class may be growing now. Poverty is no longer a major cause of death in the cities. Improvements in public sanitation and in medical and hospital care for the indigent, together with the development of antibiotics and other miracle drugs, keep many lower-class people alive, often, as it were, in spite of themselves. Through the first half of the century, when a plateau was reached, deathrates declined steadily in all age, color, and occupational groups. The lowest socioeconomic stratum (which although not constituted of the lower class nevertheless included most of it) shared in this general decline but relative to the rest of the population its deathrate (except for infants) remained at the high turn-of-the-century level.[14]

The deathrate of the lower class, although probably lower than it was half a century or more ago, seems likely to remain high in comparison to the deathrates of other classes. Many of the things that make it high — for example, early and multiple childbirth (the deathrate of women who have had five or more children is much higher than that of others), alcohol and drug abuse, accidents, and homicide — are beyond the reach of public action; further large reductions in the lower-class deathrate can occur only as the result of changes in lifestyle, which is to say, from the lower class's ceasing to be lower class.[15] Despite its high deathrate, it is nevertheless likely that the lower class is now more than reproducing itself. Its deathrate is probably no longer high *relative to its birthrate*, although the latter has probably fallen too.

If the lower-class birthrate falls far enough, the decline in the deathrate may be offset, so that the lower class will again fail to replenish itself. The appropriation in recent years of large sums for public birth-control clinics (the increase in federal subsidies was from $10 million in fiscal 1967 to $165 million in fiscal 1973), the American Medical Association's recommendation to its members in 1971 that they give contraceptive advice to unmarried girls without (if the girl insists) consulting her parents, and the Supreme Court decision of 1973 legalizing abortion during the first three months of pregnancy will all have some tendency to reduce unwanted births in the lowest socioeconomic group. Whether their effect will be dramatic is open to question, however. In 1965 there were marked educational and racial differences in the use of the most effective technique (the pill) but these had disappeared by 1970, except — significantly — that high school dropouts continued to make less use of it.[16] For several years most women having unwanted pregnancies have *known about* effective techniques (the pill and the I.U.D.) even if they did not use them or did not do so regularly or, perhaps, competently.

If there is reason to doubt that these developments will much affect the birthrate of the lowest socioeconomic group, there is even more reason to doubt that they will affect that of the lower class — that is, of the woman who cannot or will not plan ahead, who regards pregnancy (and everything else) as something that "happens to" one if one is "unlucky," who is not much troubled at the prospect of having a baby whose life chances will be poor, who may be incapable of following simple directions ("take a blue pill each day until they are all gone and then take the red ones"), and who in all likelihood must adapt herself to the demands of a man who, if he has any interest in the matter at all, wants to claim "credit" by getting her pregnant (without, of course, assuming responsibility for her or the child afterward).[17] Such a woman, it is safe to say, will make little use of birth-control clinics and, when she does use them, will often end up pregnant anyway.[18]

A particularly intractable and serious problem (although not one limited to the lower class) is presented by young girls who have illegitimate babies. The risk of mortality or of serious physical or mental impairment is high when a mother is very young, and, when she is also unmarried; having a baby adds to her economic, educational, and other disadvantages.[19] As someone has remarked, it is probably more important to delay the first child than to prevent the seventh. Birth-control services, however, are likely to have more success in preventing the seventh than in delaying the first or — if the mother remains unmarried — even the second or third. The problem here is not mainly that teen-age girls lack either knowledge about contraception or access to contraceptives (although of course many do, especially among the youngest); nor is it mainly that they are psychologically incapable of providing for the future (although doubtless many are); rather it is that the episodic nature of sex among teen-agers is incompatible with planning. "Family planning," John P. Kantner and Melvin Zenick remark in their elaborate study of the use of contraceptives by young unmarried women, "assumes both a family context and the possibility of rational planning. When, however, sexual encounters are episodic and, perhaps, unanticipated, passion is apt to triumph over reason."[20]

Philips Cutright, a demographer, estimates that, using currently available methods, a birth-control program is likely to reduce illicit pregnancies among low-income women by only 10 to 20 percent. "Contraception-only programs," he writes, "have not yet demonstrated their capacity to prevent a significant number of unwanted illicit pregnancies in any large population."[21] Abortion on request, he thinks, might cut the illegitimacy rate by 30 to 50 percent in less than a decade. To many, of course, the evil of this will appear equal to, or greater than, that of illegitimacy. The most effective and least objectionable "solution" to the problem would seem to be in the development of a "morning after" oral contraceptive, but this does not appear to be imminent.

It is reasonable to suppose, that no matter how successful improvement of opportunity proves to be as a general method of dealing with present-orientedness, there will be some persons, if only a few, whose present-orientedness will remain almost unaffected. Also, even if provision of good opportunities were sure to eliminate all present-orientedness within two or three generations, there would be good reason to look for ways by which this outcome might be secured more quickly. Without prejudice to the idea that making it in some sense profitable for people to take account of the future is in general a necessary and possibly a sufficient condition of getting them to do so, the remainder of this chapter will discuss the uses and limitations of some quite different approaches.

Psychotherapy holds almost no promise as a means of changing the lower class. It possesses no techniques for changing personality; even if it did, there would be obstacles — perhaps insuperable ones — in the way of wholesale application of them to the lower class.[22] One problem is that the nature of lower-class culture makes its bearers bad subjects. Lower-class people, write Hollingshead and Redlich,

> are not able to understand how thinking and talking can help them. They have not learned to verbalize and symbolize in the same way higher class persons have. Neither have they learned to sublimate present needs for the realization of future goals.[23]

In any case, there are not nearly enough therapists to treat the insane, let alone the present-oriented.

Two different lines of experiment and analysis in the field of child development are of special interest. Adherents of neither approach expect to be able to derive a formula for turning present-oriented children into future-oriented adults, but both approaches have clear implications, albeit perhaps mainly negative ones, for policy.

Language and class culture. In the last half-century, philosophers, anthropologists, and psychologists have all become increasingly interested in the way language shapes thoughts and feelings. A psychologist at the University of London, Basil Bernstein, has taken the lead in applying this line of analysis to problems of child development.[24] His thesis is that linguistic codes ("fashions of speaking") are shaped by social structure (by the nature of family, work, and community groups, for example) and in turn shape class culture. The lower classes (that is, semiskilled and unskilled), for example, are oriented toward the communal rather than the individual, toward the concrete rather than the abstract, and toward the here and now rather than the future. Linguistic codes thus set certain limits on what a child learns and on how it will learn it. The lower classes use only a "restricted" code, which is a language of largely implicit meanings; the speaker relies heavily upon gestures, intonation, and other nonverbal cues; his meaning is never abstract or complicated. He calls attention to features of the situation that his listener will perceive and evaluate as he does. The middle and upper classes, by contrast, use "elaborated" as well as restricted codes. Communication by means of an elaborated code employs more varied and complicated syntactic elements; the message is relatively individualized rather than conventionalized, explicit rather than implicit, and abstract rather than concrete. Bernstein illustrates these codes with two imaginary conversations, each between a mother and a child who sits on her lap in a bus.

MOTHER: Hold on tight.
CHILD: Why?
MOTHER: Hold on tight.
CHILD: Why?
MOTHER: You'll fall.
CHILD: Why?
MOTHER: I told you to hold on tight, didn't I?

MOTHER: Hold on tightly, darling.
CHILD: Why?
MOTHER: If you don't you will be thrown forward and then you'll fall.
CHILD: Why?
MOTHER: Because if the bus suddenly stops you'll jerk forward onto the seat in front.
CHILD: Why?
MOTHER: Now hold on tightly, darling, and don't make such a fuss.[25]

The low level of conceptualization in the lower-class mother's communication code influences, Bernstein thinks, the child's basic model of thinking and feeling as well as his desire and ability to learn. This low level of conceptualization constrains, among other things, the intensity and extent of his curiosity, his attitude toward authority (as opposed to power), and his ability to identify with the aims and principles of a society (as opposed to a local group), to verbalize feelings and to express them in socially approved ways, and to take an instrumental (which is to say a future-oriented) attitude toward people and things.

It seems likely that linguistic limitations are a cause, although not necessarily the only one, of present-orientedness. Without language one could have no sense of a future — one could not hope, much less plan.[26] The more limited one's linguistic (and, therefore, conceptual) equipment, it seems reasonable to suggest, the less able one will be either to take account of the future or to control impulses.[27] There is much evidence to support this view.[28]

Relation to a mother-figure in childhood. Another line of theory and experiment that appears to be particularly relevant in this context stresses the importance for normal personality development of a close and satisfying relation in the early years of life with a mother or mother substitute. The infant and young child, Bruno Bettelheim writes, "must have a star to steer by."[29] Erik H. Erikson explains that a "regular and mutual affirmation and certification" between the infant and one who cares for it will in later life reassert itself in strong emotional ties to others — family, friends, and political leaders. Failure to form such bonds "can harm an infant radically, by diminishing or extinguishing his search for impressions."[30]

Generally speaking, middle- and upper-class children get the support and stimulation that they need. They tend to have mothers (in the upper class, mother substitutes) who are supportive and who also have the verbal skills necessary to stimulate linguistic development. It is noteworthy that in one of the most upwardly mobile and presumably future-oriented of all ethnic groups, the Jewish, the pattern of child-rearing in the last generation emphasized both of these elements to an extraordinary degree. The Jewish mother, as described by Zena Smith Blau, was in this respect the exact opposite of the lower-class Negro mother, as described earlier. The Jewish mother held her son in bonds of love and mutual dependence beyond his childhood and even his youth, all the while subjecting him to intense and constant verbal stimulation.

Whatever Yiddishe Mamehs did for their children . . . was accompanied by a flow of language, consisting of rich, colorful, expressive words and phrases. Their vocabulary of endearments alone can fill a modest-sized paperback, but they also had a superb store of admonishments, curses, imprecations, explanations, songs, and folk-sayings that they effortlessly invoked as they went about ministering to the needs of their children and their husbands. The freedom that they exhibited with the spoken word invited a similar response from their children and it carried over into school. . . .[31]

The lower-class child does not get from its mother or from anyone else the support and stimulation that it needs. This is not to say that lower-class mothers do not love their children. It may be, as Rainwater asserts, that they find fulfillment in motherhood in a way that middle-class mothers, who are taught the value of outside interests for establishing their validity as persons, do not.[32] The lower-class mother or mother substitute is not, however, "a star to steer by." An account of the nature and significance of her failure to be one has been given by Lois Barclay Murphy, a psychologist who observed the behavior in a day-care center of "extremely deprived" children from "disorganized" black neighborhoods.[33] These children liked the feel of sand and water, as the others did, but they did not organize toys or solve balance, weight, and space problems with blocks. They did not come to the center with the idea of building a garage or fire station. "[T]hey may play at eating or getting whipped or other happenings but they do not project sequences which involve making a plan and carrying it out."

A child's ability to make a plan and carry it out, Dr. Murphy believes, may depend largely upon its mother's response to its earliest efforts at play. The infant's first perception of self may result from play, probably with the mother's nipple. The mother contributes to this perception by fingering the infant's fingers and toes, stroking its legs, and patting its back. When it pats and pushes her, it experiences for the first time the impact of its self on the environment and when it learns that it can *do something* with an object, such as a rattle, it is encouraged to try new explorations. After its first few months, when the mother rocks and bounces it, it forms the notion that it can do things that will *cause* the mother to play with it. This is a beginning at conceiving of positive sequences of action — that is, of planning.

The infant's impulse to make something happen will not be expressed, however, except as it is reinforced by the experience that something actually does happen. In the "severely deprived" home, Dr. Murphy says, interplay is minimal. Even feeding and cleaning are done in a random fashion and are rarely playful — "all of which makes it hardly worthwhile for the poverty child to invest in the environment." The mother who sits passively, merely holding the baby, does not create in it the expectation that reaching out, exploring, and trying to make contact with the environment will produce pleasant results. "Thus the extremely deprived baby remains at a primitive level of development, exploiting sensory experiences and immediate gratification over and over again." In order to become goal-oriented, Dr. Murphy concludes, a child evidently needs the early experiences of efforts rewarded. The deprived child, when he has reached the age of three or four, "knows his way around" and "manages for himself." He remains, however, "at the primitive sensory or motor level of playing with water and sand, without goals, or running around without a purpose."

Whether early environmental influences, such as lack of stimulation, necessarily have *permanent* effects on the individual is a disputed question. Most American psychologists agree that such effects are profound to begin with and that they extend at least into adolescence. However, one influential figure, Jerome Kagan of Harvard, believes that this view, which for many years he regarded as an "unshakable truth," requires revision.[34] In a Guatemalan village, he observed that although infants were rarely spoken to or played with and young children were moderately to severely retarded, preadolescents were remarkably competent. "Environmental experiences exert a non-trivial influence on intellectual development," he concluded. "But that influence seems to be more temporary than many have surmised." The mind, he now thinks, must have inherent properties enabling it to construct new ideas and objects — a "prior schematic blueprint" or "plan for growth" that unfolds when circumstances are right.

The view that much — but probably not all — of the damage done a child by early understimulation may be undone later under favorable circumstances is dramatically supported by a much-cited study done in Iowa over a long term of years. Two groups of children, all considered mentally retarded at the outset, were followed for about thirty years.[35] The experimental group, consisting of thirteen children under the age of three, was taken from an orphanage in which the children received "depersonalized and affectionless but otherwise adequate" care and was placed in an institution for the retarded. There the attendants and older girl inmates treated the children as guests, and each child found some one girl who was particularly interested in him or her. The contrast group included twelve children who were much like the others except for having a higher mean IQ — 86.7 as compared to 64.3. The children in this group remained in the orphanage, where they continued to get the kind of care that both they and the others had been getting before the study began.

After only two years, it was found that the experimental group had made striking gains in IQ, whereas the other group had made equally striking losses. The mean IQ's were now 91.8 and 60.5, *with the experimental group in the lead*. With one exception the members of the experimental group were then placed in adoptive homes. After another two and one-half years their mean IQ had risen from 91.8 to 101.4; in the same period, that of the contrast group had risen also, but very slightly, from 60.5 to 66.1.

Twenty years later a follow-up study was made. All those in the experimental group were found to be self-supporting, and their average education and occupational achievement compared favorably with that of the population at large. Eleven of the thirteen had married, and the mean IQ of their children was 104. The members of the contrast group had not fared nearly so well. One had died in adolescence and four were still in institutions. Only two had married. Those who were not in institutions had low-paying jobs.

A study which finds that the ability of an adult to give "conditional love" (something, it will be seen, that a lower-class person probably cannot do) to a boy before he reaches early adolescence is critical in determining his later life style was done in 1970 for the U.S. Department of Labor.[36] Edward M. Glaser and Harvey L. Ross compared two groups of men — thirty-two who had "made it" (were "successful") and thirty-eight who had not (were "unsuccessful"). All were between the ages of twenty-one and thirty, all were black or Mexican-American and had grown up in a large city "ghetto," all came from families that had been on welfare or lived in public housing, and all remembered times in childhood when they had not had enough to eat or been adequately clothed. Those who had "made it" had worked more or less steadily for the past two years, had not received welfare, did not need job training, and had not been in trouble with the law. The "unsuccessful" had been unemployed or underemployed for the past two years and *did* need job training assistance.

The men were asked to talk at length about themselves, their lives, and especially, their recollections of childhood. It was evident that the "successes" belonged to a "*mainstream*" subculture characterized by a work and achievement ethic, close family ties and loyalty, avoidance of trouble with the law, stability on the job, taking responsibility for one's own destiny, orderly planning for long-range goals, ability to sustain activity in goal-directed behavior, and ability to make a somewhat harmonious adjustment to the existing larger social order. The "non-successes," by contrast, belonged to a "*street life or gang life*" subculture characterized by an ethic of toughness, shrewdness, hustling, violence, emphasis on having a reputation among one's peers, less concern with family ties than with ties to peers, glorification of antisocial acts (in the "mainstream" sense), absence of long-range planning or goal-seeking, a disposition in favor of immediate gratification, and a rejection of most "mainstream" values.

Given that they had all come from similarly disadvantaged backgrounds, what accounted for the very different styles of life? Not intelligence; a simple "culture-free" test (the SRA nonverbal) failed to distinguish between members of the two groups. From the men's accounts of their early lives, it appeared that the choice of a subcultural "track" had been made (or at any rate was exhibited in behavior) in early adolescence. Those who had "made it" remembered liking school and participating in school activities; in adolescence their self-esteem was already related to notions of achievement. On the other hand, those who had not "made it" had not liked school (many had dropped out), and they had maintained self-esteem by having successful reputations on the street. Once on one subcultural "track," a boy became increasingly alienated from the other, which rejected him as he did it. As the boys grew into adulthood, the "tracks" became diverging life paths.

Probing into what the men recalled of their childhoods, Glaser and Ross concluded that what accounted for the adolescent's movement into one or another subculture was the presence or absence of an effective parent. Those who had "made it" told of having at least one strong parent who had high expectations for him and was effective in setting controls on his behavior. The "unsuccessful" men came from families which had presented no clear standards, made few demands, and had low expectations for their children. It was because these families failed to assimilate the child into "mainstream" subculture that he chose the only alternative — the subculture of the streets.

The effective parent, Glaser and Ross decided, employed "conditional love," as opposed to rejection on the one hand and unconditional love on the other, to discipline a boy when he misbehaved. In black families either parent might do this, although more often than not it was the mother who did. Among Mexican-Americans the situation was entirely different; that culture requires a mother to give unconditional love to her children and it permits a male to accept reproof only from another male. (Thus a boy who stole his widowed mother's welfare check in order to buy heroin was not dealt firmly with by her: it was a matter for his older brother.) In some instances, adults outside the family — a school coach, for example — served the function of an effective parent in bringing a boy into the "mainstream" subculture or, to be more precise, preventing him from turning to the street for what he could not get at home.

It would seem that, even on the most optimistic view, the individual will not develop his full intellectual and emotional capacities except as, sooner or later, he comes under normal (as opposed to lower-class) influences. Apparently he will suffer some permanent damage if he passes his first two or three years in an extremely deprived environment, but much, perhaps most, of his initial disadvantage may be overcome if by early adolescence he gets support and stimulation from peers, teachers, or fellow workers. Without this, the "plan of growth" inherent in his mind (assuming there to be one) will unfold little if at all, and by the time he has reached adulthood it will presumably have become incapable of unfolding. Insofar as the influence of his early retardation is still making itself felt when he reaches adolescence, his situation is extremely perilous, for he may then do something — for example, assimilate the subculture of "the street," take up an unskilled, deadend occupation, or (in the case of a girl) have an unwanted baby — the effect of which will be to lock him (or her) into a position from which escape is not practical even if it be psychologically possible.

The implication of all this may seem to be that the child should be taken from its lower-class parents at a very early age and brought up

252 / THE UNHEAVENLY CITY REVISITED

by people whose culture is normal. It will do little good to explain to a lower-class mother wherein her child-rearing practices are wrong: she is not really interested in improving her practices, perhaps because she cannot see anything wrong with them. In this and in other areas as well, her class culture sets sharp limits on what it is possible for her to do. It may seem, therefore, that the only thing to do is to take the child from her and put it in the care of a substitute who will bring it up properly.

However, the case is not as clear as it may at first appear. It is not certain that taking the child from its mother may not cause even greater injury to it than would leaving it with her. (It should be remembered that the Iowa children whose IQ improved so remarkably were transferred from an *institution*.) After a comprehensive review of the scientific literature, psychologist Leon J. Yarrow concludes that keeping a child with "grossly inadequate parents in a depriving and hostile environment" does not seem warranted by what is known of the dangers in separating a child from its mother; he stresses, however, that before a child is removed, strong efforts should be made to improve family conditions.[37]

Presumably, the danger to the child in taking it from its mother is a function not only of the mother's incompetence but also of the ability of the mother-substitute to give it the support and stimulation that it needs. Even supposing (as it seems plausible to do) that at present the average substitute provides a much better environment for the child than does the average mother from whom children are taken, one still cannot conclude that *all* lower-class children should be taken from their mothers. For as the number of such removals increased, the quality of the average substitute would surely fall and that of the average mother would probably increase. It is one thing to provide proper adoptive homes and institutions for a few thousand children a year and an altogether different one to provide them for several hundred thousand. With respect to institutions, at least, it is likely that "depersonalized and affectionless but otherwise adequate" care is the best that can be expected on a large scale.

Finally, it is questionable whether the state has a right to take a child from its parents in order to prevent an injury as impalpable and contingent as its socialization into lower-class culture.[38] Even if it were certain (and of course it is not) that a child brought up in the lower class would turn out to be a "social problem" of some sort, it would not automatically follow that society has a right to interfere so drastically in people's lives. If failure to provide a child with adequate linguistic equipment is considered sufficient grounds for removing a child from its parents, so in consistency ought failure to provide it with "a star to steer by." This latter criterion would probably find almost as much application in the upper classes as in the lower. As a practical matter there is, of course, not the slightest possibility of a rule being adopted that might be applied to the rich as well as to the poor; this appears from the practice of the courts at the present time. "Neglect" and "abuse," the grounds for child removal in the law of most states, are everywhere interpreted narrowly to mean abandonment of the child, failing to supply it with food, clothing, shelter, and medical care, grossly mistreating it (as, for example, beating it or locking it in a closet for a long time), or outrageously endangering its moral welfare (as, for example, by carrying on the trade of prostitution in its presence.)[39] "Emotional neglect seems the most obvious type to social workers," one of them writes, "but it is the most obscure to the courts in our experience."[40] The inability of psychiatrists to specify precisely what "emotional neglect" consists of is one reason why the courts do not take note of it.[41] One suspects, however, that if the condition were found only among the poor, it would prove no more difficult to define for legal purposes than, say, loitering.

In fact, even laws with respect to gross physical neglect and abuse are not enforced stringently or uniformly. Most cases of neglect and abuse never come to the attention of the authorities. Neighbors are reluctant to "interfere," teachers rarely report it when a pupil comes to school with cuts and bruises, and physicians frequently either fail to recognize the "child abuse syndrome" or decline to take the risk of being sued for damages if the parents are acquitted. Even when a case is reported and the facts are beyond dispute, the court may be unwilling to take custody of the child.[42]

As a matter of logic, the simplest way to deal with the problem — and one which would not involve any infringement of parents' rights — would be to permit the sale of infants and children to qualified bidders both private and public.[43] (Public bidding might be needed to ensure a price high enough to induce a sufficient number of lower-class parents to sell their children.) This assumes, of course, both that a parent who would sell a child would probably abuse or neglect it, and also that one who would buy it (especially if the price were high) would want it enough to take good care of it. The trouble with the idea, of course, is that it is wrong to represent human beings as commodities to be bought and sold.

Another possibility would be to offer "scholarships" to lower-class infants in amounts sufficient to induce their parents to place them in approved boarding schools on a year-round basis. These schools could be located in or near the children's neighborhoods and could be staffed by working-class women and girls from those neighborhoods. These arrangements would enable parents to see their children without having any responsibility for their care. This, of course, is the basic principle of *kibbutzim* in Israel. The teaching of the children could not be done entirely on a classroom basis, however. In the early stages of the acquisition of a new subject matter like reading or arithmetic, a tutorial arrangement (which is what the middle-class child gets from his parents at home) may be necessary; in effect, substitute mothers would have to be provided at least part of the time.[44]

If it is not feasible to establish boarding schools, day nurseries may be the next best thing. They are, however, a poor substitute. Even under the best of circumstances, they are not likely to succeed in bringing children out of lower-class culture. In an experimental project in Boston, twenty-one children, aged two and one-half to six, from disorganized, lower-class families spent two to three mornings a week in a nursery school generously staffed with highly trained personnel. The school was intended to help the child "gain a sense of mastery over his immediate surroundings."

Trips were followed up with related stories and play activities and we usually saw to it that there was something to carry home. By encouraging the children to tell details about these trips to parents (standing by to make sure they would be listened to and adding facts of interest specifically for the parents), we assisted communication between parents and child and gave emphasis to the importance of the experience for the child.[45]

After attendance of from one to three years, there was noticeable improvement in the children's appearance, body use, and self-esteem, and many had "learned to express their thoughts, feelings, and experiences with accuracy sufficient for communication." These gains certainly justified all the effort that was put forth, but the lives of the children did not change drastically. Language problems, for example, continued to hamper the children's ability to learn even after three years, and the experimenters doubted that these problems would ever be overcome. Reports that filtered back to them after the experiment had ended were not at all encouraging.

Many of the children were placed in situations where more demands were made on them than they were mature enough to fulfill. At least five of them repeated one of the early grades.

It is our impression that as failures began to follow one another, the inevitable regression to more discouraged, impatient, frightened, passive behavior occurred.[46]

Lower-class children could probably benefit a great deal more than they do from day nurseries were it not for the fact that they are at once confused and stultified by what they are (and are not) exposed to at home. When the influence of the nursery has made conditions for changing the child's outlook and life style feasible, even small improvements in home life might have large effects. As a rule, it is on the mother, or mother-substitute, that efforts to improve the home environment should concentrate. She is best able to give the child the support and stimulation it needs, and, fortunately, she is likely to be less — perhaps much less — improvident, irresponsible, and violent than her mate. As was noted in Chapter Three, it is the male, especially the young one, to whom lower-class culture comes most "naturally." For some reason — perhaps because extreme present-orientedness is incompatible with the childbearing function, perhaps because lower-class sex is sometimes too much like rape to be very enjoyable to women, or perhaps because "toughness" (one of Walter B. Miller's foci of lower-class culture) is usually regarded as a male attribute — women born and brought up in the lower class very often behave in ways that are not characteristic of that class. The lower-class mother — but not the father — is often very much concerned about the children's welfare: she may try to keep them in school and out of trouble; sometimes she struggles to buy a house. Usually, her efforts are futile. Her mate and, as soon as they are old enough, her sons are at best noncontributors to any "family" project and at worst active opponents. If she manages to save anything, they soon lay hands on it and squander it. "Getting ahead" is her idea, not theirs.

It would seem, then, that the aim of policy should be to encourage the mother's aspirations and to strengthen her hand as much as possible.[47] This is easier said than done, however. One suggested innovation is the "peace bond," an arrangement by which a man incurs an agreed-upon penalty, usually the forfeiture of a small sum, if he does what he has agreed not to do. It is unlikely that the lower-class male will be deterred by such a penalty, or even perhaps by the prospect of jail. Another proposal is that police powers be redefined to allow arrests for misdemeanors on probable cause (in most states a police officer who did not see a misdemeanor committed cannot make an arrest without a signed complaint). This suggestion is open to several objections. One is that such a redefinition of police powers might lead to greater embarrassment and inconvenience for those persons who (because of color, low income, or whatever) are taken to be lower class when in fact they are not. Moreover, the lower-class woman may be just as unwilling to offer the police a verbal complaint as she is to offer them a signed one. There is still another reason why workable ways of protecting the woman from her mate are unlikely to be found: the lower-class woman will often tolerate considerable abuse rather than lose the companionship of a man. Rather than risk being abandoned, she may deny that she and her children were beaten, that the welfare money was spent on a drunken spree, and all the rest. (In Illinois, the police *can* arrest for probable cause on many misdemeanors but they almost never do, partly for these reasons, partly because they do not want to create additional frictions within families, and partly because they want to avoid assaults by angry mates.[48]) Against her own unwisdom (if this is what it really is) the police, the courts, and the whole power of government cannot protect her. And so it appears that it will be very difficult if not impossible to realize even the minimum goal of policy — namely, to protect the lower-class woman and her children against the violence of her mate.

The conclusion is unavoidable that for at least several decades there will be a lower class which, while small both in absolute numbers and as a percentage of the whole population, will nevertheless be large enough to constitute a serious problem — or, rather, a set of serious problems — in the city. The question arises, therefore, as to what policies might minimize the difficulties that must inevitably exist when a lower-class minority lives in the midst of an increasingly middle- and upper-class society.

When the lower class lived on farms and in small cities like Elmtown (the population of which, it will be recalled, was about 25 percent lower class), its members were to some extent both held in check and protected by being physically isolated from each other. Also, there were few, if any, opportunities for easy money, and without money the lower-class person was effectively tied down. An even greater constraint on him, perhaps, was his visibility. In the slums of a big city, it is easy to drop out of sight. In a town or small city, on the other hand, there is no place to hide. The individual is known personally by the landlord, corner merchant, and policeman; he cannot escape into anonymity. In the big city he need never see the same merchant, landlord, or policeman twice. As an economist might put it, one who wants to lead a lower-class style of life has the advantage of numerous "economics of scale" in the big city.

Therefore, from the standpoint of a society that wants at once to protect lower-class people from each other and to protect itself from them, there are advantages in having lower-class people live in the town or small city, or, if they must live in the large one, in having them scattered in a way such that they will not constitute a "critical mass" anywhere. These considerations suggest that government programs (subsidies to large farmers, for example) that tend to push unskilled people off the land and out of rural areas ought to be stopped, that welfare programs should aim at making life in towns and small cities much more advantageous to the chronically poor than it is now (thereby reducing one of their incentives to come to the city), and that, within the large cities, there should be an end to that kind of urban renewal (almost the only kind in fact) the tendency of which is simply to shift the lower class from one place to another and not to dissipate it. As Wolfgang and Ferracuti remark with reference to the "subculture of violence," "Housing projects and neighborhood areas should be small microcosms of the social hierarchy and value system of the central dominant culture. It is in homogeneity that the subculture has strength and durability."[49]

It might be argued that the hardest cases among the lower class ought to be treated as semicompetent (incompetents being those — for example, children, the insane, the feeble-minded — who are incapable of knowing where their own interest, not to mention the social interest, lies). Such persons could be cared for in what may be called semi-institutions — small enclaves of lower-class people who, either because they wanted help in "staying out of trouble" or because they desired certain material benefits (extra-generous allowances for housing, food, clothing, and health care) would agree to accept certain limitations on their freedom. For example, they might agree to receive most of their income in kind rather than in cash, to forgo ownership of automobiles, to have no more than two or three children, and to accept a certain amount of surveillance and supervision from a semi-social-worker–semi-policeman.

Several considerations, however, argue against semi-institutional care for the lower class. As a practical matter, it is unlikely that many of the hardest cases — those from whom society most needs protection — would choose semi-affluence in a semi-institution in preference to the life of the slum. If these hardest cases are to be controlled at all, they must be controlled totally — that is, put into prison. This approach is obviously out of the question, since "being lower class" is not a crime or committable condition and is not at all likely to be made one. The tendency, in fact, is in the opposite direction: to confine fewer and fewer of those who have been convicted of crimes or have been judged mentally incompetent.

A very important danger in such efforts to restrain the lower class is that they might be applied also to people who are *not* lower class, thus abridging the freedom of these others without justification. This danger exists in part because euphemisms — e.g., "the poor" — have collapsed necessary distinctions between the competent and the semi-competent. (The blind, for example, are often lumped together in welfare programs with the lower-class poor.[50]) It exists also because prejudice or convenience sometimes causes caretakers to treat externals — skin color, speech ways, and so forth — as indicators of lower-class culture.

Another objection arises from the fact that at the present time (fifty or more years ago it was otherwise) most lower-class people in the large cities are black. Putting them in semi-institutions would inevitably appear to be a reflection of racial inferiority or an expression of racial prejudice. What is even more important, perhaps, is that taking the lower-class black out of the slum of the great city would tend to cut him off psychologically from the black community. It is by no means inconceivable that the "black pride" movement may engender morale in the mass of black people — morale that the lower class may in some degree share if it is in close physical contact with the main body of blacks. To be sure, one could argue this the other way, contending, first, that nothing would do more for the morale of the black community than to have the worst of the lower class removed from its midst and, second, that lower-class people are by the nature of their culture immune to any moral influence from the surrounding society.

Finally, there is clearly a tension if not an out-and-out incompatibility between the goal of restraining the lower-class individual and that of stimulating him. The first calls for reducing his freedom, the second for enlarging it. If it were possible to identify persons who are irremediably lower class and to place them and them alone under restraints, this objection would not apply. In fact, there is no way of knowing which individuals would respond significantly to incentives and which would not. The danger of perpetuating and increasing present-orientedness while endeavoring to restrain it makes the whole enterprise of restraint suspect. Despite the high costs to society and to the lower-class individual himself that follow from increasing his freedom, doing so may well be the best course of action in the long run.

CHAPTER ELEVEN

What Can Be Done?

Often travelers, technical advisers, or "old hands" from a given country return with tales of how disorganized, dishonest, or untrustworthy the people are; but once the tales have been told, everyone settles down to a theoretical description of, or plan for, the economy of that country which does not take into account in any formal way the psychological characteristics of the people just described.

— David McClelland

IT will be convenient to approach the question that forms the title of this chapter by distinguishing the feasible from the acceptable. A measure is *feasible* if (and only if) government (local, state, or national) could constitutionally implement it and if its implementation would result in the achievement of some specified goal or level of output at a cost that is not obviously prohibitive. For example, it is not feasible for every city dweller to have a one-acre lot (physical reality prevents), for every child to get a high school education as distinguished from a high school diploma (social and perhaps even biological reality prevent), to prohibit the movement of the poor from one city to another (this would be unconstitutional), or to replace the present cities with new ones in the space of a few years (the cost would be wildly out of relation to the benefits). The acceptability of a measure does not depend upon its feasibility: a measure is *acceptable* if those who have authority in government (elected or appointed officials or sometimes voters) are willing to try to carry it into effect. Thus, a measure could be entirely feasible but quite unacceptable or entirely acceptable and quite infeasible.

It goes without saying that it is often impossible to know in advance whether a particular measure is either feasible or acceptable. One can rarely be sure that the knowledge needed to make the measure "work" is at hand or within reach; its constitutionality may be in doubt; and there is always some possibility that unanticipated consequences will make its cost prohibitively high. ("Cost" in this context means any undesired effect or forgone advantage, not just an outlay of money or material resources.) These practical difficulties do not affect the validity of the distinction, however, or destroy its usefulness for purposes of analysis.

This chapter tries to show, first, that the range of feasible measures for dealing with the serious problems of the cities is much narrower than one might think, and, second, that within this range hardly any of the feasible measures are acceptable. If what is feasible is not, in general, acceptable, the reverse is also true: what is acceptable is not, in general, feasible. Moreover, government seems to have a perverse tendency to adopt measures which — if the analysis in the preceding chapters is not far wrong — are the very opposite of those that one would recommend. The reasons for this perversity are to be found in the nature of American political institutions and, especially, in the influence on public opinion of the upper-class cultural ideal of "service" and "responsibility to the community."

Clearly, a measure is infeasible if aimed at the simultaneous attainment of mutually exclusive ends. Two persons cannot both be satisfied if one's satisfaction is *constituted* of the other's nonsatisfaction. Insofar as the poverty problem, for example, has this relational character (that is, insofar as it is one of "relative deprivation"), it is insoluble. In Hollywood, Leo C. Rosten writes, "it is natural for the actress who earns $20,000 a year to envy the actress who earns $50,000 who envies the actress making $100,000. In a community where one can make $350,000 a year, $75,000 a year is not especially impressive — either to the group or the self."[1] The same problem arises, of course, even in the least glamorous places and with people of very ordinary income. That objective differences in income can be reduced to almost nothing does not necessarily mean that the problem of relative deprivation can be solved, for the smaller objective difference in income may come to have a greater subjective importance.

The same problem arises with the distribution of things other than income. It is in the nature of deference, for example, that some persons receive more than others. There is really no way to prevent those who receive relatively little from perceiving that fact and being made unhappy or suffering a loss of self-respect because of it. As Frank H. Knight has written, "The real scarcity which seriously afflicts individualistic civilization is the scarcity of such things as distinction, spectacular achievements, honor, victory, and power."[2] Since there can never be enough of these things to go around, the problem of poverty with respect to them is logically insoluble.

There are many other major problems which, although they differ from this one in (presumably) not having a logical structure that makes them inherently insolvable, are nevertheless unsolved and, for all anyone knows, may remain so. Although an economist of the first rank, Kenneth J. Arrow, has recently said that he thinks it "most likely that the reconciliation of full employment and price stability can be significantly improved in the future," the problem appears to be one that cannot be eliminated.[3] A problem of even greater magnitude which seems no less resistant to solution is that of ensuring that all children acquire the attitudes and skills without which they cannot live on mutually acceptable terms with society later on. Albert K. Cohen, in his path-breaking book of nearly twenty years ago, *Delinquent Boys: The Culture of the Gang*, posed a series of questions which have gone unanswered:

Of these various circumstances and features of our social system which are involved in the production of the delinquent subculture, which are subject to deliberate control? From the purely technical standpoint, exactly how is it possible to manipulate them in accordance with our wishes? How, for example, can we enable the working-class male to compete more effectively for status in a largely middle-class world . . . ? What price are we willing to pay for this or that change?[4]

When "solutions" are offered without specification of the means by which they are to be reached, it must be presumed that the means — if any exist — have yet to be discovered and that the "solution" is therefore infeasible. Doubtless a "change in the hearts and minds of men" would solve a great many problems. But how is it to be brought about? Except as the means are outlined and except as there is some real possibility of their being implemented, such "solutions" are mere words. They are seldom if ever labeled as such, however, even when put forward by highly professional social analysts. Consider, for example, the following, written not as a Commencement Day Oration but as a contribution to a leading journal of economics:

> We believe that resolution of the [urban] crisis is possible if political majorities are future-oriented enough to adopt constitutional reforms which not only benefit the lower classes but serve the majority's long-run self-interest. If these political majorities have the foresight to adopt fundamental, constitutional-type change, fulfillment can be harnessed to hope, and an urban society that is just, humane, and truly free can be a reality.[5]

The authors stop there. They offer no grounds whatever for believing that political majorities *will* change their ways and they say not a word about the steps that one (who?) might take to get them to do so.

Those who use the terminology of social science may talk of changing "culture," rather than "hearts and minds." The fact is, however, that no one knows how to change the culture of any part of the population — the lower class or the upper, whites or Negroes, pupils or teachers, policemen or criminals. Moreover, even if one *did* know how, there is good reason to suppose that doing so would be infeasible on other grounds; for example, it might require unconstitutional methods, such as taking infants from their parents at birth, or entail other disadvantages that more than offset its advantages.

What can an educational psychologist, Jerome Bruner, mean by writing that the plight of the poor in our society probably cannot be changed without first changing "the society that permits such poverty to exist" and that accordingly his "first recommendation, as a commonsense psychologist and a concerned man, would be that we should transform radically the structure of our society"?[6] Can it be that he thinks "society" is an entity having faculties enabling it to "permit" conditions to exist — that is, to exercise choice regarding them? (If so, why not criticize it for permitting *any* social problem to exist?) Assuming that society *is* able to permit, is it likely to permit "us" to transform it in such a way that it can no longer permit what it previously permitted, namely poverty? Assuming that it *will* permit this, how does one transform radically the structure of a society? (Apparently it is not always easy; Jencks remarks sadly in *Inequality* that the rate of social mobility "does not seem to respond to most of the things that social theorists expect it to respond to."[7]) Finally, assuming that the effort would succeed, what grounds are there for supposing that the new, restructured society will not permit evils even worse than poverty?

Some "solutions" are infeasible because (1) there is no reason to expect people to do the things that would constitute a solution unless government motivates them to do them, and (2) government for one reason or another cannot so motivate them. If, as Lee Rainwater asserts, "only effective protest can change endemic patterns of police harassment and brutality, or teachers' indifference and insults, or butchers' heavy thumbs, or indifferent street cleaning and garbage disposal,"[8] then (assuming that effective protest must be carried on from *outside* the government) measures to correct these abuses lie beyond the bounds of feasibility. In other words, if there *are* solutions to these problems they are not *governmental* ones, which is to say that one cannot implement them by calling into play the state's ultimate monopoly on the use of force.

Repeal of the minimum-wage laws is certainly feasible, but elimination of the *informal* minimum wage, which would reduce unemployment among the low-skilled even more, is not. Government cannot prevent the formation of a social definition of what is a "decent" wage, and (what amounts to the same thing) it cannot prevent workers from feeling some loss of self-respect in working for "peanuts." From the standpoint of the policymaker, then, the informal minimum wage presents an insoluble problem.

In the nature of the case, it is impossible to have a very clear idea of what government can and cannot do in the way of forming public opinion. Nothing except the elimination of lower-class culture would contribute as much to a general solution of the urban problem as would certain changes in public opinion — for example, greater awareness of the importance of class-cultural and other nonracial factors in the Negro's situation and a more realistic sense of what levels of performance it is reasonable to expect from such institutions as schools and police forces and from the economy as a whole. However, it is very questionable to what extent, if at all, government can bring these changes about. It is a question also whether *if* it can bring them about it *ought* to — that is, whether the unintended and long-run effects of a strenuous exercise of its opinion-forming capacities would not be likely to change American society for the worse rather than for the better.

People often respond to government measures by making adaptations the aggregate effect of which is to render the measures ineffective or even injurious. Thus, for example, the principal obstacle in the way of permanently maintaining full employment by fiscal policy devices is that investors respond to the price outlook in such a way as to check any policy except the impossible one of a continuous and accelerating inflation. Other examples of the same phenomenon are easy to find. Subsidies to induce employers to hire "hard-core" workers achieve very little because the employers tend to make adjustments (which may be perfectly legitimate) that enable them to take the subsidies while employing workers who are not significantly different from those whom they would have employed anyway. Similarly, efforts to reduce unemployment, poverty, or slum housing in a particular city may be counterproductive in that they attract more poor workers to the city. Thus, the *Wall Street Journal* reports from Detroit:

> A massive industry effort to help avert future riots in Detroit appears to be backfiring as hundreds — possibly thousands — of unemployed persons from out of state come to the city seeking work.
> The result: Some out-of-staters have failed to get a job, swelling the unemployment that many believe contributed to last July's riot.
> Others have snapped up jobs that might have gone to the city's own so-called hard-core unemployed.[9]

There is much to be said for the idea of giving small sums at any hour of day or night to persons, mostly youths, who might otherwise steal or kill to get the price of a few drinks or a "fix" of heroin. It would not be feasible to do this, however, because of the adaptive behavior that it would evoke. Once it became known that money was being given away (and of course the scheme would not work unless it *was* known), the demand would become too great to satisfy.

Essentially the same problem may exist with any welfare program that offers generous support to all who can be considered poor. Such a program may weaken rather than strengthen the self-esteem of its beneficiaries by reinforcing their impression that events are beyond their control.[10] It may also encourage them to adapt to the new situation in ways that are in the long run disadvantageous to them and destructive of the welfare system itself — for example, by taking steps to make themselves eligible (the wife leaving her job, perhaps, or lying about the number of dependents) they may "swamp" the system with their numbers. As Levitan, Rein, and Marwick remark, "Adequate benefits to relieve poverty conflict with a coherent incentive system to encourage work" and "all the good will and exhortation of welfare reformers have failed to offer a viable solution . . . to the dilemma."[11]

Some "solutions" are infeasible because the very feature(s) of social reality that constitute the problem make them impracticable. Training programs do not as a rule offer any solution to the problem of hard-core unemployment because the same qualities that make a worker hard-core also make him unable or unwilling to accept training. More generally, giving lower-class persons "really good" jobs is not a feasible way of inducing them to change their style of life, because that very style of life makes it impossible to give them "really good" jobs.

"Solutions" that deal with minor, as opposed to key or strategic, factors in a situation are also infeasible. To put the matter in another way, it does not help to create a necessary condition when there is no way of creating the sufficient conditions; similarly, in situations of multiple causation, it is of little use to set in motion a cause that contributes a trivial amount to the total effect desired when there is no way to set in motion those that would contribute a significant amount to it. It is less than likely that the McCone Commission, in its report on the background of the Watts riot, was correct in asserting that "an adequate mid-day meal is essential to a meaningful educational experience"[12] (it may be a contributing factor, but it is certainly not *essential*). Even assuming for the sake of argument that the commission *was* correct, the conclusion does not follow that a school lunch program would have an appreciable effect on the problem of preventing riots of the sort that occurred in Watts. The school lunch program "solution," however desirable it might be on other grounds, would not touch a great many much more important causes that would make riots just as likely as ever.

The assumption that an improvement in material welfare is bound to make a major contribution to the solution of almost any social problem is a pervasive one: better nutrition, better housing, better transportation, better street cleaning and refuse removal — all such things are commonly seen as ways of reducing crime, of preventing the break-up of the family, of encouraging upward social mobility, and so on. Although one cannot often find clear evidence of it, such measures probably do have *some* such effects. Even so, the policymaker must ask with regard to them the question that was raised about midday meals: Is the contribution that this *one* cause can make to the total effect (i.e. to the "solution" of the problem) likely to be more than trivial? Following such a procedure in his discussion of the efficacy of various types of social policy in reducing the "deficits" of the average Negro, James S. Coleman finds that housing, health, and public education (for example) are fields from which the contributions are likely to be small in relation to the problem.[13]

Even if it is feasible in all other respects, a measure lies outside the bounds of feasibility if its implementation would entail costs that more than offset its benefits. The proponents of a particular measure are usually blessed with both myopia and tunnel vision: they can see only the immediate and direct effects that would follow from the attainment of their objective; long-run or indirect effects, especially ones pertinent to what may be called background values, are quite invisible to them. Proponents of rent control, for example, see an immediate advantage to the poor in freezing rents at low levels. But they fail to see the harm that this will do to the whole community — and especially to the poor — because the harm will be indirect and more or less delayed. One immediate — but somewhat indirect and therefore hard to see — injury to the poor consists in preventing them from outbidding the nonpoor for housing that they (the poor) could afford because they would occupy it more intensively. (As Thomas Sowell points out, rent control drastically reduces any incentive real estate agents and landlords have to break down ethnic and racial barriers.[14]) Another immediate but somewhat indirect injury to the poor is the lowering of maintenance standards and services — heat and light, for example — that occurs when the landlord is bound to get the same (fixed) rent no matter how much or little he does for his tenants. In the longer run — and therefore harder to see — are injuries to neighborhoods and to the city as a whole: the formation of slums as buildings go unrepaired year after year, the growing frustration and anger of those who cannot move because they are not permitted to compete for housing, and the decrease in the total housing supply because investors, who in the absence of rent control would build new units or rehabilitate old ones, decide to put their money elsewhere.

An important special case of infeasibility resulting from a disproportion between costs and benefits exists when the implementation of a measure would require organization of a kind unsuitable for the implementation of other, equally desirable measures. Coleman, in making this point, remarks that it is safe to say that no city will consciously unequalize schools in order to pull suburbanites back into the city or stabilize neighborhoods. It is not for lack of social organization that cities will fail to do this, he says, but because of organization that is inappropriate; whether there could be organization appropriate to solve this problem and yet not inappropriate to solve other problems he considers questionable. "Paradoxically," he concludes, "in this instance organization itself helps bring about disorganization and disintegration of the city."[15]

There follows a list of some of the principal measures that might well be regarded as feasible by one who accepts the analysis in the previous chapters. (It will be recalled that by "feasible" is meant capable of being implemented and likely to accomplish something of more than trivial value at a cost not obviously prohibitive.) It will be seen that the list is rather short; that many of the items on it are not "constructive" — that is, they call for *not* doing something; and that far from being a comprehensive program for making the city into what one would like, it hardly begins to solve any of the problems that have been under discussion. Even if all the recommendations were carried out to the full, the urban situation would not be fundamentally improved. Feasible measures are few and unsatisfactory as compared to what it would be nice to have happen or what one would do if one were dictator. What is more to the present point, however, *hardly any of the feasible measures are acceptable*. The list is as follows:

1. Assure to all equal access to polling places, courts, and job, housing, and other markets.

2. Avoid rhetoric tending to raise expectations to unreasonable and unrealizable levels, to encourage the individual to think that "society" (e.g., "white racism"), not he, is responsible for his ills, and to exaggerate both the seriousness of social problems and the possibility of finding solutions.

3. If it is feasible to do so (the disagreement among economists has been noted earlier), use fiscal policy to keep the general unemployment level below 3 percent. In any case, remove impediments to the employment of the unskilled, the unschooled, the young, Negroes, women, and others by (a) repealing the minimum-wage and occupational licensure laws and laws that enable labor unions to exercise monopolistic powers, (b) ceasing to overpay for low-skilled public employment, (c) ceasing to harass private employers who offer low wages and unattractive (but not unsafe) working conditions to workers whose alternative is unemployment, and (d) offer wage supplements in the form of "scholarships" to enable boys and girls who have received little schooling to get jobs with employers who offer valuable on-the-job training.

4. Revise elementary and secondary school curricula so as to cover in nine grades what is now covered in twelve. Reduce the school-leaving age to fourteen (grade 9), and encourage (or perhaps even require) boys and girls who are unable or unwilling to go to college to take a full-time job or else enter military service or a civilian youth corps. Guarantee loans for higher education to all who require them. Assure the availability of serious on-the-job training for all boys and girls who choose to go to work rather than to go to college.

5. Define poverty in terms of the nearly fixed standard of "hardship," rather than in terms of the elastic one of "relative deprivation," and bring all incomes above the poverty line. Distinguish categorically between those of the poor who are competent to manage their affairs and those of them who are not, the latter category consisting of

the insane, the severely retarded, the senile, the lower class (inveterate "problem families"), and unprotected children. Make cash income transfers to the first category by means of a negative income tax, the rate structure of which gives the recipient a strong incentive to work. Whenever possible, assist the incompetent poor with goods and services rather than with cash; depending upon the degree of their incompetence, encourage (or require) them to reside in an institution or semi-institution (for example, a closely supervised public housing project).

6. Give intensive birth-control guidance to the incompetent poor.

7. Pay "problem families" to send infants and children to day nurseries and preschools, the programs of which are designed to bring the children into normal culture.

8. Regulate insurance and police practices so as to give potential victims of crime greater incentive to take reasonable precautions to prevent it.

9. Intensify police patrol in high-crime areas; permit the police to "stop and frisk" and to make misdemeanor arrests on probable cause; institute a system of "negative bail" — that is, an arrangement whereby a suspect who is held in jail and is later found innocent is paid compensation for each day of confinement.

10. Reduce drastically the time elapsing between arrest, trial, and imposition of punishment.

11. Abridge to an appropriate degree the freedom of those who in the opinion of a court are extremely likely to commit violent crimes. Confine and treat drug addicts.

12. Make it clear in advance that those who incite to riot will be severely punished.

13. Prohibit "live" television coverage of riots and of incidents likely to provoke them.[16]

There can be little doubt that with a few exceptions these recommendations are unacceptable. A politician with a heterogeneous constituency would strenuously oppose almost all of them. In most matters, the actual course of policy is likely to be the very opposite of the one recommended, whichever party is in power. Government is more likely to promote unequal than equal access to job and housing markets either by failing to enforce laws prohibiting discrimination or by "enforcing" them in a way (for example, by "affirmative action") that is itself discriminatory.[17] It is also more likely to raise expectations than to lower them; to emphasize "white racism" as *the* continuing cause of the Negro's handicaps rather than to de-emphasize it; to increase the minimum wage rather than to decrease or repeal it; to keep children who cannot or will not learn in school a longer rather than a shorter time; to define poverty in terms of relative deprivation rather than in terms of hardship; to deny the existence of class-cultural differences rather than to try to distinguish the competent from the incompetent poor on this basis; to reduce the potential victim's incentives to take precautions against crime rather than to increase them; to give the police less discretionary authority rather than more; to increase the time between arrest, trial, and punishment rather than to decrease it; and to enlarge the freedom of those who have shown themselves to be very likely to commit violent crimes rather than to restrict it.

One reason why these recommendations are politically out of the question is that there exist well-armed and strategically placed veto groups (as David Riesman calls them in *The Lonely Crowd*) which can prevent them from being seriously discussed, much less adopted. The recommendation of the Moynihan Report, that government try to strengthen the Negro family, is a case in point: official consideration of this idea had to stop abruptly when the civil-rights organizations and their allies objected.[18] What these organizations did with this proposal organized labor could do with one to free up the labor market, organized teachers could do with one to reduce the school-leaving age, organized social workers could do with one to define poverty in terms of hardship, and so on.

That interest groups have such power does not represent a malfunctioning of the political system. When they designed the system, the Founding Fathers took great pains to distribute power widely so that "factions" would check one another, thus preventing the rise of any sort of tyranny. The arrangement has worked remarkably well, but there is no denying that it has the defects of its virtues. One of these defects is that a small minority can often veto measures that would benefit a large majority.

Obviously, proposals are frequently adopted despite the opposition of such groups. Why does this not happen in the case of the measures recommended above? There are more prospective gainers than losers from each measure (if this were not thought to be so, the measures would not have been recommended); why, then, do not the prospective gainers organize themselves to overcome the opposition of the veto groups? At the very least, why do they not themselves function as veto groups when the opposites of the measures that would serve their interests are proposed? For example, if they cannot get the minimum-wage law repealed, why do they not at least prevent the rate from being raised?

Part of the answer to these questions is that in most instances the benefits from the recommended measures would be what economists call "public goods" — that is, goods such that if *anyone* benefited *everyone* would benefit. This being the case, the prospective gainers can "ride free" and therefore have little or no incentive to contribute to the support of an organization to fight for the benefits.[19] Another part of the answer is that the voter must usually accept or reject *combinations* of measures (what the candidate or the party stands for); he cannot pick and choose, he must cast his vote one way or the other. His choice therefore turns upon his evaluation of the one or two items in the "package" that touch his primary (which in many cases means his bread-and-butter) interests most closely; if he thinks that his primary interests are well served by these one or two items, he will vote in favor of the "package" even though it contains many other items that are undesirable from the standpoint of his subsidiary interests. Thus, even if the measures recommended above would benefit every voter without exception, there would nevertheless be a unanimous vote against them if they were presented in combinations such that each voter could serve one of his primary interests only by voting against them. In their effort to bring together winning coalitions of interests, candidates and parties tend to be very much aware of such considerations.[20]

Public opinion consists largely of opinions on subjects that do *not* touch the primary interests of the one holding the opinion, and if political choices were made *only* in the light of primary interests, public opinion would matter very little. In fact, of course, it matters a good deal. And there can be no doubt that it supports practically none of the recommendations on the list above.[21] Indeed, in many matters it favors the opposite. In part, then, the perversity that government exhibits in its choice of measures reflects a corresponding perversity in public opinion.

It is pertinent to inquire, therefore, why *public opinion* is perverse. An answer sometimes given is that in matters such as these it is generally dominated by the opinion of the well-educated and well-off. These people (so the argument runs) are indifferent to or downright hostile to the interest of the less well-off and the poor. In short, the "masses" are against the recommended measures because they have been misled by an elite that is looking after its own interests.

The trouble with this theory is that with respect to most measures it runs counter to the facts.[22] The well-off are not benefited by an increase in the minimum wage or by any other measures that price low-value labor out of the market and onto the welfare rolls. They are not benefited by laws that keep children who cannot or will not learn in schools that they (the well-off) must support. They are not bene- fited by the making of sweeping charges about "white racism" or by crisis-mongering of any kind.

Public opinion is indeed decisively influenced in many matters by the opinion of the well-educated and well-off. But this opinion, which reflects the "service" ideal of the upper class, tends to be altruistic. And it is precisely this altruistic bias that accounts for its perversity.

The American political style was formed largely in the upper classes and, within those classes, mainly by people of dissenting- Protestant and Jewish traditions. Accordingly, it is oriented toward the future and toward moral and material progress, for the individual and for the society as a whole. The American is confident that with a sufficient effort all difficulties can be overcome and all problems solved, and he feels a strong obligation to try to improve not only himself but everything else: his community, his society, the whole world. Ever since the days of Cotton Mather, whose *Bonifacius* was a how-to-do-it book on the doing of good, service has been the Ameri- can motto. To be sure, practice has seldom entirely corresponded to principles. The principles, however, have always been influential and they have sometimes been decisive. They can be summarized in two

very simple rules: first, DON'T JUST SIT THERE. DO SOME-
THING! and second, DO GOOD!

These two rules contribute to the perversity that characterizes the
choice of measures for dealing with the urban "crisis." From the
President on down everyone (almost everyone) enjoys the feeling of
exhilaration when a bold step is taken, and that enjoyment is no less
when, as it almost always must be, the step is taken blindfold.[23]
Believing that any problem can be solved if only we try hard enough,
we do not hesitate to attempt what we do not have the least idea of
how to do and what, in some instances, reason and experience both
tell us cannot be done. Not recognizing any bounds to what is feasible,
we are not reconciled to — indeed, we do not even perceive — the
necessity, so frequently arising, of choosing the least objectionable
among courses of action that are all very unsatisfactory. That some
children simply cannot be taught much in school is one example of a
fact that the American mind will not entertain. Our cultural ideal
requires that we give every child a good education whether he wants it
or not and whether he is capable of receiving it or not. If at first we
don't succeed, we must try, try again. And if in the end we don't
succeed, we must feel guilty for our failure. To lower the school-
leaving age would be, in the terms of this secular religion, a shirking
of the task for which we were chosen.

The recommendations listed earlier are mostly unacceptable, even
repellent, to public opinion because what they call for does not appear
to be and (although this is beside the point) may in fact not be morally
improving either to the doer or to the object of his doing. It does not
appear to be improving to a youth to send him to work rather than to
school, especially as this is what it is in one's interest as a taxpayer to
do. It does not appear to be improving to a recidivist to keep him in
jail pending trial, especially as this is what accords with one's feelings
of hostility toward him. It does not appear to be improving to a slum
dweller to say that if he has an adequate income but prefers to spend it
for things other than housing he must not expect the public to intervene, especially as it is in one's "selfish" interest that the public not
intervene. In reality, the doing of good is not so much for the benefit
of those to whom the good is done as it is for that of the *doers*, whose
moral faculties are activated and invigorated by the doing of it, and

for that of the community, the shared values of which are ritually asserted and vindicated by the doing of it. For this reason, good done otherwise than by intention, especially good done in pursuance of ends that are selfish or even "nontuistic," is not really "good" at all. For this reason, too, actions taken from good motives count as good even when in fact they do harm. By far the most effective way of helping the poor is to keep profit-seekers competing vigorously for their trade as consumers and for their services as workers; this, however, is not a way of helping that affords members of the upper classes the chance to flex their moral muscles or the community the chance to dramatize its commitment to the values that hold it together. The way to do these things is with a War on Poverty; even if the War should turn out to have precious little effect on the incomes of the poor — indeed, even if it should *lower* their incomes — the undertaking would nevertheless represent a sort of secular religious revival that affords the altruistic classes opportunities to bear witness to the cultural ideal and, by doing so, to strengthen society's adherence to it. One recalls Macaulay's remark about the attitude of the English Puritans toward bear-baiting: that they opposed it not for the suffering that it caused the bear but for the pleasure that it gave the spectators. Perhaps it is not far-fetched to say that the present-day outlook is similar: the reformer wants to improve the situation of the poor, the black, the slum dweller, and so on, not so much to make them better off materially as to make himself and the whole society better off morally.

There is something to be said for this attitude. The Puritans were surely right in thinking it worse that people should enjoy the sufferings of animals than that animals should suffer. And the present-day reformers are surely right in thinking it more important that society display a concern for what is right and just than that the material level of the poor, which is already above the level of hardship in most cases, be raised somewhat higher. There are problems here, however. One is to keep the impulse for doing good from gushing incontinently into mass extravaganzas — domestic Marshall Plans, Freedom Budgets, and the like — into which billions are poured for no one knows what or how; surely, if it is to be morally significant, good cannot be done from motives that are contrived for the individual by people who have large organizations to maintain or foisted upon him by the mass media. Another problem is to find ways of doing good that are relatively harmless — that do not greatly injure those to whom the good is done (as, for example, children who cannot or will not learn are injured by too-long confinement in school), that are not grossly unfair to third parties (taxpayers, for example), and that do not tend to damage the consensual basis, and thus eventually the political freedom, of the society (as headline-catching official declarations about "white racism" do). Still another problem is to retain, as an element of the cultural ideal itself, what Lionel Trilling has termed moral realism — "the perception of the dangers of the moral life itself."[24]

If the process of middle- and upper-class-ification tends to make public opinion more perverse, it also tends to make it more important. Half a century or more ago, the basis of city and state political power — and therefore, to a large extent, of national political power as well — was the machine. The bosses who ran it kept themselves in power by dispensing patronage and by trading in ethnic, sectional, and party loyalties, and therefore could pretty well disregard public opinion when it suited them to do so.[25] Middle- and upper-class-ification rendered this system obsolete and brought into being one in which the politician, in order to compete successfully for office, has to combine offers of benefits to *classes* of voters (homeowners, taxpayers, and so on) with appeals to general ideas and conceptions of the public interest. Whereas the old system had promised personal rewards, the new one promises social reforms. Accordingly, the smoke-filled room was replaced by the talk-filled one. "The amount of talk which is now expended on all subjects of human interest is something of which a previous age has had not the smallest conception," E. L. Godkin remarked at the end of the last century, adding that "the affairs of nations and of men will be more and more regulated by talk."[26] But even Godkin, since he did not anticipate television, had not the smallest conception of the extent to which affairs would be regulated by talk in our day.

The politician, like the TV news commentator, must always have something to say even when nothing urgently needs to be said. If he lived in a society without problems, he would have to invent some (and of course "solutions" along with them) in order to attract attention and to kindle the interest and enthusiasm needed to carry him into office and enable him, once there, to levy taxes and do the other unpopular things of which governing largely consists. Although in the society that actually exists there are many problems, there are still not enough — enough about which anyone can say or do anything very helpful — to meet his constant need for program material. Moreover, the real and important problems are not necessarily the ones that people want to hear about; a politician may be able to attract more attention and create more enthusiasm — and thus better serve his purpose, which is to generate power with which to take office and govern — by putting real problems in an unreal light or by presenting illusory ones as if they were real. The politician (again like the TV news commentator) can never publicly discuss an important matter with the seriousness that it deserves; time is short, ifs, ands, and buts make tedious listening, and there are always some in the audience who will be confused or offended by what is said and others who will try to twist it into a weapon that they can use against the speaker. Besides, the deeper a discussion goes, the less likelihood of reaching an outcome that the politician can use to generate support.

The changes brought about in the political system by the process of middle- and upper-class-ification have greatly reduced its effectiveness in finding the terms on which people will act together or even live together in peace. The upper-class ideal recommends participation as intrinsically good, but unfortunately, the more participants there are, the larger the number of issues that must be dealt with and the greater the disagreements about each. The ideal also requires that issues be settled on their merits, not by logrolling, and that their merits be conceived of in terms of general moral principles that may not, under any circumstances, be compromised.[27] In the smoke-filled room, it was party loyalty and private interest that mainly moved men; these motives always permitted "doing business." In the talk-filled room, righteous indignation is the main motive, and therefore the longer the talk continues, the clearer it becomes to each side that the other must either be shouted down or knocked down.

If we look toward the future, it is impossible not to be apprehensive. The frightening fact is that large numbers of persons are being rapidly assimilated to the upper classes and are coming to have incomes — time as well as money — that permit them to indulge their taste for "service" and doing good in political action. Television, even more than the newspapers, tends to turn the discussion of public policy issues into a branch of the mass entertainment industry. Doing good is becoming — has already become — a growth industry, like the other forms of mass entertainment, while righteous indignation and uncompromising allegiance to principle are becoming *the* motives of political commitment. This is the way it is in the affluent, middle-class society. How will it be in the super-affluent, upper-middle-class one?

CHAPTER TWELVE

The Prospect

It is probable that at this time we are about to make great changes in our social system. The world is ripe for such changes and if they are not made in the direction of greater social liberality, the direction forward, they will almost of necessity be made in the direction backward, of a terrible social niggardliness. We all know which of those directions we want. But it is not enough to want it, not even enough to work for it — we must want it and work for it with intelligence. Which means that we must be aware of the dangers which lie in our most generous wishes.

— Lionel Trilling

IT is impossible to avoid the conclusion that the serious problems of the cities will continue to exist in something like their present form for another twenty years at least. Even on the most favorable assumptions we shall have large concentrations of the poor and the unskilled, and — what, to repeat, is by no means the same thing — the lower class in the central cities and the larger, older suburbs. The outward movement of industry and commerce is bound to continue, leaving ever-larger parts of the inner city blighted or semi-abandoned. Even if we could afford to throw the existing cities away and build new ones from scratch, matters would not be essentially different, for the people who move into the new cities would take the same old problems with them. Eventually, the present problems of the cities will disappear or dwindle into relative unimportance; they will not, however, be "solved" by programs of the sort undertaken in the past decade. On the contrary, the tendency of such programs would be to prolong the problems and perhaps even make them worse.

For the most part, the problems in question have arisen from and are inseparably connected with developments that almost everyone welcomes: the growth and spread of affluence has enabled millions of people to move from congested cities to new and more spacious homes in the suburbs; the availability of a large stock of relatively good housing in the central cities and older suburbs has enabled the Negro to escape the semi-slavery of the rural South and, a century late, to move into industrial society; better public health measures and facilities have cut the deathrate of the lower class; the war and postwar baby boom have left the city with more adolescents and youths than ever before; and a widespread and general movement upward on the class-cultural scale has made poverty, squalor, ignorance, and brutality — conditions that have always and everywhere been regarded as inevitable in the nature of things — appear as anomalies that should be removed entirely and at once.

What stands in the way of dealing effectively with these problems (insofar as their nature admits of their being dealt with by government) is mainly the virtues of the American political system and of the American character. It is because governmental power is widely distributed that organized interests are so often able to veto measures that would benefit large numbers of people. It is the generous and public-regarding impulses of voters and taxpayers that impel them to support measures — for example, the minimum wage and compulsory high school attendance — the ultimate effect of which is to make the poor poorer and more demoralized. Our devotion to the doctrine that all men are created equal discourages any explicit recognition of class-cultural differences and leads to "democratic" — and often misleading — formulations of problems: for example, poverty as lack of income and material resources (something external to the individual) rather than as inability or unwillingness to take account of the future or to control impulses (something internal). Sympathy for the oppressed, indignation at the oppressor, and a wish to make amends for wrongs done by one's ancestors lead to a misrepresentation of the Negro as the near-helpless victim of "white racism." Faith in the perfectibility of man and confidence that good intentions together with strenuous exertions will hasten his progress onward and upward lead to bold programs that promise to do what no one knows how to do and what perhaps cannot be done, and therefore end in frustration, loss of mutual respect and trust, anger, and even coercion.

Even granting that in general the effect of government programs is to exacerbate the problems of the cities, it might perhaps be argued that they have a symbolic value that is more than redeeming. What economist Kenneth Boulding has said of national parks — that we seem to need them "as we seem to need a useless dome on the capitol, as a symbol of national identity and of that mutuality of concern and interest without which government would be naked coercion"[1] — may possibly apply as well to Freedom Budgets, domestic Marshall Plans, and other such concoctions. That government programs do not succeed in reducing welfare dependency, preventing crime, and so on, is not a weighty objection to them if, for want of them the feeling would spread that the society is "not worth saving." There is an imminent danger, however, that the growing multitude of programs that are intended essentially as gestures of goodwill may constitute a bureaucratic juggernaut which cannot be stopped and which will symbolize not national identity and mutual concern but rather divisiveness, confusion, and inequity. If a symbol is wanted, a useless dome is in every way preferable.

That government cannot solve the problems of the cities and is likely to make them worse by trying does not necessarily mean that calamity impends. Powerful accidental (by which is meant, nongovernmental and, more generally, nonorganizational) forces are at work that tend to alleviate and even to eliminate the problems. Hard as it may be for a nation of inveterate problem-solvers to believe, social problems sometimes disappear in the normal course of events.

One powerful accidental force at work is economic growth. Because capital tends to increase by geometric progression, a rich country becomes exceedingly rich in the space of a few years. If real per capita productivity grows at 2.2 percent per year and if the current trend toward reduced fertility continues (the norm being two children) the population by the end of the century, about 270 million, will produce and consume almost two and one-half times as much as at present. By the year 2040, the population will be approaching stability at about 320 million and will produce about seven times as much as at present.[2] These are by no means implausible assumptions, but even on more conservative ones the end of poverty, in the sense of hardship, is in sight.[3]

As this suggests, a second — and interacting — accidental force of great importance is demographic change. The baby boom that occurred after the Second War resulted in the 1960's in an unprecedented number of teen-agers. The birthrate has since fallen sharply because couples took to marrying later and having fewer children; after 1975 the number and proportion of young people in the population will probably cease to grow for about thirty years. With fewer children to support and educate, there will be more money to devote to other things. (Schools are by far the biggest item of local expenditure; the decrease in the number of children will therefore do much to relieve the "fiscal crisis" of the cities.) The problem of maintaining order will be reduced only slightly; after 1975 the proportion of males ages 15 to 24 to the total population will remain for three decades about the same as it was in 1965.[4]

A third such force — perhaps the most important of all — is the process of middle- and upper-class-ification. For the reasons that were given in Chapter Ten, it is problematic, to say the least, whether the lower class will be absorbed into the outlook and style of life of the "mainstream." With this small but nevertheless important exception, it seems highly probable that there will continue to be a general upward movement all along the class-cultural scale. This will mean a softening of manners, better performance in schools, and less violence of the sort that serves to emphasize masculinity by acts of daring and aggression. "As the larger culture becomes more cerebral," Wolfgang and Ferracuti write, "the refined symbolic forms of masculinity [for example, debating societies, musical virtuosity, and literary talent] should be more fully adopted."[5]

Middle- and upper-class-ification also implies a reduction in racial prejudice and discrimination. This should proceed with gathering momentum because of the operation of what Gunnar Myrdal, in *An American Dilemma,* called "the principle of cumulation."

White prejudice and discrimination keep the Negro low in standards of living, health, education, manners and morals. This, in turn, gives support to white prejudice. White prejudice and Negro standards thus mutually "cause" each other. . . . Such a static "accommodation" is, however, entirely accidental. If either of the factors changes, this will cause a change in the other factor, too, and start a process of interaction where the change in one factor will continuously be supported by the reaction of the other factor.[6]

It is impossible to judge how much effect these accidental forces will have on the lower class. Rapid economic growth and the prospect of high returns to investment in the "human capital" represented by oneself or one's children may, as suggested in Chapter Ten, encourage rapid mobility from the lower class. Conceivably, however, increasing affluence might have an opposite effect: generous welfare programs, for example, may destroy more incentives to provide for the future than better job and other opportunities create; moreover, the diffusion of more present-oriented ways in the middle and upper classes might lessen any pressure that lower-class people feel to change their ways or even discourage them from doing so. An increase in the absolute (if not the relative) size of the lower class is by no means out of the question. Unless the increase were very large, however, it would not necessarily lead to a radical worsening of the situation or precipitate a crisis in the life of the nation. Moreover, if an increase is not out of the question, neither is a decrease.

Although the *objective* situation does not warrant the alarmist tone of much that is said and written about the city, the *subjective* one may. However much the accidental forces may reduce the *real* importance of the problems that have been under discussion, they may have no impact on their *seeming* importance. Indeed, this is likely to grow, for some of the very same factors that improve the objective situation also raise people's standards and expectations, thus leaving the subjective situation no better — and perhaps even worse — than it was to begin with. What people *think* a situation is may (as sociologist Robert K. Merton has pointed out) become an integral part of that situation, and therefore a factor in its subsequent development. A false public definition of the situation may, as Merton says, evoke new behavior that makes the originally false definition come true, thus perpetuating a "reign of error."[7] In short, wrong public definitions of urban problems may lead to behavior that will make matters worse despite the ameliorating influence of the accidental forces.

This possibility is most painfully apparent in the case of the Negro.

That racial prejudice has long been declining and may be expected to continue to decline at an accelerating rate counts for little if the Negro *thinks* that white racism is as pervasive as ever; that his opportunities to improve his position by acquiring skills are at last fairly good counts for little if he *thinks* that "massive" government welfare, housing, and other programs — and *only* these — can help him. If he misperceives the situation in these ways, he is likely to do things that are counterproductive (for example, to cut himself off from "white" schools, jobs, and politics and to enter the fantasy world of black separatism). Such a course, if carried far enough, may validate his original (false) hypothesis — that is, he may become in fact as dependent upon government programs as he (wrongly) supposed himself to be and may revive the fact of white prejudice by giving it some objective grounds to feed upon.

Nothing could be so tragic and ironic as the acceptance of a false public definition of the situation that proves to be a self-fulfilling prophecy of racial hatred. Even if nonracial factors had not in recent years superseded the racial ones as the Negro's main handicap, it would be well to pretend that they had, for a self-fulfilling prophecy of the unimportance of racial factors would be as great a blessing as its opposite would be a curse.

Except as they create, or reinforce, counterproductive public definitions of problems and thereby encourage a "reign of error," wrong governmental measures are not likely to lead to catastrophe or even to any very significant worsening of the situation. Most wrong measures will lead to nothing worse than some additional waste and delay, usually a trivial amount. (One gets a sense of how unimportant even "important" governmental actions may be from one economist's estimate that the elimination of monopoly in the United States in 1929 would have raised income by no more than 1/13 of 1 percent, and from the estimate of another that benefits attributable to better resource allocation by virtue of the Common Market would also be much less than 1 percent.[8]) The governmental measures having the largest effect upon the city since the turn of the century are probably subsidization of truck and automobile transportation and subsidization of home ownership for the well-off; these measures certainly hastened the departure of the white middle class from the central city and, a fortiori, the entry of the poor — especially the black poor — on a large scale, but they did not significantly change the pattern of metropolitan growth; this was determined by accidental forces — the demographic, technological, economic, and class-cultural imperatives described in Chapters Two and Three.

Although it is easy to exaggerate the importance, either for good or ill, of the measures that government has adopted or might adopt, there does appear to be a danger to the good health of the society in the tendency of the public to define so many situations as "critical problems" — a definition that implies (1) that "solutions" exist or can be found and (2) that unless they are found and applied at once, disaster will befall. The import of what has been said in this book is that although there are many difficulties to be coped with, dilemmas to be faced, and afflictions to be endured, there are very few problems that can be solved; it is also that although much is seriously wrong with the city, no disaster impends unless it be one that results from public misconceptions that are in the nature of self-fulfilling prophecies.

Insofar as delusory and counterproductive public definitions of the situation arise from biases that lie deep within the culture (for example, from the impulse to DO SOMETHING! and to DO GOOD!), they are likely to persist in the face of all experience. To exhort the upper classes to display more of the quality that Trilling calls moral realism would be to offer a problem-begging "solution," since the very want of moral realism that constitutes the problem would prevent their recognizing the need of it.

The biases of the culture limit the range of possibilities, but they do not determine fully how the public will define the situation. This definition is in large part the result of a process of opinion formation that goes on within a relatively small world of officials, leaders of civic associations and other interest groups, journalists, and social scientists, especially economists; from this small world opinion is passed on to the public-at-large through the mass media, books, classroom instruction, campaign oratory, after-dinner speeches, and so on. Needless to say, a vast amount of misinformation, prejudice, and illogic enters into the process of opinion formation. (The agony of the cities, someone has remarked, is what the network executive and his fellow-commuters on the Long Island Railroad see out the window as they make their agonized way to and from their offices in Manhattan.) Within the past decade or two, developments have occurred that could make for a more realistic view of the urban situation — for example, the number of technically trained persons working on urban problems has increased greatly, their resources for gathering and manipulating data and the analytical apparatus that they can bring to bear upon policy questions are much improved, and what they have to say is taken much more seriously by politicians and administrators and therefore also by journalists.[9] It would not be surprising if the conventional wisdom were to be very much revised in the next decade or two as a consequence of these developments. Turnover within the small world of opinion-makers is rapid, and the young newcomers in that world tend to be open to new ideas and even in search of them. Because communication within the small world and between it and the public-at-large is excellent, a new definition of the situation, once formulated, could catch on very quickly.

It would be pleasant to be able to end this discussion on that relatively optimistic note. Unfortunately, another side to the matter requires mention. Technically trained persons have their own characteristic biases, and if their view of the city is different from that of the commuter on the Long Island Railroad it is not necessarily more realistic. Moreover, as the technician comes to play a more important part in policy-making he is bound to come more and more under the discipline of large organizations, especially foundations and government agencies, whose maintenance and enhancement depend in some way upon the elaboration of an alarmist, or at any rate expansionist, public definition of the situation. That young newcomers to the small world of opinion-makers tend to be open to new ideas is not altogether reassuring either, for they may tend to accept new ideas *just because* they are new. To the pessimist, the prospect is that a new conventional wisdom about the problems of the city, the product of many millions of dollars' expenditure on research, cast in the language of systems analysis and the computer, will only compound the existing confusion. The optimist, however, will see reason to believe that facts, rational analysis, and deliberation about the nature of the public interest will play a somewhat larger part than hitherto in the formation of both opinion and policy.

Note on the Size of the Social Classes

D ATA do not exist from which one can make reasonably good estimates of the size of the various social classes as defined in this book. Under the circumstances, the best that can be done is to interpret data on the size of the classes *otherwise defined*. This would be a hazardous proceeding at best, but it is all the more so because the various estimates that have been made are all extremely fragmentary. Frank Riessman, in *The Culturally Deprived Child* (New York: Harper & Row, 1962), says that in 1950 approximately one child in ten in the fourteen largest cities was culturally deprived, that by 1960 this number had risen to one in three, and that it might reach one in two by 1970. He does not say how these estimates were arrived at, however, and he uses the term *culturally deprived* interchangeably with educationally deprived, deprived, underprivileged, disadvantaged, lower class, and lower socioeconomic group.

Less impressionistic estimates have been made for particular cities or parts of cities; there is, however, no way of knowing how representative the place studied is of all urban places or even of places of about the same size and demographic type. Pierre Martineau, using a probability area sample of 3,880 households, divided metropolitan Chicago on the basis of an index of occupation, sources of income, and housing type as follows (the terms are not his): upper 8.1, middle 28.4, working 44.0, and lower 19.5. Pierre Martineau, "Social Classes and Spending Behavior," *The Journal of Marketing*, 23:2

(October 1958); reprinted in Martin M. Grossack, ed., *Understanding Consumer Behavior* (Boston: Christopher Publishing House, 1966, p. 139). Richard A. Cloward and James A. Jones constructed an index of social class on the basis of education, occupation of head of household, and total family income adjusted by number of persons in the family. ("The typical lower class person in our index has had less than an eighth grade education, is employed as an unskilled or service worker, and lives in a family whose income per person is less than the minimum wage," p. 196.) The lower East Side of New York, they found, was 44 percent lower class, 36 percent working class, and 20 percent lower-middle or above. In A. Harry Passow, ed., *Education in Depressed Areas* (New York: Columbia Teachers College, 1963). On the basis of a 5 percent sample of New Haven, Hollingshead and Redlich (*Social Class and Mental Illness*, New York: Wiley, 1958, p. 202) offer the following measures by race:

Class	White	Negro
I–II (Upper?)	11.7	1.0
III (Middle?)	20.8	4.0
IV (Working?)	50.1	36.9
V (Lower?)	17.4	58.1

Although Hollingshead and Redlich define class in terms of position in a deference hierarchy, it is noteworthy that the groups that emerge are subcultures that closely resemble the ideal types described in this book.

Lee Rainwater in *Family Design* (Chicago: Aldine Publishing Company, 1965, p. 24) says that the lower class (lower lower in his terminology) "represents about one-quarter of the working class and about thirteen percent of the population of a city like Chicago." This estimate was based (he writes in a personal communication) on studies using one or another form of W. Lloyd Warner's *Index of Status Characteristics*, especially a study by Social Research, Inc., of the

Chicago metropolitan area. Richard P. Coleman, for Social Research, Inc., using two main indices, male occupation distribution and educational background, sometimes supplemented by two others, family income and housing conditions, has prepared the following estimates on the basis of 1960 Census data (the terminology is not his):

Class	All urban total	Non-whites	Whites
Upper	14	3	15
Middle	31	13	33
Working	39	43	38
Lower	16	41	14

(*Source:* Social Research Inc., "The Urban Negro: Sampling Considerations and Statistical Overview," August 1968, p. 24.)

A U.S. Bureau of the Census report, *Socioeconomic Characteristics of the Population: 1960* (Series P-23, No. 12, July 31, 1964), combines measures of occupation, income, and education in a socioeconomic status (SES) score. If persons in the lowest 20 percent of SES scores are taken to be lower class (a janitor or kitchen worker with an income slightly below the poverty line and with seven grades of schooling would have scored near the upper limit of this class on each count), 6 percent of whites and 20 percent of nonwhites in central cities of standard metropolitan statistical areas (SMSA's) of more than 250,000 population belong to that class. For the procedure by which the scores were constructed, see U.S. Bureau of the Census, *Methodology and Scores of Socioeconomic Status*, Working Paper No. 15, 1963. The following table was prepared from tabulations run by the Census Bureau under contract for Professor Basil Zimmer of Brown University and kindly made available by him.

PERCENT DISTRIBUTION OF THE POPULATION IN SOCIOECONOMIC
STATUS CATEGORIES FOR STANDARD METROPOLITAN STATISTICAL
AREAS, 250,000 AND OVER POPULATION

SES Score	CENTRAL CITY		URBAN PART OF RING	
	White	*Nonwhite*	*White*	*Nonwhite*
80–99 (Upper?)	15	3	24	3
50–79 (Middle?)	47	22	50	21
20–49 (Working?)	32	55	23	54
0–19 (Lower?)	6	20	3	22

Selected References of
Writings Pertaining to *The Unheavenly City*

SYMPOSIA

"Banfield's Unheavenly City: A Symposium and Response": Duane Lockard "Patent Racism"; Russell D. Murphy "Challenge to Orthodoxy"; Arthur Naftalin "Unseen Hand"; Edward C. Banfield "In Reply." TRANS-action, Vol. 8, Nos. 5 and 6 (March/April 1971), pp. 69–78.

"The Unheavenly City: Acrimony and Accolades": Peter H. Rossi "The City As Purgatory"; Carl B. Stokes "The Poor Need Not Always be With Us"; Scott Greer "Put Thy Love in Order"; Robert J. Lampman "Moral Realism and the Poverty Question"; Robert E. Agger "Class, Race and Reaction: A Trivial but Dangerous Analysis," and Edward C. Banfield "Putting Social Science to Work is a Risky Undertaking." *Social Science Quarterly* Vol. 51, No. 4 (March, 1971), pp. 816–859.

"The Local Government Law Round Table Council Meets Banfield's, *The Unheavenly City*," Association of American Law Schools Round Table, *UCLA Law Review* Vol. 20, No. 2 (December, 1972), pp. 387–411.

REVIEW ARTICLES

Harvey Averch and Robert A. Levine, "Two Models of the Urban Crisis: An Analytical Essay on Banfield and Forrester," *Policy Sciences* Vol. 2, No. 2 (June, 1971), pp. 143–158.

Worth Bateman and Harold M. Hochman, "Social Problems and the Urban Crisis: Can Public Policy Make a Difference?" *American Economic Review* Vol. LXI:2 (May, 1971), pp. 346–359.

David Elesh, *The Journal of Human Resources* Vol. VI, 1 (Spring, 1971), pp. 251–256.

Joseph F. Freeman III, "Toward an Understanding of the Urban Crisis," *The Political Science Reviewer* Vol. 1 (Fall, 1971), pp. 125–153.

John Friedmann, "The Unheavenly City," *Journal of American Institute of Planners* (March, 1971), pp. 122–125.

Irving Kristol, "The Cities: A Tale of Two Classes," *Fortune* (June 1970).

David S. Mundel, "The Emporer Time Horizon — A Naked Walk Through the Urban Crisis," *Northwestern University Law Review* Vol. 67, No. 2 (1972), pp. 303–316.

Robert Nisbet, "The Urban Crisis Revisited," *The Intercollegiate Review* Vol. 7. No. 1 (Fall, 1970), pp. 1–7.

Gary T. Schwartz, "Banfield: The Unheavenly City," *UCLA Law Review* Vol. 19, No. 1 (October, 1971), pp. 148–164.

Richard Sennett, "Survival of the Fattest," *New York Review of Books* (August 13, 1970).

Richard Todd, "A Theory of the Lower Class — Edward Banfield: The Maverick of Urbanology," *The Atlantic* (September, 1970), pp. 51–55.

ARTICLES ABOUT THE BOOK'S RECEPTION

T. R. Marmor, "Banfield's 'Heresy,' *Commentary* (July, 1972), pp. 86–88.

Patricia McLaughlin, "Is Banfield Really Diabolical?," *The Pennsylvania Gazette*, Vol. 72, No. 2 (November, 1973), pp. 25–30.

Chapter Notes

CHAPTER I

Introduction

1. The 1970 Census defined as "urban" places, unincorporated as well as incorporated, with 2,500 inhabitants or more (excluding persons living in rural portions of extended cities) as well as other territory within Urbanized Areas. An "Urbanized Area" comprises at least one city of 50,000 inhabitants (the "central city") plus contiguous, closely settled areas ("urban fringe"). A "Standard Metropolitan Statistical Area (SMSA)" is a county or group of contiguous counties (except in New England) containing a city (or "twin" cities) of at least 50,000 population; contiguous counties are included in an SMSA if they are essentially metropolitan in character and are socially and economically integrated with the central city. That part of the United States lying outside of any SMSA is "nonmetropolitan." All of these definitions were somewhat different in 1960 and also in 1950.
   See Daniel J. Elazar, "Are We a Nation of Cities?," *The Public Interest*, 4 (Summer 1966), pp. 42–44.
2. Sloan R. Wayland, "Old Problems, New Faces, and New Standards," in A. Harry Passow, ed., *Education in Depressed Areas* (New York: Columbia University Teachers College, 1963), p. 66.
3. Irving Hoch, "Urban Scale and Environmental Quality," in *Population, Resources, and the Environment*, vol. III of task force reports of Commission on Population Growth and the American Future, Ronald G. Ridker, ed. (Washington, D.C., Government Printing Office, 1972), p. 243. The figures are for 1966.
4. According to the U.S. Public Health Service, the most polluted air is nowhere near as dangerous as inhaled cigarette smoke. It is of interest also that the mortality rate from emphysema is higher in rural parts of New York than in metropolitan ones (*New York Times*, October 30, 1970) and that the state with the highest death rate from respiratory disease is Vermont (*New York Times*, December 20, 1972).
5. For data see U.S. Environmental Protection Agency, *Air Quality Data*, an annual, *Air Pollution Measurements of the National Air Sampling Network, 1957–1961*, and *The Fourth Annual Report of the Council on Environmental*

Quality, U.S. Government Printing Office, September 1973, pp. 265–275.
6. This was the finding of a six-year study directed by Lawrence B. Cohen of the Department of Industrial Engineering of Columbia University and reported in the *New York Times*, December 16, 1965.
7. J. R. Meyer, J. F. Kain, and M. Wohl, *The Urban Transportation Problem* (Cambridge, Mass.: Harvard University Press, 1965), p. 359.
8. John Kain, "How to Improve Urban Transportation at Practically No Cost," *Public Policy*, 20 (Summer 1972):352. Italics are in the original.
9. Arnold J. Meltsner titles his contribution to a collection of essays "Local Revenue: A Political Problem." He explains: "Officials are sometimes reluctant to raise taxes because they believe that taxes have reached a political limit. How do you know, Mr. Mayor, that the property tax has reached a political limit? Answer: I do not know; I just feel it. A political limit is a fuzzy constraint, perhaps fictitious, that local officials worry about, but have difficulty predicting. Even social scientists cannot tell when a political limit is about to be reached." In John P. Crecine, ed., *Financing the Metropolis*, Urban Affairs Annual Reviews, vol. 4 (Beverly Hills, Calif.: Sage Publications, 1970), p. 108.

 In 1973 a survey of 30 cities with "serious financial problems" "failed to locate any cities in which conditions were such that timely action by local, or in a few cases, State officials could not avert or promptly relieve a financial emergency." Advisory Commission on Intergovernmental Relations, *City Financial Emergencies: The Intergovernmental Dimension*, (Washington, D.C., U.S. Government Printing Office, July 1973), p. 4.
10. Kenneth T. Jackson, "Metropolitan Government versus Suburban Autonomy," in Kenneth T. Jackson and Stanley K. Schultz, eds., *Cities in American History* (New York: Alfred A. Knopf, 1972), pp. 446 and 456.
11. *Final Report of the National Commission on the Causes and Prevention of Violence* (Washington, D.C.: U.S. Government Printing Office, 1969), footnote p. 29.
12. U.S. Bureau of the Census, *Census of Population: 1970, Employment Profiles of Selected Low-Income Areas*, Final Report PHC(3)-1, United States Summary — Urban Areas (January 1972). The low-income areas were defined by the Census Bureau in the middle 1960's for the use of OEO and Model Cities agencies. The following (equally weighted) criteria were used: family income below $3,000, children in broken homes, persons with low educational attainments, males in unskilled jobs, and substandard housing. Census tracts in the lowest quartile were defined as "low income." In 1970 the boundaries so established were re-examined by the Census in consultation with local planning and other officials; in most instances areas were enlarged considerably.

 A Census report (distributed after the text of this book was in type) provides data for the low-income areas of the 50 largest cities using figures from the decennial census (a 15 percent sample) and defining a low-income area to consist of all census tracts in which 20 percent or more of all persons were below the poverty line in 1969. On this basis, there were 10,555,918 persons in the poverty areas, 60 percent of whom were Negro. The median family income was $6,099; 27 percent of the families were below the poverty line and 22 percent had incomes at least three times greater than the poverty standard. About one-third of the families in the low-income areas paid rents of less than 20 percent of their income; however, of the renters whose incomes were below the poverty line, more than half paid more than half of their incomes in rent. Census tracts with a poverty rate of 40 percent or more had 2,017,513 persons nearly three-fourths of whom were Negro. U.S. Bureau of the Census, Census of Population: 1970 Subject Reports, Final Report PC(2)-9B, Low-Income Areas in Large Cities.

13. In *Dark Ghetto*, Kenneth B. Clark presents 1960 Census data showing that eight cities — New York, Los Angeles, Baltimore, Washington, Cleveland, St. Louis, New Orleans, and Chicago — contain a total of sixteen areas, all of at least 15,000 population and five of more than 100,000, that are exclusively (more than 94 percent) Negro (New York: Harper & Row, 1965), table, p. 25.

14. Commission on Population Growth and the American Future, *Population and the American Future* (Washington, D.C.: U.S. Government Printing Office, 1972), p. 74.

15. Kenneth B. Clark, "The Wonder Is There Have Been So Few Riots," *New York Times Magazine*, September 5, 1965, p. 10.

16. Alexis de Tocqueville, *Democracy in America*, trans. by Henry Reeve (New York: Alfred A. Knopf, 1945), 1: 289–290.

17. George Grier, "Washington," *City Magazine* (February 1971), p. 47, quoted by Bennett Harrison, *Education, Training and the Urban Ghetto* (Baltimore: The Johns Hopkins University Press, 1972), p. 167.

18. Cf. Robert C. Weaver, "Class, Race and Urban Renewal," *Land Economics*, 36 (August 1960): 235–251. On urban renewal in general, see James Q. Wilson, ed., *Urban Renewal: The Record and the Controversy* (Cambridge, Mass.: M.I.T. Press, 1966).

19. Scott Greer, *Urban Renewal and American Cities* (Indianapolis: Bobbs-Merrill, 1965), p. 3.

As William G. Grigsby has pointed out, the "flight to the suburbs," which most renewal projects in central cities have been intended to stop or reverse, may be a good thing from the standpoint of the society as a whole even if undesirable from that of the central city. "It is not understood that . . . exodus from the city has produced a much higher standard of housing than could otherwise have been attained, and that the market forces that produced this shift should, therefore, be stimulated." *Housing Markets and Public Policy* (Philadelphia: University of Pennsylvania Press, 1963), p. 333.

20. *The President's Fourth Annual Report on National Housing Goals*, 92d Congress, 2d Session, House Document No. 92–319, June 29, 1972. The report includes a table (p. 48) showing the revenue cost for 1971 by gross income class.

This and another form of concealed subsidy (the noninclusion of imputed net rent in gross income reported for tax purposes) are discussed by Henry J. Aaron, *Shelter and Subsidies: Who Benefits from Federal Housing Policies?* (Washington, D.C.: The Brookings Institution, 1972), ch. 4.

21. Stanley S. Surrey, Professor of Law, Harvard University, in U.S. Congress, Senate, Subcommittee on Priorities and Economy in Government of the Joint Economic Committee, *Hearings, The Economics of Federal Subsidy Programs*, 92d Congress, 1st Session, January 13, 14, and 17, 1972, p. 45.

22. *The President's Fourth Annual Report*, p. 32. The report goes on to add: "While housing programs have contributed to these problems and in many cases intensified them, it is important to emphasize that they did not *cause* them. The causes stem from the complex interaction of population migration,

community attitudes and prejudices, consumer preferences, local governmental fragmentation, and the impact of other federal programs such as urban renewal and the highway programs."

23. Richard Muth, "The Urban Economy and Public Problems," in John P. Crecine, ed., *Financing the Metropolis*, p. 454. See also Muth's book, *Cities and Housing, The Spatial Pattern of Urban Residential Land Use* (Chicago: University of Chicago Press, 1969), pp. 319–322.
24. Theodore W. Schultz, *Economic Crises in World Agriculture* (Ann Arbor: University of Michigan Press, 1965), p. 94.
25. Karl E. and Alma F. Taeuber, "The Negro as an Immigrant Group: Recent Trends in Racial and Ethnic Segregation in Chicago," *American Journal of Sociology*, 69 (January 1964): 382.
26. Executive Office of the President, Domestic Council, *Report on National Growth, 1972* (Washington, D.C.: U.S. Government Printing Office, 1972).
27. Irving Hoch, "Income and City Size," *Urban Studies*, 9 (1972): 320.
28. Peter A. Morrison, *The Impact and Significance of Rural-Urban Migration in the United States* (Santa Monica, Calif.: The Rand Corporation, #P-4752, March 1972), p. 2.
29. Dick Netzer, *Economics and Urban Problems: Diagnosis and Prescriptions* (New York: Basic Books, 1970), p. 21.
30. Christopher Jencks et al., *Inequality, A Reassessment of the Effect of Family and Schooling in America* (New York: Basic Books, 1972), pp. 141–142.
31. Andrew M. Greeley and Paul B. Sheatsley, "Attitudes Toward Racial Integration," *Scientific American*, 225 (December 1971): 13 and 15.
    Thomas F. Pettigrew has found that "white attitudes toward open housing have become increasingly more favorable over the past generation." See his paper on "Attitudes on Race and Housing: A Social-Psychological View," in Amos H. Hawley and Vincent P. Rock, eds., *Segregation in Residential Areas* (Washington, D.C.: National Academy of Sciences, 1973), pp. 21–84. See also Joel D. Aberbach and Jack L. Walker, *Race in the City* (Boston: Little, Brown and Company, 1973), which presents data on attitudes of blacks and whites in Detroit in surveys made in 1967 and 1971.
32. William Watts and Lloyd A. Free, eds., *State of the Nation* (New York: Universal Books, 1973), p. 80.
33. Irving Kristol, "The Lower Fifth," *The New Leader*, February 17, 1964, pp. 9–10.
34. Robert Blauner, "Whitewash Over Watts," *Trans-action* 3 (March–April 1966): 6.
35. Burton A. Weisbrod, "Preventing High-School Drop-outs," in Robert Dorfman, ed., *Measuring Benefits of Government Investments* (Washington, D.C.: The Brookings Institution, 1965), p. 118.
36. Wayland, "Old Problems," p. 67.
37. Elliot L. Richardson, *Responsibility and Responsiveness (II), A Report on the HEW Potential for the Seventies* (Washington, D.C.: U.S. Department of Health, Education, and Welfare, January 18, 1973).

CHAPTER 2

The Logic of Metropolitan Growth

The quotation from F. J. Kingsbury at the head of the chapter is from an article, "The Tendency of Man to Live in Cities," *Journal of Social Science*, vol. 33 (November 1895). The article is excerpted in Charles N. Glaab, *The American City: A Documentary History* (Homewood, Ill.: Dorsey Press, 1963).

This chapter owes more to the writings of Raymond Vernon, John F. Kain, and Bernard J. Frieden than the footnote references suggest.

1. There is a rich literature of theory about urban form and growth in the United States. For a good summary account of it, see Ralph Thomlinson, *Urban Structure, the Social and Spatial Character of Cities* (New York: Random House, 1969), especially ch. 8. Regional differences in urban structure are described by Lee Schnore and Hal Winsborough, "Functional Classification and the Residential Location of Social Classes," in Brian Berry, ed., *City Classification Handbook* (New York: Wiley, 1972).

   For a good general treatment of the development of the American city in the nineteenth century, see David Ward, *Cities and Immigrants: A Geography of Change in Nineteenth Century America* (New York: Oxford University Press, 1971).

2. "Report of the Select Committee Appointed to Examine into the Condition of Tenant Houses in New York and Brooklyn," transmitted to the Legislature March 9, 1857 (Albany, N.Y.), pp. 11–12. Excerpts of this report appear in Glaab, *The American City*.

3. Joel Arthur Tarr, in A. B. Callow, Jr., ed., *American Urban History* (New York: Oxford University Press, 1969), p. 205.

4. Ward, *Cities and Immigrants*, p. 131.

5. Blake McKelvey, *The Urbanization of America* (New Brunswick, N.J.: Rutgers University Press, 1963), pp. 78–79. See also Glaab, *The American City*, p. 178; and Sam B. Warner, Jr., *Streetcar Suburbs* (Cambridge, Mass.: Harvard University Press and M.I.T. Press, 1962).

6. Richard C. Wade, *The Urban Frontier* (Chicago: University of Chicago Press, Phoenix Books, 1964), p. 307.

7. In Philadelphia the outward movement was proportionately greater between 1860 and 1910 than between 1900 and 1950 (Hans Blumenfeld, "The Modern Metropolis," *Scientific American*, 213, September 1965: 67). For an account of Philadelphia's early pattern of growth, which was *not* that of the ideal type described in the text, see Sam B. Warner, Jr., *The Private City* (Philadelphia: University of Pennsylvania Press, 1968), ch. 3.

8. Edward Crapsey, *The Nether Side of New York* (New York: Sheldon and Company, 1872), p. 9.

9. Quoted in J. Leslie Dunstan, *A Light to the City* (Boston: Beacon Press, 1966), p. 91.

10. Quoted by Thomas Sowell, *Race and Economics* (New York: David McKay, forthcoming 1974), ch. 7.

11. Mabel L. Walker, *Urban Blight and Slums* (Cambridge, Mass.: Harvard University Press, 1938), pp. 18–21.

In London the course of development was strikingly similar. I am indebted to Mr. David L. Lloyd, Jr. for calling my attention to the following from R. C. K. Ensor, *England 1870–1914* (Oxford: Clarendon Press, 1936, pp. 509–510): ".... changes in urban transportation had an almost instant effect on housing. They enabled people to live farther from the centres. Soon after 1900 a building boom sprang up on the outskirts of towns and continued until 1910. The resulting movement of population was really a great social phenomenon. Seen in nearly all towns, it benefited the largest most, and London most of all..... The effect on the congested slums of east, south and north London was like the draining of marshes. It is true that the movement went by layers, and when Poplar transferred to East Ham, Walworth went to Wandsworth, or North Camberwell to Lewisham, the places left vacant might be filled from more central and crowded areas; true also, that the new houses (except those built by municipalities or trusts) took the best-off and not the neediest workers."

12. Reynolds Farley, "Suburban Persistence," in John Kramer, ed., *North American Suburbs: Politics, Diversity and Change* (Berkeley, Calif.: Glendessary Press, 1972), p. 83.

13. Constance McLaughlin Green, *The Rise of Urban America* (New York: Harper & Row, 1965), pp. 132–133.

14. Davis McEntire, *Residence and Race* (Berkeley: University of California Press, 1960), pp. 300–301. FHA discriminated against Negroes until well into the Truman administration. Afterward it discriminated against them *in effect* by insisting on very low-risk loans.

15. Gilbert Osofsky, *Harlem: The Making of a Ghetto* (New York: Harper & Row, 1963), p. 128.

16. Edith Elmer Wood, *Slums and Blighted Areas in the U.S.*, Administration of Public Works, Housing Division Bulletin Number 1 (Washington, D.C.: U.S. Government Printing Office, 1935), p. 19.

17. For an account of federal policy at this time see Roger Starr, *The Living End: The City and Its Critics* (New York: Coward-McCann, Inc., 1966), especially ch. 5.

18. It has been estimated that in the first half of the 1960 decade net out-migration of blacks from the South was about 172,000 persons annually and in the second half about 100,000 annually.

John F. Kain and Robert Schafer, "Income Maintenance, Migration, and Regional Growth," *Public Policy*, 20 (Spring 1972): 221.

19. See Richard Muth, *Cities and Housing, The Spatial Pattern of Urban Residential Land Use* (Chicago: University of Chicago Press, 1969). "One is tempted to argue," writes Raymond E. Zelder, that, far from their being a vast scarcity of "satisfactory" housing for low-income families in the past decade, "almost the reverse is the case; that is, the low-income market has been threatened by underlying conditions of chronic over-supply." "Poverty, Housing, and Market Processes," *Urban Affairs Quarterly*, 8 (September 1972): 79.

20. McEntire, *Residence and Race*, ch. 3.

21. Raymond Vernon, *Metropolis 1985* (Cambridge, Mass.: Harvard University Press, 1960), p. 141.

22. Herbert J. Gans, *The Levittowners* (New York: Pantheon Books, 1967), p.

32. See also Richard Muth, "The Urban Economy and Public Problems," in John P. Crecine, ed., *Financing the Metropolis*, Urban Affairs Annual Reviews, vol. 4 (Berkeley, Calif.: Sage Publications, 1970), p. 443, and Theodore Droettboom et al., "Urban Violence and Residential Mobility," *Journal of the American Institute of Planners* (September 1971): 319–325.

Julius Margolis has pointed out to the writer that real estate promoters have often played, and often still play, a major part in these movements. The case of Bedford-Stuyvesant illustrates his point. Stuyvesant Heights was a fashionable neighborhood until, with the Depression, many of the big brownstones became too much for their original owners to maintain. "They moved out and the prices dropped until the houses were within reach of Negro families. And the families who couldn't make the mortgage payments on their own incomes were encouraged by brokers and the lack of any zoning ordinances or regulations to subdivide the beautiful old brownstones into small apartments. Bedford-Stuyvesant is the place where 'blockbusting' developed into a fine art. Any time there was any possibility of stabilization, real estate men would spur on the process of change by paying Negroes to stage brawls on street corners to frighten white residents. Nearly every day's mail contained postcards reading, 'we have a buyer for your house.' " Fred C. Shapiro and James W. Sullivan, *Race Riots, New York 1964* (New York: Thomas Y. Crowell Company, 1964), p. 109.

23. In the Mountain and Pacific states, where the city's growth was shaped largely by the automobile, the inner parts of the city have not been industrialized and the growing middle class has not been under the same pressure to move outward to find places to build newer and more spacious housing. Consequently there are not the vast stretches of dilapidated "grey" areas that are so characteristic of the older cities that were settled in pre-automotive days. See Frederick Wirt, Benjamin Walter, Francine Rabinowitz, and Deborah Hensler, *On the City's Rim* (Lexington, Mass.: D. C. Heath, 1972), pp. 29–30.

24. Henry J. Aaron, *Shelter and Subsidies: Who Benefits from Federal Housing Policies?* (Washington, D.C.: The Brookings Institution, 1972), ch. 2.

25. Muth, *Cities and Housing*, ch. 10. "Substandard," a term used by the Department of Housing and Urban Development, includes dilapidated housing together with sound housing that lacks specified plumbing facilities. In 1966, nearly 70 percent of substandard units were so classified *only* because they lacked certain plumbing facilities. Most plumbing deficiencies are in farm and rural, not urban, areas, however. "Dilapidated," "deteriorating," and "sound" are terms used by the Census to indicate the number and seriousness ("slight," "critical," etc.) of housing defects. For a convenient account of these matters, see Aaron, *Shelter and Subsidies*, ch. 2.

26. Ibid., pp. 25 and 35.

27. Frank S. Kristof, "The 1970 Census of Housing: Does It Meet Data Needs for Housing Programs and Policy?," paper presented to Annual Conference, American Institute of Planners, San Francisco, Calif., October 25, 1971, p. 11.

28. On the problem of abandonment see George S. Sternlieb, "Abandonment and Rehabilitation: What Is to Be Done?," in George S. Sternlieb, ed., *Housing 1970–1971* (New York: AMS Press, 1972), pp. 62–119. See also Frederick E. Case, ed., *Inner-City Housing and Private Enterprise* (New York: Praeger, 1972), especially pp. 110–111.

29. See the chapter on technological change by Boris Yavitz in Eli Ginsburg et al., *Manpower Strategy for the Metropolis* (New York: Columbia University Press, 1968), especially pp. 49–55.

30. For data on employment trends from 1950 to 1967 in 11 large central cities and productivity growth by central city and suburban ring from 1947 to 1963 in 30 large metropolitan areas, see Alexander Ganz and Thomas O'Brien, "The City: Sandbox, Reservation, or Dynamo?", *Public Policy*, 21 (Winter 1973), pp. 107–123.

The 1970 Census found that in the 1960's the number of central city jobs increased from 23 to 25 million (8%) while the number in the suburban rings increased from 20 to 29 million (31%). In the 30 metropolitan areas with populations of more than 1 million, there was an aggregate increase of 1.5 million central city jobs and 4.5 suburban ones from 1960 to 1968. Census of Population, Vol. 1, Part 1. General Social and Economic Characteristics, U.S. Summary, June 1972, Table 101.

31. Jeffrey L. Pressman and Aaron Wildavsky, *Implementation* (Berkeley, University of California, 1973), p. 151.

32. This view is strenuously advanced by Anthony Downs, *Opening Up the Suburbs, An Urban Strategy for America* (New Haven: Yale University Press, 1973). Downs presents Census data (pp. 20–21) purporting to show that employment dropped sharply in most of the large central cities in the 1960's. The data, however, are based on a one percent sample and are unreliable for other reasons as well. For a view similar to Downs', see John F. Kain, "The Distribution and Movement of Jobs and Industry," in James Q. Wilson, ed., *The Metropolitan Enigma* (Cambridge, Mass.: Harvard University Press, 1968).

33. Stanley H. Masters, "The Effect of Housing Segregation on Black-White Income Differentials," Research Discussion Paper 134–72, Institute for Research on Poverty, University of Wisconsin, Madison, 1972.

34. Bennett Harrison, *Education, Training, and the Urban Ghetto* (Baltimore: The Johns Hopkins University Press, 1972), pp. 107 and 116.

35. Peter A. Morrison, "The Effects of Spatial Redistribution," *Dimensions of the Population Problem in the United States* (Santa Monica, Calif.: The Rand Corporation, Monograph R-864-CPG, August 1972), Table 12, p. 30.

36. *The Manpower Report of the President* (Washington, D.C., U.S. Government Printing Office, March 1973), p. 73.

37. U.S. Bureau of the Census, *Current Population Reports*, Series P-23, No. 37 (1971).

38. Norman M. Bradburn, Seymour Sudman, and Galen L. Gookel, *Side by Side, Integrated Neighborhoods in America* (Chicago: Quadrangle Books, 1971), p. 56. The estimates are based on NORC interviews conducted in 1967 with a national probability sample of about 4,000 households.

39. According to Philip H. Finch, "The most blatant discrimination has been all but eliminated; the more subtle methods are now under attack," "Low-Income Housing in the Suburbs: The Problem of Exclusionary Zoning," *University of Florida Law Review*, 24 (Fall 1971): 86.

40. Raymond Vernon, *The Myth and Reality of Our Urban Problems* (Cambridge, Mass.: Harvard University Press, 1962), p. 33.

41. Harrison, *Education, Training, and the Urban Ghetto*, footnote p. 206.
42. See Yavitz, in Ginsburg et al., *Manpower Strategy*, pp. 58–61.
43. Ibid., p. 59.
44. George Sternlieb, "The City as Sandbox," *The Public Interest*, 25 (Fall 1971): 14–21.
45. Irving Hoch, "Rent, Transportation and Urban Scale," Paper prepared for Symposium on Urban Growth and Development, sponsored by Washington Operations Research Council and the Urban Institute (Washington, D.C., April 17, 1973).
46. Peter A. Morrison, *Dimensions of the Population Problem in the United States* (Santa Monica, Calif. (The Rand Corporation, Monograph R-864-CPG, August 1972), p. vii, and *Urban Growth, New Cities, and the "Population Problem"* (Santa Monica, Calif.: The Rand Corporation, Monograph P-4515-1, 1970), pp. 17 and 24. For other criticism of the new towns idea see William Alonzo, "What Are New Towns For?," *Urban Studies* (February 1970), and Harvey A. Garn, *New Cities, New Communities, and Growth Centers* (Washington, D.C.: Urban Institute, March 1970), Paper No. 113–30.
47. *New York Times*, October 16, 1972.
48. Glaab, *The American City*, p. 11.
49. Ibid. Other measures proposed by the committee were regulations to ensure easy egress from tenements in case of fire, prevention of prostitution and incest by requiring a sufficient number of rooms per family and by prohibiting subletting, and prevention of drunkenness "by providing for every man a clean and comfortable home" (p. 3).
50. Code enforcement and rent control, along with apprehension about civil disorder, are held responsible for decreases in land values in Harlem in the last ten years. Because of vigorous enforcement of the building code, many buildings are vacant and have been vandalized. (*New York Times*, April 28, 1968.)
51. Before the arrival of the Irish, Oscar Handlin remarks with reference to Boston, "the rigid labor supply had made industrialization impossible." (By "rigid" he presumably means one that demanded and got relatively high wages.) And the Irish, he adds, could not have been housed without cellar holes. (*Boston's Immigrants*, rev. ed., Cambridge, Mass.: Harvard University Press, 1959, pp. 82, 110.)
52. Jacob A. Riis, in Robert A. Woods et al., *The Poor in Great Cities* (New York: Scribner's, 1895), p. 88.
53. William T. Elsing, "Life in New York Tenement Houses as Seen by a City Missionary," in *The Poor in Great Cities*, p. 76.
54. Marcus T. Reynolds, *The Housing of the Poor in American Cities* (New York: American Economic Association, March and May 1893), p. 109.
55. *Reports of the Industrial Commission, Immigration*, vol. XV (Washington, D.C.: U.S. Government Printing Office, 1901), p. 491.
56. Morris Eagle, "The Puerto Ricans in New York City," in Nathan Glazer and Davis McEntire, eds., *Studies in Housing and Minority Groups* (Berkeley: University of California Press, 1960), p. 176.

CHAPTER 3

The Imperatives of Class

The quotation at the head of the chapter is from John Dollard, *Caste and Class in a Southern Town* (Garden City, N.Y.: Anchor Books, 1957), p. 433. The original edition was published in 1937.

1. Adna F. Weber, *The Growth of Cities in the Nineteenth Century* (New York: Macmillan, 1899), p. 469.
2. U.S. Bureau of the Census, *Census of Population: 1970, Employment Profiles of Selected Low-Income Areas*, Final Report PHC(3)-1, United States Summary— Urban Areas (January 1972), Table I.
3. The *Oxford English Dictionary* defines a slum as "a thickly populated neighborhood or district where the houses and conditions of life are of a squalid and wretched character." Squalor is defined as "a combination of misery and dirt." In *The Urban Villagers* (New York: The Free Press, 1962), p. 309, Herbert J. Gans says that slums are residential districts that "have been proven to be physically, socially, or emotionally *harmful* to their residents or to the larger community" (italics in the original). Robert Hunter, in *Poverty* (New York: Harper Torchbooks, 1965), p. 108, considers it a "great injustice" to use the word to refer "to working-class districts or to poverty-stricken districts relatively free from vice."
4. Lee Rainwater, "The Problem of Lower-Class Culture and Poverty-War Strategy," in Daniel P. Moynihan, ed., *On Understanding Poverty* (New York: Basic Books, 1969), p. 241.
5. For a critical review of some of the literature on "time perspective" by a psychologist, see Vernon L. Allen's essay in the volume edited by him: *Psychological Factors in Poverty* (Chicago: Markham Publishing Company, 1970). Theodore R. Sarbin writes approvingly of some of the same concepts in the same volume, pp. 32–35. See also S. M. Miller, Frank Riessman, and Arthur A. Seagull, "Poverty and Self-Indulgence: A Critique of the Non-Deferred Gratification Pattern," in Louis A. Ferman et al., eds., *Poverty in America: A Book of Readings* (Ann Arbor: University of Michigan Press, 1963).

   The concept "time preference" as used in economics was developed largely by Irving Fisher in his *The Theory of Interest* (New York: The Macmillan Company, 1930). He drew upon an 1834 work by John Rae, which was republished in 1905 under the title, *The Sociological Theory of Capital*.
6. An ideal type "is a freely created mental construct . . . by means of which an attempt is made to 'order' reality by isolating, accentuating, and articulating the elements of a recurrent social phenomenon . . . into an internally consistent system of relationships." Julius Gould and William L. Kolb, eds., *UNESCO Dictionary of the Social Sciences* (New York: The Free Press, 1964), p. 312.

   Most of the statements about time horizons in what follows have some empirical foundation: they employ a somewhat special terminology to report facts that have been observed by social scientists and others. The main proposition, namely, that individuals and cultures have differing orientations toward the future, is of this character; so are many subsidiary propositions, such as that present-oriented persons tend to be in constant search of sensual gratifications. Some propositions, however, are *implications* of the main proposition; they are themselves deductive but they have been arrived at from premises that have been inductively established. No "data" support the statement that present-oriented persons are unconcerned about the welfare of their grandchildren yet unborn; such a statement follows from the *meaning* of present-orientedness.

7. Jerome S. Bruner, in Sterling McMurrin, ed., *The Conditions of Educational Opportunity* (New York: Committee for Economic Development, 1971), pp. 35, 36, and 65. For a representative example of a sociological study based upon the "cultural transmission" theory, see A. B. Hollingshead, *Elmtown's Youth* (New York: Wiley, 1949).

8. Elliot Liebow, *Tally's Corner* (Boston: Little, Brown and Company, 1967), p. 223. For Liebow's critique of the "cultural" approach, see his footnote p. 208. For statements of positions similar to his, see Louis Kriesburg, "The Relationship Between Socio-Economic Rank and Behavior," *Social Problems*, 10 (1963): 334–353; Kriesburg's book, *Mothers in Poverty: A Study of Fatherless Families* (Chicago: Aldine Publishing Company, 1970); and the essays by Herbert J. Gans and Lee Rainwater in Daniel P. Moynihan, ed., *On Understanding Poverty* (New York, Basic Books, 1969). For a powerful critique of this approach, see the essay by Walter B. Miller in the Moynihan volume.

9. Liebow, *Tally's Corner*, p. 66.

10. This presumably is what Liebow means when he writes (in the passage quoted above) that the "social machinery" theory is ". . . of much greater importance *for the possibility of change*." (Emphasis added). The sociologist S. M. Miller has been more explicit: "It is perhaps a 'heuristic fallacy,' as [Frank] Riessman has said, to believe that lower-class people are willing and capable of positive change. This is not always true, but if professionals and social reformers lack confidence in the poor, little can be accomplished either in the social services or in political action. An optimistic outlook may not insure success, but without optimism, it is doubtful if anything can be moved. Frequently, disenchantment and cynicism capture accurately a slice of life, but they are also immobilizing, for they ignore the constructive and energizing role of hope." "The American Lower Class: A Typological Approach," *Social Research*, 31 (Spring 1964), pp. 20, 21.

11. From a methodological standpoint, the theory advanced here has some similarity to that of Melvin L. Kohn, *Class and Conformity* (Homewood, Ill.: Dorsey Press, 1969). Kohn explains the dependent variable (life style) by an intervening one (sense of efficacy) which in turn he explains by the independent one ("the cumulative effects of educational training and occupational experience"). He dismisses the concept of time horizon as a "stereotype" in a footnote (p. 104). "The essence of higher class position is the expectation that one's decisions and actions can be consequential; the essence of lower class position is the belief that one is at the mercy of forces and people beyond one's control, often, beyond one's understanding" (p. 189).

12. The relation between social class and IQ is a worldwide phenomenon with the correlation between socioeconomic status of parents and IQ of children being

most frequently in the region of 0.35 to 0.40. When school children are grouped by socioeconomic status, the mean IQ's of the groups vary over a range of one or two standard deviations (fifteen to thirty IQ points). Arthur R. Jensen, *Genetics and Education* (New York: Harper & Row, 1972), p. 153.

13. For bibliographies of descriptive accounts of the various classes see Jack L. Roach, Llewellyn Gross, and Orville Gurslin, *Social Stratification in the United States* (Englewood Cliffs, N.J.: Prentice-Hall, Inc., 1969), ch. 4. For the lower class, see in addition an elaborate review article by Zahava D. Blum and Peter H. Rossi which appears as an appendix in Daniel P. Moynihan, ed., *On Understanding Poverty*. The works that were drawn upon most heavily in constructing the summaries in the text include Herbert J. Gans, *The Urban Villagers*, ch. 11; Walter B. Miller, "Implications of Urban Lower-Class Culture for Social Work," *Social Service Review*, 33 (September 1959), pp. 219–236 and "Lower Class Culture as a Generating Milieu of Gang Delinquency," *Journal of Social Issues*, 14 (1968), pp. 5–19; A. B. Hollingshead, *Elmtown's Youth*; Allison Davis, "The Motivation of the Underprivileged Worker," in William Foote Whyte, ed., *Industry and Society* (New York: McGraw-Hill, 1946); William Foote Whyte, *Street Corner Society*, 2d ed. (Chicago: University of Chicago Press, 1955); Mirra Komarovsky, *Blue-Collar Marriage* (New York: Vintage Books, 1967); A. B. Shostak and William Gomberg, *Blue-Collar World: Studies of the American Worker* (Englewood Cliffs, N.J.: Prentice-Hall, Inc., 1965); Albert K. Cohen and Harold M. Hodges, Jr., "Characteristics of the Lower-Blue-Collar Class," *Social Problems*, 10 (Spring 1963), pp. 305–334; Lee Rainwater, *Behind Ghetto Walls* (Chicago: Aldine Publishing Company, 1970); S. M. Miller and Frank Riessman, "The Working Class Subculture: A New View," *Social Problems*, 9 (Summer 1961): 86–97, and Peter Binzen, *Whitetown USA* (New York: Vintage Books, 1970). See also Albert K. Cohen, *Delinquent Boys: The Culture of the Gang* (Glencoe, Ill.: The Free Press of Glencoe, 1955), and Herman H. Hyman, "The Value Systems of Different Classes," in Reinhard Bendix and Seymour Martin Lipset, eds., *Class, Status and Power*, 2d ed. (New York: The Free Press, 1966).

14. Melvin L. Kohn, "Social Class and Parental Values," *American Journal of Sociology*, 64 (January 1959): 340, 344, 350. See also his "Social Class and Parent-Child Relationships: An Interpretation," *American Journal of Sociology*, 68 (January 1963): 475.

15. Kenneth Keniston, *The Young Radicals* (New York: Harcourt, Brace and World, 1968), p. 265. Keniston's observation was made with respect to the upper middle class.

16. This should help to explain the often-noted similarity between the life style of some of "high society" and that of the lower class. See, for example, the remarks of J. A. Hobson on "a lower leisure class whose valuations and ways of living form a most instructive parody of the upper leisure class" in *Work and Wealth* (New York: Macmillan, 1926), pp. 155–156. For an argument that "present-centeredness" is a "moral ideal," see the essay by Claudio Naranjo in Joan Fagan and Irma Lee Sheperd, eds., *Gestalt Therapy Now* (Palo Alto, Calif.: Science & Behavior Books, 1970), especially pp. 49–50.

17. "To him [Bertrand Russell], a family did not only mean the people who lived under the same roof: that was what he meant by the Victorian phrase 'my people.' 'My family' meant something it can mean only to those who have

grown up with family portraits: a line stretching back to the 16th century, and which he hoped would stretch for many generations after he was dead. A family was a line in which the generations he knew, long as they were, were only a very small part in which his achievement was one among a long succession.

"His concern for the posterity of the human race should be seen in the context of this sense of family posterity: of generations stretching out far beyond his knowledge." Conrad Russell, "Memories of My Father," (London) *Sunday Times Magazine*, May 14, 1972.

18. For data on the voting behavior of various income and ethnic groups on local public expenditure issues, see J. Q. Wilson and E. C. Banfield, "Public-Regardingness as a Value Premise in Voting Behavior," *American Political Science Review*, 58 (December 1964): 876–887. For data on participation in organizations, see Murray Hausknecht, *The Joiners: A Sociological Description of Voluntary Association Membership* (Totowa, N.J.: Bedminster Press, 1962).

19. W. J. Cash, *The Mind of the South* (New York: Knopf, Vintage Books, 1941), p. 80.

20. Cf. Basil Bernstein's description of the British working class, "Some Sociological Determinants of Perception," *British Journal of Sociology*, vol. 9 (1958):

> The specific character of long-term goals tends to be replaced by more general notions of the future, in which chance, a friend or a relative plays a greater part than the rigorous working out of connections. Thus present, or near present, activities have greater value than the relation of the present activity to the attainment of a distant goal. The system of expectancies, or the time-span of anticipation, is shortened and this creates different sets of preferences, goals and dissatisfactions. This environment limits the perception of the developing child of and in time. Present gratifications or present deprivations become absolute gratifications or absolute deprivations for there exists no developed time continuum upon which present activity can be ranged. Relative to the middle-classes, the postponement of present pleasure for future gratifications will be found difficult. By implication a more volatile patterning of affectual and expressive behaviour will be found in the working-classes.

21. David Riesman (in collaboration with Nathan Glazer), *Faces in the Crowd*, abr. ed. (New Haven: Yale University Press, 1965), p. 254.

22. According to Lee Rainwater, in *Family Design: Marital Sexuality, Family Size, and Contraception* (Chicago: Aldine Publishing Company, 1965), p. 55, in the "upper-lower class" (the working class as defined here):

> Though husband and wife may not go their separate ways as much as in the lower-lower class, they tend to adhere to a sharper division of labor than is true in the lower-middle class, and though they may participate together in many family activities, this seems to be more the result of default (they are thrown together in the same small home) or of a desire to keep away from unwelcome involvements outside the home than to be dictated by the values of equality and togetherness that dominate the thinking of lower-middle class men and women.

306 / THE UNHEAVENLY CITY REVISITED

23. Although Goffman's "romantic division of the world" cuts across class lines, there is no doubt on which side the lower class is to be found. Erving Goffman, in "Where the Action Is" (*International Ritual*, Garden City, N.Y.: Anchor Books, 1967, p. 268), says:

> Looking for where the action is, one arrives at a romantic division of the world. On the one side are the safe and silent places, the home, the well-regulated role in business, industry, and the professions; on the other are all those activities that generate expression, requiring the individual to lay himself on the line and place himself in jeopardy during a passing moment. It is from this contrast that we fashion nearly all our commercial fantasies. It is from this contrast that delinquents, criminals, hustlers, and sportsmen draw their self-respect. . . .

24. Herman H. Hyman, "The Value Systems of Different Classes," p. 488.
25. Cohen and Hodges, "Characteristics of the Lower-Blue-Collar Class," p. 187.
26. Daniel Rosenblatt and Edward Suchman quoted by Anselm L. Strauss in *Where Medicine Fails* (Chicago: Aldine Publishing Company, 1970), p. 18.
27. Eleanor Pavenstedt, "A Comparison of the Child Rearing Environment of Upper Lower and Very Low-Lower Class Families," *American Journal of Orthopsychiatry*, 35 (1965): 89–98.
28. Marc Fried, "Social Differences in Mental Health," in John Kosa, Aaron Antonovsky, and Irving Zola, eds., *Poverty and Health, A Sociological Analysis* (Cambridge, Mass.: Harvard University Press, 1969), p. 113.
29. On this and on lower-class culture, see the articles by Walter B. Miller cited earlier.
30. Jerome K. Myers and B. H. Roberts, *Family and Class Dynamics in Mental Illness* (New York: Wiley, 1959), p. 174. See also A. B. Hollingshead and F. C. Redlich, *Social Class and Mental Illness* (New York: Wiley, 1958), p. 175, and S. Minuchin et al., *Families of the Slums* (New York: Basic Books, 1968), p. 34.
31. Gans, *The Urban Villagers*, p. 246.
32. Ralph Barton Perry in *Puritanism and Democracy* (New York: Vanguard, 1944), p. 298, remarks of the English and colonial American yeomen, artisans, and tradesmen: "They were neither so unfortunate as to be imbued with a sense of helplessness, nor so privileged as to be satisfied with their present status. They possessed just enough to whet their appetites for more and to feel confident of their power to attain it."
33. Theodore Sedgwick, *Public and Private Economy* (New York: Harper and Brothers, 1836), part 1, p. 8. See also T. C. Grattan, *Civilized America* (London: Bradbury and Evans, 1859), 2: 376.
34. Cf. Richard C. Wade, *The Urban Frontier* (Chicago: University of Chicago Press, Phoenix Books, 1964), pp. 217–220.
35. J. Leslie Dunstan, *A Light to the City* (Boston: Beacon Press, 1966), pp. 41–43.
36. Grattan, *Civilized America*, 1: 98–99. See also Lemuel Shattuck et al., "Sanitary Evils of Foreign Emigration," *Report of the Sanitary Commission of Massachusetts, 1850* (Cambridge, Mass.: Harvard University Press, 1948), pp. 202–203.

37. Timothy L. Smith, "New Approaches to the History of Immigration in Twentieth-Century America," *American Historical Review*, 71 (July 1966): 1274.
38. Quoted by Oscar Handlin in *Boston's Immigrants*, rev. ed. (Cambridge, Mass.: Harvard University Press, 1959), p. 51. (Italics in the original.)
39. In Robert A. Woods et al., *The Poor in Great Cities* (New York: Scribner's, 1895), pp. 102–103.
40. Stephan Thernstrom, *Poverty and Progress; Social Mobility in a Nineteenth Century City* (Cambridge, Mass.: Harvard University Press, 1964), pp. 103, 107.
41. David Matza, "The Disreputable Poor," in Bendix and Lipset, eds., *Class, Status, and Power*, p. 645. In a later version of this essay (Robert K. Merton and Robert Nisbet, eds., *Contemporary Social Problems*, 3d ed., New York: Harcourt Brace Jovanovich, Inc., 1971, p. 632) the words "relatively lower intelligence, more emotional problems" have been replaced with "limited opportunities for steady employment."
42. *Reports of the Industrial Commission, Immigration*, vol. XV (Washington, D.C.: U.S. Government Printing Office, 1901), p. 480. On ethnic differences relating to mobility, see Bernard C. Rosen, "Race, Ethnicity, and the Achievement Syndrome," *American Sociological Review*, 24 (1959): 47–60.

    After citing some similar figures for the year 1878, Moses Rischin goes on to say that by the early years of the twentieth century Jewish criminals, the Americanized offspring of immigrants, were regularly making headlines. *The Promised City, New York's Jews, 1870–1914* (New York: Harper Torchbook, 1970), pp. 89 and 90.
43. William Alonso, "The Historic and the Structural Theories of Urban Form: Their Implications for Urban Renewal," *Land Economics*, 40 (May 1964): 227.
44. James Q. Wilson, in "A Guide to Reagan Country," *Commentary* (May 1967), pp. 40–41, has described vividly the care that his generation of Los Angeles boys lavished on their cars. "After marriage," he continues, "devoting energy to the improvement of a house was simply a grown-up extension of what, as a juvenile, one had done with cars."
45. In 1972 a national poll found that among suburbanites in its sample 14 percent said that they would be "happy," 25 percent that they would be "unhappy," 57 percent that it would "not make much difference," and 4 percent that they "don't know" whether to have similar-status blacks move into their communities. The corresponding figures for addition of lower-status whites were: 10, 46, 42, and 2, and for the addition of lower-status blacks (these replies included some black suburbanites): 8, 46, 43, and 3. William Watts and Lloyd A. Free, eds., *State of the Nation* (New York: Universe Books, 1973), p. 102. In general polls have shown that the higher a person's socioeconomic status, the more likely he is to favor integration of housing, transportation, and schools, as well as other forms of integration. See Paul B. Sheatsley, "White Attitudes Toward the Negro," in Talcott Parsons and Kenneth B. Clark, eds., *The Negro American* (Boston: Houghton Mifflin, 1966), p. 315.

    A study of social class and voting behavior in Little Rock found: "The higher the social class, the stronger was support for desegregation. Con-

versely, the lower the social class, the greater was support for segregation."
Harlan Hahn, L. Michael Ross, and Thomas F. Pettigrew, unpublished paper,
1966.
46. Cf. Bennett M. Berger, *Working-Class Suburb: A Study of Auto Workers in
Suburbia* (Berkeley: University of California Press, 1960), ch. 5.
47. Marshall B. Clinard, *Slums and Community Development: Experiment in
Self-Help* (New York: The Free Press, 1966).
48. Cf. John R. Seeley, "The Slum: Its Nature, Use and Users," *Journal of the
American Institute of Planners*, 25 (February 1959): 10–13.
49. Patricia Cayo Sexton, *Spanish Harlem; Anatomy of Poverty* (New York:
Harper & Row, 1965), p. 116.
50. The problem of estimating the size of the classes from these and other data is
discussed in the Appendix.
51. Blake McKelvey, *The Urbanization of America* (New Brunswick, N.J.: Rutgers University Press, 1963), p. 94; Jane Addams, "An Effort Toward Social
Democracy," *The Forum*, 15 (October 1892): 228.
52. Mrs. Helen Campbell, *Darkness and Daylight; or, Lights and Shadows of
New York Life* (Hartford, Conn.: Hartford Publishing Co., 1896), p. 170. On
brutality in general, see Richard O'Connor, *Hell's Kitchen* (Philadelphia:
Lippincott, 1958).
53. Patricia Cayo Sexton, *Education and Income* (New York: Viking, 1961), p.
200.
54. Consider, for example, the probable meaning to all concerned of the
announcement (*New York Times*, July 13, 1966) by New York City's chief
health officer, Dr. Howard J. Brown, that thousands of wooden benches
would be burnt in "a public declaration of conscience" as symbols of dehumanized medical services in the city's clinics. That the service provided by the
city to its poor was remarkably good by any standard except that of the more
affluent middle class ("No hospital in the world has better professional
talent," Dr. Brown admitted) was a fact obscured by the announcement ("dis-
graceful . . . patients . . . have to barter their dignity for their health"). That
people sat on benches rather than in chairs and waited without appointments
until a doctor could see them was not, until the rise of new class standards
made it so, an affront; it is therefore factually incorrect to use the benches as
symbols of mistreatment *in the past*. The effect of the announcement, however, must have been to make upper-middle- and upper-class people ashamed
of a city which has long treated its poor so shabbily and also to tell the poor
that if by any chance they thought they were fortunate in being cared for by
professionals as good as any in the world they were being outrageously put
upon and that they should be aggrieved and angry at not always having been
given the deference and amenities that the middle class now gives to itself.

CHAPTER 4

Race: Thinking May Make It So

The quotation at the head of the chapter is from *The Autobiography of Malcolm X* (New York: Grove, 1966), p. 344.

1. Kenneth B. Clark, *Dark Ghetto: Dilemmas of Social Power* (New York: Harper & Row, 1965), p. 11.
2. Thomas Sowell, *Race and Economics* (New York, David McKay, forthcoming 1974), ch. 7.
3. On similarities and differences between the present prospect of the Negro and that of immigrants see Sowell, *Race and Economics,* op. cit.; also Irving Kristol, "The Negro Today Is Like the Immigrant Yesterday," *New York Times Magazine,* September 11, 1966; Nathan Glazer, "Blacks and Ethnic Groups: The Difference and the Political Difference It Makes," *Social Problems,* 18 (Spring 1971); Oscar Handlin, *The Newcomers* (Cambridge, Mass.: Harvard University Press, 1959).
4. On the success of the Japanese, see Sowell, *Race and Economics,* op. cit. See also William Peterson, "Success Story, Japanese-American Style," in Nathan Glazer, ed., *Cities in Trouble* (Chicago: Quadrangle Books, 1970).
5. On the basis of extensive data, Hershberg concludes that the pauperization of Philadelphia's black population was the consequence not of the slave experience (91 percent of the city's antebellum black population was freeborn) but rather of racism and inequality experienced in the city. Theodore Hershberg, "Free Blacks in Antebellum Philadelphia: A Study of Ex-Slaves, Freeborn and Socioeconomic Decline," *Journal of Social History,* 5 (Winter 1971–72): 183–209. For support of his contention that the slave-born Negro had internalized the ethic of deferred gratification, see Robert William Fogel and Stanley L. Engerman, *Time on the Cross: The Economics of American Negro Slavery* (Boston: Little, Brown and Company, 1973).

   On the position of freedmen in the North, see also Leon F. Litwack, *North of Slavery* (Chicago: University of Chicago Press, 1961); on the rise of racial prejudice and discrimination, C. Vann Woodward, *The Strange Career of Jim Crow* (New York: Oxford University Press, 1955); on the aspirations and handicaps of urban Negroes, Timothy L. Smith, "Native Blacks and Foreign Whites: Varying Responses to Educational Opportunity in America, 1880–1950," in *Perspectives in American History,* 6 (1972): 309–335.
6. I am indebted to Professor Andrew Hacker for suggesting the word "comparable."
7. The methodological problem has been vastly over-simplified here. For a technical discussion of the problem of multicollinearity, see H. Blalock, "Correlated Independent Variables: The Problem of Multicollinearity," *Social Forces,* 42 (1963), pp. 233–237.

   For a sophisticated treatment of the concrete problem, see the essay by Otis Dudley Duncan in Daniel P. Moynihan, ed., *On Understanding Poverty* (New York: Basic Books, 1969), ch. 4. See also the finding of Blau and Duncan that when "the three major background variables — social origins, education, and career beginnings" are controlled the residual difference between white and nonwhite men living in the region of their birth — ". . . undoubtedly . . . in large part due to discrimination" — is only 4.3 points in the North and 10.7 in the South. Peter M. Blau and Otis Dudley Duncan, *The American Occupational Structure* (New York: Wiley, 1967), p. 221. See also James Gwartney, "Discrimination and Income Differentials," *American Economic Review,* 60 (June 1970): 396–408; Orley Ashenfelter and Michael Taussig, "Discrimination and Income Differentials: Comment," *American*

Economic Review, 61 (September 1971): 746–750, and James Gwartney, "Reply," same issue.

8. Pascal K. Whelpton, Arthur A. Campbell, and John E. Patterson, *Fertility and Family Planning in the United States* (Princeton, N.J.: Princeton University Press, 1966), pp. 342–348.

9. James S. Coleman et al., *Equality of Educational Opportunity*, Office of Education, U.S. Department of Health, Education, and Welfare (Washington, D.C.: U.S. Government Printing Office, 1966), pp. 454–456.

10. Robert I. Lerman, "Some Determinants of Youth School Activity," *Journal of Human Resources*, 7 (Summer 1972): 377.

11. Harry J. Gilman, "Economic Discrimination and Unemployment," *American Economic Review*, 55 (December 1965): 1077–1095. The data Gilman analyzed were for 1950 and 1957–1961.

12. Richard Muth, *Cities and Housing, The Spatial Pattern of Urban Residential Land Use* (Chicago: University of Chicago Press, 1969), p. 280. Kain and Quigley found that in St. Louis Negroes were substantially less likely to be homeowners than whites of similar characteristics. Acknowledging that the difference may be due to a greater taste for ownership on the part of whites or to whites' greater wealth, they believe housing market discrimination to be the most plausible explanation. Extending their analysis to eighteen metropolitan areas, they find that in 1960 family size and income accounted for only about one-third of the difference between black and white ownership rates, the remainder being attributable to "other factors," especially (presumably) discrimination. To whatever extent it exists, they remark, discrimination prevents Negroes from getting the tax advantages that go to homeowners and it also robs them of a hedge against inflation available to others. A family prevented in 1950 from buying a home would by 1970, they estimate, have had out-of-pocket housing costs more than double those it would have had otherwise. John F. Kain and John M. Quigley, "Housing Market Discrimination, Homeownership, and Savings Behavior," *American Economic Review*, 62 (June 1972): 263–277.

13. Katherine Anthony, "Mothers Who Must Earn," in *West Side Studies*, Russell Sage Foundation (New York: Survey Associates, 1914), p. 20.

14. Otho G. Cartwright, "Boyhood and Lawlessness," in *West Side Studies*, pp. 156, 55.

15. An elaborate study of all boys born in 1945 who lived in Philadelphia at least from their tenth to their eighteenth birthdays found that, when low socioeconomic status was held constant, Negro boys were three times more likely than whites to be chronic offenders. Marvin E. Wolfgang, Robert M. Figlio, and Thorsten Sellin, *Delinquency in a Birth Cohort* (Chicago: University of Chicago Press, 1972), p. 91. A study of arrest rates in Detroit, however, lends "no credence to the explanation of the Negro-white crime rate differential in terms of some distinctive aspect of Negro culture or in terms of racial conflict. . . ." Edward Green, "Race, Social Status, and Criminal Arrest," *American Sociological Review*, 35 (June 1970): 476–750. The Detroit study found no indication of discrimination by the police in making arrests; neither did one made in Philadelphia by Frank Cannavale and Robert Silverman under the direction of Marvin E. Wolfgang. (This unpublished work was kindly made available to the author by Professor Wolfgang.)

Studies of *unreported* crime suggest that the association of crime with both race and income may be less than appears from official statistics. Martin Gold, *Delinquent Behavior in an American City* (Belmont, Calif.: Brooks/Cole Publishing Company, 1970).

16. Studies comparing Negro and white children from the lowest socioeconomic stratum have stressed the relative lack of persistence of the Negroes when confronted with a task: a "what does it matter" attitude presumably revealing low need of achievement. See, for example, the authorities cited by Urie Bronfenbrenner in Vernon L. Allen, ed., *Psychological Factors in Poverty* (Chicago: Markham Publishing Company, 1970), p. 212.

Numerous useful cautions are offered by Hylan Lewis in "Culture, Class, and Family Life Among Low-Income Urban Negroes," in Arthur M. Ross and Herbert Hill, eds., *Employment, Race, and Poverty* (New York: Harcourt, Brace & World, Inc., 1967), ch. 6.

17. See Thomas F. Pettigrew, "Negro American Personality: Why Isn't More Known?," *The Journal of Social Issues*, 20 (April 1964): 4–23.

Rohrer and Edmonson "find reason to doubt that such a thing as '*a* Negro personality' exists at all. Despite the unquestioned fact that differences of a statistical order between whites as a group and Negroes as a group are well established in a variety of connections, there is no basis for assuming that durable patterns of behavior are related to racial status *as such* even when the emotional implications of the caste system and related stereotyped attitudes or prejudices are included in the social definition of race." John H. Rohrer and Munro S. Edmonson, eds., *The Eighth Generation Grows Up* (New York: Harper Torchbooks, 1964), p. 77. (Italics in the original.)

On the other hand, Lesser and associates have found that while class subculture markedly influences the *absolute* level of certain mental abilities in children, ethnic subculture determines the *relative* level of development of these abilities. G. S. Lesser, G. Fifer, and D. H. Clark, *Mental Abilities of Children from Different Social-Class and Cultural Groups*, Society for Research in Child Development, Serial No. 102, vol. 30, no. 4 (Chicago: University of Chicago Press, 1965).

18. Michael J. Flax, *Blacks and Whites, An Experiment in Social Indicators* (Washington, D.C.: The Urban Institute, 1971).

19. Barry R. Chiswick, "Racial Discrimination in the Labor Market: A Test of Alternative Hypotheses," *Journal of Political Economy*, 81 (November 1973).

20. Albert Wohlstetter and Sinclair Coleman, "Race Differences in Income," in Anthony H. Pascal, ed., *Racial Discrimination in Economic Life* (Lexington, Mass.: D. C. Heath and Company, 1972), pp. 68–69.

21. A. B. Hollingshead, *Elmstown's Youth* (New York: Wiley, 1949), pp. 114, 113, 119, 147, 282, 111.

22. Ibid., pp. 110–111.

23. Ibid., pp. 147, 113, 119–120, 116, 117, 331.

24. Thomas R. Brooks, "New York's Finest," *Commentary* 47 (August 1965): 31.

25. Angus Campbell and Howard Schuman, *Racial Attitudes in Fifteen American Cities* (Ann Arbor: Survey Research Center, University of Michigan, 1968).

26. Norman Bradburn, Seymour Sudman, and Galen L. Gookel, *Side by Side, Integrated Neighborhoods in America* (Chicago: Quadrangle Books, 1971), p. 134.
27. Cf. Karl E. Taeuber, "Residential Segregation," *Scientific American*, 213 (August 1965): 14.
28. Malcolm Muggeridge points out that calling a place like Harlem a "ghetto" is a perfect example of the kind of falsification of words to make them serve political ends that Orwell deplored in his essay "Politics vs. Literature." According to Muggeridge, "By equating Negro slums with a ghetto, on the one hand white racialism — in itself bad enough in all conscience — is associated with the additional horrors of Nazi anti-Semitism. On the other the white bourgeois champion of the Negro can see his wrongs in terms of pogroms and other distant and remote wickednesses, rather than of nearby and present social and economic inequalities." Letter to the editor of the *New York Times Magazine*, May 5, 1968.
29. Cited in Anthony H. Pascal, "The Analysis of Residential Segregation," in John P. Crecine, ed., *Financing the Metropolis*, Urban Affairs Annual Reviews, vol. 4 (Beverly Hills, Calif.: Sage Publications, 1970), p. 411.
30. Nathan Kantrowitz, "Ethnic and Racial Segregation in the New York Metropolis, 1960," *American Journal of Sociology*, 74 (May 1969): 693.
31. Thomas C. Schelling, "On the Ecology of Micromotives," *The Public Interest*, 25 (Fall 1971): 88.
32. Lewis G. Watts et al., *The Middle-Income Negro Family Faces Urban Renewal*, Research Center of the Florence Heller Graduate School for Advanced Studies in Social Welfare (Waltham, Mass.: Brandeis University, 1964). Similar findings for New York are reported in Oscar Handlin, *The Newcomers*, p. 92 and Appendix.
33. Ibid., p. 69.
34. Herbert J. Gans, *The Urban Villagers* (New York: The Free Press, 1962), p. 20.
35. N. M. Bradburn, S. Sudman, and G. L. Gookel, *Racial Integration in American Neighborhoods* (Chicago: National Opinion Research Center, 1970).
36. Ralph Ellison, in "Federal Role in Urban Affairs," Hearings Before the Subcommittee on Executive Reorganization, Committee on Government Operations, August 30, 1966, U.S. Senate, 89th Congress, 2d Session, Part 5, p. 1155.
37. Gerald D. Suttles, *The Social Order of the Slum* (Chicago: University of Chicago Press, 1968), p. 129.
38. Clark, *Dark Ghetto*, p. 25.
39. Wilfred G. Marston, "Socioeconomic Differentiation within Negro Areas of American Cities," *Social Forces*, 48 (December 1969): 165–176.
40. *New York Times*, September 16, 1965. The point had been made the year before by two reporters who wrote a book about the New York riots. One reason why crime in the ghetto had not been cleaned up, Shapiro and Sullivan wrote, "is that integration in the city has progressed to the point where it is easier for a Negro leader to switch neighborhoods than fight. Most Bedford-Stuyvesant leaders live in integrated Crown Heights. Most Harlem leaders pack up at the end of the day and head for Queens or Westchester." Fred C. Shapiro and James W. Sullivan, *Race Riot: New York 1964* (New York: Crowell, 1964), p. 196.

41. Urie Bronfenbrenner, "The Psychological Costs of Quality and Equality in Education," *Child Development*, 38 (1967): 910.
42. Ben J. Wattenberg and Richard M. Scammon, "Black Progress and Liberal Rhetoric," *Commentary*, 55 (April 1973): p. 43.
43. Erik H. Erikson has called attention to the danger that a majority "may, in its sudden zeal to regain its moral position and to face the facts squarely, inadvertently tend to *confirm* the minority's negative image of itself and this in the very act of dwelling exclusively and even self-indulgently on the majority's sins." Talcott Parsons and Kenneth B. Clark, eds., *The Negro American* (Boston: Houghton Mifflin, 1966), p. 238. (Italics in the original.)
44. Morris Eagle, "The Puerto Ricans in New York City," in Nathan Glazer and Davis McEntire, eds., *Studies in Housing and Minority Groups* (Berkeley: University of California Press, 1960), pp. 166, 164.

CHAPTER 5

The Problem of Unemployment

"Youth in the Ghetto," the source of the first quotation at the head of the chapter, was published (in multilith) by HARYOU (Harlem Youth Opportunities Unlimited, Inc.) in 1964. The second quotation is from James R. Dumpson and appears in the transcript of a symposium, "The Future by Design," held by the New York City Planning Commission in October 1964 (p. 130).

1. Constance McLaughlin Green, *The Rise of Urban America* (New York: Harper & Row, 1965), p. 179.
2. Nathan Glazer and Daniel Patrick Moynihan, *Beyond the Melting Pot* (Cambridge, Mass.: M.I.T. Press and Harvard University Press, 1963), p. 39.
3. Paul Goodman, *Growing Up Absurd* (New York: Vintage Books, 1962), p. 32.
4. Donald Bogue and D. P. Dandekar, *Population Trends and Prospects for the Chicago-Northwestern Indiana Consolidated Metropolitan Area, 1960 to 1990* (Chicago: Population Research and Training Center, March 1962), p. 34.
5. Thomas F. Pettigrew, *A Profile of the Negro American* (Princeton, N.J.: Van Nostrand, 1964), p. 172.
6. John Kosa, in Kosa, Aaron Antonovsky, and Irving Kenneth Zola, eds., *Poverty and Health, A Sociological Analysis* (Cambridge, Mass.: Harvard University Press, 1969), p. 28.
7. A. R. Weber, "Labor Market Perspectives of the New City," in Benjamin Chinitz, ed., *City and Suburb* (Englewood Cliffs, N.J.: Prentice-Hall, Inc., Spectrum Book, 1964), pp. 68–69.
8. Daniel Bell, "The Bogey of Automation," *New York Review of Books*, August 26, 1965, p. 24.
9. Robert M. Solow, "Technology and Unemployment," *The Public Interest*, 1 (Fall 1965): 18–19. (Italics in the original.)
10. *Monthly Labor Review*, 91 (December 1968): 36.
11. James Tobin, "On Improving the Economic Status of the Negro," in Talcott

Parsons and Kenneth B. Clark, eds., *The Negro American* (Boston: Houghton Mifflin, 1966), p. 462.

12. Finis Welch, "Relationships between Income and Schooling," unpublished paper dated March 1973, p. 24. (He cites, inter alia, his "Education in Production," *Journal of Political Economy*, 78, 1970: 35–59.) See also Stanley L. Friedlander, *Unemployment in the Urban Core: An Analysis of Thirty Cities with Policy Recommendations* (New York: Praeger, 1972), pp. 66, 102, and 104.

13. Dale L. Hiestand, *Economic Growth and Employment Opportunities for Minorities* (New York: Columbia University Press, 1964), pp. 116, 56–57.

14. Cf. Report of the National Commission on Technology, Automation, and Economic Progress, *Technology and the American Economy* (Washington, D.C.: U.S. Government Printing Office, February 1966), 1: 21–23.

15. *The Manpower Report of the President — March 1973* (Washington, D.C., U.S. Government Printing Office), p. 17.

16. *Technology and the American Economy*, p. 16.

17. Ibid., p. 23.

18. These changes are discussed by Martin S. Feldstein in "The Economics of the New Unemployment," *The Public Interest*, 33 (Fall 1973), pp. 3–42. See also his *Lowering the Permanent Rate of Unemployment*, A Joint Committee Print of the Joint Economic Committee (Washington, Government Printing Office, 1973). The latter contains comments by Professors R. A. Gordon, Bennett Harrison, Charles C. Holt, Hyman B. Kaitz, and Frank C. Pierson.

19. This was proposed by Professor William Fellner in a paper written before his nomination to the Council of Economic Advisers. See his essay in the volume by Phillip Cagan and others, *A New Look at Inflation* (Washington, D.C., American Enterprise Institute for Public Policy Research, 1973), pp. 166–167.

20. Quoted in Parsons and Clark, eds., *The Negro American*, pp. 458–459.

21. Milton Friedman, "The Role of Monetary Policy," *American Economic Review*, 58 (March 1968): 7–11; reprinted in Friedman, *The Optimum Quantity of Money and Other Essays* (Chicago: Aldine Publishing Company, 1969).

22. Martin S. Feldstein, *Lowering the Permanent Rate of Unemployment*. See also the article by William Fellner (footnote 19), pp. 156–158.

23. The Fair Labor Standards Act of June 25, 1938, also known as the Wages and Hour Act, 52 Stat. 1060 as amended; the Walsh-Healey Public Contracts Act of June 30, 1936, 49 Stat. 2036, as amended, 41 U.S.C. 35–45. The Walsh-Healey Act regulates hours and wages on federal contracts exceeding $10,000. It has not been effective as a minimum-wage law. See Herbert C. Morton, *Public Contracts and Private Wages* (Washington, D.C.: The Brookings Institution, 1965), pp. 125–126.

24. Workers covered by the $1.60 federal minimum must receive time-and-one-half pay after forty hours a week. Certain classes of workers who became subject to the act under 1966 amendments (e.g., those employed by large hotels, motels, or restaurants, or laundries, hospitals, and schools) received $1.15 in 1968, which was raised by 15 cents a year until they reached $1.60 in 1971. Some farm workers on larger farms must be paid $1.15.

25. Quoted by Robert H. Bremner, *From the Depths: The Discovery of Poverty*

in the United States (New York: New York University Press, 1956), p. 239.

26. The earnings of those in the largest categories of low-paying jobs (janitors, attendants in auto service and parking, sales personnel in food and dairy product stores, laborers in wholesale and retail trade) usually exceed the minimum wage of $2,600 for fifty-two weeks of full-time work. Laurie D. Cummings, "The Employed Poor: Their Characteristics and Occupations," *Monthly Labor Review*, 88 (July 1965): 828–835.

27. George J. Stigler, "The Unjoined Debate," *Chicago Today* (Winter 1966): 5.

The effect of the minimum wage on the drugstore soda fountain is illustrative. According to *The Wall Street Journal* (February 6, 1968, p. 1) only 30 percent of the 52,000 drugstores in the United States have fountains now, and the number declines yearly. Some druggists cited the minimum wage as the reason for scrapping the fountain: they could not afford to pay soda jerks the minimum. Others said it was cheaper to install self-service ice cream and soft drink machines. Presumably, the minimum wage is one reason why machines are cheaper. Soda-jerking is (or at any rate was) typically a job for the teenager.

For the economic theory involved, see George J. Stigler, "The Economics of Minimum Wage Legislation," *American Economic Review*, 36 (June 1946): 358–365. See also Yale Brozen, "The Effect of Statutory Minimum Wage Increases on Teen-Age Unemployment," *The Journal of Law and Economics*, 12 (April 1969): 109–122. For a less technical treatment, see The Free Society Association, Inc., *The Minimum Wage Rate; Who Really Pays? — An Interview with Yale Brozen and Milton Friedman* (Washington, D.C., April 1966).

For discussions of the minimum wage along with other matters discussed in this section, see Philip H. Wicksteed, *The Common Sense of Political Economy* (London: Routledge and Kegan Paul, 1933) — on minimum wages and unions, 2: 693–695, on overpaying public employees, 1: 343. See also Armen A. Alchian and William R. Allen, *University Economics* (Belmont, Calif.: Wadsworth Publishing Company, 1964), ch. 28.

28. Quoted in *Nation's Business*, September 1971, p. 89. Black youths are not the only ones affected, of course. Although their unemployment rate is much higher than that of white youths, in 1972 seventy-eight percent of all unemployed teenagers were white.

29. Andrew F. Brimmer, "Employment and Income in the Black Community, Trends and Outlook," Lecture Presented at the University of California, Los Angeles, March 2, 1973. In 1973 the Administration proposed an increase in the minimum wage with a differential for young workers. However, the bill passed by Congress, which raised the minimum by 38 percent, did not contain this provision and was vetoed on the grounds that "it would deny opportunities to unskilled and younger workers . . ." and "would give an enormous boost to inflation." *New York Times*, September 6, 1973.

The works cited by Brimmer in his review of the literature are: Bureau of Labor Statistics, *Bulletin* 1657 (1970); pp. 897–902. Thomas Gale Moore, "The Effects of Minimum Wages on Teenage Unemployment Rates," *Journal of Political Economy*, 79 (July/August 1971); Masanore Hashimoto and Jacob Mincer, *The NBER Survey of Research into Poverty*, National Bureau of Economic Research, forthcoming; and Marvin Kosters and Finis Welch,

"The Effects of Minimum Wages by Race, Sex, and Age," in Anthony Pascal, ed., *Racial Discrimination in Economic Life* (Lexington, Mass.: D. C. Heath and Company, 1972).

See also Douglas K. Adie, "Teen-Age Unemployment and Real Federal Minimum Wages," *Journal of Political Economy*, 81 (March/April 1973), pp. 435–441. For a contrary view see Michael C. Lovell, "The Minimum Wage, Teenage Unemployment, and the Business Cycle," *Western Economic Journal*, 10 (December 1972): pp. 414–427.

30. Martin S. Feldstein, *Lowering the Permanent Rate of Unemployment.*
31. Peter B. Doeringer and Michael J. Piore, *Internal Labor Markets and Manpower Analysis* (Lexington, Mass.: Heath Lexington Books, 1971), p. 139.
32. Walter Gellhorn, quoted by Milton Friedman, *Capitalism and Freedom* (Chicago: University of Chicago Press, 1962), p. 142.
33. Proposed by the New York City License Commissioner (*New York Times*, October 9, 1967). Under this proposal, the city, with a federal subsidy, would also train apprentices. Thus, entry into the occupations would be even further limited.
34. *Boston Globe*, March 21, 1965. A study is reported to have shown that although Negro woman toll collectors scored significantly lower on mental ability tests than did their white counterparts, they received identical ratings from their supervisors for their performance on the job. The interpretation placed on this finding was that the tests were discriminatory. Another possibility, however, is that mental ability has little to do with successful toll collecting (*New York Times*, January 21, 1968).
35. *New York Times*, June 21, 1965.
36. *New York Times*, August 11, 1968.
37. HARYOU, "Youth in the Ghetto," pp. 16–17.
38. Goodman, *Growing Up Absurd*, p. 204.
39. Cf. Bennett Harrison, *Education, Training and the Urban Ghetto* (Baltimore, Johns Hopkins Press, 1972), p. 92.
40. The 1971 Census report on the low-income areas of 51 of the largest cities found that the median lowest acceptable pay figure given by black males aged 16–21 and not in school was $83 per week; for whites the comparable figure was $84. For males with seven or less years of schooling, the median of the figures given by blacks was higher than that given by whites— $102 as against $92. For male family heads, the median for the races was the same — $108. *Employment Profiles of Selected Low-Income Areas*, op. cit. Tables 30 a and b.
41. Gloria Shaw Hamilton and J. David Roessner, "How Employers Screen Disadvantaged Job Applicants," *Monthly Labor Review*, 95 (September 1972): 14– 21.
42. *Griggs v. Duke Power Co.*, 91 U.S. 849 (1971).
43. Christopher Jencks et al., *Inequality, A Reassessment of the Effect of Family and Schooling in America* (New York: Basic Books, 1972), p. 159.
44. Ibid., p. 193.
45. Thomas Sowell, *Race and Economics* (New York: David McKay, forthcoming 1974), ch. 8.
46. *New York Times*, January 5, 1973.
47. For details on the shift to service activities in 11 large cities and aggregate

data on 30 large cities, see Alexander Ganz and Thomas O'Brien, "The City: Sandbox, Reservation, or Dynamo?," *Public Policy*, 21 (Winter 1973), pp. 108–123. See also Victor R. Fuchs, *The Growing Importance of the Service Industries*, National Bureau of Economic Research Occasional Paper 96 (New York: National Bureau of Economic Research, 1965), pp. 13–14.

48. A West Coast personnel officer explained to an interviewer who was asking about job opportunities for "ghetto" youth:

> Let's set aside the whole minority problem for a moment and take the white youngster. I maintain that I can take any young man out of the suburban area of America with his nice washed look and his good speech and his white shirt which he wears comfortably and his polished shoes which look as though they belong on his feet and his well-cut hair and send him out as a tenth-grade dropout and get him a job without a bit of trouble. It is a social image — because of the way he speaks, the way he carries himself. It has nothing to do with whether he can read or do arithmetic or anything else. It has to do with the social problem we are dealing with in the slums. . . . It is his manners, his speech, his way of carrying himself, his own self-confidence, the "neat clean-cut look". . . . Can we put the suburban image on our kids in the slums? I think part of the suburban image is how he fills out a form and how he is able to read instructions, and how he answers the telephone, and what he says when he is asked a question and how he responds.

From Hugh Curtis Clark, "The Neighborhood Youth Corps," unpublished senior honors thesis, Harvard University, 1968, p. 52.

49. Hamilton and Roessner, "How Employers Screen Disadvantaged Job Applicants," p. 18.

50. The negative income tax seems first to have been proposed in this connection by George J. Stigler. "[T]here is a great attractiveness," he wrote, "in the proposal that we extend the personal income tax to the lowest income brackets with negative rates in these brackets. Such a scheme could achieve equality of treatment with what appears to be a (large) minimum of administrative machinery. If the negative rates are appropriately graduated, we may still retain some measure of incentive for a family to increase its income." "The Economics of Minimum Wage Legislation," op. cit., p. 365.

51. For a brief description of the several federal manpower programs (". . . neither a disaster nor a roaring success . . ."), see Edward R. Fried et al., *Setting National Priorities: The 1974 Budget* (Washington, D.C.: The Brookings Institution, 1973), pp. 218–232. See also *The Manpower Report of the President — March 1973*, ch. 2.

52. Wilbur R. Thompson, *A Preface to Urban Economics* (Baltimore: The Johns Hopkins University Press, 1965), p. 113.

Raymond Vernon, in his study of the New York region, remarks that the informal minimum wage in New York is likely to force the low-wage segments of industry continually to move outward, looking for an environment in which they can survive. *Metropolis 1985* (Cambridge, Mass.: Harvard University Press, 1960), p. 51.

53. John F. Kain and Joseph J. Persky, "Alternatives to the Gilded Ghetto," *The Public Interest*, 14 (Winter 1969): 82.

54. During the hard times of 1857, when starvation was a real possibility for the unemployed, the charitable societies of New York published circulars inviting those who would accept work in the country to register. None did. K. H. Claghorn, *Report to the Industrial Commission on Immigration*, 15 (1901): 463.

55. U.S. Bureau of the Census, *Census of Population: 1970, Employment Profiles of Selected Low-Income Areas*, Final Report PHC(3)-1, United States Summary — Urban Areas (January 1972), p. 12. See also Dorothy K. Newman, "The Decentralization of Jobs," *Monthly Labor Review*, 90 (May 1967): 7–13.

56. The theory is developed in Michael J. Piore, "On-the-Job Training in a Dual Labor Market," in Arnold R. Weber, et al., eds., *Public-Private Manpower Policies* (Madison, Wis., Industrial Relations Research Association, 1969) and "Manpower Policy," in Samuel Beer et al., eds., *The State and the Poor* (Boston: Winthrop Publishing Co., 1970), pp. 53 – 83. See also Doeringer and Piore, *Internal Labor Markets*, ch. 8 and pp. 204 – 208.

57. Ibid., p. 52. See also Bennett Harrison, *Education, Training, and the Urban Ghetto* (Baltimore: The Johns Hopkins University Press, 1972), pp. 130–152.

58. Harrison, op. cit., p. 123.

59. Op. cit., p. 181.

60. Op. cit., p. 208.

61. Ibid., p. 193. See also Harrison's *Public Service Jobs for Urban Residents* (Washington, D.C.: National Civil Service League, 1969).

62. Ibid., p. 132.

63. Op. cit., p. 202. Despite this observation, the authors offer a five-fold classification of the low-income population according to its adaptability to primary employment in which the first group consists primarily of adults ("with stable, but low-wage experience"). Op. cit., p. 179.

Toward the end of his book Bennett Harrison assures the reader that the idea that some persons cannot "make it" because of personal incapacities is "one of our most unfortunate national myths." Earlier, however, he has said that it is "incontestable" that secondary labor is "significantly more unstable." Op. cit., pp. 210 and 132.

64. In the article cited above, Gloria Shaw Hamilton reports that public employers were much more likely to require a high school diploma and a passing score on a test and more likely to reject an employee because of health problems, being overweight, or having an arrest or prison record. p. 20.

65. Cf. Fried et al., *Setting National Priorities: The 1974 Budget*, p. 92.

66. For an argument in favor of it on a *more* than limited scale, see Lester Thurow, "Toward a Definition of Economic Justice," *The Public Interest*, 31 (Spring 1973), especially pp. 79–80. There is an exchange between Richard A. Posner and Thurow in the Fall 1973 issue of the same magazine which touches on the issue.

67. *Work in America*, pp. 174 and 184.

68. Fellner, in Philip Cagan et al., *A New Look at Inflation*, p. 166.

69. U.S. Congress, *Employment and Manpower Problems in the Cities: Implications of the Report of the National Advisory Commission on Civil Disorders*. Hearings before the Joint Economic Committee, 90th Congress, 2nd Session, May–June 1968, p. 66.

CHAPTER 6

Several Kinds of Poverty

1. The dependency ratios (i.e., number of children under twenty-two for every 100 persons in the "prime working ages," twenty-two to sixty-four) for poor persons living in the central cities of Standard Metropolitan Statistical Areas (SMSA's) of 250,000 or more population and for poor persons living in the entire country were 168 and 148, respectively, in 1966. By contrast, the dependency ratio of the nonpoor in the central cities was lower than that of the nonpoor in the entire country — 71 as against 79. Harold L. Sheppard, *Effects of Family Planning on Poverty in the United States* (Kalamazoo, Mich.: The W. E. Upjohn Institute for Employment Research. October 1967), pp. 3–4.
2. Richard F. Wertheimer, II, *The Monetary Rewards of Migration Within the U.S.* (Washington, D.C.: The Urban Institute, 1970), p. 26.
3. U.S. Bureau of the Census, *Current Population Reports*, P-60, No. 86, "Characteristics of the Low-Income Population, 1971" (Washington, D.C.: U.S. Government Printing Office, 1972).
4. Friedlander, in an effort to estimate illegal income in Harlem, found that one-fifth of the adult population received income in 1965 that was not from work, welfare, gifts, and so forth. His "crude" estimate is that 20 percent of those unemployed or not in the labor force and 18 percent of other workers reported some income which they could not account for and which was presumably illegal. That they reported *any* was because they could not hide their consumption of goods from the Census enumerator and gave him a figure they thought consistent with what was visible. In this way a large number of people without any acknowledged source of income reported incomes in the $4,000 and above range; a substantial number of these, Friedlander supposes, may actually have been earning $10,000 or more. If we assume a lower limit of $5,000 for the true income of those who could not account for their income and put 20 percent of the population in this group, the illegal income of Harlem would be $150 million or 37.5 percent of the total. If we assume a lower limit of $10,000, it would be $300 million or 75 percent. A "very low" estimate — 10 percent of the population (15,000 people) at $6,000 — would be $90 million or 22.5 percent. Stanley L. Friedlander, *Unemployment in the Urban Core: An Analysis of Thirty Cities with Policy Recommendations* (New York: Praeger, 1972), pp. 186–189.
5. Margaret Reid, testimony in *House Hearings on the Economic Opportunity Act of 1964*, 88th Congress, 2d Session, Part 3, p. 1429. A two-year income average, however, yields nearly as many low-income families as does a one-year average. *Economic Report of the President* (Washington, D.C.: U.S. Government Printing Office, 1965), p. 165.
6. Irving Hoch, "Urban Scale and Environmental Quality," in *Population, Resources, and the Environment*, vol. III of task force reports of the Commission on Population Growth and the American Future, Ronald G. Ridker, ed. (1972), pp. 256 and 235.
7. Rose D. Friedman, *Poverty — Definition and Perspective* (Washington, D.C.: American Enterprise Institute, February 1965), pp. 34–35.

8. Jacob Riis, "Special Needs of the Poor in New York," *The Forum* (December 1892): 493.

9. For an authoritative treatment by an economist of poverty and inequality defined in terms of income (as opposed to status, cultural deprivation, or the like), see Robert J. Lampman, *Ends and Means of Reducing Income Poverty* (Chicago: Markham Publishing Co., 1972).

10. Quoted (with italics added) in Rose Friedman, *Poverty*, p. 30.

11. Quoted by Robert Hunter, *Poverty* (New York: Harper Torchbooks, 1965), pp. 7–8.

12. A *New York Times* story (October 14, 1970) began: "The first results of a Federal study of malnutrition in New York City show that nearly half of a sample of low income children under 7 years old suffer from low levels of vitamin A." Later on in the story it developed: (1) that as between low- and upper-income children age 7–12 there was only a 2 percent difference in the frequency of vitamin A deficiency; (2) that deficiencies of other nutrients were found in less than 10 percent of the children; (3) that in the case of some nutrients no deficiencies were found; (4) that doctors disagree as to whether any of the deficiencies found constitute "malnutrition"; (5) that vitamin deficiencies found have not been linked to any specific symptoms or illness; and (6) that lack of vitamin A contributes to loss of vision in dim light but doctors do not know how great the deficiency must be to produce this effect.

    To the extent that ignorance rather than poverty is the cause of bad diets, diets cannot be expected to improve as incomes rise. Leontine Young, in *Wednesday's Children: A Study of Child Neglect and Abuse* (New York: McGraw-Hill, 1964), p. 123, reports: "Many of the mothers lack the most elemental knowledge of nutrition as well as the will to act. One mother insisted she fed her children well. She bought potato chips and Coca-Cola regularly." With a higher income, this mother might buy more potato chips and Coca-Cola.

13. For a perspective differing somewhat from the one here, see Nathan Glazer, "The Paradoxes of Health Care," *The Public Interest*, 22 (Winter 1971), pp. 62–77; see also Charles Kadushin, "Social Class and the Experience of Ill Health," in Bendix and Lipset, op. cit., pp. 406–412.

14. This paragraph is based entirely on Harold Stephen Luft, "Poverty and Health: An Empirical Investigation," unpublished Ph.D. dissertation, Harvard University (July 1972).

15. Martin S. Feldstein, "The Medical Economy," *Scientific American*, 229 (September 1973), p. 156. See also Myron J. Lefcowitz, "Poverty and Health: A Re-Examination," *Inquiry*, 16 (March 1973), pp. 3–13. This is Reprint 96 in the series of the Institute for Research on Poverty at the University of Wisconsin.

16. Adapted from Charles L. Schultze et al., *Setting National Priorities, the 1973 Budget*, op. cit., pp. 224–225.

17. Julius A. Roth, "The Treatment of the Sick," in John Kosa, Aaron Antonovsky, and Irving Kenneth Zola, eds., *Poverty and Health, A Sociological Analysis* (Cambridge, Mass.: Harvard University Press, 1969), p. 223; see also Mary W. Herman, "The Poor: Their Medical Needs and the Health Services Available to Them," *Annals of the American Academy of Political and Social Science*, 399 (January 1972): 12–21.

18. Irving Leveson, "The Challenge of Health Services for the Poor," *The Annals of the American Academy of Political and Social Science*, 399 (January 1972): 26. Pointing out that there are consistent findings of a strong impact of education upon health, the author remarks that education ". . . extends one's time horizon, and behavior may be very different when future consequences of current actions are given increased weight."

19. Richard Auster, Irving Leveson, and Deborah Sarachek, "The Production of Health. An Exploratory Study," *Journal of Human Resources*, 4 (Fall 1969): 411–436. The analysis is limited to whites. Drawing upon the same data, Leveson has shown elsewhere that environmental factors account for about seven-tenths of the differences in infant deaths among (white) income groups and that these estimates "explain" about half the white-nonwhite differential. Irving Leveson, "Determinants of Infant Mortality," *Inquiry*, 7 (June 1970): 60–61. A study of infant death in New York City, published by the National Academy of Sciences in 1973, is reported to have found that the infant death rate for the city would be reduced by "as much as" one-third if all women had the pregnancy outcome of those who received adequate health care (a way of putting it which ignores the possibility that among the women not receiving adequate care there may be many whose infants would die even if they did receive it). *New York Times*, July 8, 1973.

20. Alonzo S. Yerby, "The Problems of Medical Care for Indigent Populations," *American Journal of Public Health*, 55 (August 1965): 1215.

21. George W. Albee, in Anselm L. Strauss, ed., *Where Medicine Fails* (Chicago, Aldine Publishing Co., 1970), p. 39.

In an analysis of British experience, Martin Rein writes: "Different occupations both at the top and the bottom of the social scale generate different illness patterns. But this measure of class is not a measure of poverty. Hence, redistribution of income among these occupational groups is unlikely to alter this pattern of illness. This leads naturally to the question of what kinds of environmental manipulations are likely to reduce occupational related morbidity. Here we are led to the curious conclusion that it may be easier to alter the morbidity-generating character of the environment of the unskilled than it is to alter the occupational environment of professional and managerial groups. But by this new criterion of severity — responsiveness to prevention — we might be forced to conclude that more highly skilled white-collar occupational groups are sicker than unskilled manual groups. We should be hesitant to draw such an inference too quickly. But the example does illustrate how demanding is the task of reaching a judgment about the relationship between class and morbidity." Martin Rein, "Social Class and the Utilization of Medical Care Services," *Hospitals, Journal of the American Hospital Association*, 43 (July 1969): 50.

The poor, writes Anselm L. Strauss in *Where Medicine Fails* (p. 17), "live strictly and wholeheartedly in the present . . . To them a careful concern about health is unreal. . . ." Daniel Rosenblatt finds that the relative failure of the poor to use the many preventive health services available to them is in some measure "another dimension of the general lack of future orientation that characterizes blue collar workers." "Barriers to Medical Care for the Urban Poor," in Arthur B. Shostak and William Gomberg, eds., *New Perspectives on Poverty* (Englewood Cliffs, N.J., Prentice-Hall, 1965), pp. 72–73.

See also Eric J. Cassell, "Disease as a Way of Life," *Commentary*, 55 (February 1973), pp. 80–82.

22. Edward R. Fried et al., *Setting National Priorities: The 1974 Budget*, op. cit., p. 112.

23. U.S. Bureau of the Census, Current Population Reports, *Consumer Buying Indicators, Household Ownership and Availability of Cars, Homes, and Selected Household Durables and Annual Expenditures on Cars and Other Durables: 1971* (May 1972), Tables 1–9.

24. Quoted in N. M. Bradburn, *The Structure of Psychological Well-Being* (Chicago: Aldine Publishing Company, 1969), p. 115.

25. Victor R. Fuchs, "Redefining Poverty and Redistributing Income," *The Public Interest*, 8 (Summer 1967): 91.

26. Edward R. Fried et al., *Setting National Priorities: The 1974 Budget* (Washington, D.C.: The Brookings Institution, 1973), p. 45.

27. Lester C. Thurow finds that between 1947 and 1965, poverty (using the $3,000 line for families and the $1,500 one for unrelated individuals) declined 0.7 percentage points per year (in constant 1965 dollars). If this rate of decline continues, it would take 23 years to eliminate poverty among families and 55 years to eliminate it among unrelated individuals. Lester C. Thurow, *The Economics of Poverty and Discrimination* (Washington, D.C.: The Brookings Institution, 1969).

28. Peter A. Morrison, *Dimensions of the Population Problem in the United States* (Santa Monica, Calif.: The Rand Corporation, Monograph R-864-CPG, August 1972), pp. v–vi.

29. Benjamin A. Okner, *Transfer Payments: Their Distribution and Role in Reducing Poverty*, Reprint 254 (Washington, D.C.: The Brookings Institution, 1973). A comprehensive account of current welfare programs is provided in Gilbert Y. Steiner, *The State of Welfare* (Washington, D.C.: The Brookings Institution, 1971); a much briefer one, which emphasizes the problem of reconciling work incentives with public assistance, is Sar A. Levitan, Martin Rein, and David Marwick, *Work & Welfare Go Together* (Baltimore: The Johns Hopkins University Press, 1972).

30. The negative income tax proposal was made in Milton Friedman, *Capitalism and Freedom* (Chicago: University of Chicago Press, 1962), ch. 12. See also Christopher Green, *Negative Taxes and the Poverty Problem* (Washington, D.C.: The Brookings Institution, 1967); James Tobin, Joseph A. Pechman, and Peter M. Mieszkowski, "Is a Negative Income Tax Practical?" *The Yale Law Journal*, 77 (November 1967): 1–27; and James C. Vadakin, "A Critique of the Guaranteed Annual Income," *The Public Interest*, 11 (Spring 1968): 53–66.

31. For a detailed, vivid, and authoritative account of the formulation of the proposal and the subsequent political struggle, see Daniel P. Moynihan, *The Politics of a Guaranteed Income, The Nixon Administration and the Family Assistance Plan* (New York: Random House, 1973).

32. Michael K. Taussig, "Long-run Consequences of Income Maintenance," in Kenneth E. Boulding and Martin Pfaff, eds., *Redistribution to the Rich and the Poor, The Grants Economics of Income Distribution* (Belmont, Calif.: Wadsworth Publishing Company, 1972), p. 385.

A three-year experiment to test the disincentive effects of eight different assistance plans on "working poor" families in five cities of New Jersey and Pennsylvania indicated, according to the Assistant Secretary for Planning and Evaluation of the Department of Health, Education and Welfare, "that only small changes in family earnings should be expected in response to a negative income tax plan." Only families headed by able-bodied men were studied. *New York Times*, December 21, 1973. See also U.S. Office of Economic Opportunity, *Preliminary Results of the New Jersey Graduated Work Incentive Experiment* (Washington, D.C.: Government Printing Office, 1970).

33. The loss of output in the economy in 1963 attributable to the disincentive effect of the progressive income tax on high incomes (over $10,000) "may have been of the order of one-third of 1 percent." R. Barlow, H. E. Bracer, and J. N. Morgan, *Economic Behavior of the Affluent* (Washington, D.C.: The Brookings Institution, 1966), p. 146.

34. Elizabeth F. Durbin, *Welfare, Income, and Employment: An Economic Analysis of Family Choice* (New York: Praeger, 1969).

35. Fried et al., *Setting National Priorities: The 1974 Budget*, p. 81. Related matters are discussed by Edward C. Banfield, Nathan Glazer, and David Gordon in separate articles on welfare in *The Public Interest*, 16 (Summer 1969).

36. Martin Rein, "Poverty and Income," *American Child*, 48 (Summer 1966): 9.

37. See Simon Rottenberg, "Misplaced Emphases in Wars on Poverty," *Law and Contemporary Problems* (Winter 1966): 68–71.

38. Glen G. Cain, "Issues in the Economics of a Population Policy for the United States," *American Economic Review*, 61 (May 1971): 414.

39. Bruno Stein, *On Relief* (New York: Basic Books, 1971), pp. 86–87.

40. David Caplovitz, *The Poor Pay More* (New York: The Free Press, 1963), p. 48.

41. Lester C. Thurow, "The Political Economy of Income Redistribution Policies," *Annals of the American Academy of Political and Social Science*, 409 (September 1973), p. 150.

42. Hunter, *Poverty*, pp. 322–323.

43. Cf. David Matza, "The Disreputable Poor," in Neil J. Smelser and Seymour Martin Lipset, eds., *Social Structure and Mobility in Economic Development* (Chicago: Aldine Publishing Company, 1966), especially pp. 310–317.

44. The distinction is akin to that made by John Kosa between "acute" and "chronic" poverty. The former, he says, implies a previous period spent above the poverty level. "The chronically poor person," on the other hand, "has no personal knowledge of how to live above the poverty level and, if given some unexpected aid from a charity organization, he cannot live up to the expectations; perhaps . . . he has to be taught the rudiments of middle-class life and spending habits." Chronic poverty, he adds, is self-perpetuating and, unlike acute poverty, preserves all the traits of pauperism. "The Nature of Poverty," in John Kosa, Antonovsky, and Zola, eds., *Poverty and Health*, p. 27.

45. From an unpublished paper by Francis Duehay.

46. Cf. L. L. Geismar and Michael A. LaSorte, *Understanding the Multi-Problem Family* (New York: Association Press, 1964), pp. 56–58.

47. Gordon E. Brown, ed., *The Multi-Problem Dilemma* (Metuchen, N.J.: The Scarecrow Press, 1968), p. 8.

48. J. Leslie Dunstan, *A Light to the City* (Boston: Beacon Press, 1966), p. 106.

49. Reverend Lyman Abbott, Introduction to Mrs. Helen Campbell, *Darkness and Daylight; or, Lights and Shadows of New York Life* (Hartford, Conn.: Hartford Publishing Co., 1896), p. 53. The secret of success in dealing with the "outcast class," Reverend Abbott says, is "personal contact with men and women of higher nature," by which he presumably means higher-class culture (p. 49).

50. Roy Lubove, *The Professional Altruist* (Cambridge, Mass.: Harvard University Press, 1965), p. 16.

51. How far supervision can go even with welfare recipients who are not lower class — the blind, for instance — is described by Jacobus TenBroek and Floyd W. Matson in "The Disabled and the Law of Welfare," *California Law Review*, 54 (May 1966): 831:

> It is the agency of welfare, not the recipient, who decides what life goals are to be followed, what ambitions may be entertained, what services are appropriate, what wants are to be recognized, and what funds allocated to each. In short, the recipient is told *what* he wants as well as how much he is wanting. In the velvet glove of public aid is an iron hand: If the recipient does not comply and conform, he may be removed from the rolls or have his budget reduced. The alternatives are obedience or starvation.

52. Winifred Bell, *Aid to Dependent Children* (New York: Columbia University Press, 1965), p. 113.

A recent study compares the progress of fifty multiproblem families receiving intensive social casework (the caseworkers had earned the Master of Social Work degree, had previous field experience, and had less than half the usual caseload) with that of a control group of fifty similar families receiving normal public assistance. After thirty-one months "the essential finding was that while the demonstration group attained a slightly better degree of family functioning, its margin of progress over the control group was not significant in the statistical sense." Brown, *The Multi-Problem Dilemma*, p. 7.

53. Quoted in Harvey W. Zorbaugh, *The Gold Coast and the Slum* (Chicago: University of Chicago Press, 1929), p. 262.

54. There is no standard usage for the terms "community development," "community organization," and "community mobilization." The meanings employed here follow Patricia Cayo Sexton, *Spanish Harlem: Anatomy of Poverty* (New York: Harper & Row, 1965), pp. 140–141.

55. See, for example, various writings by and about Saul Alinsky, especially the uncritical account of his doings in Charles Silberman, *Crisis in Black and White* (New York: Random House, 1964), ch. 10.

56. Peter Marris and Martin Rein, *Dilemmas of Social Reform* (New York: Atherton Press, 1967), pp. 222–223.

57. See Daniel Patrick Moynihan, *Maximum Feasible Misunderstanding: Community Action in the War on Poverty* (New York: The Free Press, 1969).

58. *New York Times*, July 24, 1966.

59. Ralph M. Kramer, *Participation of the Poor* (Englewood Cliffs, N.J.: Prentice-Hall, Inc., 1969), p. 256.

Studies in nine cities of inner-city housing problems led to the conclusion that ". . . the poor participate less frequently than the general population in all kinds of community activities. And the white poor participate less than the black poor. But both black and white poor families tend to perceive themselves as not being a part of the community." Frederick E. Case, ed., *Inner-City Housing and Private Enterprise* (New York: Praeger, 1972), p. 34.

60. Robert A. Berliner, "Alinskism in Theory and Practice," unpublished senior honors thesis, Harvard University, 1967.
61. On Chicago, see Winston Moore, Charles P. Livermore, and George F. Galland, Jr., "Woodlawn: the Zone of Destruction," *The Public Interest*, 30 (Winter 1973): 48–52 in particular.

For discussion of "citizen participation" from a variety of points of view and for much bibliography, see Roland L. Warren, ed., *Perspectives on the American Community*, 2d ed. (Chicago: Rand McNally & Company, 1973), Section Five.

CHAPTER 7

Schooling versus Education

The "Dear Abby" correspondence appeared in the (McNaught) syndicated column on July 11, 1966.

1. Harlem Youth Opportunities Unlimited, Inc., "Youth in the Ghetto" (New York: multilithed, 1964), p. 33.
2. However, a Survey Research Center study, begun in 1968 and repeated at intervals, of a nationally representative panel of boys (there were 1,620 in the sample, including 286 dropouts, in the summer of 1970) found the weekly incomes of *employed* dropouts to be nearly identical to those of *employed* high school graduates; this was so even when the groups were matched for length of time on their present jobs. The unemployment rate of the nongraduates was twice that of the graduates, but this "is caused primarily by family background and ability factors." There was a difference of about five IQ points between the dropouts and the graduates. Jerald G. Bachman, Swayzer Green, and Ilona D. Wirtanen, *Youth in Transition*, vol. III: *Dropping Out — Problem or Symptom?* (Ann Arbor: Survey Research Center, 1971).

In an earlier Project TALENT study, Combs and Cooley, using data from the participants who were in the ninth grade in 1960, found that employment rates of male dropouts and controls were almost identical (87 and 89 percent, respectively, had full-time jobs) and the mean yearly salary of the employed dropouts was slightly more than that of the controls ($3,650 as against $3,500). Unfortunately, the authors write, the results of their study were not consistent with their expectation, which was to reveal that the graduate was much better off than the dropout, a finding that "might help dissuade some students from leaving high-school before graduation." Later follow-up studies by Project TALENT, they say, may "show more precisely the disadvantages of dropping out of high school." Janet Combs and William W. Cooley, "Dropouts: In High School and After School," *American Educational Research Journal*, 5 (May 1968): 352, 362.

3. Theodore W. Schultz, *Education and Productivity*, prepared for the National Commission on Productivity (June 1971). See also *Investment in Human Capital* (New York: The Free Press, 1971).

   An important collection of papers on the impacts of higher education, which appeared too late for mention in the text, is: Lewis C. Solomon and Paul J. Taubman, eds., *Does College Matter?* (New York: Academic Press, 1973).
4. Finis Welch, "Black-White Differences in Returns to Schooling," *American Economic Review*, 63 (December 1973). Welch finds the percentage increase in the wage rate associated with an extra year of schooling in 1966 to have been 23.0 for black urban males who entered the labor force in 1963–1965 as against 14.6 for white; for those entering in 1959–1962, 14.2 and 10.6; for those entering in 1955–1958, 7.9 and 8.2; for those entering in 1947–1954, 6.2 and 9.0, and for those entering in 1934–1946, 4.9 and 6.9.

   Barry R. Chiswick suggests that greater uncertainty of returns from investment in schooling by nonwhites may make them less responsive than whites to changes in the average rate of return from such investment. As much as one-half of their greater uncertainty may be due, he finds, to the greater instability of nonwhite employment during the year. "Racial Differences in the Variation of Rates of Return from Schooling," in G. von Furstenberg et al., eds., *Patterns of Racial Discrimination*, vol. II, *Employment and Income*, (Lexington, Mass.: D.C. Heath, forthcoming 1974).

   For data and bibliography showing *lower* returns to blacks, see Bennett Harrison, *Education, Training, and the Urban Ghetto* (Baltimore: The Johns Hopkins University Press, 1972).
5. See especially Herbert Gintis, "Education Technology and the Characteristics of Worker Productivity," *American Economic Review*, 61 (May 1971): 266–279; and Z. Grilliches and M. Mason, "Education, Income and Ability," *Journal of Political Economy*, 80 (Part 2, May/June 1972): S74–103. In this same issue of the *Journal of Political Economy*, Paul Taubman comments (pp. S106–107) that although he agrees on the relative unimportance of IQ he finds that mathematical ability *is* important — indeed as important as amount of schooling.
6. The literature dealing with the effect of "family background" is discussed in Finis Welch, "Relationships between Income and Schooling," *Journal of Research in Education*, forthcoming, 1974. On the link between mother's schooling and son's earnings see J. Hunt, "Income Determinants for College Graduates and the Return to Educational Investment," *Yale Economic Essays*, 3 (1963): 305–357. Using data from a high-income population, Leibowitz finds that mother's and father's education have equal impacts on schooling while mother's education is much more important in determining IQ. Arleen Leibowitz, "Home Investments in Children," *Journal of Political Economy*, forthcoming.
7. Gintis, "Education Technology," p. 276.
8. Sowell, *Race and Economics* (New York: David McKay, forthcoming, 1974), ch. 7. Finis Welch suggests still another interpretation of the data. "It is surprising," he writes, "that the value of schooling holding measured cognitive achievement constant is 80 to 90 percent as high as when achievement is not held constant. This says only that the attributes associated with schooling

that the market buys are not very closely associated with ability tests. Perhaps the socializing skills associated with school attendance are dominant, but I doubt that existing measures of cognitive development are accurate enough to warrant such a conclusion." "Relationships between Income and Schooling," p. 14.

9. Cited by Bennett Harrison, *Education, Training, and the Urban Ghetto*, p. 34.

10. Christopher Jencks et al., *Inequality, A Reassessment of the Effect of Family and Schooling In America* (New York: Basic Books, 1972), pp. 182–183.

11. Daniel E. Diamond, "America's Unskilled Workers: Some Problems and Solutions," dittoed paper, New York University (September 29, 1966). This paper has been helpful on many of the points discussed in this section.

12. Jencks et al., *Inequality*, pp. 182–183.

13. According to one study a fourth year of high school would cost more (in earnings forgone) than it would be worth (in increased future earnings) in 6 of 22 occupations if the future earnings are discounted at 5 percent and in 13 of the 22 if they are discounted at 10 percent. One who finishes high school and then becomes an electrician, for example, would lose $1,127 at the 5 percent discount rate and $2,255 at the 10 percent rate by investing in the fourth year of high school. (The data are for whites.) Stuart O. Schweitzer, "Occupational Choice, High School Graduation, and Investment in Human Capital," *Journal of Human Resources*, 6 (Summer 1971): 331.

14. Arthur L. Stinchcombe, *Rebellion in a High School* (Chicago: Quadrangle Books, 1964), p. 180.

   Most job-related skills are learned on the job. See the *Annual Report of the Council of Economic Advisers*, January 1965, Table 17, p. 129. See also Jacob Mincer, "On-the-Job Training: Costs, Returns, and Some Implications," *Journal of Political Economy*, 70 (Part 2, Supplement, October 1962): 50–73.

   Apprenticeship is also of small importance in training workers. See Felician F. Foltman, "An Assessment of Apprenticeship," *Monthly Labor Review*, 87 (January 1964): 33.

15. Jencks et al., *Inequality*, p. 110.

16. Ruby Jo Reeves Kennedy, quoted in Lewis Anthony Dexter, *The Tyranny of Schooling* (New York: Basic Books, 1964), pp. 114–116 (italics in the original). See also Arthur R. Jensen, "How Much Can We Boost IQ and Scholastic Achievement?" *Harvard Educational Review*, 39 (Winter 1969): 13–16.

17. See the remarks by Howard R. Stanton in Arthur J. Field, ed., *Urbanization and Work in Modernizing Societies* (Detroit: Caribbean Research Institute, Glengary Press, 1966), pp. 9–13.

18. For an important case in point, see the study by Eli Ginsburg and Douglas W. Bray of the army's prejudice during World War II against illiterates and slow learners. *The Uneducated* (New York: Columbia University Press, 1953), especially chs. 6 and 7.

19. Sowell, *Black Education: Myths and Tragedies* (New York: McKay, 1972), p. 290.

20. Cf. R. Wayne Jones, in Field, *Urbanization and Work*, pp. 57–58.

21. See, for example, Allison Davis, "Status Systems and the Socialization of the Child," *American Sociological Review*, 6 (June 1941): 352–354. Davis says

that the middle-class child is taught that he will be rewarded if he learns, whereas the lower-class one is taught that he will *not* be:

> As the middle-class child grows older, the effective rewards in maintaining learning are increasingly those of status; they are associated with the prestige of middle- or upper-class rank and culture. The class goals in education, occupation, and status are made to appear real, valuable, and certain to him because he actually begins to experience in his school, clique, and family life some of the prestige responses. The lower-class child, however, *learns* by *not* being rewarded in these prestige relationships that the middle-class goals and gains are neither likely nor desirable for one in his position. He discovers by trial-and-error learning that he is not going to be rewarded in terms of these long-range, status goals, if he is a "good little boy," if he avoids the sexual and recreational exploration available to him in his lower-class environment, or if he studies his lessons. In this learning, he is often more realistic than his teacher, if one judges by the actual cultural role which the society affords him.

22. Herbert J. Gans, *The Urban Villagers* (New York: The Free Press, 1962), p. 133.
23. Jencks et al., *Inequality*, p. 141.
24. Cf. Basil Bernstein, "Social Class and Linguistic Development: A Theory of Social Learning," in A. H. Halsey et al., eds., *Education, Economy, and Society* (New York: The Free Press, 1961), pp. 306–307.
25. C. Arnold Anderson, "A Skeptical Note on Education and Mobility," in *Education, Economy, and Society*, p. 176.
26. Philip K. Jensen, James M. O'Kane, David Graybeal, and Robert W. Friedrichs, "Evaluating Compensatory Education: A Case Study," *Education and Urban Society*, 4 (February 1972): 211–223.
27. James S. Coleman et al., *Equality of Educational Opportunity*, Office of Education, U.S. Department of Health, Education, and Welfare (Washington, D.C.: U.S. Government Printing Office, 1966).
28. For a critical review of the literature reanalyzing the Coleman Report, see the essay review of Frederick Mosteller and Daniel P. Moynihan, eds., *On Equality of Educational Opportunity: Papers Deriving from the Harvard University Faculty Seminar on the Coleman Report*, by Gerald Grant in *Harvard Educational Review*, 42 (February 1972): 109–125.
29. Harvey A. Averch, Stephen J. Carroll, Theodore S. Donaldson, Herbert J. Keesling, and John Pincus, *How Effective Is Schooling? A Critical Review and Synthesis of Research Findings* (Santa Monica, Calif.: The Rand Corporation, R-956-PCSF/RC, March 1972), multilithed.
30. Samuel Ball and Gerry Begatz, *The First Year of Sesame Street, An Evaluation* (Princeton: Educational Testing Service, 1970).
31. James S. Coleman, *Resources for Social Change* (New York: Wiley-Interscience, 1971), p. 28.
32. Alan B. Wilson, *The Consequences of Segregation: Academic Achievement in a Northern Community* (Berkeley, Calif.: The Glendessary Press, 1969), p. 61.

33. Bernstein, "Social Class and Linguistic Development," pp. 296, 307. Bernstein uses the term "working class" rather than (as earlier) lower class, but he includes in that class "all members of the semi-skilled and unskilled group except the type of family structure indicated as the base line for the middle-class and associative levels."

34. Richard A. Cloward and James A. Jones, "Social Class: Educational Attitudes and Participation," in A. Harry Passow, ed., *Education in Depressed Areas* (New York: Columbia Teachers College, 1963), p. 193.

   The midnineteenth-century high school deliberately inculcated future-orientedness. Michael B. Katz, *The Irony of Early School Reform* (Cambridge, Mass.: Harvard University Press, 1968), p. 121.

35. Bernstein, "Social Class and Linguistic Development," p. 306 (italics in the original).

36. Cloward and Jones, "Social Class," p. 194.

37. Baratz and Baratz consider it "racist" to view the Negro child as suffering from a language or cognitive "deficit" when what he has is "a handicap *in terms of the white middle class standard.*" "Many lower-class-Negro children speak a well-ordered, highly structured, but different dialect from that of standard English"; teaching should start with this language and teach them the other so as to "produce a bicultural child." Curiously they say nothing about: (a) whites who speak a similar lower-class "dialect," or (b) blacks (other than lower-class) who do not speak a dialect. Stephen S. Baratz and Jean C. Baratz, "Early Childhood Intervention: The Social Science Base of Institutional Racism," *Harvard Educational Review*, 40 (February 1970): 29–50.

38. Benjamin S. Bloom, *Stability and Change in Human Characteristics* (New York: Wiley, 1964), pp. 207–208, 127.

   Martin Deutsch suggests that it is at the three- to four-year-old level that the deprived child might most successfully be helped to catch up. "Facilitating Development in the Pre-School Child: Social and Psychological Perspectives," in Fred M. Hechinger, ed., *Pre-School Education Today* (Garden City, N.Y.: Doubleday, 1966), p. 84.

39. U.S. Office of Education, "Education of the Disadvantaged: An Evaluative Report on Title I, Elementary and Secondary Education Act of 1965, Fiscal Year 1970" (Washington, D.C.: Government Printing Office, 1971). Quoted in Averch et al., *How Effective Is Schooling?*, p. 103.

40. Jencks et al., *Inequality*, p. 135. Bachman and his fellow researchers of the Survey Research Center concluded that ". . . there are alternatives to a twelve-year diploma; perhaps one based on ten years would be sufficient." *Youth in Transition*, vol. III, p. 182.

   In Philadelphia the City Council was recently told by an associate superintendent of schools that the state's attendance law, which requires attendance until the age of seventeen unless a student has a confirmed promise of a job (in which case he may leave at sixteen) is "archaic." Many pupils, he said, are in school only because the law requires them to be there. *The Evening Bulletin*, December 27, 1972.

   J. M. Tanner, a British educational psychologist, objects to any school-leaving age as such on the grounds that there is great biological variability in the rate at which children mature:

We need not a production-line like an apple-sorter, with children falling off at age-given points of 16 or 18, some immature and some rotted by boredom and the stultifying effect of a situation they feel intuitively to be contrived. A network rather should be the model, with many paths through it, offering to the individual child a route more in accordance with his own particular speed of development and his own particular gifts. Such a system could be built if the barriers between school and industrial community were progressively removed, so that one child went to his apprenticeship as another to a new form. In neither case would the progression be dependent on chronological age, but on physical development, emotional needs, manual capabilities and intelligence. One boy might begin to spend a considerable proportion of his time in an engineering shop from age 13 onwards, though always under the ultimate control of the educational authorities. If at 16 he had after all discovered a talent for figures, he could increase the proportion of time in the schoolroom. Another late-maturing though not very intelligent boy might remain in the more protected school environment till 16 or even 17, emerging gradually into the community as science, humanism and common sense alike dictate, and not at the occurrence of an arbitrary birthday. School-leaving age could be abolished, but "education" continued for all up to 18 or 20. The economic system would have to be arranged so that passage from school to industry or vice versa did not penalize the child financially.

J. M. Tanner, *Education and Physical Growth* (London: University of London Press, 1961), p. 124.

41. Stinchcombe, *Rebellion in a High School*, p. 179.

42. Martin Trow, "The Second Transformation of American Secondary Education," in R. Bendix and S. M. Lipset, eds., *Class, Status, and Power*, 2d ed. (New York: The Free Press, 1966), p. 448.

43. Quoted in E. G. West, *Education and the State* (London: The Institute of Economic Affairs, 1965), p. 36.

44. David H. Harbreaves, *Social Relations in a Secondary School* (New York: The Humanities Press, 1967), pp. 172–173. The observations were made in a school in a "problem area" of a city in northern England. For another view of the school as a cause of delinquency, see J. R. Eichorn, "Delinquency and the Educational System," in H. C. Quay, ed., *Juvenile Delinquency* (Princeton, N.J.: Van Nostrand, 1965).

45. For proof that a white teacher who really likes children, including lower-class black ones, and is well endowed with patience and pluck can succeed in a black school, see Kim Marshall, *Law and Order in Grade 6-E* (Boston: Little, Brown and Company, 1972).

46. Howard S. Becker, "School is a Lousy Place to Learn Anything," *American Behavioral Scientist*, 16 (September–October 1972): 103.

47. Mobilization for Youth, Inc., *A Proposal for the Prevention and Control of Delinquency by Expanding Opportunities* (New York: Author, 1961), p. 112.

48. Quoted in Harrison Brown, James Bonner, and John Weir, *The Next Hundred Years* (New York: Viking, 1957), pp. 132–133.

49. Fritz Machlup, *The Production and Distribution of Knowledge in the United*

States (Princeton, N.J.: Princeton University Press, 1962), p. 128. (Italics in the original.)

50. The study was by Project TALENT; see John C. Flanagan and William W. Cooley, *Project TALENT, A Survey and Follow-up Study* (Pittsburgh: School of Education, University of Pittsburgh, 1966), ch. 10, p. 36.

51. *Work in America* (Cambridge, Mass.: The MIT Press, 1973), p. 139. Privately run vocational schools, of which there are between 7,000 and 35,000 with between 1 and 1.5 million students (data on them have never been gathered systematically), are reported to be having *in some instances* impressive successes with students many of whom dropped out of the public system. See A. Harvey Belitsky, *Private Vocational Schools and Their Students: Limited Objectives, Unlimited Opportunities* (Cambridge, Mass.: Schenkman Publishing Co., Inc., 1969).

52. Trow, "The Second Transformation," p. 448.

53. However, as Illich remarks, childhood is experienced as a burden by some: "Many of them are simply forced to go through it and are not at all happy playing the child's role." Ivan Illich, *Deschooling Society* (New York: Harper & Row, 1970), p. 27.

54. Persuasive testimony from one with special knowledge was given in the letters columns of the *Washington Post*, February 28, 1970, as follows:

> *Job Applicant*
> Why hasn't a change been made in the law regarding the hiring of 13-, 14- and 15-years-olds? This would allow more businesses to employ them for part-time jobs. There *is* a law about hiring people according to race, creed, color or religion.
> You see plenty of jobs advertised in the newspapers that a young teenager could and would handle; but when he goes to apply for it and tells his age, he is turned down.
> Jobs such as busboy, or a fellow in the back room to help sweep up or move boxes are just two things that he could do well. Furthermore, I think if more teenagers were given the opportunity to work a few hours after school, on holidays and weekends, there wouldn't be so much juvenile delinquency. Much damage and bodily harm is caused by a lack of something purposeful to do and the capability to earn one's own spending money.
>
> GARY COURTNEY,
Age 14
> Bowie, Md.

55. Of the boys among them, nearly 21 percent were clerical workers, 18 percent sales workers, 18 percent operatives and kindred workers, 16 percent service workers (not including private household), and 20 percent laborers. 1970 Census, Detailed Characteristics, New York, PC(1)-D34, Dec. 1972, Table 174, pp. 34–1008–1010.

56. *A Wall Street Journal* story of March 30, 1971 begins: "Times are tough and some companies are turning to an effective cost-cutting device. It's called child labor." According to the story, the provisions of the Fair Labor Standards Act are rarely implemented because few violations can be proved to be

willful. At that time the last case resulting in criminal penalties was in 1968, when a construction firm was fined $6,000 for employing 152 youths.

57. In a personal communication.

CHAPTER 8

Several Kinds of Crime

The quotation from Henry George at the head of the chapter is from *Social Problems* (New York, 1883), p. 12. The second quotation is from the report of the President's Commission on Law Enforcement and Administration of Justice, *The Challenge of Crime in a Free Society* (Washington, D.C.: U.S. Government Printing Office, February 1967), p. 6.

Crime statistics are notoriously unreliable for many reasons, some of which are inherent in the nature of crime. Nevertheless, it is impossible to discuss the subject without making use of them. The reader should be warned, however, that few perfectly safe factual statements are possible. For a good discussion of the limitations of the data, see Marvin E. Wolfgang, "Urban Crime," in James Q. Wilson, ed., *The Metropolitan Enigma* (Cambridge, Mass.: Harvard University Press, 1968), pp. 253–257.

Except as otherwise noted, all figures are from the *Uniform Crime Reports* published annually by the FBI.

1. Against the theory that poverty in the sense of low income causes crime, it has been pointed out that in the 1960's, when crime rates rose dramatically, the number of families with incomes below the poverty line decreased by one-third. This figure, however, must be disaggregated: there was *no* decline in the number of poor nonwhite, female-headed households that included teen-age children. It has also been argued against the poverty theory that the rate of increase was at least as high for crimes like rape and automobile theft that do not increase the offender's income (most automobile thefts are by joy-riding teen-agers) as for others. This objection would seem also to apply, although perhaps less strongly, to a "relative deprivation" theory, but empirical studies support this type of theory. Eberts and Schwirian found the rates of crime against both property and persons to be highest in SMSA's where the low-income population is a distinct local minority and the occupational gap between whites and nonwhites is greatest, and Ehrlich found that the rates for all felonies (but especially those against property) are positively related to the degree of income inequality in a community. Paul Eberts and Kent P. Schwirian, "Metropolitan Crime Rates and Relative Deprivation," *Criminologica*, 5 (February 1968): 43–52, and Isaac Ehrlich, "The Deterrent Effect of Criminal Law Enforcement," *Journal of Legal Studies*, 1 (June 1972): 276. Conklin finds "progressive deprivation" one of the most adequate explanations for the motivation of violent behavior. (This exists when *value expectations* [what one feels entitled to] are rising at the same time that *value capabilities* [what one feels capable of getting or keeping] are either declining or rising at a slower rate.) "To the extent that the whites gained as fast or faster than the

blacks [in the 1960's], the latter felt deprived. A second reason for rising expectations lay in the promises and hopes arising from the developments in civil rights in the decade prior to 1965." John E. Conklin, *Robbery and the Criminal Justice System* (Philadelphia: J. B. Lippincott Company, 1972), p. 30.

2. A study in a high-delinquency area of Philadelphia showed that boys born there were much more likely to commit delinquencies, and to commit more serious ones, than boys whose parents had migrated from places where presumably housing, schools, health conditions, and the level of living in general were much poorer. Leonard Savitz, "Delinquency and Migration," in M. E. Wolfgang, L. Savitz, and N. Johnston, *The Sociology of Crime and Delinquency* (New York: Wiley, 1962), pp. 203–204.

   A Washington, D.C., delinquency project in existence from 1964 to 1967 succeeded through the use of programmed instruction in producing educational gains of from three to six grade levels in high school dropouts from slum areas with delinquent careers. However, "the rate of delinquent acts was in no measurable way reduced by participation in the project. Those subjects passing the GED [high school equivalency] test were more delinquent than those failing the test." C. Ray Jeffery and Ina A. Jeffery, "Delinquents and Dropouts: An Experimental Program in Behavior Change," Mimeographed, 1968, Graduate School of Public Administration, New York University. The project was supported in part by contract number OE 6-85-355, U.S. Office of Education.

3. To the extent that the analysis here departs from the usual theory of rational decision-making it owes much to the work of Walter B. Miller. See especially his "The Impact of a 'Total-Community' Delinquency Control Project," *Social Problems*, 10 (Fall 1962): 168–190, and his "Theft Behavior in City Gangs," in M. W. Klein and B. G. Myerhoff, eds., *Juvenile Gangs in Context* (Englewood Cliffs, N.J.: Prentice-Hall, 1967). Miller's theoretical work will be systematically presented in *City Gangs* (New York: Wiley, forthcoming).

4. Conklin remarks that addicts tend to avoid confrontation with their victims when stealing since this would increase the chance of getting caught and therefore of a long prison term and of forced withdrawal from drugs. Addicts, he thinks, may have some responsibility for the rising robbery rate but "most robbers have never been arrested for drug law violations." *Robbery*, pp. 54 and 57.

5. Economists generally proceed on the assumption that in most cases crime "is simply a business oriented economic activity which is undertaken for much the same reasons as other types of economic activity." For a valuable set of papers, including much bibliography, based on this assumption, see Simon Rottenberg, ed., *The Economics of Crime and Punishment* (Washington, D.C.: The American Enterprise Institute for Public Policy Research, 1973). The quoted words are from the Preface.

6. Chambliss offers the hypothesis that "where a high commitment to crime as a way of life is combined with involvement in an act that is expressive, one finds the greatest resistance to deterrence through threat of punishment. At the other extreme are acts where commitment to crime is low and where the act is instrumental (such as the Snitch, the white-collar criminal, or the parking law violator). Here we would expect both general and specific deterrence to be

maximally effective." William J. Chambliss, "Types of Deviance and the Effectiveness of Legal Sanctions," *Wisconsin Law Review*, 703 (1967): 238–248.

7. The distinctions made in this paragraph are adapted from Lawrence Kohlberg, "The Child as a Moral Philosopher," *Psychology Today*, 2 (September 1968): 25–30.

8. Marvin E. Wolfgang and Franco Ferracuti, *The Subculture of Violence* (London: Tavistock Publications Ltd., 1967), pp. 154 and 260–261. See also Trasler, who stresses, as the foundation of morality, the child's anxiety about losing his parents' goodwill and who points out that if, as is typical in the lower class, the child is constantly fearful and insecure in his relationship with his parents the necessary "avoidance conditioning" may not occur. Gordon Trasler, *The Explanation of Criminality* (London: Routledge and Kegan Paul, 1962), pp. 70–83.

9. Henry Williamson, *Hustler!*, edited by R. Lincoln Keiser (New York: Avon, 1965), pp. 150–151.

10. Carroll divided three hundred Negro adolescents into "middle" and "lower" class and had them write explanations of why stealing and cheating are wrong. Some of her findings may be summarized as follows:

	PERCENT GIVING REASON	
Reasons	*Middle class*	*Lower class*
It is wrong to steal because:		
You might get caught	16	54
Your friends won't like you	43	17
You will get a bad name	28	15
It is wrong to cheat because:		
Someone will find it out	31	56
Someone will cheat you back	—	7
Children will not want to play games with you	58	64

Source: Rebecca Evans Carroll, "Relation of Social Environment to the Moral Ideology and the Personal Aspirations of Negro Boys and Girls," *The School Review*, 53 (January 1945): 32.

11. Joyce Ann Ladner, "Deviance in the Lower Class Adolescent Sub-Culture," Pruitt-Igoe Project Occasional Paper #3, Department of Sociology-Anthropology, Washington University, St. Louis (September 1966), p. 25.

12. Ibid., p. 26.

13. Allison Davis, *Social-Class Influences Upon Learning* (Cambridge, Mass.: Harvard University Press, 1948), p. 34.

14. Menachem Amir, *Patterns in Forcible Rape* (Chicago: University of Chicago Press, 1971), pp. 313 and 325–326.

15. The least skillful and experienced robbers ("opportunists" as opposed to "professionals") tend to be young and to be black. They choose victims who,

although not likely to have much money, are easiest and safest for them to handle; these are persons who are alone, female, old, or, preferably, all three. Conklin, *Robbery*, p. 91.

Friedlander, in his study of unemployment in the core areas of thirty cities, found that a record of criminal activities did not seem to present a problem for black youth in securing employment and that being arrested carried no great social stigma and "is often viewed as a mark of courage and honor among the young." The law enforcement system did not inflict substantial deterrents. "Given both the low probability of arrest and the limited penalties imposed," he concludes, "the rewards of hustling often justify the activities on rational, benefit-cost grounds." Stanley L. Friedlander, *Unemployment in the Urban Core: An Analysis of Thirty Cities with Policy Recommendations* (New York: Praeger, 1972), p. 184.

16. Kenneth Keniston, *The Uncommitted* (New York: Delta, 1965), p. 287.
17. Norman E. Zinberg, "Facts and Fancies about Drug Addiction," *The Public Interest*, 6 (Winter 1967): 76–77. Dr. Zinberg calls those who "want nothing but the immediate satisfaction of specific, pleasurable desires" *oblivion-seekers*, but it is hard to see why.

Far from being an important component of "experience" as understood by the (expressively) future-oriented individual, "pleasure" seems to be in opposition to it. Thus Dr. Timothy Leary withdrew as guru of a drug-using group because he was "dismayed over mere pleasure-seekers" in the movement. Psychedelic drugs, he said, are "too valuable to be used for mere pleasure" and "should be for developing self-knowledge." *New York Times*, November 29, 1967.

18. Cf. James Q. Wilson, "Violence," in Daniel Bell, ed., *Toward the Year 2000: Work in Progress* (Boston: Houghton Mifflin, 1968), pp. 283–284. Durkheim's discussion of the "egoistic" basis of suicide in the upper classes is relevant to the point being made in the text.
19. "Index" crimes are those used by the FBI in its Uniform Crime Reporting Program to measure "serious" common local crime problems. The "violent" category includes murder, forcible rape, aggravated assault, and robbery. The "property" category includes burglary, larceny $50 and over in value, and auto theft.
20. Peter A. Morrison, *Dimensions of the Population Problem in the United States* (Santa Monica, Calif.: The Rand Corporation, Monograph R-864-CPG, August 1972), p. 17.
21. What follows draws upon the work of Walter B. Miller cited earlier.
22. David Cumming and Elaine Cumming, "The Everyday Life of Delinquent Boys," in Irwin Deutscher and Elizabeth J. Thompson, eds., *Among the People: Encounters with the Poor* (New York: Basic Books, 1968), p. 152.
23. David Matza, *Delinquency and Drift* (New York: Wiley, 1964), pp. 89, 189–190.
24. Keniston, *The Uncommitted*, p. 184. See also pp. 398–399.
25. Walter B. Miller, "Violent Crimes in City Gangs," *The Annals of the American Academy of Political and Social Science*, 364 (March 1966): 112.
26. Walter B. Miller, "American Youth Gangs: Past and Present," in Abraham Blumberg, ed., *A Reader in Criminal Justice* (New York: Random House-Knopf, forthcoming 1974).

27. For Boston see Theodore N. Ferdinand, "The Criminal Patterns of Boston Since 1849," *American Journal of Sociology*, 73 (July 1967): 84–99, and Roger Lane, "Urbanization and Criminal Violence in the Nineteenth Century," *Journal of Social History*, 2 (December 1968): 156–163 (reproduced in Alexander B. Callow, Jr., ed., *American Urban History*, 2d edition, New York: Oxford University Press, 1973); for Buffalo, see Elwin H. Powell, "Crime as a Function of Anomie," *Journal of Criminal Law, Criminology and Police Science*, 57 (June 1966): 161–171.

28. Roger Starr, in *New York Times Magazine*, September 24, 1972, p. 95.

29. James M. Markham, "Heroin Hunger May Not a Mugger Make," *New York Times Magazine*, March 18, 1973.

30. Jacqueline Grennan, "The Age of the Person," *Seventeen* (December 1967): 168.

31. *New York Times*, March 12, 1969.

32. Eldridge Cleaver, *Soul On Ice* (New York: Delta, 1968), pp. 13–14.

33. Cf. Gresham M. Sykes and David Matza, "Techniques of Neutralization: A Theory of Delinquency," *American Sociological Review*, 22 (December 1957): 664–670. See also David Matza, *Delinquency and Drift*.

34. *Philadelphia Evening Bulletin*, March 19, 1973.

35. Personal communication to the author, March 19, 1973.

36. Joseph F. Coates, "The Future of Crime in the U.S. from Now to the Year 2000," *Policy Sciences*, 3 (March 1972): 31.

37. A winter camping program for underprivileged children was suspended after the death of an eleven-year-old South Bronx girl who struck a tree stump while sliding down a ski slope in a saucer sled. The program, which served 500 children a week, was financed by a grant of $102,743 from the Model Cities Administration. *New York Times*, February 22, 1973.

38. Llad Phillips, Harold L. Votey, Jr., and Darold Maxwell, "Crime, Youth and the Labor Market," *Journal of Political Economy*, 80 (May/June 1972): 503.

39. Stanley L. Friedlander, *Unemployment in the Urban Core*, p. 94. However, unemployment rates for the *city* (as opposed to non-whites) showed no relation to criminal activity (p. 85).

40. Quoted by Elliot Liebow, *Tally's Corner* (Boston; Little, Brown and Company, 1967), p. 43n.

    In a newspaper account of a forthcoming book about the "irregular economy" written with his wife, Professor Louis A. Ferman of the University of Michigan School of Social Work is quoted as saying that when they began studying "hard core" residents of the Detroit ghetto, "We hypothesized that they would be alienated and withdrawn from society; engaged in occasional job seeking and leisure pursuits." It turned out that most were working regularly. "Some in criminal activities — such as prostitution or narcotics — but most in conventional jobs including gardening, handicrafts, home repair, or the selling of low-priced goods." Most of the work was illegal in that it was not reported for licensing or tax purposes. *The Philadelphia Inquirer*, September 22, 1973.

41. James Q. Wilson, "Crime and Law Enforcement," in Kermit Gordon, ed., *Agenda for the Nation* (Washington, D.C.: The Brookings Institution, 1968), p. 187.

    Accounts of the effectiveness of such measures vary greatly from city to city. The Los Angeles Police Department found that better street lighting did not reduce street crimes but in Chicago, where the same experiment was tried, robbery rates dropped 10 to 15 percent in the alleys and dark streets where 51,000 lights had been installed while increasing 72.1 percent in the city as a whole. In Gary, Indiana, better lighting was credited with reducing robberies by 65 percent and assaults by 75 percent. There is, of course, no way of knowing whether the effect has been to shift these crimes to other parts of the city or to other cities. Conklin, *Robbery*, p. 185.

42. *New York Times*, January 27, 1969.

43. Gold found from interviews with a sample of teen-agers in Flint, Mich., that most of them did not regard delinquent behavior as risky: fear of apprehension was "not a strong force working to restrain delinquent behavior." In fact, the actual risk of getting caught was smaller than most of them thought. About 3 percent of offenses resulted in apprehension. Martin Gold, *Delinquent Behavior in an American City* (Belmont, Calif.: Brooks/Cole Publishing Company, 1970), ch. 6.

44. James Q. Wilson, "If Every Criminal *Knew* He Would Be Punished if Caught . . . ," *New York Times Magazine*, January 28, 1973, p. 55.

45. In animal experimentation, by contrast, it has been shown that severity of punishment is most important. Holding severity constant, however, punishment is most effective when administered simultaneously with or a few seconds after the behavior that is to be suppressed. For a review of this literature and comment on its implications for the control of crime see Barry F. Singer, "Psychological Studies of Punishment," *California Law Review*, 58 (March 1970).

46. George E. Antunes and A. Lee Hunt, "The Impact of Certainty and Security of Punishment on Levels of Crime in American States: An Extended Analysis," Paper delivered before American Political Science Association, September 1972.

47. Charles R. Tittle, "Crime Rates and Legal Sanctions," *Social Problems*, 16 (Spring 1969): 409–423.

48. Isaac Ehrlich, "The Deterrent Effect of Criminal Law Enforcement," *Journal of Legal Studies* (June 1972), pp. 259–276 and "Participation in Illegitimate Activities: A Theoretical and Empirical Investigation," *Journal of Political Economy*, 81 (May/June 1973): 521–565.

49. Morgan Owen Reynolds, "Crimes for Profit: The Economy of Theft," unpublished Ph.D. dissertation, University of Wisconsin, 1971. Table 6-3. For the framework of a benefit-cost analysis of law enforcement in general, see Gary S. Becker, "Crime and Punishment: An Economic Approach," *Journal of Political Economy*, 76 (1966): 169–217.

50. In Washington, D.C., Fred P. Graham remarks in *The Self-Inflicted Wound* (New York: Macmillan, 1970), p. 299, "with serious criminality hurtling along at a reported rate of almost 66,000 per year, the number of people being convicted each year for those same serious crimes was so small [in 1968] that they could be seated comfortably in one courtroom."

51. This paragraph draws heavily upon Robert Gold, "Urban Violence and Contemporary Defensive Cities," *American Institute of Planners Journal*, 36 (May 1970): 152.
    On city planning and defense against violent crime, see, in addition to the

article by Gold cited above, Jane Jacobs, *The Death and Life of Great American Cities* (New York: Random House, 1961), and Oscar Newman, *Crime Prevention Through Urban Design* (New York: Macmillan, 1973).

52. Mary Owen Cameron, *The Booster and the Snitch: Department Store Shoplifting* (New York: The Free Press, 1964), p. 17.

53. L. R. Zeitlin, "A Little Larceny Can Do a Lot for Employee Morale," *Psychology Today*, 5 (June 1971), pp. 22–26 and 64–66.

54. Space-General Corporation, *Prevention and Control of Crime and Delinquency*, Final Report Prepared for Youth and Adult Corrections Agency, State of California, Mimeographed, El Monte, California (July 29, 1965), p. 2.

55. These justifications are offered by Glover in support of suggestions not unlike those in the text. "Hopelessly inadequate people," he writes, "might benefit from a form of probation, very different from what we have now, where very great supervision would be exercised over their lives. They might be compelled to take certain jobs, and in some cases to live in certain hostels. Instead of the withering of necessary social skills that now takes place in prison, they could learn, under close supervision, how to adapt themselves better to the ordinary world of having a regular job." Jonathan Glover, *Responsibility* (London: Routledge & Kegan Paul, 1970), p. 169.

56. Although the discussion in the text concerns "undeterrables" only, there are obvious advantages in having a wide gradation of possible punishments in other types of cases as well. Writing about the disposition of juvenile offenders, Kittrie remarks that the choice between poorly supervised probation on the one hand and last-resort commitment on the other is much too narrow. "There is," he says, "a need for dispositions less drastic than commitment yet more meaningful than probation, which can at the same time afford juvenile authorities an effective scrutiny of the youth's rehabilitative progress. In some cities the police, through informal dispositions, have shown considerable innovation. With parental consent, they impose restrictions of varying severity upon offending juveniles, and many of these are reported to be highly effective. Kansas City, Missouri, utilizes a program called 'grounding.' A typical 'grounded' youth must attend school regularly, may leave the house only if accompanied by a parent, must dress conventionally, must cut his hair in a reasonable manner, and must study at home for a minimum prescribed period each day. After this schedule is enforced for a month, the conditions are gradually relaxed." Nicholas N. Kittrie, *The Right to Be Different; Deviance and Enforced Therapy* (Baltimore: The Johns Hopkins University Press, 1971), p. 163.

57. The constitutionality of a Connecticut law authorizing the imprisonment on a state farm of young women "in manifest danger of falling into habits of vice or leading a vicious life" was recently challenged in the Supreme Court. In a *per curiam* decision three lines long, the Court dismissed the appeal "for want of a properly presented federal question." 89 *Supreme Court Reporter* 1767 (May 26, 1969).

Massachusetts law provides for the involuntary hospitalization of any person subject to a "character disorder" rendering him so lacking in "judgment or emotional control" that he may conduct himself in a manner that "clearly violates the established . . . conventions of the community." In most states, juvenile courts may exercise wide discretion in cases where behavior is offensive without being criminal by adult standards. See Nicholas N. Kittrie, *The Right to Be Different*, especially pp. 68 and 114.

With regard to "preventive detention," i.e., detention pending trial of arrested persons who are judged likely to commit more crimes while awaiting trial, Professor Alan M. Dershowitz of the Harvard Law School remarks that the problem with the system is that it would *seem* to work: "The crime rate probably will go down slightly, and perhaps might be traceable to preventive detention, but what we won't know is how many, what proportion of the people confined, would actually not have committed crimes." He says any such plan ought to be preceded by a long test period, in which judges would select those persons they felt should be detained in order to see if, when not detained, they did actually commit more crimes than others. *New York Times*, January 30, 1969.

58. The author has discussed these matters in "How Many, and Who, Should Be Set at Liberty?", in Harry M. Clor, ed., *Civil Disorder and Violence* (Chicago: Rand McNally Public Affairs Series, 1972), pp. 27–45.

CHAPTER 9

Rioting Mainly for Fun and Profit

1. Report of the Task Force on Assessment of the President's Committee on Law Enforcement and Administration of Justice, *Crime and Its Impact — An Assessment* (Washington, D.C.: U.S. Government Printing Office, 1967), p. 121.
2. Ibid., p. 122. The "deprivation" theory has been criticized by (among others) Clark McPhail, "Civil Disorder Participation: A Critical Examination of Recent Research," *American Sociological Review*, 36 (December 1971): 1064 and 1067; Seymour Spilerman (see footnote 48 below); and Morris Janowitz. "The notion of relative deprivation may be operative," Janowitz has written, "but this sociological term seems to hide more than it illuminates. One is struck by the repeated reports of the carnival and happy days spirit that pervade the early stages of a commodity riot." (A "commodity" riot is "an outburst [within the Negro community] against property and retail establishments, plus looting"; it differs fundamentally from a "communal" riot; these occurred prior to the Second War and were attempts to prevent Negroes from moving into "contested areas.") *Social Control of Escalated Riots* (Chicago: University of Chicago Press, 1968), pp. 13 and 10.
3. Some examples: in 1966 the Dutch found it necessary to call out military police to quell a riot of construction workers in Amsterdam (*New York Times*, June 15, 1966); the next year the Tel Aviv city hall was stoned by rioters protesting unemployment, three policemen being injured (*New York Times*, March 15, 1967); in 1971 some 80,000 Western European farmers swarmed into Brussels to demand higher prices and in the ensuing melee one man was killed and 140 injured (*New York Times*, March 24, 1971); in October 1969, during a sixteen-hour wildcat strike of policemen in Montreal, a riot occurred in which two men were killed, scores injured, and an esti-

340 / THE UNHEAVENLY CITY REVISITED

mated $5 million in damage done to some 175 stores, hotels, and office buildings (*New York Times*, October 8, 1969); at about the same time, 10,000 Italian police and soldiers were vainly struggling to restore order to Reggio Calabria, a town disappointed at not having been named provincial capital (*New York Times*, February 1, 1971); that same spring Oriental Jews alleging discrimination fought street battles with riot police in Jerusalem for six hours (*Washington Post*, May 19, 1971); and in early 1973, Japanese commuters, unable to board a train, smashed a station, putting the stationmaster and his assistant in the hospital, and then went on to occupy six other stations and to stone trains and jam switches (*New York Times*, March 14, 1973).

4. David Matza, *Delinquency and Drift* (New York: Wiley, 1964), pp. 189–190.

5. Fred Powledge in *New York Times*, August 6, 1964.

6. See Richard C. Wade, *The Urban Frontier* (Chicago: University of Chicago Press, Phoenix Books, 1964), p. 90; and Howard O. Sprogle, *The Philadelphia Police, Past and Present* (Philadelphia, 1887), p. 50.

7. Wade, *The Urban Frontier*, p. 92. In Boston one house a month would not have been nearly enough; more than fifty buildings were fired by incendiaries in 1844 (Arthur Wellington Brayley, *A Complete History of the Boston Fire Department*, Boston, 1889, p. 207). In Philadelphia thirty-four boys aged five to fifteen were arrested in three summer months of 1862 for starting fires. (Sprogle, *The Philadelphia Police*, p. 318.)

8. Sprogle, *The Philadelphia Police*, pp. 90, 106. See also Eli K. Price, *The History of the Consolidation of the City of Philadelphia* (Philadelphia: J. B. Lippincott, 1873), pp. 118–119.

9. Cf. Richard O'Connor, *Hell's Kitchen* (Philadelphia: J. B. Lippincott, 1958). See also Herbert Asbury, *The Gangs of New York* (New York: Knopf, 1927).

10. Roger Lane, *Policing the City, Boston 1822–1885* (Cambridge, Mass.: Harvard University Press, 1967), p. 29.

11. *New York Times*, September 16, 1965.

12. Brayley, *Boston Fire Department*, pp. 15, 31.

13. See Mancur Olson, Jr., *The Logic of Collective Action* (Cambridge, Mass.: Harvard University Press, 1965). The theory as applied to small groups is particularly relevant here; it is summarized on pp. 33–36.

14. George W. Walling, *Recollections of a New York Chief of Police* (New York: Caxton Book Concern, 1887), p. 85.

15. Thomas C. Schelling, *The Strategy of Conflict* (Cambridge, Mass.: Harvard University Press, 1960), p. 90.

16. George Rudé, *The Crowd in History* (New York: Wiley, 1964), p. 238.

17. Michael S. Hundus, "A City of Mobocrats and Tyrants: Mob Violence in Boston, 1747–1863," *Issues in Criminology*, 6 (Summer 1971): 56. McPhail, "Civil Disorder Participation," p. 1068, gives a vivid impression of the variety of the behaviors a rioteer might engage in during one of the large riots of the 1960's: "Within a one-hour period of time, a person might walk from a bar or residence to the scene of a street arrest; chat with friends and acquaintances; curse the police; make a pass at a girl; throw a rock at a departing police car; light someone's cigarette; run down the street and join others in rocking and overturning a car; watch someone set the car on fire; drink a can of looted beer; assist firemen in extinguishing a fire as it spreads to an apartment house; and so on.

"Even if a person engages in the most extreme act of violence against person or property during a disorder, he is not likely to be continuously or exclusively so engaged. Rather, he is likely to be intermittently engaged in a wide range of routine and "illegal" activities during the course of his presence in the area of the disorder."

18. See E. C. Banfield, "Roots of the Draft Riots," *New York Magazine*, July 29, 1968.

19. This section depends heavily upon a chronology compiled by the Legislative Reference Service of the Library of Congress. It appears in the *Congressional Quarterly* Special Report on Urban Problems and Civil Disorder, No. 36, September 8, 1967, pp. 1708–1712.

20. William F. Soskin, "Riots, Ghettos, and the 'Negro Revolt,' " in Arthur M. Ross and Herbert Hill, eds., *Employment, Race and Poverty* (New York: Harcourt, Brace & World, Inc., 1967), p. 223. The Harlem and Bedford-Stuyvesant riots, together with the events leading up to them and the background situation, are described in Fred C. Shapiro and James W. Sullivan, *Race Riot: New York 1964* (New York: Crowell, 1964). An opinion survey made in Bedford-Stuyvesant shortly after the July 1964 riot is reported in Joe R. Feagin and Paul S. Sheatsley, "Ghetto Resident Appraisals of a Riot," *Public Opinion Quarterly*, 32 (Fall 1968): 352–362. Unfortunately the questions asked ("How did the trouble start, as far as you know?" "What do you think the rioters were trying to do or to show?") were so ambiguous as to make the results of very little value.

21. *New York Times*, November 7, 1964.

22. Shapiro and Sullivan, *Race Riot*, p. 204.

23. *New York Times*, September 27, 1964.

24. *New York Times*, September 11, 1964.

25. New York City Planning Commission, "The Future by Design," October 14–16, 1964, transcript, p. 55.

26. *New York Times*, October 7, 1964.

27. Allen D. Grimshaw, "Changing Patterns of Racial Violence in the United States," in Allen D. Grimshaw, ed., *Racial Violence in the United States* (Chicago: Aldine Publishing Company, 1969), p. 496.

28. Gary T. Marx, *Protest and Prejudice* (New York: Harper & Row, 1967), p. 39. Angus Campbell and Howard Schuman, in a survey made in fifteen major cities for the Kerner Commission in early 1968 found that nearly two-thirds of the Negro respondents agreed that "over the past 10 or 15 years there has been a lot of progress in getting rid of racial discrimination." "Racial Attitudes in Fifteen American Cities," in National Advisory Commission on Civil Disorders, *Supplemental Studies* (Washington, D.C.: Government Printing Office, July 1968), p. 22.

29. Comparing a sample of Negro males arrested during the Detroit riot of 1967 with a control group chosen from the area most affected by the riot, Luby found that the arrestees had no more grievances than the controls, that both arrestees and controls felt that they had made substantial progress in the past five years, and that both were remarkably optimistic about the future. Eliot D. Luby, M.D., "A Comparison Between Negro Riot Arrestees and a Riot Area Control Sample," paper presented at the annual meeting of the American Political Science Association, 1968.

30. Jerry Cohen and William S. Murphy, *Burn, Baby, Burn!* (New York: Avon Books, 1966), pp. 62–63.

31. Newspaperman Don Cormier, quoted in *Burn, Baby, Burn!*, p. 71.

32. Anthony Oberschall, "The Los Angeles Riot of August, 1965," *Social Problems*, 15 (Winter 1958): 339.

Writing of the behavior of youth gang members and not in reference to any particular riot, Walter B. Miller remarks that observers were struck "by what appeared as a current of enormous excitement — an almost ecstatic perception that all things were possible and all delights within grasp." It was, he says, the sense conveyed by ritualized events — the Bacchanalia, the Mardi Gras — when ordinary rules of conduct are suspended. "Even in those cases where the triggering incident was most clearly perceived as a racial affront, the dominant emotions of most gang members appeared to be closer to elation than anger." "American Youth Gangs: Past and Present," in Abraham Blumberg, ed., *A Reader in Criminal Justice* (New York: Random House-Knopf, forthcoming 1974).

33. Governor's Commission on the Los Angeles Riots, *Violence in the City — An End or a Beginning?*, Los Angeles, December 2, 1965, p. 24.

34. Oberschall, "The Los Angeles Riot," p. 329.

35. Ibid., p. 341. Oberschall remarks that the events "constituted a riot rather than anything else."

36. Bayard Rustin, "The Watts 'Manifesto' and the McCone Report," *Commentary* (March 1966): 30.

37. Professor Grimshaw was one who changed his views. When in 1968 he prepared for publication the remarks he had made at the symposium three years before he appended the following footnote to the passage describing the rioters as "lower-class apathetics" and "new-style indifferents": "By the middle of 1968 this assertion is *no* longer true." In a postscript he observed that a "class" as opposed to a "race" interpretation of the "disorders" (he had previously used the term "riotous behavior") "may be correct in some ways but it is even more [*sic*] startlingly incorrect in others." "Changing Patterns of Racial Violence," pp. 496 and 500.

38. *New York Times*, July 24, 1967. John Howard, a sociologist who observed the Detroit riot, later wrote that poor whites played a major role in it. He found the Detroit (and also the Newark) riot to be a "lower-class, rather than racial, revolt." William McCord et al., *Life Styles in the Black Ghetto* (New York: Norton, 1969), p. 273.

39. Quoted by E. S. Evans, "Ghetto Riots and City Politics," in Louis H. Masotti and Don R. Bowen, eds., *Riots and Rebellions: Civil Violence in the Urban Community* (Beverly Hills, Calif.: Sage Publications, 1968), p. 402. For a journalist's account of the Detroit riot, see B. J. Widick, *Detroit: City of Race and Class Violence* (Chicago: Quadrangle Books, 1972), ch. 11.

40. Fogelson and Hill, in a study done for the Kerner Commission, give data on age, sex, birthplace, occupation, and certain other characteristics of persons arrested in the major riots of 1967. They find that ". . . the rioters were a small but significant minority of the Negro population, fairly representative of the ghetto residents and especially of the young adult males, and tacitly supported by at least a large minority of the black community." From this they move to several judgments not derivable from their data: "Which, to repeat, means

that the 1960's riots were a manifestation of race and racism in the United States, a reflection of the social problems of modern black ghettos, a protest against the essential conditions of life there, and an indicator of the necessity for fundamental changes in American society." Robert M. Fogelson and Robert B. Hill, "Who Riots? A Study of Participation in the 1967 Riots," in *Supplemental Studies*, p. 243. For much more in the same vein, see Robert M. Fogelson, *Violence as Protest, A Study of Riots and Ghettos* (Garden City, N.Y.: Doubleday & Company, 1971).

41. For the distinction between "accelerating" and "background" causes, the writer is grateful to Bruce Jacobs.

42. Oberschall remarks that the Watts riot was the first in which the rioters could watch their actions on TV. The movements of the police, he says, were better reported than those of the rioters. "By listening to the continuous radio and TV coverage, it was possible to deduce that the police were moving towards or away from a particular neighborhood. Those who were active in raiding stores could choose when and where to strike, and still have ample time for retreat." "The Los Angeles Riot," pp. 335–336.

   Janowitz conjectures that the presence of the television camera "served to exacerbate tensions and aggressive behavior" but of greater importance was television's influence in spreading "the contagion throughout urban areas and the nation." "The sheer ability of the rioters to command media attention," he writes, "is an ingredient in developing legitimacy. In highbrow intellectual circles in the United States, a language of rationalization of violence has developed. The mass media serve to disseminate a popular version of such justification." *Social Control of Escalated Riots*, pp. 32–33.

43. *New York Times*, December 7, 1967.

44. In a recent study the low-income sample of an urban population was found to average 5.2 hours of television viewing daily as compared with two hours for the general population. The only significant difference between whites and Negroes in media use was that Negroes spent less time reading newspapers. Bradley S. Greenberg and Brenda Dervin, *Use of the Mass Media by the Urban Poor* (New York: Praeger, 1970).

45. *New York Times*, November 7, 1965.

46. J. Anthony Lukas, "Postscript on Detroit: 'Whitey Hasn't Got the Message,' " *New York Times Magazine*, August 27, 1967, p. 44.

47. The principal conclusion of an analysis of surveys made after the 1967 riots in Detroit and Newark was that "Negroes who riot do so because their conception of their lives and their potential has changed without commensurate improvement in their chances for a better life." Nathan S. Caplan and Jeffery M. Paige, "A Study of Ghetto Rioters," *Scientific American*, 219 (August 1968): 21. See also Nathan Caplan, "The New Ghetto Man: A Review of Recent Empirical Studies," *Journal of Social Issues*, 26 (1970): 59–73.

48. Jesse Gray, the rent-strike leader, is reported to have addressed one of the rallies that set off the Harlem riot of 1964 as follows: "We're about to witness in New York City what we have heard about in Mississippi. Somebody has said the only thing that will solve the situation in Mississippi is guerrilla warfare. I'm beginning to wonder what will solve the problem here." Shapiro and Sullivan, *Race Riot*, p. 74.

   Spilerman stresses the importance of national television in stimulating racial consciousness ("Sights of . . . Negroes being set upon by dogs, beaten, or worse, have enabled them to share a common experience, witness a common enemy, and in the process develop similar sensitivities and a community of interest") and also in creating both expectations of help from the federal government and disappointment when they were not realized. Seymour Spilerman, "The Causes of Racial Disturbances: A Comparison of Alternative Explanations," *American Sociological Review*, 35 (August 1970): 646.

49. Matza, *Delinquency and Drift*, p. 184.
50. Ibid., p. 95.

> Modern guides written for those who work with juveniles stress the importance of supporting the child. Whenever supporting the child leads to statements excusing or understanding his behavior, as they occasionally must, the precepts of subcultural delinquency are also supported. . . .
> Statements reinforcing the delinquent's conception of irresponsibility are an integral part of an ideology of child welfare shared by social work, psychoanalysis, and criminology. This ideology presents a causal theory of delinquency which, when it attributes fault, directs it to parent, community, society, or even to the victims of crime.

51. Rustin, "The Watts 'Manifesto,' " p. 30. Vice President Humphrey helped to extenuate the rioting when he said in New Orleans that if he lived in a slum tenement with rats and with no place to go swimming, "You'd have more trouble than you have already, because I've got enough spark left in me to lead a mighty good revolt [sic] under those conditions." *New York Times*, July 19, 1966.
52. "To over-simplify," Grimshaw writes, "if society at large (or significant and powerful segments of the society) agrees with linguistic labeling of events as 'criminal' and 'rebellious,' then an atmosphere will be created in which pleas for . . . 'stricter law enforcement' will strike a responsive chord." But if the same events are identified as " 'a legitimate revolt against impossible conditions'. . . then people will be predisposed to accept solutions which attack sources of the behavior rather than solely problems of control." Allen D. Grimshaw, "Theory, Taxonomic, Exotic, Psychological and Sociological," in Allen D. Grimshaw, ed., *Racial Violence*, p. 387.
53. *New York Times*, November 7, 1965.
54. There is a striking parallel between the rhetorical strategy of the civil-rights leaders in the early 1960's and that of James Mill prior to the passage of the Reform Bill of 1832. See Joseph Hamburger, *James Mill and the Art of Revolution* (New Haven: Yale University Press, 1963).
55. *New York Times*, December 16, 1966.
56. *New York Times*, December 7, 1966.
57. In March 1968, the process of explanation and, by implication, justification reached its apogee with the publication of the report of the National Advisory Commission on Civil Disorders (the Kerner Commission), which found that "white racism," poverty, and powerlessness were mainly responsible for the riots. The next month there were riots in several cities following the assassina-

tion of the Reverend Martin Luther King, Jr. These riots followed the familiar pattern of looting, burning, and vandalism, and it was apparent that despite all that had been done to give a political character to these events, most rioters were not there in order to protest. "It wasn't vengeance," a Chicago poverty worker said, "just material gain." *Wall Street Journal,* April 10, 1968. See also *New York Times,* April 12, 1968.

58. McPhail, "Civil Disorder Participation," p. 1069. He goes on to note that most riots began on weekends or in the evenings when the majority of people were free from the competing demands of work and at or near major vehicular or pedestrian intersections in densely populated areas (pp. 1070–1071).

59. Gresham M. Sykes, *The Society of Captives* (Princeton, N.J.: Princeton University Press, 1958), p. 126.

60. In the summer (June, July, and August) of 1970, 67 "disorders" were reported by the Lemberg Center for the Study of Violence, 23 of which lasted more than one day; in the summer of 1971, there were 46, 12 of which lasted more than one day. Two of the 1971 disorders resulted in the deaths of three persons. Jane A. Baskin et al., *The Long, Hot Summer? An Analysis of Summer Disorders, 1967–1971* (Waltham, Mass.: Lemberg Center for the Study of Violence, Brandeis University, 1972), pp. 9–10.

Comparable data are not available for 1972 and 1973, but these years were not without riots. On August 13, 1973, the *New York Times* reported that after the killing by an arresting officer of a man involved in the theft of a school bus bands of youths roved over an area of Queens ten or twelve blocks across, hurling rocks, bottles, and debris at police cars and other vehicles. A crowd of about 400 persons gathered, looted a liquor store, smashed plate glass windows and car windows, and overturned at least two cars. A dozen Molotov cocktails were said to have been thrown at police cars. At least three policemen and three civilians were treated for injuries in Queens General Hospital, two having been beaten by gangs of rampaging youths. Sporadic violence continued for several hours. About 150 extra policemen were moved into the precinct by bus and dozens of officers in radio cars were mustered from other precincts. Significantly, the story appeared on the next-to-the-last page of the *Times* and seems not to have been covered by national television.

On October 23, 1973 the *Philadelphia Inquirer* carried (on its front page) a story which began: "A gang of more than 200 teenagers, armed with sticks, clubs and iron bars, damaged automobiles, broke windows and fired at least two shots on busy Broad st. [a main center city street] Monday afternoon." There were no arrests.

61. After a careful review of the evidence, Seymour Spilerman concluded that the only community characteristic affecting the likelihood of disorder in the 1960's was the size of the Negro population: the larger it was, the greater the likelihood of disorder. "The Causes of Racial Disturbance," p. 645.

62. Spilerman found that the level of living of Negroes in particular cities, if it affected proneness to disorder at all (good conditions tended to be positively associated with size of Negro population), had the opposite effect from what the "deprivation" theory would imply: ". . . racial disorders are more likely to occur where the level of life for the Negro is least oppressive according to objective measures. There are more disturbances where Negro disadvantage, relative to white residents, is small and where Negro attainment surpasses

that of Negroes living elsewhere. Moreover, disorder-prone communities tend to have stable populations and better quality housing." Ibid., pp. 642–643.

63. Harlem Youth Opportunities Unlimited, Inc., "Youth in the Ghetto" (New York: multilithed, 1964), p. 20.

64. Spilerman's main conclusion is that the federal government, assisted by national television, helped develop racial solidarity among blacks and brought them to base their expectations of improvements in status largely on cues coming from Washington and, having done so, then exhibited "vacillation, compromise, expedient retreat, and unfunded promises" that "must provoke feelings of frustration and betrayal." "The Causes of Racial Disturbance," p. 646.

If the situation has not changed in some crucial respect, his analysis suggests that the likelihood of future riots depends much less upon the objective conditions of the Negro (and hardly at all upon differences in these from one city to another) than upon his response to cues conveyed to him by television from Washington. If this be the case, the prospect is poor indeed. For, despite the vacillation, compromise, expedient retreat, and unfunded promises of the middle 1960's, the attitude of Negroes toward the national government was then one of trust as compared to what — despite dramatic increases in federal spending on "people-helping" programs and dramatic improvements in black incomes and schooling — it has since become. According to a Survey Research Center report in the summer of 1973, trust in the national government has fallen steadily since the middle 1960's, the rate of decline among blacks being four times that among whites. *New York Times,* August 12, 1973.

CHAPTER 10

The Future of the Lower Class

The quotation at the head of the chapter is from Newcomb's *Principles of Political Economy* (New York, Harper and Brothers, 1886), p. 533. The one from Mrs. Fields is from *Lend a Hand* (Boston, 1886), vol. 1, p. 8.

1. Walter B. Miller, "The Elimination of the American Lower Class as National Policy: A Critique of the Ideology of the Poverty Movement of the 1960's," in Daniel P. Moynihan, ed., *On Understanding Poverty* (New York: Basic Books, 1969), ch. 10.

2. Quoted by Tom Kahn in his contribution to a symposium on "Nixon, the Great Society and The Future of Social Policy," in *Commentary,* 55 (May 1973): 43. (Italics appear in Kahn's essay but not in Harrington's book.)

3. Coleman finds the claim that a very high level of income support would establish levels of work motivation and consumer wisdom necessary for self-sufficiency "probably nonsense, even if it were economically feasible. . . ." James S. Coleman, *Resources for Social Change* (New York: Wiley-Interscience, 1971), p. 68.

4. For a somewhat different perspective on the origins of the War on Poverty see Lester C. Thurow, "The Political Economy of Income Redistribution Policies," *Annals of the American Academy of Political and Social Science*, 409 (September 1973), pp. 146–155. The origins of the Model Cities program are described in Edward C. Banfield, "Making a New Federal Program," in Allan P. Sindler, ed., *Policy and Politics in America; Six Case Studies* (Boston: Little, Brown and Company, 1973), pp. 125–158.

5. Charles L. Schultze et al., *Setting National Priorities, The 1973 Budget* (Washington, D.C.: Brookings Institution, 1972), p. 11.

6. On the New Haven experience, see Russell D. Murphy, *Political Entrepreneurs and Urban Poverty* (Lexington, Mass.: Heath Lexington Books, 1971), p. 149.

7. *Work in America* (Cambridge, Mass.: MIT Press, 1973), p. 184. It is of passing interest that Elliot Liebow was a member of the task force which prepared this report. His thesis in *Tally's Corner* (Boston: Little, Brown and Company, 1967) is that blocked opportunity mainly accounts for the life style of the streetcorner men. Coleman finds that his data are inconsistent with this thesis and suggests instead "that the whole pattern and orientation of the neighborhood as well as the disabilities in the men's relations to one another and to women, *made them unable to work steadily*" (italics added). James S. Coleman, *Resources for Social Change*, p. 66.

   As to the merits of the claim that the assurance of stable employment at a living wage will benefit marriage and the family, Reynolds Farley asserts (apropos of black, not lower-class families) that the evidence indicates that raising incomes will not significantly affect the structure of the family and that even if black and white family "stability" were the same, differences in education and occupation in the next generation would still be substantial. "Family Types and Family Headship: A Comparison of Trends Among Blacks and Whites," *Journal of Human Resources*, 6 (Summer 1971): 296.

8. Lee Rainwater, "The Lessons of Pruitt-Igoe," *The Public Interest*, 8 (Summer 1967): 123. Thurow takes a similar position: "Undoing low skill levels and poor work habits among adults is simply a slow, expensive job. As our knowledge of education increases, it appears that the critical years occur at earlier ages." The Political Economy of Income Redistribution Policies,": 151.

9. Alvin W. Gouldner, "The Secrets of Organizations," in *The Social Welfare Forum*, Proceedings of the National Conference on Social Welfare (New York: Columbia University Press, 1963), p. 175.

10. Lee Rainwater, *Behind Ghetto Walls* (Chicago: Aldine Publishing Company, 1970), p. 418. Anselm Strauss, also a sociologist, remarks that "there is usually a lag of at least one generation before life styles respond to changed incomes." *Where Medicine Fails* (Chicago: Aldine Publishing Company, 1970), p. 26.

11. Theodore W. Schultz, "The Increasing Economic Value of Human Time," *American Journal of Agricultural Economics*, 54 (December 1972): 843–850. See also his *Investment in Human Capital: The Role of Education and of Research* (New York: The Free Press, 1971).

12. Theodore Parker, *Works* (London: Trubner and Co., 1864), 7: 111. A study in Providence, R.I., in 1865 of age-specific mortality by income class showed that the infant mortality rate among income-taxpayers was 93 per 1,000 live

births as against 193 among non-income-taxpayers. Cited in Odin W. Anderson, "Infant Mortality and Social and Cultural Factors: Historical Trends and Current Patterns," in E. Gartly Jaco, ed., *Patients, Physicians, and Illness* (New York: The Free Press, 1958), pp. 10–22.

In 1911–1916 a study in seven cities showed a total infant mortality rate of 210.9 per 1,000 live births in the lowest income group (father had no earnings) and only 59.1 in the highest (father's income $1,250 and over). That the high rates had more to do with class culture than with poverty per se is suggested by the fact that the Jews, although they lived in tenements as overcrowded as any, had extremely low infant mortality rates. Robert M. Woodbury, *Causal Factors in Infant Mortality: A Statistical Study Based on Investigation in Eight Cities*, U.S. Children's Bureau Publication No. 142 (Washington, D.C.: U.S. Government Printing Office, 1925), p. 157.

13. James J. Walsh, "Irish Mortality in New York and Pennsylvania," *Studies: An Irish Quarterly Review*, 10 (December 1921): 632; see also Austin O'Malley, "Irish Vital Statistics in America," *Studies: An Irish Quarterly Review* (December 1918): 623–632.

Leonard Woolf, in *Sowing, An Autobiography of the Years 1880 to 1904* (New York: Harcourt, Brace and Co., 1960) recalls (pp. 61–64) the amazing disappearance of appalling lower-class slums in a few years.

In his remarkably vivid and authentic account of Salford (Manchester) slum life in the first quarter of the century, Robert Roberts finds the First World War to be the watershed of change. *The Classic Slum, Salford Life in the First Quarter of the Century* (Manchester: University of Manchester Press, 1971. Republished in 1973 by Penguin Books, Baltimore, Md.)

14. Data associating mortality with socioeconomic characteristics other than occupation were not collected by the Census until 1960. Some data for 1930–1960 exist for five socioeconomics areas of Chicago, however. See Evelyn M. Kitagawa, "Socioeconomic Differences in Mortality in the United States and Some Implications for Population Policy," U.S. Commission on Population Growth and the American Future, in Charles F. Westoff and Robert Parke, Jr., eds., *Demographic and Social Aspects of Population Growth*, vol. 1 of Commission Research Reports (Washington, D.C.: Government Printing Office, 1972), p. 105.

15. On the necessity of changing life style in order to reduce deaths from infant mortality, see C. V. Willie and W. B. Rothney, "Racial, Ethnic and Income Factors in the Epidemiology of Neonatal Mortality," *American Sociological Review*, 27 (August 1962): 526. On the other hand, H. M. Brenner has recently found that economic recessions and upswings have played a significant role in fetal, infant, and maternal mortality in the last half century and have probably been responsible for the apparent lack of continuity in the decline of infant mortality rates since 1950. "Fetal, Infant, and Maternal Mortality During Periods of Economic Instability," *International Journal of Health Services*, 3 (1973), pp. 145–159.

16. *Manpower Report of the President* (Washington, D.C.: G.P.O., March 1973), p. 63. For opposed views on the extent of birth-control knowledge among "the poor," see Judith Blake, "Population Policy for Americans: Is the Government Being Misled?," *Science*, 164 (May 2, 1969): 522–529; and Oscar Karkavy, Frederick S. Jaffe, and Samuel M. Wiskik, "Family Planning and

Public Policy: Who Is Misleading Whom?," *Science*, 165 (July 25, 1969): 367–373. The latter article cites (p. 371) a study which found that approximately 40 percent of births to poor and near-poor couples, as opposed to 14 percent to nonpoor couples, were unwanted by one or both parents in the years 1960 to 1965.

17. Cf. Liebow, *Tally's Corner*, p. 216. Philp, in his account of British "families with multiple problems," remarks that "many men relied excessively on the sexual relationship for reassurance about themselves. They took pride in the size of their families and some spoke openly of this as an indication of their potency and superiority over others. . . . In general the men neither took steps to limit their families nor approved of their wives doing so. . . ." The women, too, "seemed to find some reassurance" in motherhood. "Family limitation is unlikely to be accepted by them until they can come to feel that they have more value in other areas of their lives but in general they do not seem to feel this." A. F. Philp, *Family Failure, A Study of 129 Families with Multiple Problems* (London: Faber and Faber Ltd., 1961), pp. 278–279.

18. The probability of pregnancy resulting from occasional nonuse or misuse of a contraceptive is higher than one might suppose. Michael has calculated that if a couple use a technique which is 90 percent effective, in a fifteen-year period their expected fertility outcome will be 2.7 births (assuming the period of infertility associated with pregnancy to be seventeen months). Robert T. Michael, "Education and the Derived Demand for Children," *Journal of Political Economy*, 81 (Part 2, March/April 1973): S141.

19. Jane A. Menken, "Teenage Childbearing: Its Medical Aspects and Implications for the United States Population," in Westoff and Parke, eds., *Demographic and Social Aspects of Population Growth*, pp. 335–353. In 1968, more than 200,000 births occurred to girls age seventeen or younger (ibid., p. 335).

20. John F. Kantner and Melvin Zelnik, "Contraception and Pregnancy: Experience of Young Unmarried Women in the United States," *Family Planning Perspectives*, 5 (Winter 1973): 22. From interviews in 1971 with a national sample of 4,611 young women the authors found that among sexually experienced unmarried girls aged 15–19 less than half (47 percent) reported having used contraception at the time of last intercourse and less than one-fifth (18 percent) reported using it "always." As one might expect, the more schooling a girl's mother had had and the higher the income of her family, the more likely she was to report having used contraception "last time" and "always." The percentages reporting using it "last time," by schooling of mother, were: 36.7 (elementary), 45.1 (high school), and 62.0 (college). Among white respondents, 61 percent of girls from families with incomes of more than $15,000 reported using it "last time" as compared with 40 percent of girls from families with incomes below $3,000. For blacks, the percentages were 48 and 20 respectively.

A report on the experience of a cohort of adolescents who, after having had a first illegitimate child, became subjects of "an intensive effort to encourage contraceptive use" is especially instructive. Within three years, about half had become pregnant again (the same proportion as in a control group) and a majority were not using birth control continuously. However, about 40 percent of those who remained single *did* use it continuously. Frank Furstenberg,

G. S. Masnick, and Susan A. Ricketts, "How Can Family Planning Programs Delay Repeat Teenage Pregnancies?," *Family Planning Perspectives*, 4 (July 1972): 54–60.

A report based on the 1970 National Fertility Study showed that though the pill and intrauterine devices (IUD) have cut the risk of contraceptive failure in half in the last 10 years within a year's time 14 percent of a sample of 6,752 married or previously married women had an unwanted pregnancy and 26 percent got pregnant sooner than they planned. Over a five-year period, a third of the women who wanted to delay or prevent pregnancy failed to do so. The failure rate was relatively high among young women; schooling did not seem to be a significant factor. Success "depends in large part on the degree of motivation of the couple concerned," a director of the study concluded. Norman B. Ryder, "Contraceptive Failure in the United States," *Family Planning Perspectives*, Vol. 5, No. 3 (Summer, 1973), pp. 133–142.

21. Philips Cutright, "Illegitimacy in the United States: 1920–1968," in Westoff and Parke, eds., *Demographic and Social Aspects of Population Growth*, pp. 423 and 426.

22. In *Families of the Slums* (New York: Basic Books, 1967), Salvador Minuchin and his colleagues report on the effort of a team of specialists to test a technique of therapy on twelve "hard core" delinquent-producing families, with a control group of ten families that were similar except for not having delinquent children. After a series of thirty one-and-one-half-hour sessions over a period of about eight months in which two therapists and (usually) a caseworker talked to all members of the family except children under the age of six, the researchers concluded that seven of the twelve were clinically improved. The criteria of improvement were not operationally defined and varied from family to family.

On the limitations of psychotherapy as a technique for changing personality, see H. J. Eysenck, "The Effects of Psychotherapy: An Evaluation," *Journal of Consulting Psychology*, 16 (October 1952): 319–324.

23. A. B. Hollingshead and F. C. Redlich, *Social Class and Mental Illness* (New York: Wiley, 1958), p. 348. See also J. Myers and L. Schaffer, "Social Stratification and Psychiatric Practice: A Study of an Out-Patient Clinic," *American Sociological Review*, 19 (June 1954): 310, and Zahava D. Blum and Peter H. Rossi in Moynihan, ed., *On Understanding Poverty*, pp. 384–386.

24. For an empirical test of Bernstein's theories see W. P. Robinson and Susan J. Rackstraw, *A Question of Answers* (London: Routledge and Kegan Paul, 2 vols., 1972). For a critical review of work in this field, and of that of Bernstein in particular, see Denis Lawton, *Social Class, Language, and Education* (New York: Schocken Books, 1968). The writings of Bernstein on which the account in the text is based are the following: "Some Sociological Determinants of Perception," *British Journal of Sociology*, 9 (1958); "The Role of Speech in the Development and Transmission of Culture," in Gordon J. Klopf and William A. Holman, eds., *Perspectives on Learning* (New York: Mental Health Materials Center, Inc., 1967); and "Social Structure, Language and Learning" in Joan I. Roberts, ed., *School Children in the Urban Slum* (New York: The Free Press, 1967).

25. Bernstein, "Social Structure," p. 145.

26. A passage from Wittgenstein's *Philosophical Investigations* (New York: Macmillan, 1953), p. 174, is suggestive:

One can imagine an animal angry, frightened, unhappy, happy, startled. But hopeful? And why not?
A dog believes his master is at the door. But can he also believe his master will come the day after to-morrow? — And *what* can he not do here? — How do I do it? — How am I supposed to answer this?
Can only those hope who can talk? Only those who have mastered the use of a language. That is to say, the phenomena of hope are modes of this complicated form of life. . . .

27. Josephine Klein has argued that ego control presupposes the ability to take the consequences of one's actions into account, i.e., foresight, and that "words are needed to create a conception of an orderly universe in which rationally considered action is more likely to be rewarded than impulsive behavior." Quoted in Lawton, *Social Class*, p. 15.

28. For example, it has been found that illiterates tend to have a "present-tense outlook" (Howard E. Freeman and Gene G. Kassebaum, "The Illiterate in American Society: Some General Hypotheses," *Social Forces*, 34, May 1956: 375); sufferers from aphasia tend to behave in a present-oriented manner (Alfred R. Lindsmith and Anselm L. Strauss, *Social Psychology*, rev. ed., New York: Holt, Rinehart & Winston, 1956, p. 143); persons who have undergone lobotomy appear indifferent to the future (Paul Fraisse, *The Psychology of Time*, New York: Harper & Row, 1963, p. 172).

29. Bruno Bettelheim, *The Empty Fortress* (New York: The Free Press, 1968), p. 48.

30. Erik H. Erikson, "The Development of Ritualization," in Donald R. Cutler, ed., *The Religious Situation, 1968* (Boston: Beacon Press, 1968), p. 714.

31. Zena Smith Blau, "In Defense of the Jewish Mother," *Midstream* (February 1967): 47.

32. Lee Rainwater, *And the Poor Get Children* (Chicago: Quadrangle Books, 1960), pp. 82–83.

33. Lois Barclay Murphy, "Infants' Play and Cognitive Development," in Maria W. Piers, ed., *Play and Development* (New York: W. W. Norton & Company, 1972), pp. 119–126. Perhaps it should be noted that Dr. Murphy does not seem to regard the mothers' behavior as reflecting class culture. The children whose development is encouraged by play are "middle class" but the others are "extremely deprived children from disorganized, overcrowded ghetto apartments"; she suggests that it is because the mothers are "destitute" and "exhausted" that they do not play with the children.
Wilson, on the basis of longitudinal studies of twins, concludes that it requires unusual conditions, such as serious prematurity or impoverishment of the environment, to cause a major deflection from the "genetic blueprint" that normally controls the mental development of infants in their first two years. "In all likelihood, however," he adds, "there may be a cumulative latent influence absorbed from the home environment during infancy that combines with genetic predisposition and gradually becomes manifest as school age approaches; since the child's measured IQ becomes increasingly related to his parents' IQ, educational level, and socioeconomic status as he gets older." Ronald S. Wilson, "Twins: Early Mental Development," *Science*, 175 (February 25, 1972): 914–917.

34. Jerome Kagan, "Cross-Cultural Perspectives on Early Development," paper

presented as an invited address to the Annual Meeting of the American Association for the Advancement of Science, Washington, D.C., December 26, 1972.

Lawrence Kohlberg (also an educational psychologist at Harvard) asserts that "moral character" is "not fixed early in life in the family" and that no basis exists in research to doubt that a "ghetto" child put in a suburban home (or vice versa) will be morally like his age mates. "Moral Effects of Psychological Deprivation: Some Research Directions," position paper for Task Force on Socio-Emotional Development and Psychosocial Deprivation, National Institute of Child Health and Development, multilithed, undated.

35. Harold M. Skeels, *Adult Status of Children with Contrasting Early Life Experiences*, Monographs of the Society for Research in Child Development, vol. 31, no. 3, serial no. 105 (Chicago: University of Chicago Press, 1966).

36. Human Interaction Research Institute, "A Study of Successful Persons From Seriously Disadvantaged Backgrounds," Report for Office of Special Manpower Programs, U.S. Department of Labor, Mimeographed, March 31, 1970, Los Angeles. Contract No. 82-05-68-03.

37. Leon J. Yarrow, "Separation from Parents During Early Childhood," in M. L. Hoffman and L. W. Hoffman, eds., *Review of Child Development Research* (New York: Russell Sage Foundation, 1964), 1: 128.

The literature on the effect of father absence is reviewed by Urie Bronfenbrenner in his essay in Vernon L. Allen, ed., *Psychological Factors in Poverty* (Chicago: Markham Publishing Company, 1970), p. 217. Recent data, based on a small number of comparisons, are given by Thomas S. Langer and his collaborators in another essay in the same volume.

38. In 1972 the Iowa State Supreme Court, in an 8–0 ruling, held that a pair of four-year-old twins must be placed up for adoption because their mother, whose IQ was 47, could not give them proper care and attention. Expert witnesses testified that the twins were in poor condition due chiefly to "lack of stimulation" and "need of love and affection." *New York Times*, October 19, 1972.

In colonial Massachusetts children were taken from poor, incompetent, or neglectful parents as a matter of course. Noting that the Town of Boston "is grown considerably populous, and the idle and poor much increased . . ." the Province of Massachusetts enacted in 1735–36 "That where persons bring up their children in such gross ignorance that they do not know, or are not able to distinguish, the alphabet or twenty-four letters, at the age of six years, in such cases the overseers of the poor are hereby impowered and directed to put or bind out into good families, such children, for a decent and Christian education, as when parents are indigent and rated nothing to the publick taxes, unless the children are judged uncapable, through some inevitable infirmity." The author is indebted to Martin Shefter for this reference.

39. Cf. Leontine Young, *Wednesday's Children: A Study of Child Neglect and Abuse* (New York: McGraw-Hill, 1964).

40. Personal communication.

41. K. B. Cheney, "Safeguarding Legal Rights in Providing Protective Service," *Children*, 13 (May–June 1966): 86–92.

42. Cf. Larry B. Silver, M.D., "Child Abuse Syndrome: A Review," *Medical Times Magazine*, 96 (August 1968): 803–820.

43. In fact, there are "gray" and "black" markets in babies. The "gray" market (legal in all but two states) involves use of a lawyer rather than an adoption agency; in the "black" market the child is simply bought (although the payment to the mother may be called a "gift"), the birth certificate sometimes being falsified. According to the executive director of the Child Welfare League of America, it is becoming "rather normal" to pay $10,000 in a "gray" or "black" market. "The baby business," he is quoted as saying, "is expanding all over the country." *New York Times*, February 20, 1973.

44. Arthur R. Jensen, in Martin Deutsch, Irwin Katz, and Arthur R. Jensen, eds., *Social Class, Race, and Psychological Development* (New York: Holt, Rinehart & Winston, 1968), p. 166.

45. Eleanor Pavenstedt, ed., *The Drifters* (Boston: Little, Brown and Company, 1967), p. 199.

46. Ibid., p. 218. Another account, this one of an effort to establish a play center for a group of slum children in London in 1942, concludes: "I do not see much hope for my gang. What we could do for them was only patchwork and the result is most doubtful. The pattern of life in which they are growing up in that community is already shaped and has moulded the very structure of their beings." Marie Paneth, *Branch Street, A Sociological Study* (London: George Allen & Unwin Ltd., 1944), pp. 125–126.

47. An elaborate study of the WIN (Work Incentive) Program makes an opposite recommendation: that welfare payments for children be channeled through fathers instead of directly to mothers "to the end of constraining marital dissolution and buttressing paternal authority. . . ." It is not clear, however, whether the fathers in question are of the sort described here as lower class. Samuel Z. Klausner, "The Work Incentive Program: Making Adults Economically Independent" (Philadelphia, Center for Research on the Acts of Man, 1972), p. xvii.

48. Personal communication from James Q. Wilson.

49. Marvin E. Wolfgang and Franco Ferracuti, *The Subculture of Violence* (London: Tavistock Publications, 1967), p. 299. They cite (p. 304) a study showing that rates for major crimes are lower in cities where the class structure is "balanced." See also Jack Lessinger, "The Case for Scatteration," *Journal of the American Institute of Planners*, 28 (August 1962): 159–169.

50. Jacobus TenBroek and Floyd W. Matson, "The Disabled and the Law of Welfare," *California Law Review*, 54 (May 1966): 816.

Cloward and Piven complain that "the threatened denial of essential benefits is a powerful sanction to control client behavior." Presumably, the main cause of complaint is the unwarranted identification of "client" with "semicompetent." Richard A. Cloward and Frances Fox Piven, "The Professional Bureaucracies: Benefit Systems as Influence Systems," in Murray Silberman, ed., *The Role of Government in Promoting Social Change* (New York: Columbia University School of Social Work, 1965), p. 54. Reprinted in E. C. Banfield, ed., *Urban Government* (rev. ed., New York: The Free Press, 1968), pp. 666–681.

CHAPTER 11

What Can Be Done?

The quotation at the head of the chapter is from David McClelland, writing in Lucian Pye, ed., *Communications and Political Development* (Princeton, N.J.: Princeton University Press, 1963), p. 152.

1. Leo C. Rosten, *Hollywood, the Movie Colony, the Movie Makers* (New York: Harcourt Brace, 1941), p. 40.
2. Frank H. Knight, *Freedom and Reform* (New York: Harper, 1947), pp. 41–42.
3. Kenneth J. Arrow, *New York Times*, Op Ed page, March 26, 1973.
4. Albert K. Cohen, *Delinquent Boys: The Culture of the Gang* (New York: The Free Press, 1955), pp. 176–177.
5. Worth Bateman and Harold M. Hochman, "Social Problems and the Urban Crisis: Can Public Policy Make a Difference?," *American Economic Review*, 61 (May 1971): 352.
6. Jerome Bruner, in Sterling McMurrin, ed., *The Conditions of Educational Equality* (New York: Committee for Economic Development, 1971), p. 60.
7. Jencks, op. cit., p. 180.
8. Lee Rainwater, "Crucible of Identity: The Negro Lower-Class Family," in Talcott Parsons and Kenneth B. Clark, eds., *The Negro American* (Boston: Houghton Mifflin, 1966), p. 199.
9. *Wall Street Journal*, February 16, 1968, p. 9.
10. In a review of the literature of "expectancy theory," Gerald and Patricia Gurin conclude that "success experiences and reality changes in opportunities probably can be used to raise the expectancies of low expectancy people" but they add that "studies consistently stress that this be done under conditions where a person feels that the successes come *from his own skill and competence.*" (Italics supplied.) "Expectancy Theory in the Study of Poverty," *Journal of Social Issues*, 26 (1970), p. 97. Martin E. P. Seligman, in an important work relating experimental findings on animals to human psychology, suggests that what produces self-esteem and a sense of competence is not so much the absolute quality of experience as "the perception of whether your own actions controlled the experiences." Even when pleasurable, events which are felt to be uncontrollable tend to undermine "ego strength"; controllable events, by contrast, tend to produce a sense of mastery even when unpleasant. "It is highly significant," Seligman remarks, "that when rats and pigeons are given a choice between getting free food and getting the same food for putting out responses, they choose to work." *Helplessness* (San Francisco, W. H. Freeman and Company, forthcoming, 1974).
11. Sar A. Levitan, Martin Rein, and David Marwick, *Work & Welfare Go Together* (Baltimore, Johns Hopkins University Press, 1972), pp. 123–124. See also E. C. Banfield, "Welfare: A Crisis Without 'Solutions,' " *The Public Interest*, 16 (Summer 1969): 89–101. See also Henry J. Aaron, "Why is Welfare So Hard to Reform?," *Studies in Social Economics* (Washington, D.C.: The Brookings Institution, 1973).

12. Governor's Commission on the Los Angeles Riots, *Violence in the City — An End or a Beginning?*, Los Angeles, December 2, 1965, p. 55.
13. James S. Coleman, *Resources for Social Change* (New York: Wiley-Interscience, 1971), pp. 60–74. Nathan Glazer has argued that the supposed social benefits from the improvement of housing are mostly myth. "Housing Problems and Housing Policies," *The Public Interest*, 7 (Spring 1967): 21–60.
14. Thomas Sowell, *Race and Economics* (New York: David McKay, forthcoming 1974), ch. 8. See also Muth, who points out that measures which reduce the earnings of poor- relative to good-quality housing (for example, strict enforcement of building and occupancy codes, rent strikes, and public receivership of slum dwellings), while they may be beneficial to the poor in the short run, harm them in the long run by reducing the housing opportunities available to them below what they would otherwise be. Richard Muth, "The Urban Economy and Public Problems," in John P. Crecine, ed., *Financing the Metropolis*, Urban Affairs Annual Reviews, vol. 4 (Berkeley, Calif.: Sage Publications, 1970), pp. 452–453.
15. James S. Coleman, "Community Disorganization and Conflict," in Robert K. Merton and Robert Nisbet, eds., *Contemporary Social Problems* (New York, Harcourt Brace Jovanovich, Inc., 3rd edition, 1971), p. 676. For a case-study of such problems, see Jeffrey L. Pressman and Aaron Wildavsky, *Implementation* (Berkeley, Calif.: University of California Press, 1973).
16. According to Janowitz, the practice in the past "was to apply an embargo on news about a riot during the actual period of the riot. After the event, it would be covered." Morris Janowitz, *Social Control of Escalated Riots* (Chicago: University of Chicago Press, 1968), p. 34.
17. Perhaps no one reform has been more strongly urged by "urbanologists" than the loosening of zoning and other barriers that reduce movement by the poor and the black into suburban and fringe areas where job and other opportunities are better. Politicians, however, have consistently found it impossible to support such measures. Thus, a few days before the presidential election, Senator George McGovern told the press that he opposed federal efforts to force low-income, scatter-site housing on communities. "I believe fervently," he said, "that while new housing opportunities out of the ghetto are both needed and desirable for America's urban poor, that the residents of all communities where such federally backed communities are being considered should be consulted fully at every step of the planning. A Government which makes arbitrary decisions and then thrusts these decisions on the citizenry is no Government at all." *New York Times*, October 28, 1972, p. 35.

The State Urban Development Corporation of New York, a body established in 1968 with power to override local zoning ordinances, lost those powers early in 1973 by agreement of Governor Rockefeller and the leadership of the legislature. The governor was reported to have "finally decided that the opposition to the U.D.C. in suburban areas was strong enough to present a real threat to his own hopes for a fifth term. . . ." *New York Times*, May 20, 1973, p. 28.

For an account of the devices by which state laws and court decisions against "snob zoning" are frustrated in many places, see the *Wall Street Journal*, October 17, 1972.

18. See Lee Rainwater and William L. Yancey, *The Moynihan Report and the Politics of Controversy* (Cambridge, Mass.: M.I.T. Press, 1967).
19. See Mancur Olson, Jr., *The Logic of Collective Action* (Cambridge, Mass.: Harvard University Press, 1965).
20. See Anthony Downs, "Why the Government Budget Is Too Small in a Democracy," *World Politics*, 12 (July 1960): 541–563.
21. One item on the list — day-care centers for children — is popular. In July 1969 a Gallup Poll found that almost two out of every three adults favored using federal funds to set up day-care centers in communities across the nation.

    A recent report by the National Commission on the Reform of Secondary Education, a body which may or may not reflect public opinion (it consisted of educators and private citizens), recommends lowering the compulsory attendance age to fourteen and changing laws to assure those who leave school at that age employment and on-the-job training. *New York Times,* November 29, 1973.
22. With respect to one of the recommendations, the well-off have an interest that is opposed to that of the poor: In the trade-off between inflation and unemployment (and some economists deny that there is one), the well-off and the poor would in general have different optima.
23. When President Nixon devalued the dollar and inaugurated a wage-price freeze, his underlings were "invigorated," the *Wall Street Journal* reported. "Economic aides are buoyed: their concerns are no longer secondary to the President. They're 'doing something,' not just waiting for favorable statistics to turn up." *"Even those who religiously opposed wage-price controls plunge enthusiastically into planning now."* (August 27, 1971.) Italics added.

    In the opinion of a close observer, even a President wants the thrill of "doing something." In *The Politics of a Guaranteed Income, The Nixon Administration and the Family Assistance Plan* (New York: Random House, 1973), p. 165, Daniel P. Moynihan writes:

    > Men who counsel caution in a president do him no disservice, but they do not add much to his day. At the very top of government there ought to be some occasional moment of high spirits, of brave abandon: "to seek a newer world." The constraints are everywhere. No one can get to be president without knowing almost too much about them. There are uses for a measure of incaution. [Arthur] Burns was no doubt right [in his apprehensions about the proposed guaranteed income plan], but where was the glory in always being right if it meant never being bold? Why become president always to be careful? At the end of the day it was evident that the president was leaning toward FAP not least *because* of the risks involved.

24. Lionel Trilling, *The Liberal Imagination* (Garden City, N.Y.: Anchor Books, 1953), p. 213.
25. These matters are discussed in E. C. Banfield and James Q. Wilson, *City Politics* (Cambridge, Mass.: Harvard University Press, 1963), especially chs. 8–10 and pp. 329–346.
26. E. L. Godkin, "The Duty of Educated Men in a Democracy," *The Forum*, 17 (1894): 50.

Godkin would not be surprised at a British social scientist's finding that the median number of words in a half-hour essay by working-class fifteen-year-olds is 228, whereas for middle-class children of the same age it is 348. Cited in Denis Lawton, *Social Class, Language, and Education* (New York: Schocken Books, 1968), p. 105.

27. As an example of the new style of politics, consider the interfaith organization of New York City clergymen that threatened that it might support violence if it resulted from a cut in the state welfare budget (a cut that, incidentally, would have left the welfare budget at an all-time high). *New York Times*, April 4, 1969, p. 1.

CHAPTER 12

The Prospect

The quotation at the head of the chapter is from *The Liberal Imagination* (Garden City, N.Y.: Anchor Books, 1953), pp. 214–215.

1. Kenneth Boulding, book review in the *Journal of Business* (January 1963): 121.
2. The projections are from Denis F. Johnston, "The Future of Work: Three Possible Alternatives," *Monthly Labor Review* (May 1972): 9.
3. *The Manpower Report of the President* (Washington, D.C.: G.P.O., March 1973) says (p. 63): ". . . if the average net annual reduction in the absolute number in low-income groups (about 1.1 million persons per year, 1959 to 1971) can be maintained in the future, the result would be the virtual elimination of the low-income group (as presently defined) in about two decades." The report adds, however, that it may be difficult to sustain this rate of progress because the smaller low-income group is likely to consist of more difficult cases. In the opinion of Robert J. Lampman, "it appears unlikely that poverty will be completely eliminated before 1980 unless some new and extraordinary measures are taken." *Ends and Means of Reducing Income Poverty* (Chicago: Markham Publishing Company, 1971), p. 132.
4. Johnston, "The Future of Work," p. 7, projects dependency ratios (number of persons not in the labor force divided by number who are) as: 1960 (actual), 1.50; 1970 (actual), 1.39; 1980, 1.19 (assuming the two-child norm of the Census's Series E); and 2000, 1.10 (on the same assumption).

   For estimates of the effect of changes in age structure on arrest rates, see Peter A. Morrison, "The Effects of Changing Age Structure," *Dimensions of the Population Problem in the United States* (Santa Monica, Calif.: The Rand Corporation, Monograph R-864-CPG, August 1972), p. 17. The estimates used in the text of the numbers of young males in the future population are from Irene B. Taeuber, "Growth of Population in the United States in the Twentieth Century," in U.S. Commission on Population Growth and the American Future, Charles F. Westoff and Robert Parke, Jr., eds., *Demographic and Social Aspects of Population Growth*, vol. 1 of Commission Research Reports (Washington, D.C.: Government Printing Office, 1972), p. 70.

5. Marvin E. Wolfgang and Franco Ferracuti, *The Subculture of Violence* (London: Tavistock Publications, 1967), p. 306.
6. Gunnar Myrdal, *An American Dilemma* (New York: Harper, 1944), pp. 75–76.
7. Robert K. Merton, *Social Theory and Social Structure* (New York: The Free Press, 1949), p. 181.
8. Harvey Leibenstein, "Allocative Efficiency vs. 'X-Efficiency,' " *American Economic Review*, 56 (June 1966): 392–393.
9. For a description and analysis of the use of sophisticated problem-solving techniques in two cities (San Francisco and Pittsburgh), from which pessimists will probably take more comfort than will optimists, see Garry D. Brewer, *Politicians, Bureaucrats, and the Consultant, A Critique of Urban Problem Solving* (New York: Basic Books, 1973).